Saddam's Iraq

Revolution or Reaction?

Committee Against Repression
and for Democratic Rights in Iraq

CARDRI

Zed Books Ltd

Saddam's Iraq was first published by Zed Books Ltd.,
57 Caledonian Road, N1 9BU and the Committee Against
Repression and for Democratic Rights in Iraq (CARDRI),
PO Box 210, London N16 5PL, in 1986

Copyright © CARDRI 1986

Cover designed by Jabr Muhsin and Gail Cartmail
Printed in Great Britain at The Bath Press, Avon

R00601 22993

British Library Cataloguing in Publication Data

Saddam's Iraq: revolution or reaction?
1. Iraq — History — 1921-
I. Campaign Against Repression and for Democratic
Rights in Iraq
956.7'04   DS79.65

ISBN 0-86232-333-9
ISBN 0-86232-334-7 Pbk

US Distributor
Biblio Distribution Center, 81 Adams Drive,
Totowa, New Jersey 07512, USA.

Contents

Foreword

by Fenner Brockway

This is a monumental work. It describes in meticulous detail the administration and policies of the Government of Iraq, the conditions of the people, the problems of the Kurdish minority and the causes of the Gulf War. It is a revelation.

This book should be studied in every Foreign Office, by the diplomatic editors of all newspapers, by every MP concerned about the Middle East, and by all of us who wish for freedom and justice in the world. It is a classic which no one who seeks the truth about the Middle East can ignore.

Preface

This book by CARDRI (Committee Against Repression and for Democratic Rights in Iraq) is dedicated to all the victims of human rights violations in Iraq: Iraqis summarily executed, Iraqis tortured and killed, Iraqis who have "disappeared", Iraqis detained without trial by the Saddam Husain dictatorship, Iraqis deported in their tens of thousands, Iraqis forced into exile or terrorized in their homeland.

Reports of terror and repression in Iraq in late 1978 led many British Parliamentarians and others, from across the political spectrum, to sponsor the formation of CARDRI, with the aim of exposing the brutality of the Ba'th regime and developing solidarity with those in Iraq struggling for human and democratic rights in immensely difficult and dangerous conditions.

Saddam Husain's war against Iran launched in September 1980 brought the Iraqi people incalculable human misery and devastation to their economy. It has been used as a smokescreen for intensification of repression against all sections of Iraqi society.

What kind of regime would do so much damage to a country just to keep control of it? CARDRI welcomed Zed's invitation to try to answer this question. The result is this book, a serious work of scholarship by British and Iraqi academics and activists, with personal testimonies from victims of Ba'th terror.

Those in Iraq who suffer and sacrifice for democracy in their country are those the regime tries to silence with brutal repression. We hope we have helped their voices to reach you.

Ann Clwyd MP, Chair, CARDRI

Introduction

Iraq is a country three times the size of Britain with a population of 14 million. Most Iraqis are Arabs, but about 25% are Kurds, and there are ethnic minorities such as Assyrians, Turcomans and Armenians. Although Islam is the religion of the state, there are about half a million Christians and other smaller religious minorities. About 75% of Iraqi Arabs are Shi'is, but the Kurds are mostly Sunnis, with the result that the Sh'is form between 55 and 60% of the total population.

In 1947 about 35% of the population lived in towns and 65% in the countryside. According to the latest census, taken in 1977, 64% of the population live in towns and 36% in the countryside, a direct reversal of the urban-rural proportions in only 30 years. There are 1½ million industrial workers, making up to 5 million with their families. The main industries are the oil industry, textiles and transport (particularly railways and docks). Iraq exports mainly oil and dates, and imports food, consumer goods, machinery and armaments.

Iraq's main towns are the capital, Baghdad, which has a population of about 3 million; Basra, a southern oil town and the country's main port, on the Gulf, with a population of about 400,000; Mosul, the largest town in the north, with a population of about 300,000; Kirkuk, the central town of the northern oilfields, with a population of about 200,000; the Kurdish towns of Arbil and Sulaimaniya; and the Shi'i holy cities of Najaf and Karbala.

The mountainous north of Iraq borders Turkey and northern Iran; the marshy south borders southern Iran; and the desert west borders Kuwait, Saudi Arabia, Jordan and Syria. There is fertile land around Iraq's two great rivers, the Tigris and the Euphrates. Their junction is claimed to be the site of the Garden of Eden and they gave the area its Greek name, Mesopotamia, "land between the two rivers".

Mesopotamia was one of the places where human civilisation began nearly 5000 years ago and its ancient cities of Ur, Babylon, Assur, Nimrud and Nineveh were probably the source of the Old Testament stories of Noah's Flood and the Tower of Babel. The Code of Hammurabi, king of Babylon about 2000 BC, contained the world's earliest written laws. It decreed the death penalty for the builder of a badly made house if it collapsed killing the owner; and in the case of a robbery "if the robber is not caught, the man who has been robbed shall make claim, and the town and its governor shall give back to him everything he has lost."

In Iraq in the 1980s the laws decreed by the Revolutionary Command Council prescribe the death penalty for all political opponents of the Ba'th dictatorship headed by Saddam Husain and maintained in power by brutal and widespread violations of human rights. Detention without trial, disappearances, mass executions, deportations and torture are commonplace in Saddam's Iraq and have been well documented by Amnesty International and the world press.

Concern for human rights in Iraq led C.A.R.D.R.I. (Committee Against Repression and for Democratic Rights in Iraq) to investigate the nature and origins of the Saddam Husain regime. The result is *Saddam's Iraq: Revolution or Reaction?* This comprehensive history and analysis begins with two chapters on the political development of Iraq since the late 19th century.

Chapter 1, *Iraq to 1963*, outlines the formation of the state of Iraq in 1920 under the British mandate; the years of nominal independence from 1932, characterised by coups d'état; the post-war struggle for national liberation and democratic rights; the overthrow of the pro-British Nuri Sa'id regime in July 1958; and the achievements and weaknesses of the young Republic of Iraq under General 'Abd al-Karim Qasim.

Chapter 2, *Political Developments in Iraq 1963-1980*, begins with the February 1963 coup d'état which brought the Ba'th Party to power in an orgy of bloodshed until their overthrow in November 1963 by a military-nationalist coup. It examines the succession of governments that ruled Iraq until the Ba'th regained power by a coup in July 1968, and Ba'th rule since then. This covers the attempt by the Ba'th Party in the early 1970s to gain wider support by having a national alliance with some of the opposition parties; the refusal to allow any democratisation; the war in Kurdistan ended by the Algiers Treaty with the Shah of Iran in 1975; increasingly terroristic one-party rule culminating from 1978 in violent repression of all opposition; Saddam Husain's seizure of the Presidency in July 1979 and physical elimination of his opponents and rivals in the Ba'th Party; and the Iraqi invasion of Iran in September 1980.

Chapters 3 and 4 deal with the development of the Iraqi economy and its effect on Iraq's social structure and politics.

Chapter 3, *Oil and the Iraqi Economy*, shows how the oil companies' almost totally free hand in Iraq hampered the development of the Iraqi economy until the July 1958 Revolution. Under Qasim the economic power of the landlord class was broken by agrarian reform and the oil companies' monopoly rights were curtailed by Law 80. After the Iraqi state took control of the oil supply with nationalisation of the industry in 1972 the huge increase in oil revenues from 1973 led to grandiose development plans and the creation of a parasitic bourgeoisie. Economic progress has been catastrophically hit by the Iraq-Iran war but because of the size of its oil reserves, and its land and water resources, Iraq has the potential to become a very prosperous country.

Chapter 4, *The Parasitic Base of the Ba'thist Regime*, provides a detailed analysis of the role of the Ba'thist state in the development of capitalist relations of production in Iraq. It examines in particular the emergence of the parasitic bourgeoisie which is the social base of the Saddam Husain dictatorship.

Chapter 5, *Ba'thism – Nationalism, Socialism and National Socialism*, looks at the origins of Ba'thism and the history of the Ba'th Party since its foundation in 1944. Because the Ba'th Party would never have gained power through the ballot box its ideology in Iraq in the 1960s, 1970s and 1980s has primarily sought to legitimise its right to rule. The political reality is that the Ba'th came to power by a military coup and Saddam Husain now rules by right of execution and assassination. Ba'th ideology has become a national socialist cult of the personality.

Chapter 6, *Ba'th Terror – Two Personal Accounts*, contains an interview with an Iraqi mother who has had both her sons taken from her in the political repression of the Saddam Husain regime; and a speech by a representative of the Iraqi Women's League, Dr Su'ad Khairi, a well-known opponent of the Ba'thists and herself one of their many torture victims.

Chapter 7, *Women in Iraq*, traces the changes that have taken place in the lives of women in Iraq over the past few decades and, in particular, the impact on women of the Ba'th dictatorship and the Gulf War. It describes the main women's organisations in Iraq: the Ba'thist General Federation of Iraqi Women; and the Iraqi Women's League, many of whose members have "disappeared" as opponents of the Saddam Husain regime.

Chapter 8, *The Opposition*, analyses three strands of the Iraqi opposition: the Communist Movement, the Islamic Movement, and the Arab Nationalist Movement. The Iraqi Communist Party has played a fundamental role in shaping the modern political history of Iraq and is an important force in the opposition Democratic Patriotic Front (DPF). The Islamic parties have declared that their umbrella organisation, the Supreme Assembly for the Islamic Revolution, is the legitimate and sole representative of the Iraqi people, but they are distanced from other opposition forces by their dependence on the Khomeini regime in Iran. The anti-Ba'thist Arab Nationalist Movement includes the Socialist Party, the Arab Socialist Party and the pro-Syrian Ba'th Party (Iraqi Regional Command).

The fourth strand of the Iraqi opposition, the Kurdish Movement, is dealt with in Chapter 9, *The Kurds*. This provides a detailed history of the Kurds since the 19th century, including the establishment of the short-lived Kurdish Republic of Mahabad in 1946; Kurdish politics before the 1958 Revolution in Iraq; the Kurds under Qasim, the 'Arif brothers and al-Bazzaz; the campaign launched against the Kurds by the Ba'th in 1969; the 1970 Manifesto; mass deportations of Faili Kurds in 1971; bombing of Kurdish civilians in 1974; the 1975 Algiers Agreement; the burning of Kurdish villages and mass deportations in 1979 to create a cordon sanitaire along the Iraq-Iran border; and the revival of armed struggle in Iraqi Kurdistan in the early 1980s, supported by strikes and demonstrations.

Chapter 10, *The Iraqi Armed Forces, Past and Present*, traces the involvement of the army in Iraqi politics; the role of political parties and ideologies in the army; and the post-1968 Ba'thisation of the army aimed at creating *al-Jaish al-'Aqa'idi* ("the ideological army"). The structure and weaponry of the contemporary Iraqi army are examined, and the chapter concludes with a summary of the reasons suggested by military analysts for Iraq's poor performance in the Gulf War.

Chapter 11, *The Gulf War*, demonstrates that the war is neither a simple border dispute nor a conflict rooted in eternal hostility between Arabs and Persians, but was launched by Saddam Husain in an attempt to solve his internal crisis, dominate the Gulf and lead the Arab world. The course of the war is traced from the Iraqi occupation of Khuzistan in September 1980; through the Iraqi retreat by the end of 1981; the battle of Khorramshahr in May 1982; the sinking of commercial ships in the Gulf in 1983; the air attacks on cities and towns in 1984 and the use of chemical weapons. The involvement of the Arab states, Turkey and the USA is examined and the chapter concludes by looking at the effects of the war on Iraq's population, economy, army and political prospects.

List of Contributors

A. Abbas	military history researcher.
Deborah Cobbett	politics researcher.
Marion Farouk-Sluglett	tutor in Politics of the Middle East, Durham University.
Fran Hazelton	history researcher and former secretary of CARDRI.
Su'ad Khairi	historian and politician.
'Isam al-Khafaji	economist.
Jabr Muhsin	Middle East journalist.
Peter Sluglett	lecturer in Modern Middle Eastern History, Durham University.
Celine Whittleton	economics researcher and Middle East journalist.
U. Zaher	researcher in the contemporary political history of Iraq.

Editorial Group

Deborah Cobbett, Fran Hazelton (Co-ordinator), Peter Sluglett, Celine Whittleton, U. Zaher.

Assisted by Marion Farouk-Sluglett, Ken Hills, Barbara MacDermott, George Morton (former chair of CARDRI).

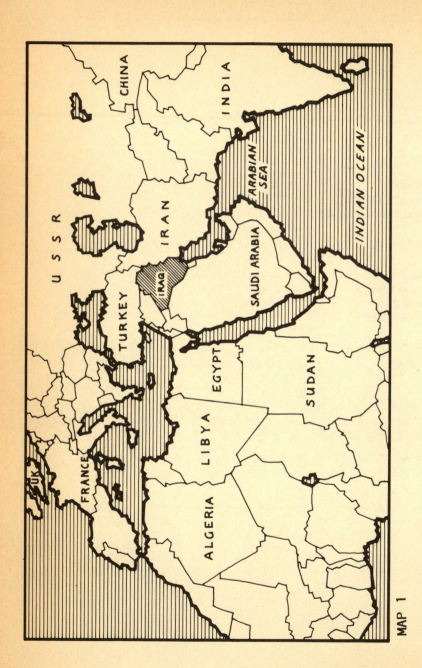

CHINA

INDIA

USSR

IRAN

TURKEY

IRAQ

SAUDI ARABIA

ARABIAN SEA

INDIAN OCEAN

EGYPT

LIBYA

ALGERIA

SUDAN

FRANCE

UK

MAP 1

xiv

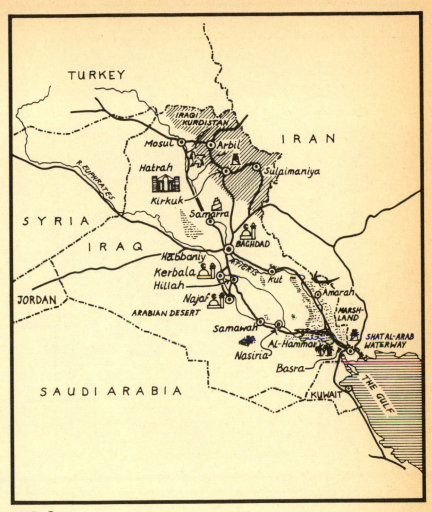

TURKEY

IRAQI KURDISTAN

Mosul

Arbil

IRAN

Hatrah

Sulaimaniya

Kirkuk

R. EUPHRATES

Samarra

SYRIA

IRAQ

BAGHDAD

Habbaniy

TIGRIS

Kut

JORDAN

Kerbala

Hillah

Najaf

Amarah

ARABIAN DESERT

MARSH-LAND

Samawah

Al-Hammar

SHAT AL-ARAB WATERWAY

Nasiria

Basra

SAUDI ARABIA

KUWAIT

THE GULF

MAP 2

XV

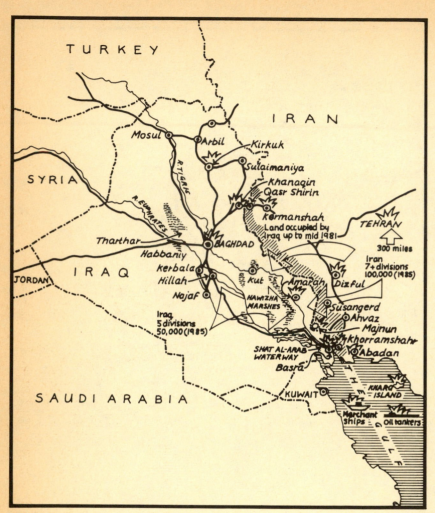

MAP 3

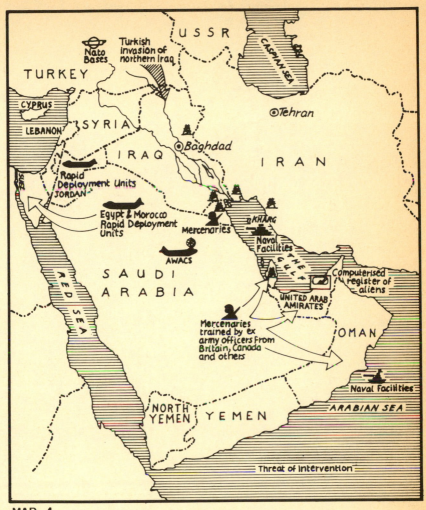

MAP 4

1. Iraq to 1963

Fran Hazelton

Before 1914 what is Iraq today was three *wilayets* or provinces of the Ottoman Empire: Basra, Baghdad and Mosul. Britain occupied this territory
during the First World War and in 1920 was awarded the mandate over Iraq
by the League of Nations. Iraq became an independent state in 1932, once
British control over Iraqi oil had been secured by concessions granted to the
Iraq Petroleum Company, and British air bases in Iraq were guaranteed
by the Anglo-Iraqi Treaty of 1930. The political system set up by the British
in the 1920s, a monarchy based on a ruling class of large landowners, persisted until July 1958 when it was overthrown in the revolutionary coup led
by Brigadier 'Abd al-Karim Qasim and supported by the opposition National
Unity Front. The 1958 Revolution achieved Iraq's national independence
and a programme of land reform, but 1958 to 1963 were years of intense
struggle between Communists, Pan-Arab Nationalists and Ba'thists about
how radical the revolution should be. The radicals were defeated in February
1963 when a CIA-backed and very bloody coup brought the Arab Ba'th
Socialist Party to power in Iraq for the first time.

19th Century European Economic Penetration

In the words of Hanna Batatu:

> under the Ottomans, Iraq consisted to no little extent of distinct, self-
> absorbed, feebly interconnected societies: and, partly, of the inter-penetra-
> tion OF a social form, oriented towards moneymaking and the expansion
> of private property and shaped essentially by Iraq's relatively recent ties
> to a world market resting on big industry, WITH older social forms attach-
> ing value to noble lineage, or knowledge of religion, or possession of
> sanctity or fighting prowess in tribal raids, and dominated largely by
> local bonds and local outlooks, by small-scale handicraft or subsistance
> agricultural production and, outside of the towns, by state or communal
> tribal forms of property.[1]

The opening of the Suez Canal in 1869 and the development of powered
river transport on the Tigris and Euphrates led to an eighteenfold increase

in the volume of Iraq's international trade between 1870 and 1914.[2] Agricultural commodities, chiefly grains, were exported; western manufactured goods were imported. Demand for Iraq's grain exports compelled mobilization of 'surplus' labour and land, and a profound shift occurred from tribal, subsistence agriculture to production for the external markets of British India and Europe. Many sarkals or sub-shaikhs became more or less free agents with work-gangs of cultivators, and succeeded in detaching themselves from the shaikhs, paying their taxes direct to the Ottoman government.[3] The nomadic population declined and the rural sedentary population increased, as did the size and number of market towns. From 1868–70 to 1897–99 the value of imports through Basra rose from £51,000 to £128,000. By 1907–08 it was £306,600[4] and the flood of imported merchandise, chiefly British textiles, had destroyed local handicraft industries. Trade was monopolized by British and local comprador elements, such as the Jewish communities of Baghdad and Basra.

> On the eve of British colonial conquest the integration into the world market of this territory and its ethnically and ecologically diverse population had produced severe demographic and social dislocations that impoverished masses of tribes people/peasants and townspeople, and benefitted a handful of merchants and tribal shaikhs.[5]

Oil

Important though this area was as a supplier of grain and a market for manufactured goods, its oil potential was recognized even before the First World War. In 1912 the Anglo-Dutch company Shell, the British National Bank of Turkey, the German Deutsche Bank and C.S. Gulbenkian, an individual Ottoman, combined to form the Turkish Petroleum Company which was in 1914 given a concession by the Ottoman authorities to prospect for oil in the Baghdad and Mosul *wilayets*. It formed a merger with the Anglo-Persian Oil Company, which had been in existence since 1903 but had only just begun producing oil. In Britain a Royal Commission had already in 1913 agreed with Winston Churchill, First Lord of the Admiralty, that 'We must become the owners or at any rate the controllers at the source of at least a proportion of the oil which we require.'[6] A few days before the outbreak of war the British government bought 51% of the shares of Anglo-Persian, which automatically gave it a large interest in the Turkish Petroleum Company.

British Occupation

Immediately war broke out, in November 1914, British Indian troops were landed in the Shatt al-Arab to protect the Anglo-Persian oil installations at Abadan, and went on to secure the port of Basra. To ensure political tranquillity and agricultural supplies for the urban population and the invading forces the British took over the Ottoman state land, as the Turkish administrators retreated with the Turkish army, and granted tracts of it to selected shaikhs as private property. In 1916 the Tribal Criminal and Civil Disputes Regulations, a piece of British-Indian legislation, was introduced, and as the Mesopotamian Expeditionary Force marched north towards Baghdad individuals picked out by the British intelligence services to act as tribal shaikhs were officially invested with juridical and later financial authority over their tribes. In March 1917, after two and a half years of fighting and 98,000 casualties, British forces captured Baghdad. Four days after the October 1918 Mudros Armistice Agreement with Turkey they took control of the oil-rich province of Mosul.

Most of Greater Syria and Iraq was now under British occupation. Damascus was being administered by Arab officials, including senior ex-Ottoman officers of Iraqi origin (the 'Sharifians') who had fought with Hussain, Sharif of Mecca, in the Arab Revolt against the Turks, in 1916, in return for British and French promises of an independent Arab state. By contrast, Baghdad was the centre of a rigid administrative system staffed entirely by British officers and officials mainly recruited from British India.

In November 1918 the French and British issued a joint declaration of intent to establish among 'those people so long. . . oppressed by the Turks . . .national governments and administrations drawing their authority from the free choice of the indigenous populations.' Expressing the ideals of President Woodrow Wilson's Fourteen Points published in January 1918, the Anglo-French Declaration was partly a sop to the USA, which had entered the war on the side of the Allies in 1916 only on condition that its economic and political aims were taken into account in the postwar settlement. 'England and France,' President Wilson wrote to his confidant Colonel House, 'have not the same views with regard to peace as we have by any means. When the war is over we can force them to our way of thinking.'[7]

The involvement of the USA, as well as the Bolsheviks' exposure of the secret deals between the European powers (the Sykes-Picot Agreement) and the emergence of an Arab nationalist movement, meant that

> Long established and hitherto almost unchallenged assumptions of British imperial policy had to be reconciled with a whole new set of requirements. In Iraq it was necessary to adapt the existing machinery, derived from Indian administrative models, to a new and less direct form of control, which was at first unfamiliar and unpalatable to those called upon to operate it.[8]

One of the first in British government circles to advocate 'indirect' rule for Iraq was Sir Arthur Hirtzel, Head of the India Office's Political Department.

> What we want to have in existence, [he wrote] what we ought to have

been creating in this time is some administration with Arab institutions which we can safely leave while pulling the strings ourselves: something that won't cost very much, which Labour can swallow consistent with its principles, but under which our economic and political interests will be secure.[9]

The 1920 Revolt

The Acting High Commissioner, Sir Arnold Wilson, took the opposite, traditional view. Outraged by the Anglo-French Declaration and believing that 'our best course is to declare Mesopotamia to be a protectorate'[10], he was in sole charge of Iraq from the end of the war until the League of Nations awarded it to Britain as a mandated territory in the San Remo Agreement of April 1920. During this time the province of Mosul, which had been allocated to France in the secret Sykes-Picot Agreement of 1916, was a cause of dispute between Britain and France. The French gave up their claim to Mosul early in 1919 in return for the Deutsche Bank's 25% share of the Turkish Petroleum Company (confiscated during the war), but final Anglo-French agreement on this issue was not reached until December 1920. In the summer and autumn of 1919 there were risings in Mosul by the Kurds, who were demanding an independent Kurdish state. In central and southern Iraq the Shia clergy were demanding an Islamic state and the chief *mujtahid* pronounced that all service under the British was unlawful. The Sharifians, many of them like Nuri al-Sa'id members of the pre-war nationalist group *'Ahd al-'Iraq* , wanted an independent Iraqi monarchy or republic, and were encouraged when the Syrian Congress in Damascus elected the sons of the Sharif, 'Abdullah and Faisal.

When the mandate over Iraq was awarded to Britain it was criticised in Parliament and the Press as being in effect a new unnecessary and expensive imperial acquisition. When news of the award reached Iraq in July 1920, resentment and opposition were such that the Sharifians, rebellious tribesmen, Shi'i *mujtahids* and ex-civil servants united in a revolt against British rule and oppressive taxation which lasted until October, with high casualties on both sides. The 1920 Revolt

is of significance as the first major manifestation of a form of Iraqi national identity and subsequently played an important role in the country's political mythology as a focus of calls to opposition to the monarchy and for anti-British sentiments.[11]

The 'Arab Solution'

The high cost of the 1920 Revolt in British lives and money (£32 million) made implementation of the 'Arab Solution' an urgent political necessity for

Britain. 'What is wanted' Kidston of the Foreign Office had written as early as January 1919 'is a King who will be content to reign but not govern and whose religious views are such that the shaikhs may acquiesce in his rule.'[12] But the British could not be seen to be forcing a particular king on the Iraqis. As Hirtzel wrote in February 1919:

> If the French remain in Syria we shall have to avoid giving them the excuse of setting up a Protectorate. If they go, or if we appear to be reactionary in Mesopotamia, there is always the risk that Faisal will encourage the Americans to take over both and it should be borne in mind that the Standard Oil Company is very anxious to take over Iraq.[13]

In July 1920 Faisal's government in Damascus collapsed as the French imposed a full colonial administration by force of arms. In Iraq the Revolt stopped British civil administration outside the towns throughout July, August and September. The British army regained control only in October, and punitive expeditions and displays of force were to continue well into 1921. Sir Percy Cox replaced Sir Arnold Wilson in October 1920, returning to Baghdad from London with a plan for the establishment of an Arab Council.

> For the post of President of the Council Cox was able to overcome the genuine reluctance of the venerable Naquib of Baghdad, Sayid Abd al-Rahman al-Gaylani; and the latter on 25 October issued invitations to eminent fellow countrymen selected by himself and Cox for Cabinet positions.[14]

The Council of Arab Ministers had no jurisdiction in foreign affairs but was responsible for drafting an electoral law, setting up a national assembly and approving Faisal as constitutional monarch when he eventually arrived at Basra, on Iraqi soil for the first time, in June 1921.

Installation of Faisal as king of Iraq was one of the decisions taken by the Cairo Conference held in March 1921, organized by the recently established Middle East Department of the Colonial Office, presided over by Winston Churchill, the new Colonial Secretary, and responsible for making the political, financial and military arrangements for the mandated territories. The main object, according to Churchill, was to maintain firm British control as cheaply as possible, and the Conference decided 'to give responsibility for the control of Iraq to the Royal Air Force thus recognizing the ability of air power to maintain effective control of a mandated territory with the maximum economy in the deployment of forces'.[15]

Faisal was crowned in Baghdad on 23 August 1921 and a national government was formed from Sharifians he brought with him and high-ranking urban Sunni Muslims.

> In the course of the years that followed, Faisal did not prove quite the pliant instrument that his British masters had expected him to be, although their monopoly of the means of coercion meant that ultimately, the advice they gave had to be taken. The king and his circle were con-

stantly involved in a delicate balancing act, having to satisfy the exigencies of British policy, while at the same time trying to retain some degree of credibility with what may loosely be termed Iraqi national aspirations.[16]

The British quickly dropped the word 'mandate' which, as Gertrude Bell explained 'produces the same effect here as the word Protectorate in Egypt'[17] but sought to preserve Britain's mandatory powers and responsibilities as defined by the League of Nations in an Anglo-Iraqi Treaty, negotiated from December 1921 to August 1922, while Iraqi opposition to it grew and the new Turkish regime was sending raids across the northern frontier and supporting Kurds in Mosul. Faisal and his government delayed ratification of the treaty for nearly two years, firstly with the adoption in April 1923 of a protocol stipulating that the treaty should expire when Iraq became independent, or not more than four years after a peace settlement with Turkey. But the shaikhs, whose land and authority came from the British, supported it; the Shia clergy opposed it, but also resented Faisal's Sunni government. The Kurds still sought the independent Kurdistan promised in the non-ratified Treaty of Sèvres, 1920. The 1922 Anglo-Iraqi Treaty was finally ratified by Iraq's Constituent Assembly in June 1924, in return for a British commitment to secure Mosul for Iraq.

Oil Concessions, Air Bases and Iraqi 'Independence'

That Mosul should be a part of Iraq was the one issue over which there was no disagreement between the British and the Iraqi government in its early years. For Britain, exploitation of Mosul's oilfields required political control of the area, through the Iraqi government, but Faisal's regime had little chance of survival in an Iraq dominated by the Shia, as it would be without the Sunni population, Arab and Kurdish, of the Mosul *wilayet*. Iraqi dependence on the British in resisting Turkish demands and silencing Kurdish pressure for autonomy had a price: Iraqi agreement to the concession terms laid down by the oil companies. At the 1923 Lausanne Conference, Lord Curzon, the Foreign Secretary told the Italian representative 'that when we have definitely settled the question of Mosul (which we had no intention of relinquishing) we would give them a share of the oil.'[18] The Americans, who challenged the validity of the Turkish Petroleum Company's Ottoman-granted concession, and whose interests, like those of the French, might have been better served by Turkish control of Mosul, only dropped their Open Door policy once they had acquired a quarter of the TPC's share capital in 1923. The TPC refused to allow any share equity participation by the Iraqi government, which was anyway unable to raise the capital, but it eventually agreed to the Iraqi demand that royalties should be based on gold rather than sterling, and on a sliding scale.

The Mosul boundary problem, unresolved at the Lausanne Conference, was transferred to the League of Nations. Throughout the autumn of 1924

Turkish pressure on Mosul increased and the RAF bombed the Kurdish city of Sulaimaniya in November. In July 1925 the League's boundary commission recommended that Mosul should be part of Iraq, on condition that Britain's mandatory powers be extended for 25 years or until Iraq entered the League of Nations. When the Anglo-Iraqi Treaty of January 1926 was signed, accepting this condition, a Baghdad secret police report noted that 'Those in favour of the Treaty, on whatever grounds, use the argument that the treaty is not only essential for the retention of the Mosul *wilayet* but is also essential for the actual existence of the independence of Iraq and its monarchy.'[19] The Turkish-Iraqi Treaty of July 1926 agreed the inclusion of the Mosul *wilayet* into Iraq, and gave Turkey 10% of Iraq's oil royalties for 25 years.

Exploration for oil began in April 1927 and enormous amounts were found near Kirkuk in October. But production proceeded slowly and Iraq's main export was still grain in 1930 when a sharp fall in world prices of grains forced the Iraqi government to seek an advance on royalties from the TPC which had in 1929 become a consortium of Anglo-Iranian, Shell, Mobil and Standard Oil of New Jersey, known as the Iraq Petoleum Company. The TPC granted the advance in return for an expansion of its concession area from 192 sq. miles to 35,000 sq. miles, leading to its monopolization of the entire country by 1938.

Meanwhile Faisal and the Baghdad politicians tussled with *al-Wadha' al-Shadd*, the 'perplexing predicament', in which they found themselves as Iraqi nationalists in a government dependent on an outside power, Britain. They pursued the 'escape' clause in the 1926 Anglo-Iraqi Treaty which provided for admission of Iraq to the League of Nations before expiry of the mandate in 1951, and sought entry in 1928. At the end of 1927 Britain agreed to an Anglo-Iraqi treaty which relaxed its formal rights to intervention in Iraq but maintained firm control over everything affecting British interests and external obligations, in particular retention of the RAF air bases in Iraq for an indefinite period. The British Labour government elected in 1929 decided to review the relationship between Britain and Iraq, but the new Anglo-Iraqi treaty signed in 1930 'although promising some as yet unspecified form of independent status for the country, was soon to be almost universally recognized as a major sacrifice of Iraqi interests for Great Britain's benefit.'[20]

Iraqi independence was finally conceded by Britain in 1932 to give a freer hand to Faisal and his officials and to restore tranquillity after widespread strikes and demonstrations in 1931. Since 1920

the construction and imposition of the state apparatus (had) placed an almost imperceptible shift of political and economic power to the urban areas, especially Baghdad. This process included the formation and reproduction of a new urban petty bourgeoisie, operating small stores and workshops and staffing the lower levels of the bureaucracy. Dependent on the expansion of the state apparatus and the urban trading and manufacturing sectors, these elements came to articulate resentment of control by the British and the parasitic ruling class.[21]

They provided the membership of Iraq's first trade union, the *Jam'iyyat Ashab al-Sana'a* (Artisans' Association) founded in 1929 by Muhammad Salih al-Qazzaz with the encouragement of veteran nationalist leader Ja'far Abu'l-Timman and under the aegis of his *Watani* (National) Party. The *Jam'iyyat* also recruited railway workers from the Baghdad headquarters of the Iraqi railways, probably the largest single economic enterprise in the capital at the time. It was not simply concerned with the direct economic interests of its members but began by organizing a literacy campaign and courses of lectures on political and social problems.[22] In 1931, when popular resentment against the government was already high because of the 1930 Anglo-Iraqi Treaty and the massive new concessions to the IPC, the *Municipal Fees Law* was introduced, imposing new taxation on small merchants. The response was strikes and demonstrations initiated by the *Jam'iyyat* in Baghdad which spread to the provincial towns after al-Qazzaz was imprisoned and the opposition party leaders took charge, Ja'far Abu'l-Timman, Yasin al-Hashimi, and Rashid 'Ali. The situation in July 1931, the British High Commission informed the Secretary of State for the Colonies, 'reveals surprising lack of support for present Government, and unpopularity of King Faisal. Republican cries have been openly raised in the streets . . . except in the Government newspapers, there had been no sign of loyalty to the King or support for the Government.'[23] To quell the unrest the RAF flew demonstration flights over the towns of the mid-Euphrates and Basra. In January 1932 the Council of the League of Nations agreed to Iraq's admission, subject to the signature of various guarantees including the administration of justice and the general safe-guarding of minority rights. Iraq became an independent state but 'the British authorities still retained supreme power, and the vast majority of the population still possessed no power at all.'[24]

With Independence 'the urban ruling elements . . . continued along the path of compromise with the colonial power and repression of the newly conscious strata of the petty bourgeoisie and workers in the urban area.'[25] The *Consumption Tax Law* of 1931 had ended efforts to tax the landowners directly; the 1932 *Land Settlement Law* legalized the shaikhs' landholdings as private property; and the 1933 *Rights and Duties of Cultivators Law* bound peasants to landowners and restricted the circulation of labour. Although a city-wide boycott of the British-owned Baghdad Electric Light and Power Company, from 5 December 1933 to 3 January 1934, organized by al-Qazzaz, achieved a slight lowering of electricity prices, a ban was then imposed on trade unions, their leaders were imprisoned and the movement was forced almost completely underground for the next ten years.[26]

The Political System

Under the British mandate 'Largely Western-devised political forms were imported into a tribal society ethnically and theologically fragmented, with an urban crust of sophisticated largely Turkish educated leaders.'[27] The *Organic Law* of 1924 which remained Iraq's constitution until 1958, set up a bi-cameral parliamentary system but the king had the power to appoint and demand the resignation of ministers, and in practice the cabinet controlled the legislation through manipulation of elections and the power to dissolve parliament. Formal political life 'operated in an almost entirely artificial atmosphere, and occupied itself very little with the major political and economic concerns of the population.'[28] Political parties were essentially followings for individuals. Two parties established since the time of Ottoman rule were the *'Ahd al-'Iraqi* and *Hara al-'Istiqlal*, which aimed at defending Arab rights against the Turks. After 1921 three other parties were set up: the *Watani* (National) Party, the *Sha'b* (People's) Party and the *Taqqadum* (Progressive) Party. These three parties had the aim of ending the mandate and winning independence. After the signing of the 1930 Anglo-Iraqi Treaty there was a re-grouping of parties. Nuri al-Sa'id reformed the *'Ahd*, which aimed to end the mandate but was pro-Treaty. Former members of the *Sha'b* and *Watani* came together in the anti-government *Ikha' al-Watani* (National Brotherhood) Party, which rejected the Treaty as incompatible with Iraqi national aspirations. By the mid-1930s, once Iraq had gained independence, these parties 'died a natural death since their raison d'etre had disappeared.'[29] Parties other than the clandestine Iraqi Communist Party (ICP), founded in 1934, were only to reappear on Iraq's political scene after the Second World War.

The Army

When Faisal died in 1933 and was succeeded by his much less politically and diplomatically skilled son, Ghazi, the pre-Independence equilibrium he had maintained began to break down. Between 1934 and 1936 rival political factions forced the resignation of three cabinets by inciting tribal uprising. As these could only be put down militarily the army acquired a crucial political role. The Iraqi Army had been set up immediately after the creation of the Arab government in 1920, with Ja'far al-'Askari as Minister of Defence and his brother-in-law Nuri al-Sa'id as Officiating Commander of the General Staff, when the army consisted of a skeleton Headquarters Staff of ten Iraqi officers. In March 1921 the Cairo Conference decided that 'immediate steps should be taken to raise an Iraqi army of 15,000 and that British forces should be progressively reduced as the army grew.'[30] From the start the new army was equipped and trained on British lines. A British Military Mission was established, British military advisers were attached to the Ministry of Defence and the Iraq Military College

9

which opened in July 1921 was largely staffed by Britons and used British training manuals. From 1924 four Iraqi army cadets were sent each year to Britain and India for further training, and between 1932 and 1936 an annual average of 25 were sent. But the British prevented the introduction of conscription throughout the Mandate since a large Iraqi army would have made the King independent of the pro-British tribal shaikhs, and 'the army featured more prominently in political bargaining than in military action.'[31] Its first victory was the crushing of the Assyrian Revolt in 1933. The Assyrian community had been brought from Turkish Kurdistan to Ba'quba during the First World War under the protection of the British who in 1919 tried to settle them on land taken from rebellious Kurds. They served the British, with great loss of life, in the 1920 Revolt, in the Assyrian Levies, which remained, paid by Britain, until Independence. The Iraqi Army's massacre of rebellious Assyrians in August 1933 enhanced its public image and brought fame and promotion to the commanders of the expedition, including the Kurdish general Bakr Sidqi. The following year conscription was introduced 'with *acclaim*'[32] and the army's strength, which was less than 12,000 at the end of 1933, rose to 15,000 by the end of 1935, and on the eve of Iraq's first military coup was 20,000.[33]

The Coups d'État 1936–1941

The first coup d'état, which took place on 29 October 1936, led by Bakr Sidqi, installed a civilian government of reformist ministers drawn from the left-liberal *al-Ahali* group, under the leadership of Hikmat Sulaiman. But in March 1937 Sidqi, an admirer of Mussolini, launched a vigorous attack on liberals and the left which was met by protest strikes throughout the country: at Basra port, at the National Cigarette Factory in Baghdad, and at the IPC's works in Kirkuk.[34] When these strikes were suppressed by displays of military might the *al-Ahali* ministers resigned. Sidqi was assassinated a few months later and 'the army became virtually the sole deciding factor in the rise and fall of almost all Cabinets from 1937–1941.'[35] There were six coups d'état before the outbreak of the Second World War, with a key role being played by the 'Four Colonels'. When King Ghazi died in a car accident in 1939 he was succeeded by 'Abd al-Ilah as Regent for Ghazi's four-year-old son Faisal. 'Abd al-Ilah was dominated by the pro-British politician Nuri al-Sa'id, who was to be the effective ruler of Iraq until the revolution of 1958. Nuri al-Sa'id and the royal family were forced to flee Iraq briefly during the May 1941 revolt against the British led by Rashid 'Ali al-Gailani. The revolt occurred after the 'Four Colonels' and anti-British politicians sympathetic to Nazism challenged Britian's right under the 1930 Anglo-Iraqi Treaty to land and deploy troops in Iraq. The British crushed the revolt militarily and in January 1943 Iraq declared war on the Axis powers.

The Labour Movement and National Liberation

The wartime British-Soviet alliance and the international atmosphere at the end of the war brought Iraq a degree of democracy, with less vigorous persecution, for a while, of the Iraqi Communist Party (ICP), and the licensing of some trade unions in 1944–45 and some political parties in 1946. This led Arshard al-'Umari, who became Prime Minister in June 1946, to complain that the Allies 'were responsible for spreading progressive and communist ideas.'[36] The relative freedom did not survive the advent of the Cold War but 'it provided a vital formative experience for those who came of age politically at the time and who were to participate in the bloody battles between the authorities and "the people" which raged throughout the late 1940s and 1950s.'[37] During the ministries of Hamdi al-Pachachi and Tawfiq al-Suwaidi between 1944 and 1946 permission was granted for the formation of 16 trade unions, twelve of which were controlled by members of the ICP. The Railway Workers Union at its first congress in November 1944, a month after it was finally licensed, adopted a charter stating its aims of improving wages and conditions by strictly legal means, and within a few months a third of the 11,000 railway workers had joined. When the demand for wage increases of 30–50% was turned down by the British-managed Railway Directorate a national rail strike was called which was solid for ten days among the 1,250 workers in Baghdad. The Railway Directorate threatened to cut the supply of water to the workers' living quarters and replace the strikers with imported Indian labour. The strike committee was arrested, the union was suppressed, and eventually the workers went back to work with 20–30% wage increases. Despite the banning of the union railway workers struck again for higher wages in 1946 and three times in 1948. Similarly, at Basra port the Union of Port Employees was licensed in August 1945, and more than half the port workers joined it. When wage demands were refused a strike took place in May 1947, and more strikes followed even after the union was suppressed. The workers at the Kirkuk oilfields asked permission to form a union in May 1946 but were refused. When the Iraq Petroleum Company rejected demands for higher wages a strike was called and on 3 July 5,000 workers, members of the two hostile tribes from which the company mainly recruited, marched through Kirkuk in a peaceful demonstration. On the tenth day when the strikers assembled in the evening, as usual, at the Gawurbaghi gardens outside the city, to hear the latest news and instructions from the strike committee, they were suddenly charged by mounted police and ten were killed. This savage and totally unprovoked attack proved to the population throughout the country that the government was ready to sacrifice the lives of Iraqi workers in defence of British economic interests.[38] The strikes of 1944–47 were for economic demands, but because all the major industrial concerns—railways, ports, oilfields and textile mills—were British-run, those who died were honoured as martyrs to the cause of national liberation from British imperialist domination.

Britain, USA and the Middle East

British postwar policy for the Middle East had been outlined in a Foreign Office memo in March 1944.[39] Whilst hoping for some form of United Nations organization and an increase in US interest and involvement, Britain was to use existing arrangements with Middle East countries, concerning defence, internal security, administration and foreign political commitments, to maintain unilaterally the stability which protected the sea, air and land communications between the UK and India and the Far East. When Ernest Bevin became British Foreign Secretary after the election of a Labour government in July 1945 he said he wished to 'leave behind forever the idea of one country dominating another.' But Britain was thrown into tight financial dependence on the USA after the abrupt cancellation of Lend-Lease on 21 August 1945. In March 1946 Opposition Leader Winston Churchill, with prior approval of President Truman, called, in his Fulton speech, for an Anglo-American Alliance against the Soviet Union. By the end of 1946 the British government could no longer provide financial and military support for the regimes in Greece and Turkey and the USA assumed the responsibility with the announcement of the Truman Doctrine on 12 March 1947. To the British military establishment the Middle East, which ended the war 'littered with bases, airfields, landing grounds, depots and countless administrative units only a fraction of which would be needed once peace-time policy was formulated and implemented'[40], was of such vital importance that when Prime Minister Attlee in January 1947 pressed the idea of withdrawing and concentrating on Africa, all three service chiefs were prepared to resign rather than give way over the area.[41] They valued it not only because of the oil and imperial communications (even after Indian independence) but as a base from which Africa could be defended and British forces would be able to attack the Soviet flank.

> By the late forties these considerations were taken to be conclusive. Whatever political doubts existed in the early years of the Labour government, the service chiefs had steered the UK back to its traditional understanding of the need to hold the Middle East.[42]

The 'Portsmouth' Treaty

Between March 1946 and January 1948, when a new Anglo-Iraqi treaty was signed but not ratified, the British attempted treaty renegotiations everywhere, 'and everywhere they failed except Transjordan – the one country so small and poor that even the impoverished British exchequer could offer something worth having.'[43] The 1930 Anglo-Iraqi Treaty, which 'virtually reduced Iraq to an appendage of the British Empire'[44] was not due to expire until 1952, but in March 1946 the Iraqi Prime Minister Tawfiq al-Suwaidi announced his intention to seek revision of the treaty. Throughout the next

22 months there was widespread popular agitation demanding the lessening or abolition of British military rights in Iraq, but the strength of Iraqi feeling, particularly for removal of the British airbases, was not fully appreciated during the negotiations for a new treaty which took place between the British government and the Iraqi government in 1946 and 1947.

> I contemplate [Mr Baxter of the Foreign Office wrote to the British Ambassador in Baghdad in April 1946] the possibility either of extending the scope of the Egyptian negotiations, if all goes well, to develop into some new regional partnership defence arrangements covering not only Egypt, but also Palestine, Transjordan and Iraq, or alternatively of making a bilateral arrangement whereby our defence requirements under a new Anglo-Egyptian treaty would be drawn up in such a way as to be capable of fitting into an above area.[45]

At the end of May 1946 the al-Suwaidi Government was manoeuvred out of office in a Senate plot encouraged by the Regent and Nuri al-Sa'id, and the 'Umari Government which took over repudiated the memo produced by a Ministerial sub-committee, calling for the 1930 treaty to be scrapped and replaced by a Treaty of Friendship, with no mention of bases. Prime Minister al-'Umari and the new Minister of Foreign Affairs, Fadhil al-Jamali, who was later to sign the Portsmouth Treaty, 'agreed,' said the British Chargé d'Affaires, 'that this was nonsense, and I left them in no doubt that we would take the same view.'[46] When Dr Jamali met Bevin in London on 18 September 1946 his main concern was 'the question of the Communists, who were making things difficult, and yet they were not really all of them Communists at all.'[47] In March 1947 Salih Jabr became Prime Minister of Iraq when Nuri al-Sa'id, having manipulated elections to ensure the success of his own supporters, resigned 'in favour of a successor who was to carry out a policy outlined to him by the Regent and General Nuri. The Regent invited Senator Salih Jabr to form the new government on 29 March while General Nuri returned to the Senate to guide his protege from behind the scenes.'[48]

Secret military talks which were 'educative and exploratory' took place in Baghdad on 8–17 May 1947 at the end of which Prime Minister Salih Jabr made an unexpected speech warning that 'The present Treaty is not popular with the nation, and if we force the people to continue to accept it we will be preparing the way for growing hostility towards Great Britain which we both want to avoid.'[49] In July the British Embassy warned the Foreign Office that sooner or later the British would be faced with a demand for evacuation of the bases and advised that it would be unwise to try to hold positions which in the long run were untenable; even if for the next ten years there were friendly governments in Iraq pressure of public opinion for evacuation was likely to remain strong and probably increase in strength.[50]

While the Regent was under pressure from Iraqi public opinion when he met Bevin on 18 August 1947, the British Foreign Secretary was in difficulties with Anglo-Egyptian treaty revision. Baxter of the Foreign Office wrote:

What we and the Iraqis would really like is a reciprocal defence arrangement with all the Arab countries of the Middle East, but that cannot be secured by negotiations with Iraq alone, and no wider negotiations with the Middle East countries as a whole seem possible until the Palestine and Egyptian problems are on their way to settlement.'[51]

On 17 September 1947 the Chiefs-of-Staff, advised by the Foreign Office that 'in the light of growing pressure of nationalist opinion in Iraq for revision. . .we have better prospects of reaching a satisfactory agreement with the Iraqis now than if we refuse to consider revision before the existing Treaty expires in 1952,' agreed in principle to early treaty revision on the basis of sharing the air bases with the Iraqis. 'We appreciate,' they said, 'that it may be necessary to acquiesce in some arrangement which has the appearance of complete equality. We should emphasise, however, that, whatever the *de jure* arrangements, we must retain the *de facto* control.'[52] In October Bevin advised Stafford Cripps that

The significance of Iraq for Great Britain is clearly growing, particularly in the light of the situation in Egypt. Egypt is a broken reed. . .The Iraqis need and want our help. If we do not give it their external position might deteriorate and externally they might be tempted to turn elsewhere.'[53]

As a result the Treasury sanctioned financial concessions which were eventually made by the British, including the handing over free of charge the fixed assets at Camp 57 and Camp 67 and the Hull Bridge; and a contribution towards the cost of officer courses in Britain, previously paid for by the Iraqis, initially of £10,000, later raised to £20,000.

Further secret talks took place in Baghdad from 22 November to 3 December 1947. 'The main thing,' said Pyman of the Foreign Office reporting on the talks, 'was to find a form of words which would enable the present Iraqi government to give us what we want in fact, without signing a document which is liable to make them the butt of Iraqi and Arab opinion.'[54] The two conflicting views were put clearly at a meeting on 27 November. Busk, leading the British side, said '. . . the presence of adequate forces was the crucial point in the Treaty and unless the military requirements of HMG were granted the Treaty was valueless.' But Salih Jabr's position was 'I am master in my own house, and I want to be able to show my people the country with no forces in it, only staff to run the bases', and he would not agree to the stationing of foreign troops in peacetime. The Regent suggested Salih Jabr should go to London. 'I think,' wrote Busk to the Foreign Office, 'he feels that the Prime Minister must be faced with realities in a very different atmosphere.'[55]

It was essential for the British to have the RAF at Habbaniya and Sha'iba in peacetime and 'in consequence of developments in Palestine,' wrote the Ambassador on 24 December 1947, 'we have only a very brief period during which we can hope to secure our objectives.'[56] Consultations involving the Chiefs-of-Staff, the Embassy and Nuri al-Saʻid resulted in a proposed definition of 'peacetime' as being when all postwar treaties came into effect (by which time a Joint Defence Board would be established and making recommendations on military decisions in Iraq). The Treasury, told that 'the Foreign Office regard the conclusion of this Treaty as of the highest importance for our whole position in the Middle East,'[57] agreed to provision of a special plane to bring Salih Jabr and the rest of the Iraqi signing party from Iraq to Britain. The new Anglo-Iraqi Treaty was signed at Portsmouth (where Bevin was holidaying on doctor's orders) on 15 January. 'The letter is changed,' commented *Le Monde*, 'the spirit remains the same.'[58]

Al-Wathbah

The signing of the Portsmouth Treaty precipitated *al-Wathbah* — the Leap — 'most formidable mass insurrection in the history of the monarchy'.[59] As early as November 1947 the organ of the ICP, *al-Qaʻidah*, had called for the overthrow of the Salih Jabr Government, charging it with conducting secret negotiations on revision of the treaty and concealing their substance from the people. The Communists having united the left parties under a Cooperation Committee, stepped up the attack in December, warning of the dangers that lurked in the forthcoming final talks in London, and calling on all honest citizens to unite in a common struggle for severance of the treaty ties and the replacement of the Jabr Government by a democracy. On 3 January 1948 Foreign Secretary al-Jamali was reported as having said in London that party politics rather than justice were behind much of the criticism levelled at the 1930 treaty, and that if attacks on it had continued unabated a large number of Iraqis had, in the meantime, become sensitive to its merits. The statement was immediately disavowed by Salih Jabr but it had stimulated the Independence Party to meet and decide to call a demonstration, which took place on 5 January. A peaceful demonstration of law students, carrying banners decrying the statement attributed to Jamali, was confronted by mounted police, and beaten back from the Law School with clubs and firearms. Several students were wounded, 39 were arrested and the Law School was closed down. On 6 January students at all the other colleges went on strike. This preliminary phase of *al-Wathbah* ended when the authorities relented and on 8 January released the arrested students and reopened the Law School.

From 8 to 15 January, while the formal negotiations were taking place in Britain, the opposition in Iraq paused. Fahd, Secretary of the ICP, imprisoned with other leading Communists since January 1947, sent word from Kut prison that the party should make serious preparations to send its forces into the street. The Cooperation Committee, headed by Mosul lawyer and friend of the Communists, Kamil Qazanchi, was augmented by the Student Cooperation Committee, and the publication of the Portsmouth

Treaty on 16 January sparked a three-day strike and continuous demonstrations by college students. These were led by the Student Cooperation Committee, which had the support not only of the Communists and their confederates, the Progressive Democrats, the Populists and the Kurdish Democrats, but also of students from the National Democratic and Independence Parties. On 19 January the most right-wing of these parties, the Independence Party, ordered its students to separate from the Cooperation Committee and bide their time; but the National Democrats held on. From this point the Communists emerged unmistakably as the fundamental driving force behind *al-Wathbah*. On 20 January a Communist-initiated mass march participated in by workers and shanty-town dwellers as well as students, was fired upon and people were killed, some of them women and children. The following day the faculties of Pharmacy and Medicine and physicians at the hospital all resigned following the example of the Dean of the Pharmacy School, who had done so after students brought him the brains of one of their number, blown out by a police bullet. The streets were filled with angry crowds, armed with huge canes and clashing with the police. 'An atmosphere redolent of social revolution enveloped Baghdad,' says Batatu.

The Regent, unsure of the army, did an about-face. On the night of 21 January he summoned a palace council, this time inviting the representatives of the political parties, and he openly disowned the treaty, promising that 'no treaty will be ratified that does not assure the rights of the country and the national aspirations.'[60] This split the opposition: the National Democrats enjoined the people to remain on their guard because though the treaty was laid aside the government which signed it was still in power; the Communists were determined that the popular movement should continue to overthrow the Salih Jabr government. They were helped by Salih Jabr's statement in London on 22 January that the movement was the work of a few seditionists. On 23 January enormous crowds, roused by the Communists, streamed through Baghdad's main streets, meeting with no resistance, the uniformed police having withdrawn. The secret police recorded the event, including the unplanned calls of 'Long Live the Republic!' The Communist organizers did not intend to call the monarchy into question, but to split the Regent from the British, Nuri al-Sa'id and Salih Jabr.

On 26 January Nuri al-Sa'id and Salih Jabr returned from London, intent on salvaging the treaty. The Regent was persuaded by them to wheel about again and Salih Jabr broadcast an appeal for calm, promising a detailed explanation of the treaty. The crowds which took to the streets were met by Nuri al-Sa'id's answer to the problem: machine-guns. By the next morning the police were positioned at strategic points throughout Baghdad with orders to break up demonstrations and shoot to kill. The Communists published a declaration that there was no danger of civil war or revolution. They called on the Baghdadi citizens to struggle arm in arm to defeat the Portsmouth Treaty and overthrow the Salih Jabr cabinet; and for the formation of a national democratic government. That day, 27 January, 300 to 400 people were killed by the police. By the evening Salih Jabr was fleeing for his life to the Euphrates. The regent charged Muhammad al-Sadr, a Shi'i *sayyid* (man of religion), and a leader of the 1920 Revolt, with forming a new government. On 4 February the new government formally rejected the Portsmouth Treaty.

Solidarity and Repression

The next few months saw virtual anarchy in parts of Iraq, the manager of the largest Iraqi bank describing the situation as 'desperate', with the regime 'helpless to stem the mounting tide of unemployment, inevitably leading to riots and a political crisis of the first magnitude.'[61] In April 1948, after oilworkers' demands for 25–40% wage increases were turned down, the K3 pumping station on the pipeline near Haditha was brought to a halt by a strike of 30,000 workers, led by the ICP. After two and a half weeks, the government and the Iraq Petroleum Company (IPC) cut off the strikers' supplies of food and water but they were fed by neighbouring villagers. After three weeks the strikers decided to march on Baghdad, some 250 km. away. In the first two days of the march people in the small towns and villages on the way gave the marchers food and hospitality, and even lent them cars and trucks. They were eventually arrested outside Fallujah, about 70 miles from the capital. 'The collapse of the march in the face of government pressure is far less important than the fact that it was undertaken at all, and the sympathy which it attracted. The "great march" (*al-Masirah al-Kubra*) occupies an almost legendary place in modern Iraqi history.'[62] On 15 May 1948 British forces withdrew from Palestine, and the Israeli-Arab war broke out. Under the guise of waging the war, and 'in order to safeguard the rear of the Army' the government forces in Iraq, which had regrouped themselves, declared martial law and made hundreds of arrests in a wave of repression against all who played an active part in *al-Wathbah*. The repression continued throughout 1949, when several prominent members of the ICP were executed, and the Party organization was temporarily shattered.

Oil, Foreign Control and Social Dislocation

The reconstruction and expansion of the industrialized capitalist countries which began in the 1950s, under the leadership of the USA, required a rapid and protracted increase in the production and export of Middle Eastern crude oil. In 1952 the American oil companies adopted a 50-50 policy to 'get more money into the hands of conservative governments in the Arab world.'[63] For Iraq this meant oil revenue jumped from 10% of total government income to 60%. Control of oil output and prices, however, remained firmly in the hands of IPC executives in New York and London. Furthermore, the Iraqi dinar was linked to sterling, so Iraq's economy was regularly affected by changes in the value of the pound. Even though the Portsmouth Treaty was never ratified, Britain still had air bases at Habbaniya and Sha'iba under the terms of the 1930 Treaty, and in 1955 was instrumental in recruiting Iraq into the US-sponsored Baghdad Pact. The Iraqi regime had been dependent on oil revenue simply to balance the country's budget since 1934, but the additional revenue after 1952 enabled Nuri al-Sa'id to resolve Iraq's postwar financial crisis, and undertake development projects such as dams and irrigation schemes which benefitted the large landowners.

> Iraq in this period is a society enduring tremendous dislocations. The largest source of national wealth is under foreign control. The locus of domestic production is the agricultural sector, but there land tenure, income distribution and the sharply polarized class structure contribute to the continued deterioration of the means of production – the land – and the immizeration of the producers. There is accelerated growth in the urban centres, especially Baghdad: the oil rent and agricultural surpluses are concentrated there in trade, construction and speculation. Great numbers of the peasants flee the land and crowd the slums, finding even the miserable, part-time, unskilled, poorly paid jobs there an improvement over conditions in the countryside.[64]

Iraq's Pre-revolutionary Social Structure

The society thus dislocated in the 1950s had been virtually re-structured by the British.

> When the British came to Iraq in 1914 they adapted the Ottoman machinery and combined it with British Indian administrative practice, which arrested the decline in shaikhly power and gave wide-ranging powers to the tribal shaikhs and landlords. . .local notables made use of their powers to acquire vast semifeudal estates and to reduce 'their' tribesmen to the status of debt-bonded serfs; this eventually led to the virtual isolation of the rural area from the rest of the economy, and tended to arrest the emergence of capitalist relations of production in the countryside. The acute contradiction set in motion by this process resulted in severe distortions in the country's economic and political systems, which continued until, and indeed long after, the Revolution of 1958.[65]

By the late 1950s, 70% of all cultivable land in Iraq was divided into some 3,400 large estates.[66] 55.1% was owned by 2,484 individuals (out of a total population of 6 to 7 million); and 16.8% belonged to the 49 families who formed the core of the landlord class.[67] Although the landlords were mainly tribal shaikhs, since the British occupation

> an organic relationship (had) evolved among the indigenous segments as urban officials used their position to secure vast estates for themselves and partnerships with the large merchants; shaikhs took up residence in the

towns as absentee landlords and acquired interests in urban real estate and the import trade.[68]

With the *Lazma Law* of 1952, adding to the laws of 1931, 1932, and 1933, the landlords' virtual immunity from taxation and their power to rule almost directly, particularly in Kut and 'Amara, was confirmed.

> On the eve of the 1958 Revolution, large land ownership, together with the power of Nuri and the Monarchy, were correctly identified by many Iraqis as the creation of the British. Abolition of the landlords and the political apparatus which sustained them were desired not simply on the grounds of economic efficiency or social justice, but to achieve the goal of full independence from British control.[69]

The Iraqi peasantry was particularly poverty-stricken, even by Middle Eastern standards. Most of the rural population of 3.8 million in 1957 were completely landless.[70] In 1953 a British medical expert described the Iraqi peasant as 'a living pathological specimen' and noted that the average life expectancy was between 35 and 39 years.[71] Apart from occasional peasant risings this section of Iraqi society was generally inarticulate and passive, as well as being landless, illiterate and heavily in debt.

In the towns, especially Baghdad, Basra and Mosul, the pre-revolutionary bourgeoisie consisted largely of traders, ranging from well-to-do import and export wholesalers to owners of small shops. 90,000 individuals were engaged in foreign and domestic trade in 1957–8 and 9,000 in real estate transactions for profit.[72] As well as this commercial fraction there was also an emerging industrial fraction of the bourgeoisie, whose capital accumulation accelerated after the Development Board was established in 1950, enabling Iraqi contractors to take advantage of major government investment in construction and public works. By the late 1950s profits from manufacturing exceeded those from trade. Despite its growing size and diversification of wealth and property,

> the bourgeoisie as a whole was no match for the real powers in the country, namely the monarchy and its entourage, the great landowners, the Iraq Petroleum Company, and British economic and military domination. In many important ways therefore the grande bourgeoisie were as excluded from political power as the other strata of the population below them.[73]

Below those who were unmistakably bourgeois in their outlook and material conditions but above the mass of peasants and workers were the petty bourgeoisie, a growing class of small businessmen, shopkeepers, professionals and semi-professionals employed in services and the public sector such as teachers, doctors, civil servants and army officers. There were also thousands of students looking for careers in commerce or scarce posts in the government bureaucracy. Remembering hardships in their own families many were believers in social justice, but their main concern was to progress up the social ladder and they were often contemptuous of manual labour. Since the petty bourgeois were the most educated Iraqis they were the most important carriers of nationalist and anti-imperialist ideas, which were, however, also held by members of the bourgeoisie, the peasantry and the working class.

The Iraqi working class was still in the making on the eve of the 1958 Revolution, a process checked by the basic weakness of the industrial bourgeoisie. In 1954 only 90,291 workers were employed in industrial production and a further 15,249 in the oil industry. Of the 22,460 enterprises in existence 45% were one-man businesses and 93% employed less than five workers. Only 294 firms employed more than 20 workers and between them they employed 44% of all industrial workers. Only 30,000 workers worked for manufacturing units employing ten or more workers. The total numerical strength of the working class including those employed in transport and services was estimated to be 442,000, out of a total urban population of 2.6 million. A very large proportion of the working class was illiterate and, since many of them had only recently migrated from rural areas, most were unskilled.[74]

Poverty

Between 1939 and 1957 the cost of living in Iraq increased fivefold. On the eve of the 1958 Revolution 80% of the population was illiterate; 90% of Iraqi women were illiterate; and less than 20% of Iraqi children went to school. There was only one doctor for every 6,000 people; one dentist for every 500,000; one nurse for every 12,000. There was no form of social security for unemployment, old age or ill health, except for a small number who were in government service. At a meeting of the Baghdad Pact countries (Iraq, Iran, Pakistan and Turkey), in 1956, the Pakistani Health Minister admitted that 'The proportion of undernourished persons in the region has, during the past few years risen from 33% to 56%, and the incidence of tuberculosis, which is increasing is four times that obtaining in the European countries.'[75]

Repression and Resistance

In the last years of the monarchy

> The disarticulation between the political system (a parliament monopolized by the landlords and handpicked government supporters) and rapidly changing social reality became untenable with the increasing pace of urban-based economic activity following the growth of oil revenues. Strikes and demonstrations by workers and students increased in tempo and severity. Repression was harsh and democratic rights systematically denied. When the regime's alignment with the US and Britain against Egypt led

to the Baghdad Pact, this affront to Iraqi and Arab nationalism heightened the already explosive confrontation over basic democratic rights, and, more importantly, the allocation of economic and political power in Iraqi society . . . The ascendant bourgeoisie, petty bourgeoisie and working class demanded that the state represent their interests. As even the armed forces came to reflect the shifting balance of social forces, the immunity of the regime to radical alteration evaporated.[76]

Iraq's ruling clique was compared by one contemporary observer to a pack of cards who 'comprise the elite, with seats in the Senate, rotten boroughs to elect them to the lower house and American commerical agencies to pay their bills. It is an ill-assorted pack, with no kings, no queens, but many knaves.'[77] The *New Statesman*, describing the regime in 1958, wrote: 'All political parties were banned, the press censored, there were 10,000 political prisoners, torture was regularly employed.'[78] Nuri al-Sa'id had

a very efficient, British-trained police force, innumerable spies and agents provocateurs, a controlled press and a complacent Parliament dominated by the big southern landowners who are his main natural supporters. His chief hatchet-man, Sa'id Quazzaz, has been Minister of Interior about as many times as Nuri has been Premier. . .Most of the time martial law is in force and Quazzaz has a very efficient card-index system for checking on the movements of known nationalists and troublemakers, so that they can be rounded up at a few hours notice if there is a sudden change in the political situation and a threat of street riots.[79]

In 1952, inspired by the Egyptian Revolution, an uprising took place in Iraq demanding democratic rights, particularly direct elections. There were marches in Baghdad in which 40 people were killed when police opened fire on demonstrators; a strike for higher wages by the Iraqi workforce at the British bases in Habbaniya and Sha'iba, in which officially two strikers were killed and nine wounded; and strikes at the ports of Fao and Basra, also suppressed with bloodshed and loss of life.[80] Even after 2,000 arrests the police did not have the situation fully under control and to save itself the ruling clique played on the popularity of the army. Military units were sent into the streets, where there was fraternization between soldiers and people; and the Army Chief-of-Staff was made Prime Minister, despite this being unconstitutional. Although the principle of direct elections was conceded, the repressive apparatus and corrupt political system remained intact.

Article 79 of the *Criminal Procedure Act* Appendix permitted the arrest of persons 'who for some reason, it is believed, may disturb the peace.' There was no limitation to the length of time a prisoner could be held before being brought to trial; and 'Nuri never hesitated to use force, if necessary – from police beatings to deliberate torture to extract information.'[81] Political prisoners were kept in gaols at Nugrat al-Salman, Kut and Ba'quba. In June 1953 political prisoners in Baghdad gaol refused to move to the much more savage Ba'quba gaol, but were machine-gunned, many were killed and all

153 were injured. At Kut two political prisoners were killed in August 1953 when they presented a petition demanding improvements in conditions; in September eight were killed and 92 wounded.

The Baghdad Pact

The removal of British troops from Egypt, the spread and popularity of Nasserist ideas throughout the Arab world, and the enhancement of Nasser's status to that of international statesman, when he embraced the principle of non-alignment at the Bandung Conference in 1953, gave Nuri al-Sa'id's reactionary, pro-Western regime a special role to play in the formation of the Baghdad Pact which developed from US Secretary of State John Foster Dulles' 'Northern Tier' foreign policy concept, of bringing the countries bordering the Soviet Union into a military pact with the West. Nuri al-Sa'id shared Dulles' obsessive anti-Communism, and also believed that the Soviet Union had the same 'southward thrust' aim as Tsarist Russia. He resumed the post of Prime Minister in 1954, to take Iraq into the Baghdad Pact, to which most Iraqis were opposed. When the 1954 elections returned groups other than Sa'id's henchmen the parliament was dissolved and new elections held, which were boycotted, 122 out of 135 seats being uncontested.

> The Prime Minister Nuri al-Sa'id, [commented *The Times*] may, however, have been too thorough this time. His election not only eliminated the extremists, but some influential Conservative statesmen of the Pasha's own generation. . . Since Nuri Sa'id returned to office all political parties have been dissolved, including his own. The application of a new press ordinance has reduced the number of newspapers licensed in Baghdad from sixty or so to seven. . .The colleges and schools have been purged of their fiery element. The dismissed teachers and students, and also the civil servants dismissed for political misconduct, have been made liable under an amendment to the army law for nine months' military service.[82]

The Parliament thus created ratified the Baghdad Pact after only ten minutes' discussion, with tanks and army units surrounding it and on the streets of Baghdad to prevent any demonstration. So disastrous for the country were the 'Special Agreements' and 'Memoranda' of the Pact that the Iraqi people only learned of them from discussions in the British House of Commons. They were concealed from the Iraqi parliament because Nuri al-Sa'id could not be sure that even his hand-picked deputies would accept them.

In 1956 following the Anglo-French-Israeli invasion of Egypt there were demonstrations in support of Egypt in Baghdad, Mosul, Najaf and Hai, near Kut. The Iraqi regime attacked the crowds with aeroplanes and field artillery, killing and wounding dozens, including prominent political, intellectual and civic leaders. Two patriots were executed at Hai. 'Nuri survived the Suez storm by acting quickly and with great energy. Altogether he locked up nearly 500 people.'[83]

The National Unity Front

By early 1957 the three main opposition parties banned in 1954 – the National Democratic Party (NDP), the Iraqi Communist Party (ICP) and the Ba'th Party – had formed the National Unity Front, together with Nasserists, whose influence increased after 1956, and other opposition groups.

The NDP, which developed from the liberal *Ahali* group founded in the 1930s, was the party of the Iraqi bourgeoisie, its lack of organization and influence accurately reflecting the complexities and lack of differentiation within the bourgeoisie. It was small in numbers but its leaders were men of substance and importance: Muhammad Hadid became Minister of Finance and Hudaiyyib al-Hajj Hmud, a 'liberal' landowner, became Minister of Agriculture after the 1958 Revolution. 'What the middle class and the upper strata of the bourgeoisie actually wanted, of course, was a revolution which would promote social reform and development with a socio-economic system that safeguarded and promoted their own private interests and property.'[84]

The ICP, founded in 1934, was unquestionably the most effective political party in Iraq, small by European standards, but tightly organized throughout the country and widely supported. Many of the ICP's supporters had only a vague understanding of socialism but saw the party as standing for social justice and improvements in their living conditions. ICP members, who were very active in the independence movement and led organizations such as the Partisans for Peace, the League for the Defence of Women's Rights, the Federation of Democratic Youth, several trade unions and an organization for soldiers, with its own newspaper, bore the brunt of the repression which intensified after 1954. The tremendous popularity of the ICP in 1958 and after was largely a result of its courageous stand in the pre-Revolutionary years, when its main aim was the mobilization and unification of all political forces opposed to the regime.

The Ba'th Party, founded in Iraq in 1954 on the basis of ideas formulated in Syria, was essentially a party of the petty bourgeoisie, and thus had many potential supporters in Iraq. On the eve of the Revolution it was still very small, split into a number of factions and lacked any mass support, but it was militant and tightly organized.

The Nasserists, or *qawmiyyum*, were devoted admirers of Nasser, but they had no formal political organization. As Pan-Arab Nationalists, they sought the union of Iraq with other Arab countries, particularly Egypt and Syria, an idea as yet untarnished by Syrian experience of Egyptian domination in the United Arab Republic. Before the 1958 Revolution Iraqi Nasserists were barely discernible as a separate group, because all the opposition was pro-Nasser at that time.

The National Unity Front was a very loose alliance whose goals of independence, social reform and land reform corresponded to those of the conservative NDP but were also on the programme of the ICP. Its formation stimulated the Free Officers within the army who, like many Iraqis, were highly politicized. None of the political parties however, were directly in touch with the Free Officers, and the actual timing of the revolutionary coup d'état took them all by surprise.[85]

The Revolutionary Coup d'État 14 July 1958

In May an article in the illegal communist newspaper *Ittihad al-Sha'b* declared: 'The rule of the traitors is collapsing. Let us prepare ourselves for the awaited moment'. On 18 June 4,000 people demonstrated in Diwaniyah and in a three-hour battle with police 43 were killed, 120 wounded and 500 arrested. The paramilitary police were used because Nuri al-Sa'id could no longer rely on the army. On 12 July the ICP advised its underground members that 'the political atmosphere in Iraq is now extremely tense' and that they should 'rally the masses around the chief slogans and demands of our national democratic movements'.[86] The opportunity in hope of which the Free Officers had long conspired now presented itself, as a result of three events which had occurred earlier in 1958. These were: the formation of the United Arab Republic of Egypt and Syria (UAR), which brought Nasser's jurisdiction to the borders of Iraq; the civil conflict in Lebanon, which led to conflict among army officers as well as among civilians; and the declaration by the Iraqi regime of a union between Iraq and Jordan.[87]

On the eve of the Revolution Nuri al-Sa'id, his leading ministers and senior army officers were engaged in preparing the framework of the Iraq-Jordanian 'Arab Union', some of the army officers being in Amman, to organize a Joint General Staff for the unified army. On the night of 13–14 July, when a brigade of the Iraqi army located in north-east Baghdad was ordered to move to Jordan some of the Free Officers suspected that the government intended to use it in support of President Chamoun against the Lebanese opposition. At 4.30 in the morning of 14 July 'Abd al-Salam 'Arif, who had gained control of the whole brigade, entered Baghdad at its head. He seized the radio station and from it announced the downfall of the regime, and urged people to take to the streets. He sent detachments to the Royal Palace, where the royal family were shot dead, to the Ministry of Defence and the South Gate police station to establish communication with the Free Officers in the Rashid Army Camp. 'Abd al-Karim Qasim, then commander of the 19th Infantry Brigade, arrived with his forces and appointed Brigadier Salih al-'Abdi as Military Governor of Baghdad. Martial law was declared in the afternoon and tanks were stationed at the important points in Baghdad. The new regime announced on the radio that:

> The affairs of the country must be entrusted to a Government emanating from the people and working under its inspiration. This can only be

achieved by the formation of a popular republic to uphold complete Iraqi unity, to bind itself with bonds of fraternity with Arab and Muslim countries to work in accordance with UN principles, to honour all pledges and treaties in accordance with the interests of the homeland, and to act in compliance with the Bandung Conference resolutions. This national government shall be known from now on by the name of the Iraqi Republic.[88]

Within a few days, during which Nuri al-Sa'id was captured and killed, order was restored.

Wahda

The new Iraqi Republic was ruled by a Revolutionary Council of top army officers, one of whom was Prime Minister Qasim, and a Cabinet of NDP leaders and middle class independents. Qasim's social and political policies were welcomed and applauded by a wide spectrum of Iraqi society, since they met many of the demands of the pre-Revolutionary independence struggles: withdrawal of Iraq from the Baghdad Pact and Sterling Area; evacuation of British bases; establishment of diplomatic and trading relations with socialist countries; a programme of land reform; negotiations with IPC for a greater share of oil royalties; a housing programme for the shanty-town dwellers on the outskirts of Baghdad; an amnesty for all political prisoners; a draft constitution; legal recognition for trade unions, peasant unions and similar democratic organizations; profits on consumer goods limited to 15%; rents reduced; and substantial cuts in the price of food and other necessities. So great was the immediate popularity of the Revolution, with the Iraqi people giving their full support to Qasim and the Iraqi army, that, although US marines had just landed in Lebanon and the British moved Jordanian troops to the border with Iraq, direct Western military intervention was not attempted.

The main contradiction in Iraq immediately after the Revolution was that of a basically national bourgeois regime confronted by, yet at the same time relying upon, a politically conscious radical left. The issue of how radical the Revolution should be became symbolized by the struggle over whether or not Iraq should join the union of Egypt and Syria, which would mean that Nasserist political and economic doctrines would be applied to Iraq. For the Communists and their sympathizers this would mean persecution, and for Qasim it would mean subservience to Nasser. Thus, for different reasons, the left and Qasim were equally opposed to *wahda* (union). 'Wahda developed into the rallying cry for opposition to the left since, for many union with Egypt was the lesser evil in the face of radical socio-economic change or a government in which the Communists were actually represented.'[89]

Suppression of the Communists

In March 1959 a pro-*wahda* revolt took place in Mosul, with Egyptian support, led by Colonel al-Shawwaf, a Nasserist, which failed only after much bloodshed. In April the situation in Iraq was, in the opinion of Allen Dulles, Director of the CIA, 'the most dangerous in the world today' and the Communists were close to a 'complete takeover'. In fact the ICP had no plans to seize power, but was calling for reconstruction of the National Unity Front and free elections, in which it could expect to win many seats. In July 1959, in the days following the first anniversary of the Revolution, 31 people were killed and 130 injured in violence provoked in Kirkuk between pro- and anti-government forces. In August the ICP Central Committee stated that 'we utterly condemn any transgression against innocent people . . .or the harming or torture even of traitors. . .We condemn these methods in principle'[90] but the Kirkuk violence was used to drive a wedge between the Communists and Qasim. He still, however, needed to satisfy left public opinion, and to this end ordered the execution in September 1959 of Sa'id Qazzaz, Minister of the Interior under Nuri al-Sa'id. This execution convinced the Ba'thists and Pan-Arab Nationalists whom Qasim had dropped from the Cabinet in February 1959, that he was not turning seriously against the Communists, and in October a Ba'thist assassination attempt on Qasim's life was carried out, but failed, one of the would-be assassins being a youthful Saddam Husain.

Withdrawal of democratic rights and suppression of Communists accelerated in 1960. More than 6,000 trade unionists were dismissed from their jobs and the government took control of the trade unions, peasants' unions and organizations of lawyers, teachers and students, after attacks on their offices and the homes of their democratic leaders. Even the moderate paper *al-Istiqlal* in February 1961 described this process as 'acts of forging the wishes of the voters and violating their freedoms by blackmailing them in their means of livelihood and hurling them into prisons and places of detention.'[91] Circulation of the ICP's newspaper was restricted and the ICP's application for a licence was turned down. Later the NDP's *al-Ahali* newspaper was suppressed and the licence of the Kurdistan Democratic Party (KDP, founded 1945) was withdrawn. Nuri al-Sa'id's secret police and repressive apparatus were still in existence and it was second nature to them to resume persecution of the left.

The Overthrow of Qasim

One of the main achievements of the Qasim period, from July 1958 to February 1963, was the agrarian law reform programme, largely a result of the ICP's efforts. This broke the political strength of the landlords. The power of the grande bourgeoisie was also broken at this time. Political and economic power were reconstructed in favour of the urban and petty bourgeoisie while maintaining the principle of private ownership. In addition to these internal achievements Iraq's revolution cut the link with Britain and took Iraq out of the Baghdad Pact. Another very important achievement was the passing of Law 80 in October 1961, which ended futile negotiations with the Iraq Petroleum Company (IPC) and limited the company's rights to 0.5% of the concession actually being exploited, and secured prospecting and oil rights in the other 99.5% of the country for the government.

Although Qasim retained his personal popularity he isolated himself from all political parties. The Ba'thists and Pan-Arab Nationalists he dismissed from power then sought to unseat him; the Communists never sought to unseat him, but by dismissing army officers suspected of membership of, or sympathy with, the ICP Qasim deprived himself of those who would have defended him against a coup. He created a power vacuum around himself, so that the alliance of Ba'thists and Pan-Arab Nationalists who plotted to overthrow him only had to kill one military man, the Commander of the Air Force, in order to seize power. Then began the slaughter of their political opponents.

References

1. Hanna Batatu, 'Class Analysis and Iraqi Society', *Arab Studies Quarterly*, vol. 1, no. 3, Summer 1979, pp. 229–230.

2. Batatu, *The Old Social Classes and Revolutionary Movements in Iraq: a Study of Iraq's Old Landed and Commercial Classes and of its Communists, Ba'thists and Free Officers*, (Princeton, 1978) pp. 239–240.

3. Peter Sluglett and Marion Farouk-Sluglett, 'Some Reflections on the Sunni/Shi'i Question in Iraq', *British Society for Middle Eastern Studies Bulletin* vol. 5, no. 2, 1978 p. 81.

4. Batatu, *The Old Social Classes*, pp. 239–240.

5. Quoted by Sluglett, *Britain in Iraq 1914-1932*, (London, 1976) p. 104.

5. Joe Stork, 'Oil and the Penetration of Capitalism in Iraq', in Petter Nore and Terisa Turner (eds.), *Oil and Class Struggle* (London, 1980), p. 174.

6. Quoted by Sluglett, *Britain in Iraq*, p. 104.

7. Ibid., p. 19.

8. Ibid., p. 14.

9. Ibid., p. 37.

10. Ibid., p. 28.

11. Farouk-Sluglett and Sluglett, 'Labor and National Liberation: the Trade Union Movement in Iraq, 1920-1958', *Arab Studies Quarterly*, vol.5, no. 2, 1981, p. 144.

12. Quoted by Sluglett, *Britain in Iraq*, p. 31.

13. Ibid., p. 32.

14. S.H. Longrigg, *Iraq 1900-1950*, (London, 1953), p. 127.

15. Sir David Lee, *Flight from the Middle East*, p. XV.

16. Farouk-Sluglett and Sluglett, 'Labor and National Liberation', p. 145.

17. Quoted by Sluglett, *Britain in Iraq*, p. 78.
18. Ibid., p. 111.
19. Ibid., p. 125.
20. Farouk-Sluglett and Sluglett, 'Labor and National Liberation', p. 147.
21. Stork, 'Oil and the Penetration of Capitalism in Iraq', p. 174.
22. S. Khairi, *Min Ta'rikh al-Haraka al-Thawriyya al-Mu'asira fi'il-'Iraq*, (Baghdad, 1975), quoted in 'Labor and National Liberation'.
23. Quoted by Sluglett, *Britain in Iraq*, p. 208.
24. Sluglett, *Britain in Iraq*, p. 222.
25. Stork, 'Oil and the Penetration of Capitalism in Iraq', p. 175.
26. Farouk-Sluglett and Sluglett, 'Labor and National Liberation', p. 149.
27. Edith and E.F. Penrose, *Iraq: International Relations and National Development*, (London, 1978).
28. Farouk-Sluglett and Sluglett, 'Labour and National Liberation', p. 145.
29. Khadduri, *Independent Iraq: 1932–1958* (London, 1960).
30. Quoted by Mohammad A. Tarbush in *The Role of the Military in Politics: A case study of Iraq to 1941*, (London, 1982), p. 77.
31. Sluglett, *Britain in Iraq*.
32. Quoted Tarbush, *The Role of the Military in Politics*, p. 94.
33. Tarbush, *The Role of the Military in Politics*, p. 94.
34. Batatu, *The Old Social Classes*, pp. 442–443.
35. Khadduri, *Independent Iraq*.
36. Report by the British Ambassador, quoted by Farouk-Sluglett and Sluglett, 'Labor and National Liberation', note p. 146.
37. Farouk-Sluglett and Sluglett, 'Labor and National Liberation', p. 147.
38. Khairi, *Min Tarikh*, pp. 150–152.
39. Lee, *Flight from the Middle East*.
40. Ibid.
41. Montgomery of Alamein, *The Memoirs of Field Marshal the Viscount of Alamein, KG* (Collins, London 1958) p. 436.
42. Philip Darby, *British Defence Policy East of Suez 1947–1968*, (OUP, London, 1973) p. 26.
43. Elizabeth Monroe, *Britain's Moment in the Middle East, 1914–56*, (Chatto and Windus, London, 1963) p. 156.
44. Batatu, *The Old Social Classes*, p. 545.
45. FO 371 52401 E2831, quoted by Fran Hazelton in *Military Aspects of the Portsmouth Treaty*, MA diss. S.O.A.S. London, 1981.
46. FO 371 52401.
47. FO 371 52402 E9355/226/G.
48. Khadduri, *Independent Iraq*.
49. FO 371 61591.
50. FO 371 61592.
51. FO 371 61594 E7069.
52. FO 371 6194.
53. FO 371 61595 E9513.
54. FO 371 61599 E11608.
55. FO 371 61599 E11566.
56. FO 371 61601 E12235.
57. FO 371 61601 E12259.
58. *Le Monde*, 17 January 1948.

59. Batatu, *The Old Social Classes*, p. 545.

60. *The Times*, 22 January 1948, quoted by George Kirk, *The Middle East 1945–1950*, p. 157.

61. Remark reported to Washington by US Embassy, quoted by Stork, 'Oil and the Pentration of Capitalism in Iraq,' see his note 6.

62. Farouk-Sluglett and Sluglett, 'Labor and National Liberation', p. 154.

63. US Ambassador George MacGhee, quoted by Stork, 'Oil and the Penetration of Capitalism in Iraq', see his note 7.

64. Stork, 'Oil and the Penetration of Capitalism in Iraq', p. 178.

65. Farouk-Sluglett and Sluglett, 'The Transformation of Land Tenure and Rural Social Structure in Central and Southern Iraq c 1870–1958', *Int. J. Middle East Stud.*, 15(1983), p. 491.

66. Farouk-Sluglett and Sluglett, 'Iraq: The Path to Independence,' *Gazelle Review*, 6, 1979, p. 41.

67. Batatu, 'Class Analysis and Iraqi Society', p. 237.

68. Stork, 'Oil and the Penetration of Capitalism in Iraq', p. 174.

69. Farouk-Sluglett and Sluglett, 'Iraq: The Path to Independence', p. 42.

70. M. Farouk-Sluglett, 'Contemporary Iraq: Some Recent Writing Reconsidered', *Review of Middle East Studies*, 3, 1978, p. 91.

71. R. Gabbay, *Communism and Agrarian Reforms in Iraq*, (London, 1978) p. 29.

72. M.S. Hasan, 'The Role of Foreign Trade in the Economic Development of Iraq, 1864–1964: A Study in the Growth of a Dependent Economy,' in M.A. Cook, ed. *Studies in the Economic History of the Middle East* (London, 1970).

73. Farouk-Sluglett, 'Contemporary Iraq', p. 92.

74. Ibid., p. 91.

75. *Times*, 4 December 1956, quoted by Idris Cox in *End Terrorism in Iraq* (CPGB pamphlet 1962), p. 5.

76. Stork, 'Oil and the Penetration of Capitalism in Iraq', pp. 179, 181.

77. Desmond Stewart and John Haylock, *New Babylon*, (London, 1956).

78. *New Statesman*, 19 July 1958.

79. Paul Johnson, *Journey into Chaos*, (London, 1958).

80. Khairi, *Min Tarikh*, pp. 186–187.

81. Johnson, op. cit.

82. *Times*, 23 February 1955, quoted by Cox in *End Terrorism in Iraq*.

83. Johnson, op. cit.

84. Farouk-Sluglett, *'Contemporary Iraq'*, p. 93.

85. Ibid., p. 95.

86. Cox, *End Terrorism in Iraq*, p. 6.

87. Penrose and Penrose, *Iraq*, p. 202.

88. Ibid., p. 204.

89. Farouk-Sluglett, 'Contemporary Iraq', p. 97.

90. Ittihad al-Sha'b, 2 August 1959, quoted by Batatu in *The Old Social Classes*.

91. Cox, op. cit., p. 9.

2. Political Developments in Iraq 1963-1980

U. Zaher

The Fascist Coup of February 1963

The Fascist coup of 8 February 1963, which brought the Ba'th Party to power, found ready allies among diverse political forces. It was welcomed by all reactionary forces and the enemies of the 14 July 1958 Revolution. The Ba'th was also able to win the support of senior army officers who had lost their positions or been banished from political life, or, in some cases, had been waiting for a chance to avenge the death of fellow officers executed under Qasim's rule for taking part in unsuccessful plots. The coup was even supported by Kurdish groups who had been at war with the previous regime, despite the fact that the Ba'thist internal publication *al-Ishtiraki* (The Socialist) had only a month earlier described the Kurdish movement as a 'suspect colonialist movement' and that the Ba'th had criticized Qasim for not dealing severely enough with the Kurdish revolt.

An important factor in favour of the Ba'thist plotters and their allies was the growing isolation of the Qasim regime from the people and the democratic forces. It had gradually surrendered to reactionary elements key posts in the army, the state and the economy. From mid-1959 the danger of counter-revolution was indeed looming, fluctuating but steadily increasing. Democratic forces who warned of the danger were ignored and even suppressed. On the eve of the coup, many of Qasim's own men were in despair and ready to compromise with the enemies of the revolution. At the critical moment they surrendered shamelessly to the camp of the plotters. Thus it was that when masses of people surged forward from their slums in Baghdad to confront the conspirators and their tanks, they faced not only their old enemies but also some of Qasim's own aides.

The coup was marked by its extreme brutality towards the revolutionary forces which had played a principal role first in the struggle against colonialism and the monarchy and later for the defence and development of the July 1958 revolution. The Ba'th Party itself acknowledged its bloody deeds when it looked back to the 'lessons' of its first experience of power in 1963 and their application to its second bid for power in July 1968. The Political Report of the Eighth Regional Congress of the Ba'th Party held in Baghdad in January 1974 openly stated: 'In the revolution of 8 February 1963 blood was shed freely. . . Therefore the leadership of the Party determined that this time power must be taken over without such bloodletting as would spoil the image and divert the course of the Revolution'.[1]

The coup was not merely reactionary. It was carried out to bring a fascist-style party, the Ba'th, to power, a party influenced by the national socialist ideology of its principal founder and spiritual leader, Michel 'Aflaq. It set up a para-military body, the National Guard, whose brutal and barbarous activities were reported in the international press with undisguised revulsion. 'This sounds like an open incitement to a massacre which would make St. Bartholomew's Day look like a Sunday school picnic' (*Sunday Times* 10 February 1963). '. . .I have left behind many hundreds of people for whom the future holds only firing squads' (*Daily Express* 12 February 1963). 'According to the best informed sources there are at least 1,000 dead in Baghdad alone' (*Le Monde* 14 February 1963).

In the pamphlet 'Report from Iraq' issued by the British Committee for the Defence of Human Rights in Iraq, dated February 1964, Leslie Hale M.P. pointed out that 'the National Guards were actually set up in a fashion closely similar to the Hitlerite shock troops, except that the National Guards were immature, untrained and even less responsible. They were enlisted in the main on the basis of anti-communism, and their solution for every problem was: violence.' Bands of the National Guard roamed the streets and carried out summary executions, arbitrary arrests and savage torture. Sports grounds, military camps and schools were turned into concentration camps and interrogation centres for tens of thousands of people from all walks of life. At the top of the list were leaders, cadres and activists of the trade unions and the mass democratic organizations, including the Iraqi Women's League and the General Union of Students of the Iraqi Republic (GUSIR). The regime installed and imposed its own Fascist-type 'mass' organizations which acted as extensions of the National Guard.

Hanna Batatu[2] has described the terrible torture chambers in *Qasr al-Nihayah* (Palace of the End) in Baghdad, a palace from the time of the monarchy which became a centre for detention and interrogation. The headquarters of the National Guard in all towns became torture centres. A pamphlet entitled *al-Munharifun* (The Perverts), a semi-official publication circulated in 1964, after the fall of the Ba'th, provided horrific photographic evidence and documents exposing the crimes committed under the direct orders of the notorious 'Special Bureau of Investigation'. It included lists of names of the murdered and 'disappeared' victims, and a description of the instruments of torture. Hands and fingers were chopped, women were raped and victims were killed by poison then dissolved in acid tanks leaving no trace behind. Mass graves were later unearthed where victims had been buried alive.

Massacre of Communists

The National Guard and their Ba'thist masters viewed the Iraqi Communist Party as a special target for their countrywide barbarous crimes. Their leader Michel 'Aflaq later declared in an interview with the French daily *Le Monde*: 'Communist Parties will be banned and suppressed with the utmost severity in any country where the Ba'th Party comes to power'.[3] The fact was that despite a systematic campaign of repression under Qasim's dictatorial rule, with hundreds of Communists imprisoned, sentenced to death and assassinated[4], the Iraqi Communist Party had remained a formidable political force and a threat to the new rulers.

On the evening of 8 February 1963, at 8.20 p.m., Baghdad radio broadcast Order Number 13 which called for a massacre of Communists. It stated:

> As a consequence of the attempts of Communist agents, supporters of God's enemy 'Abd al-Karim Qasim, to disturb the ranks of the citizens and disobey orders and instructions, we hereby confer authority on the commanders of military units, Police and National Guards to annihilate anyone who disturbs the peace. Faithful sons of the people are called upon to co-operate with the authorities by informing on these criminals and annihilate them.

CIA Connection

Evidence of the direct involvement of the CIA in the anti-communist witch-hunt came to light in later years. Muhammad Haikal, then editor of the Egyptian daily *al-Ahram*, stated on the authority of King Husain of Jordan that 'an American espionage service' which had been in touch with the Iraqi Ba'th conveyed to the latter, on a secret broadcasting service, the names and addresses of the Iraqi Communists.[5] The American agency referred to was almost certainly the CIA. This fact is confirmed by Penrose and Penrose[6] who quote well informed Iraqi officials, including Ba'thists. The French *Service de Documentation Extérieure et de Contre-Espionnage* also helped to overthrow Qasim and harass the Communists.[7]

Armed with the names and whereabouts of individual Communists, the National Guards carried out summary executions. Communists held in detention under the Qasim regime since the clamp down in 1959 and 1960 were dragged out of prison and shot without a hearing.[8] Iraqi Communist Party sources put at 5,000 the number of their members and supporters killed during the first three days of the coup while resisting the Ba'th take-over or the house-to-house witch-hunt.[9] Other sources claimed that by the end of the rule of the Ba'th, its terror campaign had claimed the lives of an estimated 3,000 to 5,000 Communists.[10]

Popular Resistance

As soon as the coup became known early in the morning of 8 February 1963 tens of thousands of people came out on the streets from the poorer districts of Baghdad, such as *al-Thawra* township. They took control of vantage points and bridges and converged on the Ministry of Defence to block the advance of the tanks. Qasim, who arrived there at 10 a.m., turned down their demands for arms and decided to barricade himself in the Ministry of Defence with about 1,500 troops and resist the plotters there. The Communist Party distributed a statement at 10 a.m. calling on the people to defeat the coup and to take up arms. Street battles continued until the following day when Qasim and his aides were seized and summarily executed by the Ba'th. The fighting continued, however, and many districts of Baghdad remained in the hands of popular forces led by the Communists for three days after the coup. In Basra, the workers led the resistance which continued up to the evening of 12 February 1963.

During the night of 19 February, the First Secretary of the ICP, Husain Ahmed al-Radhi (Salam 'Adil) was arrested. For 15 days he was savagely tortured in the dungeons of *Qasr al-Nihaya*, after which he was crushed to death. On 7 March, the regime announced his 'execution' together with two of his comrades in the Communist Party leadership, following a trial that had never taken place.

International Solidarity

The international campaign of solidarity with the Iraqi people played an outstanding role in exposing the barbarous crimes of the Ba'th, deepening their isolation internationally and in the Arab world. On 21 February 1963, Iraqi democrats abroad set up the 'Committee for the Defence of the Iraqi People'. Among the prominent personalities in the Committee were the celebrated poet Muhammad Mahdi al-Jawahiri and Dr. Naziha Dulaimi, the first woman Minister after the 1958 Revolution and a leading figure in the women's movement. In May 1963, a British Committee for the Defence of Human Rights in Iraq was formed. Its Chairman was Lord Chorley, with Labour M.P. William Griffiths as its Secretary and novelist Ethel Mannin as Treasurer. At a House of Commons press conference on 14 May 1963, it declared its intention to raise money to send a fact-finding mission to Iraq, and urged the Iraqi Government to bring to trial or to release the thousands of detainees.[11] Solidarity committees were also set up in France and Italy. Telegrams of protest, public meetings and demonstrations demanded an immediate halt to the massacres. Petitions and memoranda were addressed to the United Nations, the Human Rights Commission, the Organisation of Non-Aligned States, as well as to state leaders and prominent personalities all over the world. The campaign of genocide against the Kurdish people, unleashed only a few months after the fascist coup, was also widely exposed and condemned by the solidarity movement.

Oil and Economy

The first proclamation broadcast on Baghdad radio by the National Council of the Revolutionary Command (NCRC) stated: 'The new movement will work to increase our financial potential and guarantee that oil will continue to be exported'.[12] The coup leaders declared that the rights of the oil companies in Iraq would be respected and that they would be permitted to continue their operations.

Thus it became clear from the outset that the coup had the blessing and support of the foreign oil companies. The Iraq Petroleum Company had rejected Law 80 of December 1961 which limited its concession rights to the area actually being exploited, amounting to only 0.5% of the original concession area covering virtually the whole of Iraq, and reserved all rights in the other 99.5% of the country to the Iraqi State. Ever since the breakdown of the negotiations between the Qasim Government and the IPC in October 1961, the oil companies had been manoeuvring to have Law 80 repealed. One of the main objectives was to recover the North Rumaila oilfield where abundant deposits had been discovered but left untapped. Meanwhile, they kept the volume of oil production in 1961 and 1962 unchanged, while that of other oil-producing countries was rising rapidly.[13] The stagnation of oil production meant the stagnation of oil revenues, and consequent economic problems for the Iraqi Government.

Soon after the coup, negotiations were resumed by the new so-called moderate rulers, and the companies had high hopes of a reasonably favourable agreement. Edith and E.F. Penrose say of the Iraqi negotiating team headed by the Oil Minister 'Abdul 'Aziz al-Wattari: 'here, at last, was a man the companies could talk to, one who had some understanding of the industry and of their problems, a moderate negotiator who sincerely believed that Iraq would gain more from partnership with the foreign companies than if she tried to "go it alone", at least in the near future.'[14]

But though an interim compromise was reached in June 1963, Law 80 proved to be an irreversible step. Its popularity with the Iraqi people was such that the Ba'th did not dare to try to rescind it. As part of the interim agreement, the IPC stepped up the volume of oil production, with the result that the revenue from oil reached ID186.2 million (ID = Iraqi dinar) during the first nine months of 1963, an increase of 13.8% over the same period of 1962.[15] This additional income compensated for the drop in the national income from other domestic production more especially in dustrial and agricultural output. The value of exports of grains reached only ID800,000 in 1963, representing only 13.7% of its level of 1962. The economy was also hard hit by the enormous cost of the military campaign in Kurdistan which started in June 1963.

War in Kurdistan

Immediately after seizing power on 8 February, the Ba'th made overtures to the Kurdish national movement which had been at loggerheads with the Qasim regime. They invited two or three Kurds to join the government and proclaimed their intention to start talks towards a negotiated settlement.[16] The Kurdish leadership observed a cease-fire and negotiations began on 19 February, the Kurdish delegation being led by Jalal Talabani. The ruling NCRC announced on 10 March that it had agreed to grant the Kurds national rights 'on the basis of decentralization', as an answer to Kurdish demands for autonomy.

But it soon became clear that the NCRC was only buying time while trying to consolidate the hold of the Ba'th on the reins of power and suppressing popular resistance. By early May 1963, fighting between government forces and Kurdish nationalists was resumed.[17] On 10 June 1963 the regime declared an all-out war against the Kurdish movement, its hopes of an early success apparently fired by the assertions of Army Officers that they could have disposed of the Kurdish forces at the time of Qasim had he given them a free hand and sufficient equipment.

A large-scale offensive was launched which exposed the true chauvinist character of the Ba'th party. The war turned into a genocidal campaign, with aircraft and tanks razing Kurdish villages and killing hundreds of people, many of them women and children. The Military Governor of the North declared: 'We warn all inhabitants of villages in the provinces of Kirkuk, Sulaimaniya and Arbil against sheltering any criminal or insurgent and against helping them in any way whatsoever. We shall bomb and destroy any village if firing comes from anywhere near it against the army, the police, the National Guards or the loyal tribes'. Hundreds of Communist Party cadres and members who had set up partisan bases in Kurdistan after the coup, joined in the armed resistance of the Kurdish national movement led by the veteran leader Mulla Mustafa Barzani.

False Arab Unity

The demagogic slogan of Arab Unity and the hysterical calls for 'immediate unity' with the United Arab Republic (Egypt), raised by the Ba'th Party and other groups, were exposed as mere manoeuvres to divert attention from a fierce hostility to the democratic changes brought about by the 14 July 1958 revolution.

Soon after a military coup which brought the Ba'th Party to power in Syria in early March 1963, 'unity discussions' between Egypt, Syria and Iraq took place in Cairo from 14 to 20 March and from 6 to 14 April 1963.[18] Sharp differences arose at an early stage. Jamal 'Abd al-Nasir (Nasser) adopted a hostile attitude, notably towards Michel 'Aflaq and other leaders of the Ba'th. He said during one of the sessions: 'I say that there is no ideological conflict for a very simple reason. . . because I do not know what is the ideology of the Ba'th Party. . . Where is the theory of the Ba'th Party? Where is the ideology? I have never found any ideology behind the three words: unity, freedom and socialism, in all that has been published.'[19]

On 17 April an agreement called the Cairo Charter was announced which envisaged a transition period towards unity. But by May, open discord was obvious and Cairo radio was attacking both Ba'thist regimes.[20] After an unsuccessful coup by pro-Nasser forces in Syria in July 1963, the so-called 'union' was abandoned and allowed to die a natural death.

Uprising in the Army

The increasing isolation of the Iraqi regime and the fierce resistance to its military attacks on Kurdistan reinforced the opposition movement in the country. Despite the boast by Ba'th leaders that the Communist Party had ceased to exist, its clandestine Central Committee issued its first communiqué in mid-June 1963 calling on the people, including the armed forces, to organize, resist the rulers and support the Kurdish people 'for the salvation of the homeland. . . for democracy, land, bread and work.' An armed uprising became the aim, and a number of Communist Party officials took the initiative of organizing hundreds of soldiers and NCOs to prepare for it. A plan was drawn up which envisaged taking over army camps and the broadcasting station in Baghdad. A particular target was the army camp at al-Rashid where nearly 900 officers, pilots and military personnel were detained in No. 1 Prison. But the uprising was prematurely started on 3 July 1963. It achieved an early success by taking control of the airport at al-Rashid and seizing leading figures of the fascist regime, including the Foreign Minister, the Minister of the Interior and the Commander of the National Guard who had rushed to the camp. But military and organizational factors contributed to the failure of the uprising which was crushed after a heroic resistance. It remained however a significant political victory in the sense that it exposed the weakness of the regime and showed the strength of popular feeling against it.

On 21 July 1963 leading Communists were arrested and killed under torture. Leaders of the armed uprising headed by Sergeant Hasan Sirei, were executed after courageously facing a military tribunal. The tortured bodies were hanged in working class districts to strike terror among the population.

Fall of the Ba'th

The forces that participated in the 8 February coup were heterogeneous and had no agreed programme of action beyond the seizure of power. They were only united by their anti-Communist hysteria. The Ba'th Party strove to impose its hegemony, not satisfied with its control of 16 out of 18 seats in the NCRC. Soon after the coup, it manoeuvred to oust the Nasserists and other nationalist elements. It then turned against its nationalist allies after accusing them of conspiring against the regime on 25 May 1963. With the rapid deterioration of relations with Egypt, the Nasserists and nationalists began to plot against the Ba'th. Their activity coincided with the growth of resentment within the army ranks.

The crisis was soon reflected within the leadership of the Ba'th Party itself. The Sixth Pan-Arab Congress of the Ba'th Party, held in 1964, presented a dramatic description of the in-fighting. It admitted that the coup 'did not differ from military coup d'etats and did not achieve any gains. Rather, there were reactionary achievements such as the abolition of the Law on Personal Status'. The Congress also confessed to the crimes committed by the National Guard. According to the Ba'th's own analysis of that period, it had 'gradually split into right-wing and left factions'.[21]

In an attempt to absolve some at least of the Ba'th leadership, the Regional Congress of the Iraqi Ba'th held on 11 November 1963 dismissed the Party's General Secretary, 'Ali Salih al-Sa'di who was also Deputy Prime Minister, and blamed him for all the crimes committed during the previous nine months. But the gesture failed to impress anyone. The internal split developed into an open armed clash on 13 November with air raids on the presidential palace and on military targets.

The relations between the Ba'th and the military had begun to deteriorate soon after February 1963. They had shared a common objective in the overthrow of Qasim. Some army officers had joined the Ba'th Party because of its claims to nationalism, its anti-Communism and its proclaimed sympathy with Nasserism. They became disenchanted before long for a number of reasons, more particularly the deepening rift between the Ba'th and Nasser and the prominent influence of the National Guard whose numbers had grown to 34,000 by August 1963 and who had in fact much more power than the army and other government organs.

The armed in-fighting, which tore apart the Ba'th leadership, was exploited by the army, including some Ba'thist officers. On 18 November 1963, the military seized power in a swift coup d'état. Tanks were positioned at strategic points in Baghdad and the headquarters of the National Guard were hit by four rockets. The new leadership of the Ba'th Party, appointed only a week earlier, was arrested. Some of its members immediately collaborated with the new government headed by 'Abd al-Salam 'Arif, a nationalist with Nasserist leanings who had been made President after the coup in February. Other Ba'th leaders were sent abroad into exile without offering any resistance.

As for the National Guard, their cowardly collapse and surrender when faced by a single regiment of the army became a laughable episode to be remembered by the Iraqi people for a long time. The fall of the Ba'th on 18 November 1963 was as disgraceful as their rule had been oppressive and barbarous.

Military-Nationalist Rule: 18 November 1963 to 17 July 1968

In the first few months of its existence, the regime headed by 'Abd al-Salam 'Arif was a loose coalition of military pan-Arab nationalists, Nasserists and some Ba'thists. The latter, discredited by the crimes committed by their Party in power, were soon eased out of their official posts. The former Ba'thist Prime Minister Ahmad Hasan al-Bakr was given the rank of Ambassador at the Ministry of Foreign Affairs and his office of Vice-President was abolished.

The Nasserists, given a free hand by 'Arif, came to the fore and moved fast in another effort to achieve unity with Egypt. On 26 May 1964, Iraq and Egypt agreed to form a Joint Presidential Council. As a token of their political alignment, the agreement also envisaged close bonds between Egypt's single political party – the Arab Socialist Union – and a similar state-run organization to be set up in Iraq. On 14 July 1964 it was announced that such an organization had been formed, embracing various nationalist groupings among them some ex-Ba'thists who had turned Nasserists.

On the same day the government announced the nationalization of all banks and insurance companies as well as 32 private manufacturing and trading establishments. The move was meant to underline the desire to conform with the economic system in force in Egypt. But it was directed against the interests of the national bourgeoisie which had monopolized power after the 14 July 1958 revolution. The nationalization decrees, though increasing the share of the State sector in the country's industrial base, did not produce any radical change in the prevailing semi-feudal and capitalist relations of production. Retired senior army officers were appointed to leading posts in the management of the nationalized firms. The operations of these firms were mismanaged and disrupted, business stagnated, speculation became rife and there was a heavy flight of capital to banks abroad. The oil sector, controlled by the monopoly companies, retained its dominant position in the economy. Meanwhile, the worsening living conditions and growing unemployment were the cause of mounting discontent among the population.

Though the regime eased the grip of terror, dissolved the National Guard and released a number of detainees, it continued to suppress democratic freedoms. Thousands of political detainees remained imprisoned under harsh conditions. Between February 1963 and late 1965 the desert prison of Nuqrat al-Salman alone received 2,368 prisoners and 1,671 detainees.[22] Many were subjected to torture at the hands of the Public Directorate for Security. The Provisional Constitution announced on 29 April 1964 did not end the State of Emergency and specified a three-year transition period before the return to normality. In an attempt to hide the fact that power remained with the military and that martial law was still in operation, the powers of the Military Governor General were transferred to the Prime Minister (himself a military man) and the military courts were renamed State Security Courts. The Prime Minister was also given powers to suspend all civil laws.

Nor did the policy of the new regime towards the Kurdish problem show any real change. The war in Kurdistan continued for nearly three months. Then a cease-fire was announced, due mainly to widespread opposition to the war and to international pressure, and negotiations to search for a peaceful settlement started on 11 February 1964. But although political prisoners were released and the economic blockade of Kurdish towns and villages was lifted, most of the army units were not returned to barracks and the mercenary forces of *al-Fursan* (The Knights), which were Kurdish tribes fighting on the side of the central government, remained on the government payroll. There was no reinstatement of the hundreds of Kurdish officials and employees suspended from their posts.

The truce lasted only until March 1965 when government forces launched a new military offensive, hoping to deal a crushing blow at the Kurdish movement before the end of the summer. The offensive failed, the army suffered heavy casualties, and the regime found itself in a deep internal crisis.

In its dealings with the oil companies, the 'Arif Government tried at first to manoeuvre in the same way as its predecessor. The setting up of the Iraq National Oil Company (INOC) was announced, and widely welcomed, in February 1964. Then, yielding to right-wing elements who advocated the development of the oil wealth in partnership with foreign private or State companies, and even with the Iraq Petroleum Company (IPC), the government resumed the negotiations with the IPC in May 1964. In June 1965 an agreement was reached restoring the North Rumaila oilfield to the IPC in return for a joint INOC-IPC concession over an area of 32,000 square kilometres, a guaranteed rise in production and a cash payment of £20 million.[23] But the news of the agreement was met with such an outcry that it was not ratified and never even formally presented to the Cabinet.

In September 1965, the reputedly pro-Nasser Prime Minister Brigadier 'Abd al-Razzaq attempted a palace coup against the President with the intention of seeking immediate unity with Egypt, but he failed and fled to Cairo where he was granted political asylum. Attempts at unity with Egypt were thus brought to an end. Despite efforts to hush up the whole affair, contempt for the military in power was openly expressed throughout the country and 'Abd al-Razzaq was ridiculed as the man who staged a coup against himself.

The military rulers now thought that the appointment of a civilian at the head of the government might defuse the political crisis and attract public support. 'Abd al-Rahman al-Bazzaz, a former diplomat and a law scholar, became Prime Minister on 21 September 1965. He was, however, immediately denounced by the opposition for his close association with reactionary circles and supporters of the monarchy.

Under a programme of 'prudent socialism', al-Bazzaz sought to lessen the impact of the nationalization measures of July 1964 by removing restrictions on private investment, encouraging joint ventures with foreign capital for the exploitation of raw materials, and seeking to restrict the public sector and even to dismantle it to some extent.[24] The Land Reform legislation was also amended in such a way as to treble the financial compensation paid to the big landlords while suspending the further distribution of land to the peasants. Promises of steps towards representative government and the resumption of elections never materialized. The fear of Communism continued to predominate, and al-Bazzaz declared his opposition to allowing the Communist Party to carry on its activities openly.[25]

When President 'Abd al-Salam 'Arif died in a helicopter crash on 13 April 1966, a brief struggle for the Presidency was resolved by the choice of a compromise candidate in the person of 'Abd al-Rahman 'Arif, the brother of the late President.

Meanwhile military operations in Kurdistan, which were estimated to cost nearly $270 million a year, continued unabated but with no end in sight. The financial burden on the economy caused by the war and its unpopularity in the country led the government to seek an alternative way out. On 29 June 1966, it declared a cease-fire and invited Kurdish leaders to resume negotiations for a peaceful settlement.

These steps did not, however, hide the growing instability of the Government. In June 1966 former Prime Minister 'Abd al-Razzaq attempted yet another unsuccessful coup d'état. The top ranks of the ruling clique remained divided. Prime Minister al-Bazzaz was dismissed in August 1966 and succeeded by a series of governments run by military men clearly favoured by the oil companies and Western multinational firms seeking a foothold in Iraq.

In early 1967, Iraq's economic difficulties were aggravated by a drop in oil revenues caused by a dispute between the IPC and Syria over the transit fees for the shipment of oil through the trans-Syria pipeline, and the consequent interruption of Iraqi exports of oil through this pipeline from December 1966 to March 1967 when the dispute was finally settled.

Then came the Israeli aggression against Egypt in early June 1967 which exposed the demagogy of the Pan-Arab nationalist movement which had for years posed as the arch-enemy of Zionism and persecuted democratic forces under the false slogan of 'Arab Unity'. Only a token military contingent was sent by Iraq to assist the Arab cause, and this only after a series of mass demonstrations. Diplomatic relations with Britain and the USA were severed, and oil exports to pro-Israel countries were banned, but only for a short time. Normal oil exports were re-started soon after the Arab Summit held in Khartum in August 1967, and diplomatic relations with Britain were resumed in 1968.

Upsurge of the Democratic Movement

Throughout 1965–68 the military government proved unable either to tackle the urgent problems of the country — more especially the economic difficulties and the Kurdish question — or to contain the popular opposition to its rule. The latter found expression in strikes by large numbers of workers. The construction workers went on strike in November 1965 and again in May 1968. In Baghdad there was a strike by 3,000 workers at the 'Army Martyrs' factory in 1966, another involving 3,000 textile workers and a solidarity strike by 10,000 workers in the soft drinks industry. In May 1968, thousands of workers in light industries, mechanical workshops, tailoring, building and power generation staged numerous solidarity strikes and sit-ins. Alarmed at the strength of working-class unrest, the government made a tentative promise of trade union elections.

The democratic students movement was also stepping up its actions during the same period. Its organization, the General Union of Students in the Iraqi Republic (GUSIR) was campaigning in defence of academic and welfare rights. The government's reaction was a violent one. Colleges were surrounded by armoured cars which opened fire and injured a number of students. On 14 January 1968 all the colleges in Baghdad and Basra decided on a strike which lasted 13 days, in support of their demands for the punishment of their attackers, the release of detained students and the withdrawal of security and intelligence men from the colleges. The Ba'thist student organization – National Union of Iraqi Students (NUIS) – was against the strike, and its leaders, among them Saddam Husain, used firearms to break it. Student elections were eventually allowed which gave GUSIR an absolute majority but were shortly followed by a government decree declaring the elections illegal and therefore invalid.

In the elections of the Teachers Union, 65% of the teaching profession in Baghdad boycotted the election because of intimidation and harassment by the authorities. In other cities, the Democratic List won an absolute majority.

In the countryside, peasants claiming their rights came under government fire. Armed policemen were rushed to help semi-feudal landlords in the Nasiriya, Kut and Middle Euphrates of Southern Iraq using armoured cars and helicopters against peasant risings.

Ba'th Rule: 1968–1980

It was against the background of a deepening crisis of the military regime and a rising tide of resistance that the Ba'th Party returned to power on 17 July 1968 in a military coup carried out with the help of non-Ba'thist army officers. From the outset, it prepared itself for its task of containing and defeating any attempts at popular revolt and true democratic changes.

The Ba'thist Coup – But the Struggle for Democracy Continues
The Ba'th Party's right wing, headed by the 'Aflaq-Bakr-Saddam trio, was determined to assert its rule, though mindful — initially at least — of the lessons of the coup of February 1963. It was clearly aware of the mounting demand for democracy, the strength of the Iraqi Communist Party and the Kurdish national movement, and of the fact that the memory

of the crimes committed by the Ba'th and the National Guard against tens of thousands of people was still fresh in the minds of all Iraqis.

Without renouncing its anti-Communism and its chauvinistic contempt for the Kurds and other minorities, the Ba'th Party evolved a new policy which combined the suppression of all opposition and any expression of dissent[26] with economic and political moves intended to win a measure of popular support. In the main, however, it manoeuvred to split the opposition.

The principal characteristic of the Ba'th remained its fierce hostility to any advance towards political democracy. Amid a relentless flow of demagogic propaganda – made possible by its monopolization of all media – 'laws' devised by the 'Revolutionary Command Council' opened the door wide for the use of State terror. New repressive bodies were created, which were placed above the law and given a free hand to use any means of intimidation, from general harassment of innocent people to arbitrary arrests, torture and political assassinations. One such body was the 'National Security' apparatus, functioning under the direct control of the Ba'th leadership and headed by Nadhim Kazzar, a Ba'thist who had earned a notorious reputation as a torturer during the period of terror which followed the coup of February 1963. His headquarters, the scene of barbarous crimes, was known as *Qasr al-Nihaya* (Palace of the End). Few who entered it ever came out, nor did their bodies receive a decent burial. Political prisoners of the Ba'th often simply 'disappeared', as far as their relatives and friends were concerned.[27]

The new concept of 'popular democracy' put forward by the Ba'th in 1969 meant in practice a one-party rule with terrorist organs under strict party directives, used to suppress all opposition including dissent within the ranks of the Ba'th Party itself. But the demands for a democratic system could not easily be stifled. The Iraqi Communist Party was calling for a parliamentary system within a constitutional framework embodying democratic principles, free elections, a solution of the Kurdish problem based on autonomy, the abolition of all oil concessions to foreign companies, and the intensification of the struggle against imperialism and Zionism. The ICP also called for the formation of a patriotic front of all progressive forces, and a coalition government.[28]

Throughout 1969 and 1970, while the process of Ba'thisation of all State organs and particularly the army was being stepped up, a ruthless campaign of terror was unleashed against the opponents of the Ba'th, marked by frequent public executions.

> For eight hours on the day of the hangings, the police virtually handed over central Baghdad to the youths. Directed by Ba'th party commissars they erected the gibbets in flower beds, patrolling the approach roads, controlled the tens of thousands of watchers and chanted for more executions. Each of the three soldiers among the executed had a bandage on an ankle or wrist; the joints were so clearly misshapen that they had clearly been broken.[29]

Aware of its unpopularity and of the persisting demand for democratic freedoms and a coalition government, the regime resorted to demagogic slogans speaking of 'the alliance' and of a 'patriotic front' but making it quite clear that political parties, trade unions, peasants associations and other such organizations had no existence without the full control of the Ba'th. They were offered the choice between functioning under complete Ba'th control or stopping all political activity. The Kurdistan Democratic Party, the Iraqi Communist Party and the Nasserist groups exposed these manoeuvres. The government retorted with intensified terror and executions and with military operations against the Kurdish national movement in Iraqi Kurdistan in 1969.

The Kurdish Question
The war in Kurdistan had exhausted the economic and military potential of the country over the period 1961–69. Yet the problem remained unsolved and the regime was faced with continuing demands for a peaceful and democratic solution of the Kurdish question. Its very recognition that there was a Kurdish question was a partial retreat from its previous policy of all-out war against the people of Iraqi Kurdistan and attempts to isolate the Kurdistan Democratic Party from the democratic movement in Iraq.

On 11 March 1970, al-Bakr (then President) announced the conclusion of an agreement with the Kurdistan Democratic Party which provided for autonomy in local affairs in Kurdistan. Until then, the Ba'th had supported a breakaway minority of the KDP led by Jalal Talabani and corrupt tribal elements hostile to the leader of the KDP, Mustafa al-Barzani. According to the agreement, the central government was to retain control of foreign affairs, the customs administration and economic resources including oil-fields. But there would be a Kurdish Vice-President of the Iraqi Republic, and Kurds would be given posts in the government and in the Revolutionary Command Council, in proportion to their numbers, during the interim period before the election of a new legislative body.[30]

The democratic forces, while welcoming the prospect of an end of the bloody war against the Kurdish people, pointed to the inherent danger of the notion that the Kurdish problem could be solved in the absence of democratic rights and freedoms and while opponents of the regime were ruthlessly persecuted. They stressed that in such conditions it would be extremely difficult, even impossible, for the Kurdish people to have a real voice in the decision-making process either in the central government or indeed in Kurdistan itself. They therefore called once again for a representative democratic regime in Iraq as a whole.

Clearly, the Ba'thist regime looked at the agreement only as a necessary instrument for the suppression of all opposition to its totalitarian rule. Its response to the call for democracy was an escalation of the campaign of terror and the re-opening of the 'Palace of the End', with the Iraqi Communist Party as the main target. Scores of Communist cadres and members, among them 'Ali Husain al-Barazanchi (a member of the Central Committee of the ICP in the oil city of Kirkuk) were tortured to death in the summer of 1971.

There was in fact a wide gap between the words of the March 1970 Agreement and the actions of the Ba'thist rulers. It soon became evident that Kirkuk, at the centre of an oil-rich area, was to be excluded from the 'autonomous region'. In early 1971 thousands of Kurdish families were deported, some to Iran and others, especially from the Kirkuk area, to the southern part of Iraq. The notorious 'National Security' body was identified as being responsible for an attempt on the life of Barzani. Bitter experience once again demonstrated that the solution of the Kurdish question could not be isolated from the struggle for a democratic political system in the country as a whole.

Hegemony versus Democracy

On coming to power by the coup d'état of July 1968 the Ba'th party had many characteristics of a 'petty bourgeois nationalist party'. There were diverging trends within its leading group and internal conflicts were often resolved by conspiratorial and bloody methods. But there was also a general realization that its most pressing task was to put an end to the country's economic backwardness, still persisting after four decades of exploitation of its oil riches. As far as the Ba'th was concerned, the only way to achieve economic progress was to modernize capitalism in Iraq and this in turn meant finding the means for a rapid accumulation of capital.

However, this task could not be tackled while the foreign multinational companies remained in full control of the oil wealth. A ministerial committee under a senior Ba'thist army officer, Salih Mahdi 'Ammash, was 'understood to have initiated the strategy of limited reconciliation with the Iraq Petroleum Company',[31] even though the nationalization of the IPC group had been a major public demand for some time. But the Ba'th leadership was now realizing that it could not confront the oil companies – and indirectly the governments of the Western countries supporting them – without the support of the Communist Party and without an improvement in Iraq's relations with the Soviet Union.

The Ba'th leadership was of course fully aware of the popularity of socialist ideas in the country and of the influence of the Communist Party and the democratic left in general. As regards relations with the Soviet Union, a first step had been taken in 1969 when, unable to obtain the IPC group's assistance for the start of oil production in areas taken over by the State under Law 80 of 1961, the Iraqi Government had turned to Soviet enterprises with whom it signed agreements for the development of untapped oil-bearing areas, more especially the North Rumaila field.

By 1972, the continued intransigence of the IPC left the Iraqi government with no alternative but to nationalize the company. This was done by Law 61 of 1 June 1972 (which did not immediately affect the two affiliates of the company).

The deterioration of the economy, the conflict with the oil group and the popular pressure for a radical change, now compelled the Ba'th leadership to forget its empty boast that it was capable of 'overcoming the Communists politically and taking over their popularity through radical socio-economic changes'.

A tactical step to re-assure public opinion was taken in July 1973 when the Ba'th entered into an alliance with the Communist Party, formalized in the National Action Charter which was the programme of a newly formed Patriotic Front. This was agreed upon after a prolonged dialogue between the two parties over a number of disputed issues, more especially those relating to the 'leading role of the Ba'th Party' and the need for democratic institutions.

The ICP maintained that no political party could lead another party or occupy a 'leading role' in the Front. On this issue, the agreed text of the Charter read as follows: 'The relations between the parties of the Progressive and National Front are based on mutual respect for the independence of each Party, ideologically, politically and organizationally'.[32]

On the question of the political system, the ICP maintained its strong criticism of the undemocratic methods of government adopted by the Ba'th. While positively evaluating a number of socio-economic measures and foreign policy moves, it insisted on concrete steps towards the introduction of a democratic system. The National Action Charter signed in July 1973 guaranteed all political and cultural democratic rights, including freedom of action for the patriotic political parties, the social and vocational organizations, the workers' trade unions and peasants' organizations, as well as the freedom of the press, of opinion and belief, and other basic freedoms. It stipulated the termination of the 'transitional period' and provided for the 'preparation of the draft of a permanent constitution', 'the elimination of the emergency conditions and the establishment of constitutional organs and institutions, legislative and executive' and 'the implementation of the formula of local government and elected people's councils in all administrative units of the Republic of Iraq'.

The Charter also called for the setting up of 'an Executive Regional Authority in the Kurdish region, stemming from a Legislative Assembly elected along the above-mentioned democratic lines'. But conditions in Iraqi Kurdistan had meanwhile deteriorated. The Kurdistan Democratic Party having rejected a 'Draft Law for the Autonomy of the Kurdish Region', the government responded with the use of force. While the Communist Party continued to call for a peaceful application of the March 1970 agreement regarding Kurdistan, the Ba'thist rulers ordered a new fierce military campaign. From March 1974 to early 1975 casualties were high on both sides, and they included civilians of all ages and both sexes on the Kurdish side. Phosphorous shells were used by the Iraqi army.[33] Orders were issued to the army to advance at any cost and Ba'thist officers were placed in the rear with orders to shoot soldiers who tried to retreat.

The hostilities against the Kurds were the direct cause of a momentous step that was to have long-term repercussions for Iraq and the whole region.

During a meeting of Heads of State of the members of the Organization of Petroleum Exporting Countries held in Algiers in March 1975, the Shah of Iran and Saddam Husain (then Iraq's Vice-President) reached an agreement on the demarcation of their common borders. As regards the Shatt al-'Arab, the wide estuary of the river Tigris forming the southernmost border of Iraq, the Iraqi Government abandoned its former claim to the whole width of the waterway and accepted a settlement by which the frontier became the median line. This was part of a deal which included an agreement to 're-establish security and reciprocal confidence along the length of the common borders' and an undertaking 'to exercise strict and effective supervision. . . with the aim of putting a final end to all infiltration of a subversive character from either side'.[34] In the words of a commentator in the Middle East Economic Survey: 'In plain words this translates into an Iraqi concession over the Shatt al-'Arab border problem. . . in return for an Iranian undertaking to close the Iranian border to the Kurdish insurgents from Iraq and suspend military aid to them'.[35]

The signing of the 1975 Algiers Accords with Iran and the defeats inflicted on the Kurds were two of the causes of the reversal by the Ba'th party of its tactical rapprochement with the Iraqi Communist Party. Another important cause was the sudden sharp increase in oil income following the big rise of oil prices in 1974.

In violation of the National Action Charter, the Ba'th set out to declare itself as the 'leading party' not only in terms of State powers but concerning the life of the 'whole society'. Calls by the Communist Party for the implementation of the Charter provisions relating to political democracy were met with harassment and arrests of ICP members and supporters. The anti-Communist campaign was then stepped up after the publication of the report of the IPC's Central Committee plenum meeting of 10 March 1978. The report sharply criticized Ba'thist policies and actions. It called for an end to the state of emergency, for free general elections, for a constituent National Assembly, for a halt to the process of Arabization and Ba'thization of Iraqi Kurdistan. The response of the Ba'th was to intensify its anti-Communist campaign and its terrorism. In May 1978, 31 members and supporters of the ICP were executed under the pretext that they had set up Communist Party cells in the armed forces.

Nearly all ICP representatives of the Patriotic Front were arrested or forced to cease all political activities, and meetings of the Supreme Committee of the Front were effectively stopped. The Front was reduced to an executive body for the implementation of government policy and of the directives of the 'leading Party'. In an intensive propaganda campaign, members of the Front were told that it was their duty to adopt 'the policy and thought of the Revolution'. By early 1979, one-party rule was the predominant theme in statements by the Ba'th leaders and in their press. 'The equality of the political parties in the Patriotic Front is out of the question. . .', stated the Ba'th party newspaper *al-Thawra*, 'and this means that any other ideologies, opinions or practices, disguised as socialism, are impermissible'.[36] During a visit to Basra province in February 1979, the then Vice-President Saddam Husain declared: 'All citizens are Ba'thists, irrespective of their ethnic origins. . . I am entirely confident. . . that even those who are not organized in other political parties feel the need to be Ba'thists not only through sympathy and conviction but through their desire to be organized in the Ba'th Party'.

In April 1979 the Iraqi Communist Party declared that the Patriotic Front 'has ceased to be an alliance of patriotic forces. . . it has indeed been transformed into an instrument of the Ba'th Party'.[37] In the course of the same month the offices of the ICP's newspaper *Tariq al-Sha'b* in Baghdad were closed down and its printing equipment confiscated. At a meeting held in late July 1979, the Central Committee of the ICP declared its open opposition to the Ba'th regime and called for 'a Democratic Patriotic Front to end the dictatorship and establish a democratic system of government in Iraq'. Later that year, Communist partisan units were set up in Iraqi Kurdistan.

Multi-millionaire Ba'thists

By 1975 Iraq's income from oil had reached $8000 million, nearly 16 times its level of 1972. A very important effect of this huge increase was to transform the Ba'th Party into a tool of a new parasitic section of the local bourgeoisie, and not — as its leaders had boasted in 1972 — to push it 'to the left of the Communist Party'. The whole orientation of the Ba'th Party had always been, of course, towards the development of capitalist relations rather than their abolition.

With the unexpected and massive influx of oil revenue, both the state sector and the private sector expanded rapidly. Between 1973 and 1976, the private sector trebled in size and the number of small enterprises increased from 26,377 in 1973 to 41,000 in 1977.[38] But the most remarkable development was the flourishing of a numerous body of private middlemen — contractors, brokers, etc. — and top bureaucrats in the state sector.

This parasitic section of the bourgeoisie came rapidly into its own, swelling its own wealth by all available means. In 1980 there were more than 700 multi-millionaires, most of them officials, members and supporters of the Ba'th Party and its 'special-type socialism'. Such fortunes could not have been accumulated without the cooperation of the top bureaucrats in charge of state expenditure who were only too eager to secure for themselves the largest possible share of the bonanza in the shortest possible time. This type of 'alliance' was the driving force behind the expansion of a non-productive sector of the economy which held back any real socio-economic development. The rural upper class, for its part, was also growing thanks to the hundreds of millions of dollars injected by the State in the agricultural sector. Most of the new elements of the rural middle class were cadres of the Ba'th Party in the countryside, sons of landowners and rich farmers.

Multinational companies from Japan, France, West Germany, Britain and other countries including the USA (diplomatic relations with the US were severed in 1967 but the value of Iraq-US trade in 1975 was 15 times its level of 1965) made full use of the prevailing economic climate to secure huge and most profitable contracts. Iraq's dependence on the world capitalist market was especially marked in the second half of the 1970s, as the country became more and more important as an exporter of crude oil and an importer of capital goods, consumer goods and luxury goods from developed capitalist countries. By 1978 over 90% of the investments in the industrial sector were committed to capitalist corporations and multinationals.

The new parasitic body of entrepreneurs, middlemen and bureaucrats flourished in the conditions of 'special type' Ba'th 'democracy' which suited them so well that they became the social base of the Ba'th Party and its most ardent supporters. And it is especially significant that they had no interest in economic stability and were firmly opposed to the financial controls and regulations usually needed for capital investment by the productive sections of the bourgeoisie.

It was only natural that, with the huge and continuous increase in oil revenues from 1974-80 and the increasingly widespread use of repression and demagogy, the number of those employed in local government and in the security apparatus almost doubled from 346,000 in 1969 to 663,000 in 1976.[39] At their head was a group of governors, senior officials and senior army officers who formed a 'special' stratum with a common interest in political power and shared opportunities to enrich themselves, added to their tribal, sectarian and family links. Almost all of the members of this 'special' stratum were members and supporters of the Ba'th Party and vehemently opposed to any kind of democratic advance.

At the same time, and beyond the control of the Ba'th Party, the working class had also grown on a large scale. One third of the labour force was engaged in material production in the industrial, farming and construction sectors. The rapid growth of the demand for labour in the manufacturing and service industries resulted in a large transfer of population from the rural areas to the urban areas, and a corresponding increase of the influence of the working class in various aspects of social life.

Ba'thization

But despite the massive income from oil, the regime was in crisis. The policy of economic development on capitalist lines through dependence on the West and its multinational companies amounted to a distorted type of capitalism, i.e. bureaucratic state capitalism. At the same time, the political repression was proving insufficient to stifle the popular demand for democratic rights and institutions. Under the illusion that it had solved the Kurdish problem, the regime decided to speed up the process of Ba'thization by which it hoped to secure the tightest possible control over the whole population.

Already in 1977, Saddam Husain had declared that 'every Iraqi citizen is a Ba'thist even if he has not joined the Ba'th Party'. The regime now proceeded with the Ba'thization of the State organs, the social organizations, the educational system and the cultural life of the whole country. Non-Ba'thists were banned from employment in the Ministries of Defence, Interior, Foreign Affairs, Education, Culture and Information. Trade Unions, peasant co-operative societies, women's organizations, student and youth organizations and vocational associations were monopolized and transformed into tools for the implementation of Ba'th policies.

'Laws' were enacted banning the formation of parallel organizations and punishing with life imprisonment anyone who dared to exercise this right. A campaign of terror was launched to force people, especially civil servants, into affiliation to the ruling party and the organizations attached to it. Workers were deprived of their right to strike and thousands fell victim to Government persecution and ill-treatment by management.

Non-Ba'thists were denied scholarships to study abroad, and a penalty of 15 years imprisonment with hard labour was imposed on offenders. They were also denied admission to military colleges, teachers training colleges and the Institute of Fine Arts. Thousands of qualified students were denied university or school higher education or were expelled from both. Thousands of teachers were also dismissed, causing a sharp decline in the standard of education and the emigration of large numbers of teachers and specialists in various fields. The head of the ruling junta, Saddam Husain (a self-proclaimed Field Marshal with no military training or education) admitted that 'there are university lecturers who even write whole theses for students who are relatives of senior officials in the State and the Party. . . and yield to the pressure of senior Party officials to award academic degrees to their relatives'.[40]

Death 'Laws'

Those who opposed Ba'thization faced arrest, torture and 'disappearance'. The use of torture became widespread as a means to obtain confessions or to force the victims to renounce their convictions and pledge themselves not to engage in any political activity other than through the ruling Ba'th party. Article 200 of the Iraqi Penal Code 111[41] provides for the death sentence as punishment for any of the following activities:

> Concealment by Ba'th Party members of their former political affiliations.
> Joining the Ba'th Party while maintaining contact with another political party or organization.
> Leaving the Ba'th Party and joining another political party.
> Persuading a Ba'th Party member to leave the Ba'th Party.

In April 1980 Amnesty International published a list of 257 Iraqis executed between January 1978 and December 1979 with details of their place of residence, their occupation and the date of their execution. They included Kurdish activists, members and supporters of the Iraqi Communist Party, Shi'ites and even members of the Ba'th Party itself. As already mentioned, 31 members and supporters of the Iraqi Communist Party were executed in May 1978. They had been arrested several years previously and kept imprisoned, charged with having pursued non-Ba'thist political activity within the army. Though they had been arrested at different times and from various military units, the propaganda machine presented their case as a 'conspiracy against the revolutionary regime'. That this charge was a fabrication was implicitly admitted by the ruling party itself, when the Ninth Congress of the Ba'th Regional Command heard a complaint that they should have been executed immediately after their arrest so as to avoid international action in their favour, and that the long delay was 'a tactical error'.[42]

The Kurdish people, representing about 25% of the Iraqi population, had more than their share of terror, bloodshed and executions. During the four years 1975-78 alone, over a thousand Kurds were executed under various pretexts.

Chauvinism

Under the illusion that the border agreement with Iran concluded in Algiers in 1975 had given the regime a measure of security, the Ba'th revived its long-standing policy of forced Arabization of ethnic minorities. In Iraqi Kurdistan, this meant a new effort to destroy and scatter whole communities. The central government carved predominantly Kurdish administrative units out of the 'autonomous region'. Thousands of Kurds were removed from their homes. Along the hundreds of kilometres of the borders with Iran and Turkey, the inhabitants of a band of territory 15 km. wide were forcibly removed from their homes. The deported families were re-housed in barrack-like 'complexes' sited near army camps and were denied the right to engage in any productive work. No legal means of expression were left to the Kurdish people: the Kurdish press, their political, social and vocational organizations were banned. Even the Kurdish branches of the official state-backed trade unions were eliminated.

Over the period 1975-78, more than 350,000 people were deported from Kurdistan and 240 villages were burned down. Fertile lands were turned into unpopulated areas, their villages and fields having been replaced by military installations and new military roads. Subjected to such brutality, the Kurdish people had no alternative but to resume their struggle in defence of their existence and their national rights.

The Supreme Ruler

By 1979 the Iraqi Communist Party as well as the Kurdistan Democratic Party and other opposition forces, all driven into clandestinity, were waging an armed struggle against the dictatorship of a party inspired by a philosophy inherited from Fascism and based on a combination of mass terror, demagogy and bribes.

In July 1979 Saddam Husain managed, with the help of the security apparatus, to deal a blow at the remaining opposition within the Ba'th Party by having 21 of its senior officials, including members of the Revolutionary Command Council and senior ministers, summarily executed. This was soon after the removal of al-Bakr from the Presidency (he resigned 'for health reasons') and his replacement by Saddam Husain as Iraq's Head of State.

Iraq's oil revenues in 1980 reached $21.3 billion, over a hundred times their size in 1968, and foreign reserves amounted to $35 billion. Unlimited funds thus became available to the ruling party to expand and strengthen its organs of repression – especially the security apparatus, the intelligence services and the para-military bodies – and at the same time to seek popularity by the creation of new jobs in public services and large construction projects.

Saddam Husain, the head of the Ba'thist junta, was now presented by his propaganda machine as 'The Knight', 'The Leader with a Strategic Mind and Precise Calculations'. As early as January 1980, the Ba'thist media started to build his image as 'Leader of the Non-Aligned Movement', in anticipation of the conference of Heads of State of Non-Aligned Countries which was due to take place in Baghdad in late 1982.

But behind the sham picture of stability and prosperity, the dictatorship was in fact isolated from the people under its rule. Its growing resort to mass executions, arrests and torture, murders of political opponents both in Iraq and abroad, exposed its own lack of confidence in its ability to keep in power without terrorist methods.

Preparations for War
The overthrow of the Shah of Iran in February 1979 had a traumatic effect on all the reactionary rulers in the Middle East. In Iraq, the ruling junta was more especially alarmed by the example of the millions of unarmed Iranians who faced the might of the Shah's army and secret police and overthrew his tyrannical regime with amazing speed.

The Ba'th, headed by Saddam Husain, gave refuge to the deposed Shah's generals, to his former Prime Minister Shahpur Bakhtiar and remnants of his Savak secret police. It also hastened to strengthen its ties with Saudi Arabia and the Gulf States. Anti-Communism was now raised to a hysterical pitch. In a speech in February 1980 to celebrate the anniversary of the fascist coup of February 1963, Saddam Husain described the Iraqi Communist Party as part of the 'rotten, renegade, atheistic storm that had broken over Iraq'.[43] In the spring and summer of 1980, the deportation of tens of thousands of Shi'ite Iraqis on the allegation that they were of Iranian origin triggered off a wave of racist hostility against the Iranian people.

On the eve of the invasion of Iran, huge arms deals worth $4.5 billion were signed with France and Italy. Iraq's dictator saw it as his mission to provoke the overthrow of the new Iranian regime, blinded by his own fear and dreaming perhaps of the prospect of laying his hands on Iran's oil wealth.

Amid frenetic calls for a new 'Qadisiya of the Arabs' (the Arabs conquered Persia after defeating the Persian army at Qadisiya in 635 A.D.) and ravings about differences between 'the Muslim Arabs and the heathen

Persians', the Iraqi Head of State announced in September 1980 the abrogation of the treaty that he had himself signed with the late Shah in 1975. On 22 September 1980, the Iraqi armed forces stormed across the Iranian border and quickly seized 4,126 sq.miles of Iranian territory. But the advance had ground to a halt by the end of 1980.[44]

The Ba'thist regime's war against Iran was an extension of its policy of terror, suppression of all opponents, and chauvinism. It deepened the crisis of the dictatorship. The opposition forces condemned the bloody adventure, they exposed the phoney calls for 'peace' by the aggressor, and they reiterated the call for a true autonomy for Iraqi Kurdistan, the overthrow of the regime of fascism and war and the establishment of a democratic regime throughout Iraq.

References

1. *The 1968 Revolution in Iraq, Experience and Prospects: The Political Report of the 8th Congress of the Arab Ba'th Socialist Party in Iraq*, January 1974, (Ithaca Press, London 1979) p. 30.

2. Hanna Batatu, *The Old Social Classes and the Revolutionary Movement in Iraq: A Study of Iraq's Old and Commercial Classes and of its Communists, Ba'thists and Free Officers*, (Princeton University Press, 1978).

3. *al-Akhbar*, Baghdad, 24 February 1963, Interview with Aflaq.

4. Dilip Hiro, *Inside the Middle East*, (Routledge and Kegan Paul, London, 1982), p. 170.

5. M.S. Agwani, *Communism in the Arab East*, (Asia Publishing House, New Delhi and London), 1969, p. 143.

6. Edith and E.F. Penrose, *Iraq*, (Boulder, 1978) p. 288.

7. *The Middle East*, August 1981, p. 33.

8. Penrose, op. cit., p. 33.

9. *al-Thaqafa al-Jadida*, monthly magazine of the Iraqi Communist Party, No. 138, February 1982, pp. 78–82.

10. *Economic and Political Weekly*, 10 June 1978, p. 932.

11. *Guardian*, 15 May 1963; *Daily Worker*, 15 May 1963.

12. *Evening Standard*, 8 February 1963.

13. Penrose, op. cit., p. 269.

14. Ibid., p. 282.

15. *Statistical Bulletin of the Iraqi Central Bank for the Fourth Quarter of 1963*.

16. *Guardian*, 15 May 1963.

17. *New York Herald Tribune*, 15 May 1963.

18. Penrose, op. cit., p. 303.

19. *Transcript of the Union Talks*, al-Ahram Institute, Cairo, 1963, p. 143. (in Arabic).

20. *Daily Telegraph*, 21 May 1963.

21. Preparatory Committee of the Seventh Pan-Arab Congress, *The Crisis*

of the Arab Socialist Ba'th Party as Seen from the Experience in Iraq, a theoretical document (in Arabic).

22. *Tareeq al-Sha'b*, clandestine organ of the Iraqi Communist Party, late June 1966.

23. Petter Nore and Terisa Turner, ed. *Oil and Class Struggle*, (Zed Press, London, 1980) p. 184.

24. Ibid., p. 184.

25. Penrose, op. cit., p. 341.

26. Penrose, op. cit., pp. 359–360.

27. Ibid., pp. 264–365.

28. Dilip Hiro, op. cit., 1982, p. 171.

29. *Sunday Times*, 28 February 1969.

30. Ismet Cherif Vanly, *Le Kurdistan Irakien, Entitlé nationale* (Neuchatel 1970).

31. *MEES*, 1 October 1969.

32. *National Action Charter and the Rules of Action of the Progressive Patriotic and National Front*, Publication of the Ministry of Information, Documentary Series (29), al-Huriyah Printing House, (Government Press, Baghdad) 1974.

33. *The Times*, 13 December 1974.

34. Penrose, op. cit., 1978, p. 373.

35. *MEES*, 7 March 1975.

36. *al-Thawra*, 10 January 1979.

37. *Iraqi Letter*, published by the Iraqi Communist Party, no. 2, April 1979, p. 9.

38. Special Report from the journal *al-Sina'ah* (Industry), Ministry of Industry and Minerals, 1978.

39. Dr. Sabah al-Durrah, *al-Quita' al-'amm fi'l-'Iraq*, (The Public Sector in Iraq)

40. *al-Sharq al-Awsat*, London-based Arab daily, 23 April 1984.

41. CARDRI – pamphlet on 'Human Rights in Iraq', 1981.

42. Central Report of the 9th Congress of the Socialist Arab Ba'th Party (June 1982), Baghdad, January 1983, p. 72 (in Arabic).

43. *The Guardian*, 12 February 1980.

44. *Strategic Survey 1983–84, The Middle East*, Report of International Institute of Strategic Studies, London, May 1984.

3. Oil and the Iraqi Economy

Celine Whittleton

Pre-1958 Background – An Economy in Decay

In a book published almost on the eve of the revolution of 1958 a former Middle East correspondent of the London Times singled out Iraq from all other countries of the Middle East for its exceptional economic backwardness as well as for its 'unlimited material promise':

> For generations she has been in a state of semi-dereliction.
> Her medieval population of thirty-five million has dwindled to about five million. Here wide farmlands have, all too often, gone to waste. Health, eductional, techniques – all are in a condition of decay. . . But Iraq still possesses the raw material of national wealth: two great rivers and three secondary ones; a population far too small for its territories; agricultural lands of wide resource; great reservoirs of oil.[1]

This description by an experienced observer was written in 1957, thirty years after Iraq's first commercial production of crude oil: 45,000 tonnes from a northern oilfield in 1927.

Oil production was kept very small for a number of years. The British-controlled group of foreign companies in charge of the industry had fought long and hard to obtain their concession rights, which they knew to be an extremely valuable long-term asset. But they were in no hurry to speed up production during a period of low world demand. And the deposits in northern Iraq were far inland, without easy access to an export outlet. In 1933 their ouput was still only 123,000 tonnes.

It was raised to 4 million tonnes in 1935 thanks to the completion of the first pipeline from Kirkuk to the Mediterranean, then remained limited to the capacity of this small pipeline until 1950, with a temporary drop during the war.

But with the steep rise of demand for oil after the war, the companies were eager to expand their exports of Iraqi crude. This was achieved through the opening of major pipelines from the northern oilfields and large-scale development of the southern oilfields which started production in 1951.

In 1956 production of Iraqi crude reached 30 million tonnes and the government's revenue from it was ID69 million (ID = Iraqi dinar)[2] representing half the profits declared by the companies for their operations in that year. This revenue amounted to 21% of Iraq's national revenue.

Discontent with the size of the country's income from its immense oil wealth had been mounting for some time. Another bone of contention between the government and the oil companies was the question of employment of Iraqis in the industry. In the early 1950s their total number was 10,430[3] few of whom had reached the high technical or administrative positions virtually monopolized by foreign employees.

The Iraq Petroleum Company and its two subsidiaries — the Mosul Petroleum Company and the Basra Petroleum Company — were owned by four different national groups: British Petroleum Company, the Anglo-Dutch Royal Dutch/Shell group, the Compagnie Francaise des Petroles and the American-owned Near East Development Corporation, each of which had a share of 23.75% in the IPC. The balance was held by the Gulbenkian Estate. Their concessions to extract crude oil covered the whole of Iraq with the exception of about 680 sq. miles close to the border with Iran. The concession rights of the IPC were the subject of very long and complicated manoeuvres, both before and during the period of the British mandate over Iraq.

The right to exploit Iraq's oil deposits had originally been promised by the Turkish Grand Vizir to the Turkish Petroleum Company which had been formed for this purpose by British, German and Dutch interests in 1914, when Iraq was still a province of the Ottoman Empire. After the defeat of Germany and Ottoman Turkey in the first World War, the German share was transferred to French interests, an arrangement which was formally ratified by the Iraqi government in 1925, and the TPC soon started production.

There followed a period of intense diplomatic pressure by the US State Department which culminated in the allocation of 23.75% share to an American group.

The name of the Turkish Petroleum Company was changed to Iraq Petroleum Company in 1929, and the final concession agreement was signed in 1931, a year before the formal ending of the British mandate. This agreement secured for the IPC the whole of the provinces of Baghdad and Mosul east of the Tigris and was intended to last until the year 2000. The Mosul Petroleum Company had all the areas west of the Tigris and north of latitude 33°N, up to the year 2007, while the Basra Petroleum Company's concession, intended to continue until the year 2013, simply referred to all the Iraqi territory not covered by the IPC and MPC concessions.

The share of the Iraqi State consisted at first of a royalty paid by the companies on a per-tonne-produced basis. This led to continuous demands by the Iraqi government to increase production in order to raise its income. The political parties opposed to the regime of Nuri al-Sa'id denounced the concession agreements with growing anger, and the first demands for nationalization were heard in the early 1950s.

The royalty system had to be abandoned by the companies in 1952 when the interruption of Iran's oil exports made it easier for the Iraqi authorities to insist on the adoption of the 50–50 profit-sharing system previously introduced by Aramco in Saudi Arabia. However, hopes of fairer treatment by the companies following the new arrangement were disappointed. As the companies' activities were limited to the production and marketing of crude, they were able to keep their profits on their Iraqi operations at a minimum level since they remained free to sell the crude to partners abroad at very low prices, unrelated to prevailing market prices.

After the 1952 agreement, oil production was considerably stepped up from 8.4 million tonnes in 1951 to 29.5 million in 1954, an increase of just over 350%. The Iraqi share of the profits was ID13.7 million in 1951 and ID68.4 million in 1954.[4]

Both the level of production and the income from oil were adversely affected by the Suez crisis. The Suez Canal was closed to navigation on 31 October 1956 and the flow of oil through the pipeline from Kirkuk to the Mediterranean was stopped by the action of the Syrian government in protest against the tripartite invasion of Egypt. Iraq's income from oil fell to ID48.2 million in 1957, then recovered to ID83.8 million in 1958 after the re-opening of the pipeline.

Despite these fluctuations the increase in the oil revenue had a remarkable impact on the structure of the Iraqi state finances. It has been calculated that as a result of the 1952 agreement on profit-sharing, oil revenue as a proportion of Government revenue jumped from 10% to over 60% between 1952 and the end of the 1950s.[5]

The Nuri al-Sa'id Government hoped that this would enable it to surmount the acute economic and social crisis it was facing. But such a regime could not, or would not, solve the crisis.

In theory the Development Board set up in 1950 was to be allocated 70% of the oil income, in an attempt to remedy the worst effects of decades of neglect of the economy, and the Board did spend large amounts of money for the construction of flood control systems, dams and irrigation canals.

But the very nature of the antiquated land tenure system ensured that the beneficiaries would be the big landowners whose predominance over the agricultural sector was matched by their influence over the Government's policies and actions. As for the use of its profits from the land, this class of powerful landowners — mostly tribal shaikhs who had been allocated huge tribal lands under the British mandate — favoured investments in real estate and in trade rather than industry.

Industrial development was anyway virtually impossible in a country such as Iraq relying on oil revenue for a very large part of its income and governed by a monarchical regime propped up by foreign interests and semi-feudal landowners.

The oil industry does not provide the infrastructure essential for industrial growth. No railway or road networks or well-equipped ports are built where all that is needed are suitable oil terminals and pipelines. No native skills are required either, where the technical and administrative posts remain in the hands of foreign staff.

In such conditions, existing natural resources other than oil were left untapped while agriculture became of secondary importance to the economy even if — as in Iraq in the 1950s — nearly two-thirds of the population lived off the land.

Well into the 1960s, the Iraqi railway system consisted of 1,661 km. of narrow-gauge track, linking Baghdad to Basra and Samarra in the south, Kirkuk and Arbil in the north.

Manufacturing industry was primitive compared with that of other developing countries. It consisted mainly of light industries for the production of textiles, foodstuffs, construction materials, soap, leather, glass and cigarettes.

As for oil processing, the only installations until the mid 1950s were a small refinery erected in 1927 at Alwand, near Basra, to meet part of the local demand, and an asphalt plant at Qayyara, south of Mosul, with an annual capacity of 60,000 tonnes. The first major development in this field was the completion in 1955 of an oil refinery at Daura, near Baghdad, with a capacity of about one million tonnes a year, to which was added in 1957 a plant to produce lubricating oil at an annual rate of 25,000 tonnes.

The July 1958 Revolution and the Economy

The use or misuse of the relatively large revenue by a government propped up by a foreign power, semi-feudal landowners and courtiers was one of the root causes of the political upsurge which led to the overthrow of the monarchy and its state institutions in July 1958.

The leaders of the revolution were faced with the problem of reconstructing a decaying economy. Having promised economic independence and an equitable social system, they had to tackle three essential preliminary tasks: to remove the economic and political influence of the big landowners and improve the standard of life of the peasantry; to re-negotiate the agreements with the oil companies in order to give the Iraqi state a decisive say over future plans for the industry and a larger share of its profits; and to provide the infrastructure necessary for industrial development.

The government led by 'Abd al-Karim Qasim introduced the first Agrarian Reform in Iraq and it drastically reduced the powers of the oil companies. But the problems of industrial development could not be tackled during the very short life of the Qasim regime.

The Agrarian Reform

The *Agrarian Reform Law* of 30 September 1958 — barely two and a half months after the July Revolution – limited the size of agricultural holdings, encouraged the establishment of agricultural co-operative societies and dealt with the respective duties of the landlord and his tenants.

A look at the state of agriculture under the monarchy is necessary to form some idea of the degree of mismanagement of the land in a country blessed with a potentially rich soil and abundant water resources. True, much of the country is desert, but reclamation schemes are possible and some indeed have been carried out. Given efficient management and adequate financing, the existing plans to harness the two great rivers and the affluents of the Tigris can expand the cultivated area, drain many areas rendered sterile by over-salination, and make Iraq self-sufficient in food supplies.

The total area of Iraq is 434,000 sq. km. (about 173 million dunums) of which 38.5% is arid desert and 21.2% high mountains. Of the rest of the country, only a small part is cultivated, for a number of reasons. The flow of the rivers varies from year to year, periods of flood alternating with periods of drought. Further, in the vast alluvial plain between the Euphrates and the Tigris south from the Baghdad area, the flatness of the land and the impervious nature of the soil often prevent the run-off of irrigation water. Due to the hot climate and fast evaporation, excessive quantities of salt are deposited leading to declining yields and eventual sterility of the soil.

A Census by the Iraqi Department of Agriculture found that the cultivable area in 1952–53 was only 23 million dunums (5,750,000 ha.) of which about half were cultivated in any one year. Then the 1958–59 Census of Agriculture put the cultivable area at the higher figure of 30.1 million dunums (7.5 million ha.) of which 50 to 55% were cultivated annually.[6]

The first Agrarian Reform Law of 1958 set two ceilings on land ownership, depending on irrigation facilities: the limit was 250 ha. in the irrigated areas and 500 ha. in the rain-fed areas (the latter are mostly in the north of the country). These were high ceilings as it is estimated that it takes at least 20 and up to 200 share-croppers to till such holdings.[7]

As well as compensation for their excess land, the 1958 legislation gave the landlords 'the right of choice' which meant that those who had to surrender part of their properties could keep the most fertile and best irrigated parts of their lands and give up the least profitable tracts.

The excess lands as well as Crown lands were to be distributed in such a way as to allow rural families from 7.5 to 15 ha. of land under direct or pump irrigation, or 15 to 30 ha. of rain-fed land.

It had been intended to complete the land reform in five years. Ten years later it was still far from complete. After a fairly quick start, land distribution slowed down after the 1963 coup d'état. Between 1959 and 1962, 1.4 million dunums were distributed to 28,638 beneficiaries, an average of 50.6 dunums (about 12.5 ha.) each. Between 1963 and 1967 only 1.1 million dunums were distributed to 23,992 beneficiaries, an average of just under 46 dunums (11.5 ha.) each.[8]

The regime which came into power in 1968 introduced a number of amendments. In 1969 further compensation to the landlords was abolished. In 1970 a new Agrarian Reform Law was promulgated which reduced the ceiling on ownership of irrigated land to a maximum of 150 ha. while that on rain-fed land remained practically unchanged. At the same time, the new law reduced the size of allotments for distribution to a minimum of 1.5 ha. and a maximum of 15 ha. for irrigated land, while the ceiling for holdings of non-irrigated land was slightly increased.

There is little doubt that the main achievements of the agrarian reform have been to do away with the influential role of the semi-feudal landowners, both political and economic, and to create a rural petty bourgeoisie by means of a large increase in the number of owners or tenants with holdings of between 5 and 25 ha. Whatever the intentions of the legislators in 1958, these were the most notable effects of the reform as operated and administered over a period of 25 years by a state in complete control of the whole of the country's economy.

In the absence of official data on the implementation of the agrarian reform after 1971, estimates of land tenure in the late 1970s have been made on the basis of statistical tables appended to the Iraqi Planning Ministry's Research into the Family Budget, published in 1977.

The 1958–59 Census of Agriculture showed that 1.7% of the landowners held between them 63.1% of the cultivated land, while 64% of the total held between them only 3.66% of the land. Before 1959, there were 51 owners of over 300,000 dunums (75,000 ha.), including some with hundreds of thousands of dunums. By 1977 it was estimated[9] that there were 23,846 holders with an average of 305 dunums each (approximately 76 ha.), representing about 31% of the total farmed area and 5% of the total number of holders.

At the bottom of the rural pyramid, there were still nearly 48,000 holders with an average of about 0.5 ha., and over 71,000 with an average of just under 3 ha.

But the largest section of the rural population in 1977 consisted of 333,849 holders — owners or tenants — with an average of between 7 and 26 ha., a remarkable contrast with the pre-1958 situation when holders of 5 to 25 ha. numbered only 41,305.

However, in terms of agricultural production the expected benefits of the agrarian reform failed to materialize, especially in respect of the two main crops — wheat and barley. Wheat production had doubled between the 1930s and the 1950s, thanks to the construction of flood control works and irrigation canals. By the mid 1950s wheat output averaged 800,000 tonnes a year, and barley was in the region of one million tonnes.

Wide fluctuations in the first two decades of the agrarian reform in both the yield and the size of the cultivated areas reflected the continued misuse of the land. The completion of dams and reservoirs put an end to damaging floods, but maladministration, neglect of the agricultural co-operative societies and failure to control salination, all combined to produce erratic crop yields and to spread discouragement among the peasant population.

As regards wheat, the best result so far was achieved in 1972 when 2,465,000 tonnes were harvested. Since then, the wheat crop has fallen in some years to less than its level of the 1950s. In the ten years 1973-1982 the annual average was just under 1.1 million tonnes. Like wheat the barley crop reached a peak of 859,000 tonnes in 1972 then fluctuated in the following nine years with an annual average of 488,100 tonnes.[10]

The distortion of the role of the co-operatives and the increasing obstacles created by successive governments are one of the main reasons for the failure of the land reform to reach its economic targets.

Originally intended to provide a full service, including the supply of agricultural equipment, pumps, tractors, etc., the function of the co-operatives became gradually restricted to the provision of credits and assistance with marketing. By 1976 there were 1,895 agricultural co-operatives with a total of 280,142 members holding 4.6 million ha. But only 81 of them, with 11,000 members holding 125,000 ha. were production co-operatives. The rest were mostly service units, providing finanical facilities and marketing assistance.[11]

The early hopes that the social imbalance in the countryside was soon to be eradicated were gradually frustrated by the lukewarm attitude of the authorities to some of the more progressive aspects of the agrarian reform. While a large proportion of the peasants remained share-croppers, the larger landowners were granted special privileges. For example, Law 43 of 1977 allowed an individual member of a co-operative society to acquire up to ten per cent of its shares. In practice, since the profits of a co-operative society are distributed in proportion to the number of shares held by a member, this made it possible for the richer landowners to acquire most of the profts. At the same time, the holders of less than three shares were denied any part of the society's profits.

The large-scale migration of peasants to the urban areas, especially since the mid-1970s, must be attributed to the frustrated hopes of the poorer peasants and the contrast between their stagnant economic condition and the opportunities for work that the oil wealth offered in the towns. The number of people gainfully employed in agriculture in 1958-59, when the total population was about 6 million, was 1.6 million (including 301,411 children under 14 years of age). By 1977 when the total population had risen to 12 million, there were only 943,890 gainfully employed in agriculture (of which 91,134 were children)[12]. The downward trend was certainly accentuated when the peasants were called up to fight against Iran in the early 1980s.

To compensate for this loss of rural manpower, foreign — mainly Egyptian — agricultural labour was imported in vast numbers variously estimated at between three quarters and one and a half million.

Meanwhile, thanks to the various projects already completed, some 250,000 ha. of land had been reclaimed by 1982. Other major schemes for dams and irrigation systems were planned in order to enlarge the cultivated area and ensure self-sufficiency in food. But their implementation had to be postponed when war expenditure grew beyond all expectations and took the lion's share of the country's income.

Confronting the Oil Companies – 1958–72

The regime which took over the government of Iraq in July 1958 was all too conscious that the country's finances rested on its revenue from its oil wealth and that promises to modernize the economy and improve the quality of life of the mass of the population could not be kept without a much larger income from this source.

There had indeed been a considerable increase in Iraq's oil revenue after the 1952 agreement which had established the principle that the government would receive half the companies' profits on their operations in Iraq. By 1958, however, it had become clear that the rate of growth of this revenue was linked to a large extent to the rate of growth of crude oil production.

According to the annual statistical bulletin of the Organization of Petroleum Exporting Countries[13] Iraq's annual average revenue from oil in the period 1952–57, at ID55.5 million, was just over three and a half times its level of 1951. But since the annual average output of crude oil during the same period had tripled, claims that Iraq had derived a real advantage from the new arrangement were seen to be greatly exaggerated.

The IPC and its sister companies were very willing to step up Iraqi production of crude for sale to their parent companies – the British, Dutch, French and American groups already mentioned – at a time when demand was rising on the world market. Iraq was a very desirable source with its easily accessible oil and cheap operating costs. It has been estimated[14] that in the early 1960s the total cost of operating and developing oil (not including the cost of finding it) was 7 cents per barrel in Iraq, compared to 10 cents in Saudi Arabia, 46 cents in Algeria, 62 cents in Venezuela and 151 cents in the USA.

As for the 50–50 profit sharing agreement, the government of Nuri al-Sa'id itself had challenged the cost-accounting methods of the IPC group on the basis of which the profit-sharing was calculated. Differences between the government and the IPC were many and deep, from the calculation of fixed costs, exploration costs and drilling costs, to the inclusion in the companies' crude production costs of such items as 'company overheads, expenditures on public relations, corporate grants, and the like'.[15] But the talks over these differences dragged on for two years with no sign of a firm stand on the part of the Iraqi negotiators.

Meanwhile, popular hostility to the Nuri al-Sa'id Government had reached new heights during the tripartite invasion of Egypt in 1956. In 1957, members of the Chamber of Deputies were also voicing their discontent with the conduct of the oil negotiations and demanding urgent action to end the companies' monopoly of the country's oil.

Formal negotiations were resumed in June 1958 and continued until July 12, almost the eve of the July revolution.

From the outset, the new regime spoke of the need to secure larger oil revenues. The IPC group for its part, fearful of drastic changes and attempting to ward them off, announced in January 1959 new plans for a quick expansion of export facilities sufficient to raise crude exports from 34 to 57 million tonnes a year by the end of 1960. Not surprisingly, these plans met with little enthusiasm on the part of the Iraqi authorities. They were announced at a time when crude oil prices on the world market were beginning to fall. The crude oil price index (1954 = 100) was 98.6 in 1959, 92.5 in 1960 and 89.2 in 1961. It remained on a downward trend until 1967 when the Israeli invasion of Sinai and Egypt's closure of the Suez Canal boosted oil prices to much higher levels.

In 1959 Iraq and most oil producing countries with profit-sharing agreements realized that higher output would not be accompanied by a proportionate rise in their oil income.

Iraq's negotiations with the companies were resumed in August 1960. By then the conflict had been aggravated by the Basra Oil Company's decision to stop production at its Rumaila field as a protest against an increase in port dues. The Rumaila field had then a capacity of about 4 million tonnes a year.

The new talks were held intermittently between August 1960 and October 1961. Besides minor issues they had to deal with Iraq's demands for a 20% share in the capital of the IPC group, the relinquishment of 90% of the untapped concession areas and the discontinuation of the wastage of gas from the oilfields or money compensation if it continued to be flared.

The Iraqi negotiators, now headed by General 'Abd al-Karim Qasim, were encouraged by the enthusiastic popular response to these far-reaching demands. In April 1961 they ordered the companies to stop all exploration or drilling in the undeveloped portions of the concession areas until a successful conclusion of the talks had been reached. Support for Qasim in stopping all exploration activities was wide and unreserved. Organizations and individuals throughout the nation, and some beyond its borders, expressed strong approval in public statements and telegrams.[16]

The companies for their part apparently discounted the danger of outright cancellation of their concessions. They refused to budge from the 50–50 profit-sharing formula. As regards the concession areas, they offered to relinquish 75% of these territories immediately and a further 15% within seven years without, however, allowing the Iraqi government the right to choose the areas to be returned.

When the talks collapsed in October 1961, the next move was up to the Qasim Government. On 11 December, it promulgated a law enforcing the measures which the companies had chosen to consider as empty threats. This was the first radical step to curtail the monopoly rights of the oil companies since the unsuccessful Iranian attempt to nationalize its oil ten years earlier, a step of considerable importance for the future of the oil industry in Iraq and in the Middle East as whole.

Law 80 of 1961 reduced the concession areas of the three oil companies to about 0.5% of their original size. It left them a total of 748 sq. miles: 288 sq. miles for the IPC in the north-east of the country, 24 sq. miles for the MPC in the Mosul area; and 436 sq. miles for the BPC in the Rumaila and Zubair regions. Their former rights over practically the whole of Iraq's territory were abolished.

This law made no mention, however, of three other basic issues in dispute: the revision of the 50–50 profit-sharing formula, the use of natural gas and Iraq's claim to a 20% share in the capital of the IPC group. These issues, and the companies' efforts to obtain amendments to Law 80, which they never accepted, continued to be in dispute for another eleven years until the nationalization of Iraq's oil industry in 1972.

After the coup d'état of February 1963 and the social upheavals that accompanied and followed it, relations between the successive governments and the companies remained in a position of stalemate in which production and revenue expanded very slowly. Between 1961 and 1965, the average annual increase in oil output was only 6.5%.

Apart from its deep domestic political problems, the chief concern of the government of 'Abd al-Salam 'Arif was to determine the oil potential of the areas taken back under Law 80 of 1961 and to elaborate a programme for their development, despite the hostility of the IPC group.

The Qasim government had previously decided that this development had to be carried out by a national oil company and had prepared a draft law to this effect. In February 1964 the new government announced the formation of the Iraq National Oil Company (INOC) and issued a law which put it in charge of all phases of the oil industry, including exploration and prospecting, production, transportation, refining, storage and distribution of crude oil, oil products and petrochemicals.

It took several years for the INOC to start to function in this manner. Meanwhile there was the urgent question of a specially rich oilfield – the North Rumaila field in the former BPC area expropriated under Law 80 but still untapped. Opinions of Iraqi oil experts and economists differed widely on the best way to make a start. Proposals to exploit North Rumaila as a joint venture in partnership with the IPC group reached an advanced stage, while opponents of the scheme advocated the development of the field by INOC independently.

Matters were brought to a head by the Israeli attack on Egypt, Jordan and Syria in June 1967 which firmly crystallized opinion against any stronger links with foreign oil companies. In July 1967, during the regime of President 'Abd al-Rahman 'Arif who had succeeded his brother in 1966, legislation was promulgated which specifically prohibited the Iraq National Oil Company from developing oil in any part of the country by the granting of 'concessions or the like'.

The IPC group did not recognize the legislation in respect of the INOC any more than it had accepted the expropriations of 1961. Further, in an unwise show of its remaining power to control Iraqi finances, it kept oil production below its potential capacity with an annual average of only 68.3 million tonnes during 1965–69.

While the conflict with the companies continued to deepen, the Iraqi authorities were looking for the best way to exploit the expropriated oil-bearing areas, and especially the promising North Rumaila field. They finally turned to the Soviet Union with whom two agreements were signed in 1969, one between the governments of the two countries and one between the INOC and the Soviet Machine Export Organization.

The Soviet government agreed to put into operation the North Rumaila oilfield with an initial output of 5 million tonnes by early 1972 to be gradually raised to 18 million tonnes a year. It also undertook to conduct a large programme of work for the development of several other oil-bearing areas in south Iraq, to finance the whole operation and to accept Iraqi oil in payment of a credit equivalent to $70 million.

This momentous step taken by the 'Arif Government before 1968 was intended as an assertion of Iraq's newly-found independence in its running conflict with the IPC group. The conflict was in the very early 1970s exacerbated by two IPC moves, first a threat to take legal action to prevent the sale of crude oil from North Rumaila, then a decision to reduce output from Kirkuk in contravention of an earlier agreement to step it up, under the pretext that a fall in oil prices had made its export uneconomic.

This proved to be the breaking point. On June 1 1972, the Iraq Petroleum Company was nationalized. Its two affiliates were not immediately affected, and indeed IPC itself was by then trying to salvage what it could. It accepted the nationalization of the Kirkuk producing area, surrendered the Mosul Petroleum Company and paid Iraq $141 million of outstanding royalty backpayments, in return for a promise that the Basra Petroleum Company would retain its oil concession.

Nevertheless, the BPC was in its turn nationalized seven months later in protest at the support given to Israel by the US and Dutch governments during the June 1973 Arab–Israeli war.

The first oil from North Rumaila flowed in April 1972. From there on and until the disasters inflicted by the war which started in September 1980, oil production followed a rising curve reaching a record level of 170.6 million tonnes in 1979 (equivalent to 3,475,000 barrels a day).[17]

The Seven Fat Years of the Ba'th

The nationalization of the IPC group could hardly have taken place at a more opportune time. The fourth Arab-Israeli war started on 6 October 1973. On 17 October a meeting of the oil ministers of the Arab producing countries announced the first use of the 'oil weapon' in response to the support given to Israel by the US. This took the form of the immediate doubling of crude oil prices, plus an unpracticable embargo on oil exports to the US and

Holland.

As far as Iraq was concerned, the doubling of the price coupled with a much increased output meant a sudden huge rise in oil revenue which continued to grow at a fast rate on a tide of still higher prices and increasing production until 1981 when the war on Iran devastated Iraq's oil industry. The amazing increase in wealth from this one source developed as follows:

	Crude Oil Production[18] *in million metric tonnes*	*Oil Revenue*[19] *Estimates in million US $*
1972	72.1	575
1973	99.0	1,900
1974	96.7	6,000
1975	111.0	8,000
1976	118.8	8,500
1977	115.2	9,500
1978	125.7	11,600
1979	170.6	21,200
1980	130.2	26,500
1981	44.2	10,400
1982	45.1	9,500
1983	46.7	9,651
1984	58.5	11,247

Long before this huge increase in the oil income successive Iraqi governments had proclaimed that planned economic development was one of their most cherished aims. In 1964, after the overthrow of the first Ba'thist government, a five-year economic development plan for the financial years 1965-66 to 1969-70 was devised by the Planning Ministry. It aimed at investments of ID668.1 million ($1,870.4 million at the then official rate of exchange of three dollars per dinar). Its two largest allocations were for industry and agriculture which accounted between them for over half the proposed total expenditure. It is clear however that funds for development were diverted to current expenditure, as the actual expenditure at the end of the period was only 62% of the original allocations. Significantly, the amount spent on agriculture was only 31.3% of the original target for this sector.[20]

The 1970-75 plan suffered a similar fate, but for different reasons. After a modest start it was revised annually when the planners came to expect more and more money after the nationalization of the oil industry and the quadrupling of oil prices in 1974. However, they did not manage to invest the vast sums put at their disposal. Of receipts estimated at the equivalent of $5,203 million, actual development expenditure in this five-year period was put at a total of slightly under $4,000 million.[21]

Development plans for subsequent five-year periods were reportedly devised on a grandiose scale against the background of continuously rising oil prices. In the case of Iraqi crude, the posted price for Basra Light rose from $2.45 per barrel in early 1972 to $11.67 in January 1974. By December 1979 it had jumped to $25.96 and it reached a peak of $35.96 in January 1981.

But the targets of the development programmes appear to have been abandoned in practice by the middle 1970s. Official figures are not available, however, as the publication of the yearly allocations and expenditures ceased after 1978, the last year for which official information on many other aspects of the economy was published.

According to economic reports prepared by Lloyds Bank, the proposed investments for 1976–80 amounted to ID15,211 million ($51.5 billion)[22] and those for 1981–1985 were raised to ID43,017 million ($130 billion).[23]

These very impressive figures became quite irrelevant in the economic chaos which followed the decision to attack Iran in September 1980 when the five-year plan ending in 1980 was still far from completion. Most of the projects other than those contributing to the war effort had to be postponed or abandoned for lack of funds or because they were situated in the areas coming under Iranian fire.

The war itself has been estimated to cost 'at least one billion dollars a month'[24] while income from oil exports fell catastrophically with the destruction of the southern export terminals in the early stages of the war and with the closing by Syria on 10 April 1982 of the pipeline taking Kirkuk crude to the Mediterranean across Syrian territory. By then the only outlet for the export of Iraqi oil was the small pipeline to the Turkish port of Dortyol with a capacity of about 700,000 barrels a day.

The war put an end to a period of steady economic progress throughout the 1970s, more especially after the rise of oil prices which started in 1973. This progress is illustrated by the very fast growth of the Gross Domestic Product in the 1970s.

Gross Domestic Product – in Million Dinars[25]

Year	At Current Prices	At Constant Prices 1975 = 100
1965	863.2	–
1970	1,139.8	2,618.8
1973	1,512.1	3,167.0
1974	3,331.5	3,394.7
1976	5,113.8	4,376.4
1977	5,593.4	5,135.0
1978	6,838.2	5,762.7

The GDP in 1974 was thus double its level of 1973. Between 1974 and 1978 it grew again by 105%, an average annual growth of 26.2%. Estimates of the post-1978 fluctuations of the GDP indicate further rises of 35% in 1979 and 15.6% in 1980, then a decrease of 30% in 1981.[26]

The swelling of the revenue from the oil industry in the 1970s accruing entirely to the state is reflected in the upward trend of the contribution of the state-owned sector in the total GDP: it rose from 25.6% in 1971 to 77.6% in 1978. Exports of crude oil alone accounted for 56.17% of the GDP in 1979. The share of manufacturing industry remained small. The following assessments of the contributions of the principal economic sectors to the GDP during the fattest years of Iraq's economy appeared in a study sponsored by the Arab Industrial Development Organization (AIDO) and published in Baghdad in 1982.[27]

Contributions to the Gross Domestic Product by Principal Economic Sectors, in Percentage (at Constant Prices 1975 = 100)

	1975	*1976*	*1977*	*1978*	*1979*
Crude Oil	49.76	53.12	52.49	52.93	56.17
Agriculture, Fisheries and Forestry	7.59	7.79	7.43	6.33	5.36
Manufacturing Industry	6.59	6.77	7.41	6.86	6.85
Building Industry	8.67	8.23	6.74	7.51	7.02
Transport, Communications and Storage	4.49	4.72	4.93	5.14	4.51
All Others	22.90	19.37	21.00	21.23	20.09
	100.00	*100.00*	*100.00*	*100.00*	*100.00*

Industrial Development – One Step Forward

Iraq's manufacturing sector has always been a small one. Until the 1970s it consisted of light industries producing construction materials and consumer goods, as described earlier in this chapter. In 1969, the 'larger' industrial establishments (those employing more than ten people) numbered 1,248 of which 179 were state-owned and employed 44,610 people. 1,069 were privately owned and had a total workforce of 40,300, i.e. an average of just under 32 workers each compared with an average of about 2,500 in the state-owned factories. The latter included, of course, the oil refineries already mentioned.

The ambitious targets for industrial development set in the early 1970s were based on the justifiable expectation of a very large income from the nationalized oilfields for many years to come. On this basis, the government strategy aimed at widening the range of privately-owned light industries and financing them through the state-controlled banking system. Projects involving high technology and heavy investments were kept for the state sector.

It is evident that manufacturing industry as a whole did progress between 1975 and 1979, as shown by the fact that its share of the Gross Domestic Product remained practically unchanged during this period despite the very large increase in the total GDP. Up to 1978 at least, much of the growth must be attributed to the state sector. Between 1969 and 1978, the number of state-owned industrial establishments increased by 79.3% and their workforce by 144%, while the number of 'larger' privately owned ones rose by 24.7% and their workforce by only 5.4%.

Up to the end of the decade, and even in 1980 and 1981, international engineering firms and consultants were awarded contracts worth huge sums of money in order to provide an industrial base capable of sustaining a steady development in the 1980s. Spending on industrial development in six years, from 1974 to 1979, added up to ID4,284 million[29] a quarter of which was for projects to expand the production of crude oil and oil products. ID950 million were spent on power projects and about 1D900 million on the chemicals and petrochemicals industries. Most of these investments benefited, of course, the private sector by providing cheap energy, better communications as well as materials for the light industries.

The greatest emphasis was placed on three major industries: iron and steel, fertilizers and petrochemicals. All three had become potentially viable after a substantial improvement of the port installations.

Apart from two oil terminals at Mina al-Bakr and Khor al-Amaya, Iraq's only port until the early 1970s was Basra, on the Shatt al-'Arab. Despite limitations imposed by the nature and small extent of Iraq's coastline, two others have been added. The port installations at Um Qasr, south of Basra, include facilities for the export of the high-value sulphur from the rich deposits in the Mosul area. Nearer Basra a larger port Hawr al-Zubair was completed towards the end of the decade and equipped for bulk handling of phosphates, other minerals and fertilizers. This was an exceptionally costly enterprise as it involved the digging of a canal capable of taking merchant ships of up to 60,000 tonnes deadweight.

Hawr al-Zubair is also the site of an iron and steel plant with an annual capacity of 1.2 million tonnes of sponge iron and 400,000 tonnes of steel, as well as two large plants using gas from the southern oilfields as feedstock to produce respectively nitrogen fertilizers and plastic resins.

The much needed and long delayed fertilizers industry had at last become a reality by the end of 1970s, with the completion of three major projects: two nitrogen plants at Hawr al-Zubair and at Basra and a very large plant at al-Qayim, in the north-west of the country, using the important phosphate deposits in that region for the production of phosphatic fertilizers, with a potential annual output of over one and a half million tonnes.

The production capacity of Iraq's oil refining installations was also expanded from 185,000 barrels a day in 1974 to 305,000 in 1981. Actual production from the refineries rose from 106,000 to 188,000 barrels a day during the same period.[30] The capacity of the Basra refinery alone was raised from 70,000 to 150,000 barrels a day.

Most of the completed industrial plants were still producing well below their capacity by September 1980. Nevertheless the total value of industrial production at current prices rose from ID428.1 million in 1975 to ID1,110 million in 1979.[31] The largest part of the increase was due to the growth of two manufacturing groups: petroleum products and by-products and food processing.

In the proposed development programme for 1981–85 — interrupted and much of it abandoned after 1981 — priority was given to the infrastructure and more especially to the railways and roads networks. Designs for the construction of modern high-speed railway tracks, intended to supersede eventually the two major lines linking Baghdad with the north and the south of the country, were completed, and some of the new tracks had reportedly been put in place and even damaged by enemy action by the end of 1983. The planned network of some 3,000 km. altogether includes several new lines linking Baghdad with the southern ports, with the northern cities of Mosul, Arbil and Kirkuk, and with Qusayba near the Syrian border with a branch line to the phosphate mines at Akashat and the fertilizers plant at al-Qayim. Long-term plans envisage the linking of Iraq's railway system with those of Kuwait, Saudi Arabia and Turkey.

The construction of new major roads, notably two six-lane motorways — one designed to link Iraq with Jordan, Syria and Kuwait and the other to run between Baghdad and the Turkish border — were begun on the eve of the war.

Guns Before Butter

Economic planning cannot be blamed for the fact that so many of the major industrial schemes conceived and started during the 1970s were located in the area which proved the most vulnerable to enemy attacks from the early stages of the war with Iran. This was the only area with easy access to the country's only outlet to the sea at the head of the Gulf as well as to the energy and feedstocks needed for the new steel and petrochemicals industries.

The blame for the virtual wiping out of the extremely costly equipment so recently installed belongs to those reponsible for the conduct of Iraq's foreign policy, even more so because they had earlier claimed personal credit for the pre-war economic progress.

Early on in the war, the Basra refinery was bombed and put out of action. The two oil terminals at Mina al-Bakr and Khor al-Amaya, the southern section of the 'strategic' pipeline system completed in 1975 to link the terminals with the northern oilfields, the pumping stations and the petrochemicals plants, all were also hit by air raids after the start of the Iraqi military attack across the Shatt al-'Arab. The exact extent of the damage to these installations was not revealed. Nor has there been an estimate of the length of time needed for repairs and of their possible cost.

From the economic point of view, they were not however the only disasters. The whole of the Iraqi economy became in fact a war casualty. By 1983 oil revenue and foreign exchange reserves had become a fraction of their pre-war level, exports had slumped while imports soared, and payments to international contractors in charge of major projects could no longer be met.

The closing down of the southern terminals meant the interruption of oil production from the southern oilfields, but oil exports continued on a more limited scale by means of the two pipelines to the Mediterranean terminals. When the pipeline linking the northern fields to Banias, on the Syrian coast, was closed by Syria in April 1982 the only outlet became the pipeline from these oilfields to the Gulf of Iskenderun, at the Turkish port of Dortyol, commissioned in 1977 with a capacity of 700,000 barrels a day. But already by 1981 total oil production had fallen to just under 900,000 barrels a day, compared to 3.4 million in 1979.[32] When the pipeline across Syria was closed, it fell still lower despite some export by road tankers through Jordan and Turkey. When it became clear that the war with Iran was no blitzkrieg, it was decided to expand the capacity of the line to Dortyol and to start planning for another pipeline across Saudi Arabia to the Red Sea. Financing was however a major problem for the latter project, but a small increase of the volume of crude oil exports to slightly over one million barrels a day became possible in 1984 by the costly expedient of sending about 200,000 barrels a day by road tankers via Jordan and the port of Aqaba.

No official figures are available regarding government finances for this period. It is thought however that the revenue from oil exports dropped to around $10 billion a year in 1981 and 1982, only 37.7% of its peak of $26.5 billion in 1980, and that foreign exchange in hand at the end of 1983 was as low as $2 billion whereas it amounted to $35 billion before the war.[33] Apart from expenditure on armaments, the largest drain on foreign exchange reserves was the debt to foreign companies for work already completed or still being done. At end 1983 the government's debt to France alone, partly for civil contracts and partly for arms supplies, was thought to be at least five but perhaps as much as $7 billion and the total foreign debt including unpaid interests was estimated at a minimum of $50 billion in 1983.[34]

Generous financial aid came in 1981 and 1982 from Saudi Arabia as well as, to a smaller extent, Kuwait and other Arab neighbours in the Gulf. This aid became however somewhat more restricted in 1983 when the donor countries found their own oil income seriously reduced by a fall in oil prices and in oil demand on the world market.

The rush to secure foreign loans and credits began in earnest in 1983. In most cases, the foreign companies involved in contracts in Iraq as well as their respective governments agreed to re-payment by long-term credits, rather than forfeit the prospect of post-war contracts. Meanwhile, the regime of austerity imposed on the country was tightened month by month, and the outlook remains bleak for many years to come. The cost of repairing the material damage caused by the war, of rebuilding the devastated ports, oil terminals, pipelines, factories, towns and villages, is bound to delay a return to economic development for a long time.

But the potential for a prosperous Iraq exists beyond any doubt. In 1973, at the time of the turmoil in oil circles in the wake of the nationalization of the IPC group and the sharp increase in oil prices, Iraq's proved reserves of oil were assessed at 31.5 billion barrels (approximately 4,300 million tonnes). Some 6.4 billion barrels were extracted in the following eight years. Yet the reserves were still estimated at some 30 to 35 billion barrels in the early 1980s[35] on the basis of new fields identified in the late 1970s.

The size of the oil reserves has been further upgraded by the Iraqi National Oil Company. In the course of 1983 it estimated them first at 59 billion barrels[36] then at some 100 billion barrels, after identifying other major fields for future development.[37] While the latter figure is probably on the optimistic side, an upward revision of the size of the oil reserves was certainly justified. A report prepared by three US experts for the Eleventh World Petroleum Congress estimated Iraq's 'demonstrated' reserves at the end of 1980 at 7.26 billion tonnes[38] i.e. approximately 53 billion barrels.

Clearly Iraq's oil wealth is such that it can sustain a high level of all-round economic development for many years to come. At the rate of the peak 1979 level of 3.4 million barrels a day, the above estimate could keep production going for a minimum of 45 years, or 80 years if the higher estimate proves correct. This alone would provide a revenue more than adequate to enlarge both the agricultural and the industrial sectors of the economy and to finance social services on a scale that no Iraqi government has considered so far.

The inherent strength of the economy consists of the large resources of oil and minerals, the vast tracts of land to be reclaimed, the big rivers to be harnessed, and above all the human resources. The population of about 14 million in 1982 was nearly three times that of 1957.

With natural assets richer than ever, the means to develop them to benefit every member of an even bigger population should present no problem to the democratic and peace-loving government that the Iraqi people sooner or later will give themselves.

References

1. J. Morris, *The Market of Seleukia*, (Faber and Faber, London, 1957) pp. 298–299.
2. OPEC Annual Statistical Bulletins.
3. B. Shwardran, *The Middle East, Oil and the Great Powers*, 2nd edn. revised, (Council for Middle Eastern Affairs Press, New York, 1969) p. 278.
4. Ibid., p. 262.
5. P. Nore and T. Turner, *Oil and Class Struggle*, (Zed Press, London, 1980) p. 176.
6. R. Gabbay, *Communism and Agrarian Reform in Iraq*, (Croom Helm, London, 1978) p. 30.
7. J.M. al-Helwai, 'Rural Iraq, Changes and Problems', *World Marxist*

Review, July 1978, pp. 83–89.

8. Gabbay, op. cit., p. 117.

9. I. al-Khafaji, *The State and Capitalist Development in Iraq 1968–1978*, Dar al Mustaqbal for U.N. University Third World Forum, Middle East Office, Cairo, 1983. p. 123 (in Arabic).

10. F.A.O. Yearbook of Food and Agricultural Statistics.

11. al-Helwai, op. cit., pp. 83–89.

12. al-Khafaji, op. cit., p. 126.

13. C.W. Stocking, *Middle East Oil*, (Allen Lane, The Penguin Press, London 1971) pp. 462–63.

14. Ibid., p. 423.

15. Ibid., p. 208.

16. Ibid., p. 243.

17. British Petroleum Company, *Annual Statistics of World Energy*, 1981.

18. Ibid., and *Petroleum Economist*, January 1985.

19. International Monetary Fund, *International Financial Statistics*. Estimates include income from refined products and natural liquid gas. 1983 and 1974 figures from Economist Intelligence Unit Review, *Iraq*, No 3 and No 4 1985.

20. Economist Intelligence Unit, *Iraq – a New Market in a Region in Turmoil*, Special Report No. 88, October 1980.

21. Ibid.

22. Lloyds Bank Ltd. Overseas Department, London. *Iraq*, June 1981.

23. Lloyds Bank Group, London, *Economic Report Iraq*, 1983.

24. Ibid.

25. al-Khafaji, op. cit., p. 26.

26. Lloyds Bank Group, London, *Economic Report Iraq*, 1983.

27. M. al-Quraishi, *Industrial Development in the Republic of Iraq 1975–1979*, The Arab Industrial Development Organization, Regional Study, Baghdad, August 1982, p. 52 (in Arabic).

28. al-Khafaji, op. cit., p. 92.

29. *Middle East Economic Digest*, London, 14 December 1979.

30. OPEC, *Annual Report* 1981.

31. al-Quraishi, op. cit., p. 125.

32. *British Petroleum Statistical Review of World Energy*, 1981.

33. *Middle East Economic Digest*, London, 16 December 1983.

34. Economist Intelligence Unit Review, *Iraq*, No. 4, 1983.

35. Ibid.

36. *Petroleum Times*, London, August 1983.

37. *Middle East Economic Digest*, London, 23 December 1983.

38. *Petroleum Economist*, London, September 1983.

4. The Parasitic Base of the Ba'thist Regime

'Isam al-Khafaji

Since its advent to power in 1968, and more particularly since the early 1970s, the Iraqi Ba'thist regime has attempted to present itself to the world as engaged in building up a form of 'socialism' or 'Arab socialism', independent of both East and West.[1] Furthermore, its propaganda machine has tirelessly proclaimed its intention to create both an equal and just society, and a diversified and independent economy. More recently, however, with rather less fanfare, the Ba'thist regime has tended to play down its 'socialist' stance, and has strengthened its political and economic ties with the West and the 'moderate' Arab states, a course of action which some commentators have rationalized in terms of purely personal decisions on the part of the present leadership. As will become clear from the analysis presented in this paper, this development is by no means accidental, and is in fact the logical outcome of the economic and social policies which the regime has been pursuing for some time.

The usual explanations given for this apparent 'change of heart' are either that the regime has somehow 'reappraised' its economic policy and 'discovered' the importance of individual initiative, or that the growing burdens of the war with Iran have now compelled it to assign to local capitalists some of the tasks that the state had previously been able to undertake. However, a thorough examination of the relationship between the state and private economic activity will show that this development cannot be explained in terms of a sudden 'reappraisal' or the circumstances created by the war. This chapter will attempt to prove the opposite, namely that capitalist relations of production, which became dominant under the present regime, were in fact the very forces which required intensive intervention by the state. Capitalist relations later forced the gradual liberalization of economic activity in such a way that official economic policies increasingly came to serve the needs of a form of capitalism whose main characteristics were essentially parasitic. Furthermore, the unleashing of the war against Iran can also be partially explained by the desire of this new capitalist formation to secure and stabilize oil exports, in order to finance its activities and perpetuate its income. This paper will begin by examining the validity of the widely held notion that the 'omnipotent' Iraqi state has hitherto been controlling virtually all economic activity, not in the interests of certain classes, but in some sense independently of them.

The Private and Public Sectors in Iraqi State Capitalism

In less than 30 years, oil revenues in Iraq rose from ID49.75 million in 1953 (ID = $3.39) to ID144 million in 1980.[2] This enormous and rapid influx of new wealth had a profound impact on the whole structure of society and the economy. Perhaps its most significant effect was on the relationships of all social classes, particularly the dominant classes, with the state power. In general terms, the sudden availability of these huge sums enabled the regime to claim that it was 'building prosperity' and constructing a 'socialist society'. However, the mere availability of such huge sums does not *of itself* imply a 'socialist' orientation. It is sufficient to cite the example of Saudi Arabia, which has major state investments in public services and productive industries, but which could not by any stretch of the imagination be described as socialist. Similarly, the share of the pre-revolutionary Iraqi state in gross fixed domestic capital formation averaged 50% of the total over the years 1953-58.

Hence, given the fact that a state's share in gross fixed capital formation is no indication of its political orientation, it is useful to ask who benefited most from this level of investment, and to investigate the ways in which they were able to do so. This would help to explain the fact that while the Iraqi state sector contributed nearly 80% of fixed capital by the late 1970s, this was accompanied by a vigorous and unprecedented growth in the strength of private capital.

The rise in oil prices and in the volume of oil exports since 1973-74 has resulted in oil revenues exceeding gross state expenditure for consumption and investment combined. The oil sector alone provided more than 60% of GDP. This has meant that the state is in control of the largest source of economic surplus in the society, making government expenditure the principal source of demand in the economy. In brief, the state itself has become the economy's largest single customer, and governmental expenditure has grown at a rate more than three times that of GDP. This factor has helped to unite and capitalize the market, by breaking up pre-capitalist forms of exploitation and by expanding the market through the intensive demand created by government expenditure. However, although the state has become the principal consumer and the major source of surplus in the economy, it has failed to become the major employer of labour or the largest producer. Hence, although the oil sector alone constituted 58.09% of GDP in 1975, this did not manifest itself in the form of the creation of products or services within the economy, but rather in the form of financial revenues which were spent on imports or purchases from domestic capital. The oil sectors of the economy shared the remaining 41.91% of GDP, divided between the state sector (22.86%) and the private sector (19.05%). Of course, the state sector includes areas such as public administration, security and defence, whose contribution to GDP consists of the sum total of wages and salaries of employees as well as smaller sums in the form of rents paid to the owners of buildings which house government offices. If this area, which contributed 12.48% to GDP, is excluded, the state's contribution is reduced to a modest 9.3%, compared with the private sector's 19.05%.

Because of its relatively small participation in the productive sectors of the economy, the state's ability to absorb labour outside public administration, security and defence has been limited. Thus, although the state was in formal control of 80% of GDP and the most profitable sectors of the economy, it employed less than a quarter of the labour force in 1977; in consequence, agriculture, construction and other parts of the private sector actually control and determine the labour market. However, the state's most obvious field of activity as a purchaser of domestic and foreign capital is in investment expenditure. As a result of the huge increases in investment allocation — largely undertaken without any proper consideration of the availability of essential resources such as construction materials, power supplies, appropriate technical and administrative cadres, port and airport capacity — foreign and domestic contracting has gradually emerged as the most dynamic sphere within the economy, and its general orientation vitally determines that of other sectors. Activities in this sphere, where private sector participation has amounted to about 92% since the Ba'th takeover in 1968, have acted as a major stimulant in accelerating demand for the products of domestic industry, in accumulating enormous profits, and in firmly establishing an important new stratum of the Iraqi bourgeoisie.

Government Policy and the Contracting Bourgeoisie

During the 1970s, the state's sole asset was the income it derived from oil, and the commodities it wished to purchase with this income could only be provided by the private sector, either from domestic or from foreign sources. Its ambitious 'dash for growth' led to an unrealistic approach to the process of economic development, exemplified by purchases of sophisticated technological equipment which took no account of the level of local expertise. Government investment increased from ID71.7 million in 1968-69 to ID1214.6 million in 1975-76, under a programme officially described as 'explosive development'. Comparable growth took place in investment on the part of self-financed government corporations, and there were major increases in consumption and private investment. Hence demand mounted rapidly for what were even then fairly meagre physical resources, thus creating an inflationary cycle which was itself stimulated by forecasts on the part of private capital that the state's demands for its commodities and services would continue to increase. One specialist study of this process has estimated that the average cost of capital formation increased threefold over the period 1973-76 as a result of these and other pressures.[4] The contracting bourgeoisie was able to put up its prices continually because of its monopoly in the domestic market; by 1974–75 there were already 2,788 contractors registered officially with the Planning Council classified into six grades according to their financial standing.

However, this relatively small number of contractors was not capable of providing all the goods and services required by the investment sector, especially when it is considered that the vast majority of contractors were concentrated in the lower grades. Thus there were only 159 in the first three grades, and 1826 in the sixth.[5] In addition, most of them were newcomers and had no previous experience of the complex activities demanded by the investment programme; only 829 had been registered in 1970–71. The rapid rise in the number of contractors and of their importance within the economy has greatly affected the behaviour of the rising bourgeoisie, particularly since 1968. This key field of activity continued to be backward and underdeveloped in organizational terms, largely because entry into the 'world of contracts' was an easy matter, only requiring some relationship or connection with political personalities. With the general expansion of contracting, there were 63 foreign contractors registered with the Ministry of Planning in 1975, and three Arab (non-Iraqi) contractors, as well as 151 engineering bureaux of which only eight were Iraqi and eight other Arab, while 31 were American, 29 British and 21 West German.[6]

In another study[7] we have attempted to present initial estimates of profits in the private building and construction sector, based on official national accounts with some reservations expressed about the figures offered by the contractors. Profits in this sector alone in 1975 reached ID35.04 million, and leaped to ID155.77 million in 1976[8], a rate of growth of more than 400% within a single year. Of course, contractors did not only benefit from increased government demand; there were several other avenues in which profits could be made. Thus contractors purchased or hired machinery or equipment (generally imported free of taxes) from the state at subsidized rates, and either used it on several projects at the same time or leased it to smaller contractors. The state generally places about 40% of the total value of the contract at the contractor's disposal, enabling him to use it for his own purposes for a relatively long period.

In a memorandum to the President in mid-1977, one of the Iraqi Communist Party's representatives in the government, who was a member of the Planning Council asked:

> What does the contractor need? He needs the capital which he obtains from the state, the machinery which he also obtains from the state, the raw materials which are supplied by the state at subsidized prices, and technical expertise, which is available as a result of the state's training programmes. Since he does not have to provide any of these items himself the contractor has nothing left to do except to open an elegant office, and even this may not be necessary.[9]

The very nature of this activity and the closeness of its ties with the political power has made those influential within it acquire characteristics which differ from other strata of Iraqi capitalism. The *Economist* has described the relationship as follows:

> The presence of a private contracting sector within the economy, which often achieves enormous profits, seems to the regime to be preferable to employing foreign companies. It is possible that the presence of this sector gives the regime some flexibility in rewarding its supporters and also enables it to make monetary transfers outside the official framework.[10]

The truth of this observation can be gauged from the close relationship which has been noted between the activity of the contractors and the needs of government, and is also confirmed by a study carried out to plot the rise of a sample of 31 individuals who were 'first grade' contractors in the late 1970s. Of the sample, eleven could not be traced; eight were connected by family relationships with senior figures in the regime; six had joint business ventures with such figures; two were former leaders of the ruling party, and four belonged to families traditionally sympathetic towards the party and had family members in it.[11] Of course, this stratum has not been the only beneficiary of the government's policies, but we have chosen to concentrate on its activities because these seem generally to have passed unnoticed, and because observers outside Iraq have often concluded, quite erroneously, that the absence of large private industrial projects is somehow equivalent to the absence of *capitalism*, another reason for the inappropriate 'socialist' label. Furthermore, the importance of distinguishing the 'parasitic' bourgeoisie from the other strata of Iraqi capitalism is of major political significance for those forces currently struggling for an alternative democratic regime in Iraq.

In calling for a democratic regime, the opposition forces are not simply trying to win over some sectors of Iraqi capitalism by opportunistic means. There is a genuine desire for democratic change in these circles as well, and unless a clear distinction is made between the interests of the parasitic strata and of the other wings of the bourgeoisie, it is difficult to account for their different political attitudes. Hence our intention here is very definitely *not* to lump together the whole capitalist class, but to concentrate on that part of the class whose activities depend generally on the depletion of the state's resources, whether by legal, quasi-legal or illegal means. As we shall see, this does not apply only to contractors; it also includes the entire stratum known as the 'bureaucratic bourgeoisie', as well as various brokers, speculators and agents of multinational companies whose interests are served not by increasing the productive capacities of the economy and diversifying its base, but rather by the perpetuation of technological and financial dependence upon multinationals, the militarization of the economy and the maintenance of the country's dependence upon exports of crude oil.

New Dependence under the Ba'th

In 1970-71, about 50% of government investment in industry was directed towards the extractive industries, that is, gas, oil, sulphur and phosphates.[12] This strategy, which was accompanied by laws and other directives issued in the 1960s and 1970s, brought the private sector both cheap raw and intermediate materials from the state industries and low interest loans from government banks. Loans and facilities granted by the Industrial Bank alone to the private sector increased from ID0.61 million in 1967-68 to ID12.5 million in 1977.[13] It also gave the private sector wide-ranging exemptions and immunities from taxation. Some entrepreneurs did not need to contribute any capital of their own at all in order to open a new factory. The Industrial Bank was committed to granting loans of up to 80% of the total cost of construction projects, while loans for other projects were given up to 40% of cost in the three central provinces and of up to 50-60% of cost in the other provinces.[14] In other words, the industrialist had only to inflate the cost of his project (a device regularly resorted to) in order to obtain a loan which would cover the total cost. A combination of rising demand and financial protection thus provided a monopolistic situation for industries which add little to the country's productive capacity and do not require large initial capital investment. In particular, this has encouraged the growth of 'final touch' industries, in which manufacturers import semi-finished products and then 'finish' them, a procedure which allows the products to be classified as locally manufactured goods, and thus to benefit from a variety of privileges and immunities.

By such methods, therefore, the private sector reaped immense rewards from the industrialization strategy. The value added in this sector reached 84% of that in the public industrial sector, although here of course investments were hundreds of times greater. This great expansion in activity is reflected in two recent decrees, the *Law regulating Industrial Investment in the Private and Mixed Sectors*, No. 115 of 1982 and *Company Law*, No. 36 of 1983. These permit an increase in the maximum capital allowed for private sector projects from ID200,000 to ID2 million in the case of companies with limited liability and to ID5 million for joint stock companies; they also empower the Industrial Bank to grant up to 120% of the capital for projects which are accepted.[15] With the state assisting private industry in this way, two points should be emphasized, concerning both the quality and the rate of industrial growth.

In the first place, the claim made by the regime that industrialization is being planned in such a way as to be related to the country's own resources is totally false. It is sufficient to point out that the percentage of imported inputs to total industrial inputs rose from 16.3% in 1970 to 70.4% in 1976[16]; the dependent nature of Iraqi industry will be discussed in more detail below. Secondly, the official industrial growth rates as published in the national statistical tables must be studied alongside both the rate of inflation and the rate of growth of the economy as a whole, in order to obtain a more realistic picture. Thus while the official rate of growth of national income shows an extremely favourable annual rate of 27.9% over the period 1969-80,[17] it should not be forgotten that oil revenues increased by 1,974.2% between 1970 and 1978, which grossly inflates the figure. However, the rate of growth in manufacturing industry should not be underestimated, since this is about 14% for the period 1968-81.[18] This would be even more impressive were it not for the rate of inflation, which was estimated officially at about 16% per annum between 1968 and 1975 and at about 25% between 1975 and 1980. Hence a comparison between the two rates suggests that there may have been no growth at all in this sector in terms of constant prices! In general, the pattern of distorted growth has other serious consequences which will be discussed in more detail below.

After the nationalization of the Iraq Petroleum Company and its subsidiaries in 1972, it was government policy to try to control the volume of oil exports and maximize revenues without any participation on the part of the foreign oil companies. The feverish search for new market outlets soon led to the appearance of a new stratum of brokers and middlemen. E. and E.F. Penrose describe this as follows:

> Before INOC production was established, bids were invited for long-term oil contracts on either cash or barter terms. This attracted speculative brokers and middlemen of all kinds, many of whom were foreign, but most of whom were Iraqis who had set up offices in Baghdad to represent foreign firms which wanted to sell their products in Iraq and were willing in return to take oil (which they would then resell). Thus pharmaceutical firms, tea traders and engineering firms, among others, all entered the lists. When INOC was faced with the prospect of selling large quantities of nationalized oil (perhaps in the teeth of IPC opposition) it again appealed to middlemen to help in the disposal of it: . . . The 'national' appeal brought to the doors of INOC a flood of all sorts of persons, firms and organizations (solicitors, teachers, chemists, retired men, in fact people from many walks of life) which only added to an already confused picture.[19]

In this way the euphoria of oil began to leave its mark on the social structure of Iraq. Between 1968 and 1973 imports increased from ID14.9 million to ID270.3 million, but then went up in a single year to ID700 million in 1974, escalating to ID3981 million in 1980. As a result, 38.8% of GDP was imported from outside Iraq in 1980, compared with only 14% in 1968. Hence it is ludicrous to talk in terms of achieving independence from inflationary pressures or from subordination to the world market, particularly as Iraqi exports do not consist of manufactured or diversified products but of a single substance, crude oil. Although the great increase in oil exports brought severe pressure on the capacity of ports, storage facilities and the transport sector in general, it was the source of huge profits for transport contractors and traders, and also gradually caused the state to give up its monopoly over foreign trade, permitting the private sector to gain import licences once more and also granting them to construction contractors, factory owners and foreign contracting companies. At the same time, little more was heard about the necessity of making the country self-sufficient in food by the end of the 1970s, since imported foodstuffs and consumer goods began to constitute an increasing proportion of imports because of the marginalization and decline of the agricultural sector.

A further feature of these developments, related to the general overall direction of economic policy, was the widespread belief that the mere fact of the state's possession of substantial financial resources was sufficient for it to be able to establish a balanced or equal relationship with the party selling it the complex technology. This was soon proved wrong, since the rush to purchase turnkey projects seriously weakened the regime's bargaining power; there were only a very limited number of companies and organizations actually capable of undertaking such complex projects as the construction of an entire petrochemical industry. The total cost of the turnkey projects completed in mid-1977 was about ID1870 million, about 50% of the cost of all industrial contracts (ID3573 million).[20] Such projects were generally carried out by 'Closed Box Technology' in which contractors prepare studies and designs, procure equipment and machinery and carry out the civil engineering, construction and installation work. This method allowed the companies to make far higher profits than would have been possible under more competitive conditions. They made skilful play of transport problems, the lack of raw materials and skilled labour, inadequate port facilities and of risks such as the possibility that work might have to be terminated before the project was completed in order to obtain major concessions from the regime, which, in sum, amounted to a major departure from the declared intentions of the development policy. Thus a law was passed in 1973 which gave the Revolutionary Command Council the right to exempt any project which it defined as of sufficient importance from all legal restrictions. In such projects, contractors were given the right to ignore or bypass income tax and labour laws, and overall supervision was vested in a special committee of the RCC (Law 157 of 1973, the *Law for the Execution of Major Development Projects*).

As a result, the mechanism of economic planning, to which the regime had always declared itself committed, became virtually paralysed, especially as the largest projects, and those having the most widespread effect on the rest of the economy, such as the petrochemical, iron and steel and phosphate complexes, came under the provisions of Law 157. In addition, the RCC had the right to award projects to Iraqi and foreign contractors without advertising them, which made a further mockery of planning procedures; the planning authorities did not have proper access to information on present or future economic variables, and could not take balanced decisions on other projects. The role of the Planning Council was relegated to the collection of secondary projects referred to it by the specialized ministries, and then to constructing a list in order of priorities, called the Investment Plan, which was generally subject to such constraints as the presence or absence of the appropriate raw materials. In addition, the principal economic sectors remained outside the scope of the Investment Plan; thus agriculture, building, construction, and most other private sector activities proceeded according to their own laws of motion. The directives and decisions for these areas of the economy were necessarily shaped or determined by the private sector, since they would otherwise remain purely paper projects with no-one to carry them out. As we have seen, the *Major Development Projects Law* had also excluded a large proportion of public sector activities from the scope of the Plan; in addition, major factors such as the movement of the labour force, pricing, and wages were all subject to market forces which the state had to reflect rather than attempt to control. Lastly, an economic framework largely defined by oil prices and the volume of oil exports is in fact subject to forces outside the national economy, and this has caused the Plans to become collections of forecasts devoid of any true function or purpose. Thus in 1980 the *Economist* commented that the Plan had ceased to have any meaningful political or economic content by 1976. Official objectives were no longer published; emphasis switched backwards and forwards from manufacturing industry to the oil industry, according to the personality of particular ministers, and in general the Plan's 'priorities' were more matters of propaganda than of fact. No sector forecasts were published for the last two years of the 1976–80 Plan, only the gross allocations.[21]

The increase in the size of the contracts signed with multinational companies, and the activities of private domestic contractors have meant that both groups have gained substantial influence over the decision makers, forcing them to give out more concessions as far as profits and tax exemptions are concerned, clear proof that the state's financial resources are no match for the power of these socio-economic strata. Furthermore, the spread of the activities of contracting companies has given the contractors themselves greater consciousness of their own coherence as a social stratum with homogeneous interests. This had already become apparent by 1976, when a plan to form a 'Contractors' Union' was defeated by democratic forces, which described it as the nucleus of a political party. The contractors gradually demanded facilities to enable them to act on the same footing as foreign companies, and the regime has responded positively to such pressures since the late 1970s. Thus in 1981 Iraqi contractors (main contractors, subcontractors and consultants) were included in the provisions of the *Major Development Projects Law*,[22] and in 1982 regulations were issued exempting Arab and foreign companies executing projects covered by this Law from the provisions of the Income Tax Laws.[23] Such indicators give some idea of the size of the profits won by foreign companies since the oil price rise of 1973.

Between 1970 and 1975 the value of the contracts awarded to foreign companies was ID682.4 million.[24] This rose sharply in the second half of the 1970s, reaching ID1065.5 million in 1978, ID4077.2 million in 1980 and ID7134.3 million in 1981.[25] This increase has not only affected the country's foreign reserves, but has also had drastic effects on the state's industrialization policies. In general terms the technology introduced by the turnkey projects in particular means that the rest of Iraqi industry has had to adapt its production to utilize the products provided by these projects, particularly petrochemicals. The turnkey method has virtually ensured that Iraqi cadres do not gain knowledge or experience of operating such projects, which means that the local economy will continue to be dependent on foreign sources of intermediate and capital goods, as well as foreign maintenance and experience. Foreign contracting has also tended to prevent the Iraqi side from confirming the feasibility of many of the projects, and from judging whether they can be operated efficiently and profitably within existing production capacity. It has also enabled some of the companies which were expelled from the Iraqi market in the early 1970s to return, making use of their 'experience' and the increasing demand for complex integrated technology.[26] Thus, in the 1970s, technological dependence replaced the financial dependence which was so much talked about before the explosion in oil prices. This did not of course mean that financial dependence was no longer a danger, but rather that it followed the pattern familiar from other oil producing countries with large financial surpluses.

Some Consequences of Recent Economic Policies

Such policies have had wide ranging effects on the whole of Iraqi society, and it is difficult to provide a comprehensive picture. Furthermore, foreign observers have often gained the impression, largely by taking the regime's claims at their face value, that progress has generally been uniform throughout the country, at least before the outbreak of the war with Iran in September 1980. In fact, in spite of the construction boom taking place very visibly in the city centres, there are whole areas on the outskirts of these same cities which do not have even minimal housing or living standards. Such areas house the bulk of the urban labour force, most notably Madinat al-Thawra outside Baghdad, which has a population of at least 1.5 million living in accommodation originally designed to house less than a fifth of that number.

The most recent Annual Abstract of Statistics, issued in 1978, indicated that more than half a million people were still living in *sarifas*, shacks made from mud and reeds; 4 million lived in mud houses (*kukh*), and a quarter of a million in tents.[27] Thus out of a total population of some 14 million, more than one third were not adequately housed. Again, although no official statistics on income distribution have ever been produced, the findings of research on family budgets carried out in 1976 give some idea of the huge disparities in income. Surveys showed that the share of the bottom 5% of families is 0.6% of the gross income of all families, while the top 5% get 22.9% of all incomes, making the gap between the top and bottom of the scale of the order of 38.2 : 1. The action taken by the regime at the end of the 1970s and the freedom which has been accorded to private economic activity in general makes it most likely that this gap will have widened in both directions since then. For comparative purposes, it is possible to consult the research carried out by the World Bank in which the data for Iraq goes back to 1956. From this it appears that the share of the lowest 20% of the population was 2.1% of total income, while the share of the top 20% was about 62%.[28] The data for 1976 shows that during the 18 years of 'socialism' the share of the lowest income group rose only to 4.7% of the total, while the top 20% continued to receive as much as 50.4% of the total. Although these indicators are only approximate, they must cast serious doubt on the real success of the much vaunted policy of closing the gap between rich and poor.

Although the official national accounts do not give any information about the gap between incomes the decline in the proportion of wages and salaries as shown under the heading 'Remuneration for Employees' is a useful illustration of these tendencies. This section remained almost constant in the period between 1966 and 1973, representing 28.03% of gross value added in 1966, 27.7% in 1968, 28.7% in 1970, 26.4% in 1971, 28.7% in 1972 and 27.5% in 1973. In 1974 the proportion fell to 18.82%, rose briefly to 20.99% in 1975, then fell again to 18.8% in 1977 and 18.66% in 1978.[29] These figures show that the spectacular rise in oil revenues did not bring about a parallel increase in wages and salaries, while an attempt to estimate the net revenue of the private sector suggests an increase from 12.4% of national income in 1975 to 39.6% in 1977.[30]

These results, it will now be clear, were not the unforeseen consequences of an erratic economic policy. Pumping government expenditure into both investment and consumption brought about a huge rise in the demand for labour in the cities, particularly for skilled labour. It also caused runaway inflation because of the general scarcity of goods and services. One result of this was a rising gap between the income of rural and urban dwellers as a consequence of the fall in agricultural prices and the rise in the cost of goods, services and material inputs. This has accelerated mass migration from the countryside to such an extent that the countryside has been virtually denuded of its population and agriculture provided less than 6% of GDP in the late 1970s, in comparison to 23% in the early 1960s. During the decade 1968-78, the agricultural sector lost about 310,000 workers, while the workforce in the construction and building sectors increased from 67,000 in 1970 to 185,000 in 1978. Competition for labour certainly brought about improvements in living conditions, but not in proportion to the rise in profits or the size of the national income. Again, increases in wages were generally absorbed by inflation, and it is even possible that the standards of living of some workers deteriorated in comparison with their situation in the late 1960s.

The consumer price index in 1980 reached 252 on the base of 1968 = 100. However, the way in which this figure has been calculated gives rise to some doubts about its accuracy. Thus the Annual Abstract of Statistics shows a rise in rents of 54.7% between 1973 and 1978, and Batatu commented in 1981 that 'the present monthly rent for what the Iraqi worker contemptuously calls a "garage", that is a miserable house with one bedroom and one sitting room and the minimum essential services, now costs between ID50 and ID60, compared with ID10–15 only a decade earlier'.[31] Furthermore, the average annual rise in prices to 1976 was around 10%, while the average growth in wages was about 3.2%, which clearly indicates a drop in real wages. The growth of wages only started to increase faster than the rate of inflation between 1977 and 1980 in the manufacturing industries and between 1975 and 1980 in the construction sector. Official publications and statements ignored the fact that the rise in wages was a natural result of the rise in the demand for labour as a market commodity, since there was intense competition for a very limited labour force. However, as we have shown, wages remained relatively modest in comparison with the incomes of other classes. The Minister of Labour admitted in July 1980 that rises in wages and salaries were not granted for reasons of 'principle' but 'to stop the flow of technicians and specialists from the state sector to the private sector'.[32] Similar explanations were given for the flood of Arab and foreign labour to Iraq at the end of the 1970s. The regime claimed that the Arab labour force was imported for 'pan-Arab considerations', although an official admitted in 1982 that the presence of foreign workers had played an important role in combatting pressures to raise wages from Iraqi workers.[33]

It was against this socio-economic background that the war against Iran was launched in September 1980. Since that time, of course, a host of new economic and political variables have been introduced which will certainly influence the future development of both economy and society in Iraq. We must now try to include the various factors mentioned above in an analysis of the war from the point of view of the newly emerging classes.

The Economic Function of the War

So far we have not referred to any of the political aspects of the development of Iraq under Ba'thist rule. Although this is not our main concern, it is necessary to relate our subject matter to recent political developments. So far, our explanation has attempted to show the inadequacy of the notion put forward by a number of commentators, including radical writers, of the so-called petty bourgeois nature of the Ba'th regime,[34] or the claim that it represents the interests of the middle classes.[35] We have made it clear that the main beneficiaries of Ba'thist rule have been the representatives of the more parasitic section of Iraqi capitalism, contractors, brokers, bureaucrats and speculators. This discussion has echoes of the theory which was prominent in the 1920s and 1930s, that Fascist regimes should be considered petty bourgeois in spite of the fact that they provided vital services for capitalism, simply because the leaders of the Fascist movements did not themselves originate from the *grande bourgeoisie*. The Ba'th 'experiment' was not limited to providing the circumstances under which an unprecedented flowering of capitalism could take place, and it is now necessary to make brief reference to a number of other important factors.

In the first place, it is the case that, in common with the bourgeoisie in other Third World countries which have arrived at the capitalist stage relatively late under the circumstances of the technological revolution and of increasingly complex and expensive capital units, the Iraqi bourgeoisie has remained and will remain fundamentally dependent on the state. The state not only provides infrastructural facilities such as roads, bridges and electricity, but also the major industrial investments essential for capitalist development, which private capital cannot afford to undertake by itself. In addition, the availability of oil revenues strengthened the relationship between the Iraqi state and the bourgeoisie, a phenomenon which I have called 'National State Capitalism'.[36] The term 'National' in this context is not meant as a political label, but describes the action of a regime which is attempting to unify the domestic market and to destroy precapitalist relations by bringing agricultural and craft industrial production into the cycle of capital, which was one of the principal reasons for the land reforms of 1970 and 1975. Contrary to what appear to be widely held beliefs, the impetus to capitalist development not only requires the elimination of existing feudal relations but also the restriction of the scope and nature of the activities of the 'old' bourgeoisie, which associated its own activities with those of the feudal landlords and with commercial, real estate and other activities.

Secondly, the political heritage of the democratic movement in Iraq and the leading role played by the Iraqi Communist Party has meant that every right-wing movement has been faced with the urgent necessity of repressing the left, by a combination of verbal demagogy and terror. The Ba'th ideology and slogans are an extreme expression of a political movement's efforts to give leftist form to a fundamentally rightist content. The regime has attempted to play the part taken by the Nazis in Germany, to try to win over the mass movement after attempting to paralyse the left and simultaneously putting forward slogans which appear superficially similar to those of the democratic movement. The coexistence of these two factors, the dependence of the bourgeoisie upon the state and the strength of the democratic movement, point to major structural weaknesses in Iraqi capitalism.

At its peak in 1980, oil production reached 3.7 million barrels per day, and the Iraqi regime was attempting to increase oil exports in order to give Iraq greater bargaining power in OPEC. After the Iranian revolution and the decline in Iranian oil production Iraq became the second largest oil producer in OPEC after Saudi Arabia. One of Iraq's major problems was that almost all her oil export outlets involved crossing other countries, with the exception of the less profitable Gulf seaboard, which cannot receive supertankers and whose distance from the Mediterranean involves higher transport costs. Here it should be remembered that the two oil pipelines passing across

Syria have been and are often exposed to shut-downs or stoppages because of factors connected with Iraqi-Syrian relations, to such an extent that these pipelines have always functioned as the Achilles heel of the Iraqi economy. In contrast, of course, Saudi Arabia has port facilities on both the Gulf and the Red Sea, and Iran also has a long coastline. In spite of the pan-Arab sloganizing of the Ba'th, no unity scheme with Syria would give Iraq hegemony over such a union, in contrast, for example, to a similar type of relationship with one or more of the smaller Gulf states. The regime has always shied away from any close relationship with countries with a similar or higher level of development which might threaten its own hegemony, but it has shown itself eager to achieve such a relationship with weaker states. Hence its 'Unity' aspirations were directed southwards, where the main obstacle until 1979 was Iran, Iraq's principal challenger for hegemony in the region.

Before the fall of the Shah, a move was made to bypass Syria, and a pipeline across Turkey was constructed in 1976. Later, the so-called 'Strategic Pipeline' was completed, which could pump oil either towards the Gulf or the Mediterranean, depending on political and other considerations. Of course, the routes of the pipelines were related to the political choices or orientation of the Iraqi regime; Turkey or any other country could also obstruct the flow of Iraqi oil if Iraqi policies clashed with Turkish interests.

All these expedients were necessarily partial solutions, and the golden opportunity only came with the fall of the Shah and the decision of the new regime that it would cease to play the role of the United States' policeman in the area. As a result, Iraq's main competitor in the region suddenly disappeared. If the Iraqi regime could exert a dominant role in the region, it would then be able to ensure its control over all decisions of OPEC in a manner which accorded with its notions of its own proper importance. Many details of the preparations for the current war have appeared in the international press, and cannot be discussed fully here.[37] The Iraqi regime seems to have based much of its planning on the deluded notions put forward in the Western media that the situation in Iran had caused the fragmentation of the central institutions of government and brought about chaos in the armed forces. However, history has many lessons about paper calculations made by leaders obsessed with the pursuit of 'glory', which brought catastrophe for their peoples and themselves to perdition.

References

1. As in, for example, Majid Khadduri, *Socialist Iraq: a Study in Iraqi Politics since 1968* (Washington D.C., 1978), and in the official English translation of the Ba'th Party's political report for 1974, *Revolutionary Iraq*.

2. Figures for 1953 from the Ministry of Finance, General Directorate of Accounts, and for the following years from Economist Intelligence Unit,

Quarterly Economic Review of Iraq, Annual Supplement, 1981.

3. Calculated from the *Annual Abstract of Statistics*, (*AAS*), 1976.

4. Fadhil 'Abbas Mahdi, 'Tadqirat l'il-taghayyir fi kulfat al-takwin al-ra'smali fi'l-'Iraq' (Estimates for changes in the cost of capital formation in Iraq), *Dirasat 'Arabiyya* (Beirut), November 1980, p. 155.

5. Sabah al-Durra, *al-Qita' al-'Amm fi'l-'Iraq*, (The Public Sector in Iraq), (Baghdad, 1977), p. 141.

6. Ahmad Abraihi al-'Ali, *al-Bina' w'al-Tashyid: Mabhath fi'l-'Ard w'al-Talab w'al-Muzharat al-Iqtisadiyya li-Suq al-Muqawalat*, (Building and Construction: a Study on Supply and Demand and the Economic Symptoms of the Contract Market), unpublished paper, Ministry of Planning, Baghdad, Unit for the Follow up and Analysis of Economic Variables, 1977, pp. 26–27.

7. 'Isam al-Khafaji, *Ra'smaliyya al-Dawla al-Wataniyya* (National State Capitalism), (Beirut, 1979) pp. 200–201.

8. 'Isam al-Khafaji, *al-Dawla w'al-Tatawwur al-Ra'smali fi'l-Iraq 1968–1978* (The State and Capitalist Development in Iraq 1968–1978) (Cairo, 1984) p. 71.

9. Amir 'Abdullah, 'Hawl Aslub (al-Mashru' al-Jahiz) fi'l-Ta'aqid ma' al-Sharikat al-Ajnabiyya fi'l-Qita' al-Sina'i' (On the turnkey project approach to contracts with foreign firms in the industrial sector) and 'Hawl Qita' al-Muqawalat w'al-Siyasa al-Tabaqiyya l'il-Dawla' (On the contract sector and the class policy of the state). Texts of two memoranda presented by the Minister without Portfolio (Amir 'Abdullah) to the President of the Republic and the Director of the Planning Board, 21 June 1977, *al-Thaqafa al-Jadida*, 133, August 1981, pp. 17–18.

10. Economist Intelligence Unit, *Iraq: a New Market in a Region of Turmoil*, 1980, p. 7.

11. al-Khafaji, *The State and Capitalist Development*, op. cit., p. 82.

12. Makram Sader, 'Le Développement Industriel de l'Irak', mimeo, CERMOC, Beirut, 1981, p. 17.

13. Figures for 1967–68 from *AAS* 1974, p. 243; for 1977, from *AAS* 1978, p. 337.

14. *Alif Ba'*, 4 November 1981.

15. Economist Intelligence Unit, *Iraq . . .* op. cit., p. 35.

16. ECWA (Economic Commission for Western Asia), *Industrial Development in Iraq: Problems and Prospects*, 2 vols. (Beirut, 1979); vol. 1, p. 66.

17. Ministry of Planning, Baghdad, *Iraq: 13 Years of Progress*, (Baghdad, n.d. [1981]) p. 9.

18. These figures have been taken from the text of the Political Report of the Ninth Congress of the Arab Ba'th Socialist Party (held in Baghdad in July 1982), published in *al-Thawra* newspaper between 25 January 1983 and 3 February 1983.

19. Edith and E.F. Penrose, *Iraq: International Relations and National Development* (London and Boulder, 1978) p. 440.

20. Amir 'Abdullah, op. cit., p. 9.

21. Economist Intelligence Unit, *Iraq . . .* op. cit., p. 20.

22. Decree No. 873 of 1981, *al-Thawra*, 3 July 1981.

23. *al-Waqai'a al-'Iraqiyya*, 7 June 1982.

24. al-Khafaji, *National State Capitalism*, op. cit., p. 201.

25. Figures for 1978 and 1979 from Economist Intelligence Unit, *Iraq . . .*

op. cit., p. 87; for 1980 and 1981 from John Townsend, 'Economic and Political Implications of the War: the Economic Consequences for the Participants', in M.S. El Azhary (ed.) *The Iran-Iraq War* (London, 1984) pp. 60–62. (ID = $3.39.)

26. For information on the restoration of contacts on the part of the government with foreign oil companies since the early 1980's see *Business Week*, 13 October 1981. For cooperation with Mobil Oil and possibilities of cooperation with Royal Dutch Shell, see *The Economist*, 6 June 1981 and the *Financial Times*, 1 August 1981.

27. AAS, 1978, p. 48.

28. S. Jain, *Size Distribution of Income*, World Bank, (Washington DC, 1975).

29. Calculated from information in *AAS* 1976, p. 175, and *AAS* 1978, pp. 136–137.

30. al-Khafaji, *The State and Capitalist Development*, op. cit., p. 162.

31. Hanna Batatu, 'Iraq's Underground Shi'a Movements', *Middle East Journal*, Autumn 1981, p. 581.

32. *Middle East Economic Digest*, 25 July 1980.

33. Mushin Khalil Ibrahim, 'Hawl Tajriba al-'Iraq al-'Amala al-Wafida' (Iraq's experience of imported labour), *al-Mustqbal al-'Arabi* (Beirut), May 1983, p. 103.

34. See for example Joe Stork, 'Oil and the Penetration of Capitalism in Iraq: an Interpretation', *Peuples Méditerranéens*, 9, Oct–Dec 1979.

35. See Hanna Batatu, *The Old Social Classes and the Revolutionary Movements of Iraq . . .*, (Princeton, 1978).

36. al-Khafaji, *National State Capitalism*, op. cit.

37. See the report in the *Guardian* on 6 January 1984 about Iraq's attempts to buy anti-tetanus serum in August 1980, some two months before the war began. The amount sought was about ten times the annual UK consumption, and the population of the UK is about four times that of Iraq. See also the *International Journal of the Armed Forces*, November 1980, which reported that Saddam Husain had invited senior NATO officers to discuss his war plans, informing them that the question of control of the Gulf for the next 50 years had been settled. In fact, the *Journal* noted, this control 'did not last 50 minutes'.

5. Iraqi Ba'thism: Nationalism, Socialism and National Socialism

Marion Farouk-Sluglett and Peter Slugett

This chapter is an attempt to trace the historical origins of Ba'thism and to give a history of the Ba'th Party both in and out of power since its foundation in 1944. We begin with a brief description of the origins of Arab nationalism, showing how the idea of the Arabs as a separate ethno-linguistic entity gradually took shape in the Arab provinces of the Ottoman Empire in the latter part of the 19th century. With the effective division of the Arab Middle East between Britain and France after 1920, Arab nationalism subsequently developed in two different but essentially inter-related directions. First, it took the form of a movement for national liberation, seeking independence from foreign rule or foreign influence. Secondly, a number of writers, most notably Sati' al-Husri, put forward ideas of pan-Arabism, the notion that the Arabs form a single entity stretching from Morocco to Iraq, which has been divided artificially by colonialism, imperialism, and (since 1948) Zionism.

Ba'thism developed out of the second strand, pan-Arabism, and the doctrines which still form its basic ideology were elaborated by the Syrian Christian writer Michel 'Aflaq in the mid 1940s and 1950s. 'Aflaq and his associates gained considerable influence in Syrian politics until 1958, when the Syrian Ba'th, founded formally in 1944, agreed to dissolve itself as the price demanded by Nasser for the creation of the union of Syria and Egypt, known as the United Arab Republic. The failure of the union in 1961 precipitated a major and permanent split in the Ba'th, which has been in some sense institutionalized ever since by the existence of two separate 'Ba'th Parties' in Syria and Iraq.

In Iraq, where pan-Arab ideas did not really gain a substantial following until the 1950s, the Ba'th organization developed more slowly, and the Party could only claim some 300 members by the time of the Revolution of July 1958. After the Revolution, the Ba'th joined forces with the Nasserists in opposition to the government of 'Abd al-Karim Qasim, and managed to organize a coup in 1963 which brought them both to power for a brief period. After a few months the Ba'th fell out with the Nasserists, and were ousted from power. A series of highly unstable Nasserist-nationalist governments followed until the second Ba'th coup in 1968; the Ba'th have been in effective control of Iraq since that time. We shall examine the nature of their ideology, and in particular the way in which its vagueness and lack of specificity have enabled the present rulers of Iraq to justify and rationalize a whole range of apparently contradictory policies under the slogans of 'Unity, Freedom, and Socialism'.

The Origins of Arab Nationalism

The body of ideas from which Arab nationalism later emerged developed only gradually during the second half of the 19th century.[1] The earliest notion of the Arabs as a separate ethno-linguistic entity was essentially secular, and derives initially from the writings of Syrian and Lebanese intellectuals who were themselves inspired by European nationalism, liberalism and constitutionalism. Many, though not all, were either Christians or had been educated in the schools and colleges founded in Greater Syria during and after the 1830s and 1840s. A little later, again to summarize in very broad terms, Muslim writers like 'Abd al-Rahman al-Kawakibi and Rashid Rida, under the inspiration of European liberalism and the ideals of Islamic reform put forward principally by Muhammad 'Abduh, sought to identify the Arabs more closely with Islam, asserting that only the Arabs could purge the Islamic polity of the corruption into which it had fallen during the centuries of Ottoman control. Naturally both these notions were a direct challenge to the 'official' ideology of the Ottoman Empire as the universal Islamic state (*dawla*) ruled over by the Ottoman sultan–caliph, who was in some not quite explicit sense[2] the descendant of the Prophet Muhammad, in which the non-Muslim monotheistic communities also lived, as second-class but protected citizens. In this state, religion rather than language or ethnicity was the primary focus and indeed the only means of identity, and 'Abd al-Hamid attempted to encourage the association between pan-Islamism and Ottomanism in the course of his long reign.

In general therefore, the first manifestation of Arab feeling in the latter years of the 19th century took the form of the belief, on the part of a small but influential number of individuals, that their position within the Empire could only be improved, or in some sense adequately fulfilled, through some recognition by the Ottoman authorities of their separate and specific status as Arabs. These vague notions were gradually transformed into political shape, in the course of the general opposition to 'Abd al-Hamid's autocratic rule, and found expression in the formation of a number of 'decentralization' societies, which flourished in various provinces, but particularly in Syria-Lebanon, in the first decade of this century.[3] On the eve of the First World War, therefore, there was a strong tide of opposition to Ottoman rule, although a more general changeover to Arabism only took place when the Ottoman Empire was finally defeated in 1918. Apart from the Arab Revolt there was no generalized anti-Turkish rising by Arabs in the course of the First World War; those Syrians who might have wished to lead one were either hanged in Beirut in 1916 or forced into exile.

The experience of the ex-Ottoman provinces in the next two decades was not uniform, which goes some way to explain the different forms which nationalism came to assume in Iraq and Syria. In Iraq the British continued the direct rule which they had been extending over the area since 1914 until 1920, while in Syria an Arab government, admittedly financed and supported by Britain, was actually running the country. However in July 1920 the French defeated the Arab government by force of arms and introduced a system of direct rule. In Iraq, in response to the national rising known as the Revolution of 1920, the British introduced a system of indirect rule, under which Arab ministers and provincial governors were backed by British advisers whose advice had to be taken. Those who held office under the monarchy, men like Nuri al-Sa'id, Ja'far al-'Askari and 'Ali Jawdat al-Ayyubi, would have regarded themselves as nationalists in the sense that they had indeed fought to liberate the Arab provinces of the Ottoman Empire from the Ottomans, and were participating in the government of an Arab country.

However, it gradually became clear, if not to those in office in Iraq and elsewhere in the Arab world, that the price of liberation from the Ottomans was European control. For some, notably the new landed aristocracy, the emerging comprador bourgeoisie, and some of the minorities, particularly the Lebanese Maronites whose historical ties with their French protectors went back to the 15th century, if not to the Crusades, the change of masters was perfectly acceptable, but for the majority, the introduction of European control became more and more intolerable.

Arab Nationalism after 1918: the Ideas of Sati' al-Husri

In the 1920s and 1930s, therefore, the nationalist movement in the Arab world took on a new complexion. The Ottomans had gone, and the caliphate with them. On the edges of the Arab world, two new states, Turkey and Iran, were taking shape, based essentially on a combination of economic, political and social modernization and militarism. In Iraq in particular, where many still spoke Turkish, the example of Atatürk exerted a powerful attraction. Further away, other new forms of state were also developing.

> One of the reasons [says Bassam Tibi] for the rising popularity of Germany among Arab nationalists in the period after the First World War was the hostility which they felt towards British and French colonial rule in the region. Until this time they had been predominantly francophile, and their thinking was in the Western tradition of Natural Law and rationalism. By the 1930s, however, they were turning their attention to the Third Reich, which they believed to have no colonial intentions, and which might free them from British and French colonial rule.[4]

Tibi goes on to analyse the role of Sati' al-Husri in this process, in particular his comparison between the divided and scattered German nation, unified

91

under Bismarck, defeated in war and yet revived and renewed by a new spirit of nationalism, and the once great Arab world, divided by British and French imperialism, but capable of exercising a commanding role on a regional and international level if reunited into a single political entity.

It seems certain that Husri was the first person to articulate this idea in the form expressed here, and as an educational administrator and author of text-books which were used in many Arab countries, he was able to ensure its widespread diffusion. The doctrine, which also lies at the heart of Michel 'Aflaq's writings, has exerted a powerful influence on those of a widespread variety of political persuasions in the Arab world. Although it took some time to gain general acceptance outside Greater Syria and Iraq — largely because of Egypt's earlier *de facto* departure from the Ottoman Empire, which had confronted Egyptian intellectuals with different choices — it is not difficult to see its attractions for a people aspiring to independence from European rule. Since the Arabs share a common language and a common history, the theory runs, they are members of one nation. They are prevented from realizing their aspirations to nationhood by the artificial political divisions into which they have been herded by imperialism; only by breaking these bonds, and by achieving unity, can they become truly free.[5]

In the 1930s and 1940s, this notion was more obviously more appealing in some parts of the Arab Middle East than in others. In Iraq, which was less urbanized than Syria and also had a more heterogeneous population, the notion of unity did not begin to take deep roots until as late as the 1950s. In Syria and Palestine, on the other hand, where the divisions made at Versailles, San Remo and the Quai d'Orsay were far more painful, ideas of a re-united Syria, and by extension a united Arab world, were greeted with enthusiasm. These ideas were developed in detail by the founders of the Ba'th Party, a group of French-educated Syrian intellectuals in Damascus, under the leadership of Zaki al-Arsuzi, Salah al-Din Bitar and Michel 'Aflaq, who constituted themselves formally as a party in 1944. 'Aflaq, who was born in 1910, is generally considered as the principal ideologue of the Party, and is now settled permanently in Iraq, having led the Party in Syria until 1966.[6]

The Origins of the Ba'th Party: the Political Situation in Syria and Iraq, 1920–1945.

Before examining 'Aflaq's ideas more specifically, it is useful to try to place the Ba'th in the context of the other 'nationalist' political parties and group-ings of the 1940s. In Syria, the older generation of nationalists, who had not had the same opportunities for collaboration with the colonial power as their counterparts in Iraq, were organized into two main groupings, *Hizb al-Sha'b* and *al-Kutla al-Wataniyya*. Both these bodies opposed the mandate as constituted, and had been instrumental in conducting the abortive negotiations with the French which had begun in 1936. In general, both believed in 'Syria for the Syrians', fiercely opposed the ceding of Alexandretta to Turkey in 1938–39, and sought an independent united Syrian state. This united Syria — with or without Lebanon — might continue to have strong economic and cultural links with France, but would be politically independent under their own rule. As younger men, this generation had opposed the Turks or been part of Faisal's short-lived Arab government in Damascus in 1920, but had generally been excluded from power ever since. *Hizb al-Sha'b* and *al-Kutla al-Wataniyya* were both 'conventional' political organizations which might attract votes at elections in which electoral registration was normally dependent on property qualifications, but had no mass base. Other important parties of a rather different nature were Antun Sa'adeh's Parti Populaire Syrien and the Syrian Communist Party.

In Iraq, political organizations were far less developed, since formal politics were more a matter of musical chairs with the same fifty or so individuals exchanging the various offices of state. Naturally, there were occasional rivalries within this elite, but there were few differences of principle. The entire apparatus of government, the king, the cabinet, the bicameral legislature, had been imported by the British and the whole edifice was widely seen as an elaborate pretence at an independent political structure. In 1936, for example, on the occasion of the first military coup in the Middle East, the first act of the new Prime Minister, Hikmat Sulaiman, was to assure the British ambassador that the abrupt change of regime would not mean the slightest change in Iraq's relations with her ally Britain,[7] and even Rashid 'Ali's attempt to break away from British control in 1941 seems in retrospect a somewhat quixotic venture. The only opposition grouping of any importance before the Second World War, *Jam'iyyat al-Ahali*, enjoyed a very brief period of political access rather than political power in 1936, and although individual members later became influential, the group as such was never a serious challenge to the *status quo*. The Communist Party, founded in 1934, became more widely influential after the Soviet Union broke with Germany in 1941.

The defeat of Germany and Italy left Britain and France, though much weakened, still in political control of the Arab Middle East. In 1946 Syria became formally independent, thus attaining the same status which had been conferred on Iraq 14 years earlier. For both countries the War marked an important watershed, since it raised hopes and expectations of greater political freedom, especially in Iraq, which were not to be fulfilled. Since the political mechanism which existed in Syria and Iraq had no indigenous roots, they had no institutionalized means of 'regular' or peaceful reproduction; hence any opposition which did not in some sense adhere to the political rules was seen as a serious challenge.

The Ba'th in Syria 1944–66

The rise of the Ba'th in Syria as a mass political organization dates from the end of the War, and more specifically from the subsequent defeat of the Arab armies in Palestine in 1948. Like its competitors, it had no chance of gaining power by conventional means, by being voted in at elections, although 16 Ba'thists were elected to the Syrian parliament in 1954,[8] and by the middle 1950s, the doctrines which can now be found in the pages of the Baghdad Ba'thist daily *al-Thawra* had already been articulated. Nationalism, and a 'spirtualized' notion of unity,[9] were the means by which Arab society should be revitalized; Islam was the prime 'moment' of Arabism in which Christians and Muslims alike[10] could and should participate; the Ba'th Party was to be the standard bearer and vanguard of the new Arab nation. Some ideas of 'Aflaq's rhetoric may be conveyed by the following quotations from the 1950s:

> Our attachment to the Spirit of the nation and its heritage will increase our drive, strengthen our forward march and ensure our orientation; thus we shall not be irresolute for we shall then be confident that everything will be consistent with the spirit of our nation. When our point of departure is strong which is the saturation of the spirit of our nation and the clear understanding of ourselves and our reality, truly sensing our needs, we shall not be susceptible to the assumption of artificial ideas or imitating others.

and

> Our strength therefore is not only the strength of the large number of the Arabs at this time but it is also the strength of Arab history, for we are marching in the direction of the genuine Arab spirit, we are acting according to what our heroic ancestors would want us to do at all times.[11]

Some more specific notions of the future were embodied in the Party's constitution, although this is full of internal contradictions. For example:

> Article 26. The Party of the Arab Ba'th is a socialist party. It believes that the economic wealth of the fatherland belongs to the nation.

> Article 34. Property and inheritance are two natural rights. They are protected within the limits of the national interest.

Of course, the party is also anti-imperialist; it believes in land reform, free social, educational and medical services. Its notion of socialism is somewhat vague; here is article 4, the only place in the whole 48 article constitution that it is mentioned specifically:

> Article 4. The Party of the Arab Ba'th is a socialist party. It believes that socialism is a necessity which emanates from the depth of Arab nationalism itself. Socialism constitutes in fact the ideal social order which will allow the Arab people to realize its possibilities and to enable its genius

to flourish, and which will ensure for the nation constant progress in its material and moral output. It makes possible a trustful brotherhood among its members.[12]

It is difficult to resist the temptation to quote another thinker writing about a different nation some 30 years earlier:

Whoever is prepared to make the national cause his own to such an extent that he knows no higher ideal than the welfare of his nation; whoever has understood our great national anthem, 'Deutschland Über Alles' to mean that nothing in the wide world surpasses in his eyes this Germany, people and land — that man is a Socialist.[13]

Devlin summarizes another curious lacuna in early Ba'th ideology: 'Aflaq and Bitar had very little to say in their writing about the specifics of the system of government the Ba'thists should strive for.'[14] This is of course a common failing of nationalist writing of this type; there is no indication of how power should be achieved, or how it is to be wielded later.

It is not possible to chronicle the later history of the Ba'th in Syria in any detail here.[15] Very briefly, by 1953, 'Aflaq and Bitar and some 500 Ba'thists had joined forces with Akram Hawrani's Arab Socialist Party, and were in exile in Lebanon plotting against the dictatorship of Adib Shishakli, whom they and army associates of Hawrani were able to oust in 1954. By this time, the Ba'th was also gaining adherents in other Arab countries; for example, the Iraqi party was founded in 1951 and had 300 members by 1955.[16] Devlin gives details of the constant infighting and factionalism which plagued the main party at this stage and which was to make the creation of a truly pan-Arab party ultimately impossible.

The Syrian Party, which had managed to capture certain crucial political positions in 1956, agreed to dissolve itself as the price to be paid for entering the United Arab Republic in 1958, since Nasser distrusted parties, and in any case, the Ba'th never made the slightest headway in Egypt. This decision caused a major crisis when, as happened very quickly, the Union began to turn sour and became little more than a mechanism for the exploitation of Syria by Egypt. In the course of this episode, different factions appeared within the Syrian Ba'th, who were deeply critical of what Devlin describes as the 'old guard' (of 'Aflaq and Bitar) for having agreed to accept both the unity scheme and the dissolution of the party. In 1963, one of the Ba'th factions seized power in Syria; there was a further intra-Ba'th coup in 1966 and another in 1970, which brought the regime that is now ruling Syria to power. 'Aflaq enjoyed chequered fortunes in these years; when the Iraqi Ba'th came to power briefly in 1963, he acted as an intermediary in the negotiations with their Nasserist partners By 1966, the Syrian and Iraqi wings of the party had split irrevocably; 'Aflaq went to Baghdad in 1968, and, as we have already noted, has been there intermittently ever since.[17]

The Ba'th in Iraq, 1949–58

Originally, Ba'thist ideas were brought to Iraq by a few Syrian teachers late in 1949. By 1951, Fu'ad al-Rikabi (a Shi'i), an engineer from Nasiriyah, had taken control of an organization that numbered about 50 persons. By 1955, according to police records, there were 289 of them. Interestingly, most early Ba'thists were Shi'is, and from generally fairly humble origins. By 1957, the Ba'th had joined the opposition National Front, which consisted of itself, the Communists, the National Democratic Party and the Istiqlal. The heterogeneous nature of this alliance, and the fact that the actual Revolution of July 1958 was carried out by military officers who were largely unconnected with formal political parties, meant that, in Batatu's words, in the months immediately following the Revolution there was no 'indubitable focus of political authority. No one person, force or institution dominated the scene.' In this period of sudden political freedom and fluidity, the Ba'th claim to have attracted '300 active members, 1200 organized helpers (*ansar*), 2000 organized supporters and 10,000 unorganized supporters', according to al-Rikabi.[18]

At the end of July 1958, a few days after the Revolution, Michel 'Aflaq arrived in Baghdad to press the new government to join the recently formed United Arab Republic of Egypt and Syria, of which he himself had been a prime mover. This prospect naturally found favour with the Iraqi Ba'th and their associates the Nasserists, a loose political grouping who were attracted by Nasser's achievements but who had no formal organization. Unity, *wahda*, is generally taken as having been the principal point of difference between the Ba'th–Nasserists and the much larger and more influential Iraqi Communist Party. Here it is useful to clear up some common misconceptions which have unfortunately become the received wisdom of many accounts of this period.

In the first place, what now seems to be the fundamental and irreconcilable divide between Communist and Pan-Arab Nationalist parties in the Arab world (with the possible and somewhat artificial exception of Syria and the equally singular situation in Lebanon) was not so clear in the 1940s and early 1950s as it is in the 1980s. Here Rodinson's article, 'Marxist Communism and Arab Nationalism Compared' is quite suggestive, principally, perhaps, because it does not make specific reference to the Iraqi case.[19]

In the Iraqi context, it has already been mentioned that pan-Arab ideas had not gained particularly widespread currency before the Egyptian revolution of 1952. It is quite clear from the accounts of both Dann and Batatu – and a host of examples can be cited – that the only political party to make any major impact between 1945 and 1958 was the ICP. As well as having led the labour movement during and immediately after the war, it had organized the great demonstrations against the British in the late 1940s, and its martyrs, notably Fahd, were self-evidently disinterested, totally committed and sincere individuals of humble origins who had shown great courage and indeed been prepared to sacrifice themselves for beliefs whose general principles, particularly those of anti-imperialism and social reform, were evidently widely shared by the politically conscious. Secondly, the notion of integration or reintegration into the Arab world had naturally found greater resonance in Syria than in Iraq, because of the nature of the recent political struggle in Syria, the divisions which the French had made, and the parcelling out of the whole of greater Syria between France and Britain.

Nevertheless, although pan-Arabism was not a particularly pressing issue in Iraq in the post-war years, the Iraqi Communists themselves were prepared to accommodate to it, and in particular to its anti-imperialist tenets. Thus the Communists, the Ba'th, the National Democrats and the Nationalists of the Istiqlal joined together with the Kurdistan Democratic Party in a National Democratic Front in opposition to the monarchy in 1957. With the rise of Nasser, of course, and in particular with the nationalization of the Suez Canal in 1956, the success of pan-Arab nationalism in Egypt brought it many followers in Iraq. In keeping with the spirit of the times, the Communist Party's Second Conference in 1956 took place under the banner 'For a national Arab policy', stressing that the Arabs are one nation with 'a fervent desire for unity.' More cautiously, perhaps, the Party tied 'the fulfilment of the pan-Arab idea to the "disappearance of imperialism from the Arab world and the carrying out of democratic reforms".'[20]

Thus in the quasi-colonial situation which existed in Iraq before 1958, there were possibilites for Communist/Nationalist accommodation and cooperation, particularly from the Communist side, since the Communists were both more numerous and better organized. However, in Egypt since 1952 and in Syria since 1956, countries where Arab nationalists were actually in power, the attitudes of the nationalists towards the Communists did not bode well for future relations between the two groups in Iraq. Thus in Syria in 1956, 'Aflaq and his colleagues, who were nominally in alliance with the Syrian Communist Party, produced a document which emphasized that Communist internationalism was wholly uncongenial to them, and made clear their alarm at the rise of Soviet popularity in Egypt and Syria, which had further increased the appeal of the Syrian Communist Party.[21] Furthermore, the Syrian Ba'th was actually disintegrating in 1957 into a number of warring factions, and it seems to have seized on the prospect of a constitutional union with Egypt as a kind of *deus ex machina*; although the Union required the Ba'th to dissolve, the Party command seems to have believed that their positions would in fact be secured by the distribution of office to senior Party members in Syria, and it had the further advantage that the Egyptian anti-Communist laws would be introduced, forcing the Syrian Communist Party to dissolve itself as well. As far as the Iraqi Communists were concerned, their opposition to *wahda*, unity, was not so much a matter of opposition to unity *as such*, but rather the result of their profound suspicion of the motives and good faith of the Ba'th and the Nasserists.

Thus it is hardly surprising that 'Aflaq had hurried to Baghdad at the end of July 1958 to press the Iraqis to join Egypt and Syria in the Union, and equally unsurprising that the Iraqi Communists were entirely averse to doing so, under, let it be stressed, such circumstances. In particular, as the drive towards unity had the support of the powerful 'Abd al-Salam 'Arif, the Deputy Prime Minister and Minister of Interior, who was profoundly and notoriously anti-Communist, the Iraqi Communists had no illusions about the dangers it would bring. The Party organized a massive demonstration in Baghdad on 7 August 1958, calling for a Federal Arab Union and friendship with the Soviet Union, which was equivalent to stressing Iraqi particularism.[22] As we have shown elsewhere, this aversion to Union was also congenial to 'Abd al-Karim Qasim, who had no desire to defer to Nasser.[23]

Thus *wahda* was the symbol rather than the substance of the rift between the ICP and the Nationalists. Even if the Qasim regime decided to maintain the existing social system, there was still a wide range of possible options. For example, how far should land reform, or the nationalization of oil and of industry, actually go? These were important issues which divided the population, particularly the urban middle class, an influential section of society which feared the pressures being exerted from the left. Thus an alliance soon emerged between those forces who believed that their interests were being threatened by Qasim, and those who believed that the Communists would take over and thus exclude them from power. As a result, *wahda* developed into a rallying cry for the opposition to the left, since for many, union with Egypt was a lesser evil than the radical social and economic changes which they feared the Communists might introduce. Ironically, therefore, those vested interests which had not been swept away in July 1958 now sought and found common cause with the Ba'thists and Nationalists. This is an important part of the explanation for the bitter divide between the Communists and the Ba'thists-Nationalists after 1958, which continues to bedevil all aspects of political life in Iraq.

Although Qasim was identified with the Communists, he never threw his whole weight behind them. Only two Communists ever held ministerial portfolios, those of National Guidance and Municipalities, for a few months in 1958 and 1959. In spite of 'Arif's attempt on his life in October 1958, the abortive nationalist coup in Mosul in March 1959, and the second attempt at assassination which involved Saddam Husain and other Ba'thists in November 1959, Qasim became gradually convinced that he should dissociate himself from the Communists at all costs. In the autumn of 1959 he began to dismiss Communists from all senior positions in the civil service and the armed forces. Eventually, his policies had the effect of cutting the ground from under his own feet, since although he purged the left, which was generally well-disposed towards him, he allowed his rightist opponents to continue to hold positions of power. By 1961, therefore, when the fruitless and expensive war against the Kurds began, he found himself almost completely isolated.

Meanwhile, the Ba'th had suffered a serious, if temporary setback in the failure of the attempt to assassinate Qasim in November 1959. After al-Rikabi's flight to Syria, the party organization was taken over by 'Ali Salih al-Sa'di, who had somehow managed to escape arrest at the time. The party was further weakened by arrests and al-Rikabi's founding a rival body in 1961, but by 1962 it had forged a broad alliance with nationalist officers in the armed forces and was planning a military coup. This coup actually took place in February 1963, and a Ba'th–Nationalist coalition came to power. As is well known, thousands of Communists and leftists were rounded up and arrested, and many were subsequently tortured to death or executed in prison. It is true that the Nationalists and Ba'thists had some old scores to settle; a number of Nationalists had been killed in the course of the failed coup attempt in Mosul in 1959, and in the course' of the Turkoman-Kurdish race riot in Kirkuk the same year,[24] but the scale of the atrocities committed by the regime, and its militias were out of all proportion to the offences against them. This is amply illustrated by a 1964 government publication, *al-Munharifun*. 'Aflaq himself wrote a few months later that 'our differences with the Communists cannot possibly justify such means . . . How was it possible to give free rein to . . . elements who had a basic interest in the killing of Communists?'[25]

The Ba'th/Nationalist Coalition, February-November 1963

As far as it is possible to ascertain, there were about 15,000 Ba'thist supporters in February 1963, and some 850 full members. There were very few Ba'thists in important positions in the armed forces, with the exception of Salih Mahdi 'Ammash, Hardan al-Takriti and Ahmad Hasan al-Bakr. This led the Ba'th to rely on the paramilitary National Guard, a highly un-disciplined body, 'which, by its vindictiveness towards its political enemies and its considerable cruelty succeeded in making itself generally hated and severely damaged the image of the party in the public mind'.[26] Of course the new regime was totally unprepared for power and had no idea how to carry on the actual business of government. There was in any case no detailed Ba'th analysis of the situation in Iraq for them to consult. Competing groups soon began to struggle for power, both within the Ba'th and between the Ba'th and their Nationalist allies. In October 1963, at a Ba'th conference in Syria, al-Sa'di suddenly declared himself a leftist, and branded his rivals as right wing deviationists, a tactic we shall see frequently employed in the future to demonstrate ideological purity. On November 13 the Ba'th faction in the government was ousted, unceremoniously but bloodlessly, and sent into exile. The eighth political report of the party in 1974 says of this period:

> The 1963 experiment did not fail because of too much so-called left or too much so-called right. The main reason for failure was the leader-ship's failure to achieve a balance between the ideal and the possible and

its consequent inability to make accurate calculations of stages and possibilities and a graduated practical programme to achieve essential targets. The leadership of the 1963 revolution failed to practice its role as a leadership of a revolutionary Party. The party machine was left without precise and comprehensive central guidance. The Party consequently was unable to act as a vanguard revolutionary institution leading the Revolution as it should.[27]

The Return of the Ba'th, July 1968

The main problem facing the Iraqi Ba'th on its return to power in 1968 was its extremely narrow social and political base in the country. They were largely remembered for the brutality and ruthlessness of the few months that they had been in power in 1963, and were generally distrusted by the other major political groupings in the country, including the Communists and the Nasserists. The policies which they pursued immediately after 1968 did not give the lie to this image. After they had taken power through the army and the National Guard, and had managed to out-manoeuvre their Nationalist accomplices Generals Nayif and Da'ud, they made clear that they would brook no opposition. There followed numerous arrests among Nasserists, Communists and 'Zionist and Imperialist agents'; in 1969, 53 'spies' were officially executed, and a further 41 opponents were executed in 1970. This continuing reign of terror was accompanied by campaigns of arbitrary imprisonment and torture of potential opponents.

Gradually, however, a different form of emphasis appeared at the same time. Although the kinds of activity we have just described are evidence of the Party's determination to make its return to power felt, sections within the Party realized that it was necessary to end its almost total political isolation and to make some sort of accommodation with its former enemies. Furthermore, it needed to produce positive economic policies which would be both popular and effective. Thus in 1969 and 1970 the Ba'th began to make official overtures to the Communist Party and the Kurdistan Democratic Party and other 'progressive forces', calling upon them to participate with it in the 'national struggle' against Imperialism and Zionism, and in the 'construction of an independent Iraq and a free and prosperous Arab nation'. Thus the Ba'th alternately cajoled and pressurized the Communists and the anti-Barzani Kurds to join them in a National Front early in 1972. This coalition, which came into being in 1973, enabled them to broaden their power base very substantially. For their part, the KDP and the Communists were permitted a certain degree of political freedom, and in particular were allowed to publish their own newspapers and magazines. These journals adopted a considerable degree of self-censorship, implying generally that the Ba'th Party could never be seriously at fault, or Ba'th rule questioned or doubted. At the same time, the Ba'th began to make overtures to the socialist countries, which bore fruit in the Iraqi-Soviet Friendship Treaty of 1972, a vital precondition for the oil nationalization of the summer of that year. Naturally the Friendship Treaty was another important reason for the Communists joining the National Front. Quite fortuitously, the nationalization was shortly followed by the war of 1973, and the subsequent oil embargo, which led to unparalleled rises in oil prices. The Ba'th were able to use the increased revenues from oil to buy popularity, or at least acquiescence, through increases in wages and salaries, infrastructural and industrial projects, and by extending health, welfare and educational services.

Alongside these displays of largesse, the Party was quietly tightening its hold on the main instruments of control, the army and the security services. By mid-1973 another 'plot' against the government was discovered, led by the secret police chief Kazzar, who was executed with 36 of his followers. The security services were expanded to the extent that in 1978 125,000 people, some 20% of all public employees, were working for them.[28] All non-Ba'th officers were gradually purged from the armed forces, which are now only open to loyal Ba'thists, a development whose effects have been particularly apparent during the present war with Iran. Further consolidation was made possible through the regime's alliance with the anti-Barzani Kurds and the various manoeuvres leading up to the Algiers Agreement with the Shah in 1975, which stilled effective opposition from that quarter for several years.

For their part, the Communists made use of the relatively liberal atmosphere of the National Patriotic Front to strengthen and widen the support for their Party and to consolidate their positions within the framework permitted to them. Although continuing to be guarded and moderate in their criticism of Ba'th 'socialist' policies, the Communists gradually came to be viewed less as allies by the Ba'th and more as a general impediment and threat to its claim to be the 'leader of the nation'. Moreover, the vast oil wealth which the Ba'th now controlled meant that they were no longer dependent upon Communist support.

Thus, from 1976 onwards, the Ba'th leadership began to clamp down on the Communists and the more radical left, and intense persecution became the order of the day. By this time the Ba'th had organized an elaborate security system in which the Party organization was an active participant; individual members were made responsible for their street or quarter and had to report on their families and neighbours. Over the next few years the Communists were depicted as the supreme traitors to the *umma 'arabiyya* (Arab people); Saddam Husain accused them of electrocuting their opponents and burying them alive, crimes of which he and his own followers were guilty — tactics reminiscent of the aftermath of the Reichstag fire in 1933. Anyone associating with these 'foreign agents' and 'traitors' was declared to be 'a traitor to the Iraqi homeland, a traitor to the air and soil of Iraq and to the waters of the Tigris and Euphrates'.[29] At the same time, the Ba'th were building up a series of mass organizations, of youth, women, children, peasants, workers and so on whose main task was to propagate the superiority and legitimacy of the Party's rule.

Towards an Understanding of Baʿthist Ideology

Before attempting to piece Baʿthist ideology together, certain preliminary remarks may be useful. Having quarrelled with their colleagues on the National (that is, pan-Arab) Command in Syria in 1966, the Iraqi Baʿth had to establish themselves as the only true manifestation of the Party. This they did by inviting ʿAflaq, who had left Syria in 1966, to become secretary general of the 'sole legitimate Baʿth Party'. It is also important to differentiate between the Iraqi Baʿth *as an organization* and Baʿth *thought* as articulated by ʿAflaq, Bitar, Arsuzi, al-Atasi, Razzaz and other Baʿth writers. Since, as we have stressed, the Baʿth had an extremely narrow base and a relatively small number of active supporters both in 1963 and 1968, it is inconceivable that it would ever have gained power through the ballot box, and on both occasions it took power through a military coup. Hence the real point at issue is the seizure and consolidation of political power; when individuals within the Party succeed in achieving power they immediately attempt to legitimize their right to govern within the broad framework of Baʿthist doctrine. It is this fact which makes any systematic analysis of Baʿthist ideology in Iraq in the 1960s, 1970s and 1980s a somewhat daunting task.

When the Baʿth seized power in 1968 it had no definite or developed plan of action, and thus had to fall back on the generalities of doctrine elaborated by ʿAflaq. In the beginning it tended to justify its own position almost entirely within the framework of Arab unity, the issue on which it had been fighting the left since 1958. Thus a report written in 1970 reads:

> Our party is characterized by its insistence, from the beginning, on the reality of the nation and its unity and the rejection of the present state of division . . . The national struggle is a complete and original whole and not a mere grouping of local strategies . . .'[30]

Despite the fact that there is no indication in this or any other of the Party's contemporary publications of how such unity could be brought about, the Baʿth chose to make unity its main point of departure, and the feature which differentiated it from any other political force or organization in Iraq, or, indeed, elsewhere. By denying Arab unity, it is claimed, the Communist Party has found itself 'in the camp of the petite bourgeoisie, both left and right', and in that of the reactionaries, 'all fighting the unionist tide'. Similarly guilty are the Nasserists, 'who placed the interests of a single nation above the interests of the (Arab) nation'.[31] The following passage gives some flavour of the general tenor of this sort of writing, and above all of its extreme vagueness:

> The party's task is to undertake serious and speedy work to change the features of Arab realities with the object of attaining the objective conditions necessary to confront the Zionist-Imperialist alliance. This is to be achieved by tireless endeavours to realize unity in its progressive form.

Our view of the structure of the Arab condition is to be totally revised, and we must make the mental and psychological preparation to link up Arab life fully with the exigencies of long term confrontation. Economy, politics and everyday life must all be directed towards leading the Arab struggle towards the battlefields.'[32]

Apart from the issue of Arab unity, which was particularly prominent in the first few years after 1968, the overall ideological framework of the Party in Iraq has essentially remained within the original mystical notion of the Arab nation, the Arab homeland, *al-watan al-'arabi*, and the Arab masses– *al-jamahir* – who wage 'a fierce and bold struggle against the imperialist and Zionist enemy and its local reactionary hirelings'.[33] Thus 'The political strategy of the Party aims, in a scientific and practical way, at developing Arab trends and tendencies towards the higher national aspirations of the Arab nation in its present stage of historical development.'[34] The general ideological position assumed at the Eighth Party Congress of 1974 is still presented as the line pursued today and extracts from this conference appear on almost every front page of *al-Thawra*. A study of the terminology of these documents shows that this degree of continuity is possible because of the extreme vagueness and generality of the concepts used. Words like socialism, democracy, the masses, the toiling masses and so forth are constantly used and can of course be made to fit almost any day to day contingency. Nevertheless, a certain inner logic may be discerned, as we shall now try to show.

In the first place, this inner logic derives from 'Aflaq's original view of the nation as a harmonious whole. Thus, the Eighth Congress of 1974 defines socialism as 'a vital prerequisite for the liberation, unity and renaissance of the Arab nation',[35] and the Arab masses as the main participants and objects of socialism. The working class is part of the Arab nation, whose priority is the struggle with Zionism and Imperialism, whose continued strength requires the national and the class struggle to be balanced in such a way that the energies of the nation can be directed against the main enemy. This is later summarized in a statement that the main contradictions in the Arab world today are those between the Arab masses on the one hand and Zionism and Imperialism on the other. Despite some occasional lip-service to notions of class struggle and the working class, the emphasis on the fundamental unity of the people and the nation remains the basis of all other definitions. Thus, on 28 February 1980, in a discussion of the socialist state, *al-dawla al-ishtirakiya, al-Thawra* says: 'The actual producer is the foundation of the socialist process and the working class has a historical (*tarikhi*) and national (*qawmi*) role to play within society.' The article goes on to emphasize that above everything: 'The worker is a citizen (*muwatanun*) because he is a son of the people (*ibn al-sha'b*); the relationship which defines his rights and duties. Thus his class, *tabaqa*, is secondary to his role as a citizen. As the role of the citizen is defined by his role in the struggle as a son of the people, the people will therefore define his rights and duties. As the socialist state is the state of the people, there can be no class conflict. It goes without saying that the relationship between the working class and the Ba'th is equally harmonious, since the Ba'th is the Party of the toiling masses!

Also in February 1980, when visiting a state factory, Saddam Husain gave the following statement of his views. Having emphasized the importance of the 1968 revolution, he assures the workers that man (*al-insan*) lies at the centre of Ba'thist concern. Radical change must take place not only in society, but also in man. This transformation of man will be accomplished by his continued participation in the struggle, and his assuming an optimistic attitude towards the aims of the nation (*ahdaf al-umma*). The new man that will arise is *al-insan al-Ba'thi*, of whom Saddam Husain is the shining example. The quintessence of the *jamahir* and the *sha'b* is of course the Ba'th Party itself. Thus Saddam says: 'Why do we consider the Ba'th to be the Party of every one of you, whether you are actual members of the Party or not? This is because the Ba'th expresses the conscience (*damir*) of the people and its ideological aspirations in its struggle for the realization of its principles.' Elsewhere, *al-Thawra* says that it is obvious that the party is in its essence an expression of the will of the masses, *iradat al-jamahir*. Such a party can only come into existence when society reaches a certain degree of consciousness and will for change. Thus 'the Ba'th has not fallen from the sky and has not been imported and has not been created by nature, and is not the result of the will of an individual' (10 January 1980). In a similar discussion about democracy, we learn that 'democracy is not the relationship between the leading party (*al-hizb al-qa'id*) and the citizens; the leading party itself is the basic pillar of democracy'. Thus 'democracy is the extension of the bond between the vanguard party, the state (*al-sulta*) and the masses', another expression of the concept of harmony noted earlier (10 January 1980).

As liberal democracy in capitalist societies serves primarily to maintain the capitalist system and man 'is not free to elect those who serve him, although he is free to go to the ballot box every four or five years', the Ba'th believes that socialism is necessary for freedom. Only socialism will make man really free by freeing him from his material needs and guaranteeing his future, and giving him education to enable him to enjoy his freedom. Such a system leads to popular democracy (*dimuqratiya sha'biya*) in which the Ba'th is the central element. Apart from such references to an ideal socialist society, readers of *al-Thawra* are only given occasional glimpses of the 'precise' nature of *al-ishtirakiya* (socialism). Thus *al-Thawra* quotes the following statements of Saddam Husain:

> We have chosen socialism and shall not depart from it. We want a living and a better socialism, which is the road to happiness (*al-sa'ada*), constructive development, which will enable us to face the enemy (*al-'adu*).

> Socialism does not mean the equal distribution of wealth between the deprived poor and the exploiting rich; this would be too inflexible. Socialism is a means (*wasila*) to raise and improve productivity.'

In recent years such generalizations have undergone a certain modification. As the abstractions become vaguer and vaguer Saddam Husain moves more prominently to the centre of the stage. At the same time Iraq, rather than the Arab nation, becomes the principal focus of attention. In a speech on the seventeenth anniversary of the 'revolution' of February 1963, Saddam Husain assures his audience that Iraq will continue to be the faithful guardian (*haris*) of the soil of the Arab nation, and that the Ba'th Party is the knight (*faris*) which has restored honour to the Iraqi people and the Arab nation. In the same speech he says

> Western journalists say that Saddam Husain is a Takriti. I say to them with pity: Saddam Husain was born in a village in the southern part of Takrit province; Takrit province is a part of the *muhafaza* of Salah al-Din, and he is an Iraqi. Saddam Husain was born in the *muhafaza* of Salah al-Din but he is not (only) a son of the *muhafaza* of Salah al-Din because he is a son of the province of Arbil, of Sulaimaniya, he is a son of Anbar, a son of the Tigris and Euphrates, a son of Barada, and of Jordan, and of the Nile, of Damascus and Amman, Cairo and Casablanca, and a son of every Iraqi city and a son of the Iraqi people, of the Iraqi soil and of the Iraqi air and of the Arab homeland and of the Arab nation.'

Ideology, in fact, has become the cult of personality.

References

1. See Albert Hourani, *Arabic Thought in the Liberal Age 1798–1939*, (OUP, London, 1970).

2. This is discussed briefly by Bassam Tibi: see *Arab Nationalism: a Critical Enquiry*, (ed. and trans. Marion Farouk-Sluglett and Peter Sluglett, Macmillan, London, 1981), p. 53 and in more detail, note 65, pp.233–234.

3. See here Z.N. Ziene, *The Emergence of Arab Nationalism*, (Khayats, Beirut, 1966) and Albert Hourani, op. cit.

4. Tibi, op. cit., p. 100.

5. See for example, Abdullah al-Alayili, 'What is Arab Nationalism?', in Sylvia Haim (ed. and trans.) *Arab Nationalism: an Anthology*, (California UP, London and Berkeley, 1962, 1976) pp. 120–127.

6. There is considerable dispute about the relative primacy of the early leadership. Thus in Kamal Abu Jaber's *The Arab Ba'th Socialist Party* (Syracuse UP, Syracuse, 1966) al-Arsuzi is not mentioned at all, and J.F. Devlin's *The Ba'th Party: a History from its Origins to 1966*, (Hoover Institution, Stanford, 1976) contains only a few references. However, perhaps because of their Iraqi rivals' close association with 'Aflaq, the present Syrian Ba'th leadership claims al-Arsuzi as the source of its ideology. For 'Aflaq, see N.S. Babikian, 'Michel 'Aflaq; A Biographic Outline', *Arab Studies Quarterly*, vol. 2, no. 2, (Spring 1980), pp. 162–179.

7. See the useful article by H.H. Kopietz, 'The Use of German and

British Archives in the Study of the Middle East: the Iraqi Coup d'État of 1936', Abbas Kelidar (ed.) *The Integration of Modern Iraq*, (Croom Helm, London, 1979) pp. 46–62.

8. Devlin, op. cit., p. 68.

9. See the Constitution of the Ba'th Party in ibid., p. 28.

10. 'L'Islam est cette pulsion vitale qui a mis en branle les forces latentes de la nation arabe . . . Muhammad fut l'incarnation de tous les Arabes; que chaque Arabe soit donc aujourd'hui Muhammad! . . . Les Chrétiens arabes . . . lorsqu'ils retrouveront leur caractère originel, reconnaitront que l'Islam est pour eux une culture nationale au sein de laquelle ils doivent s'immerger et de laquelle ils se rassasieront, afin de la comprendre et de l'aimer au point d'êtres attachés a l'Islam comme a l'événement de plus précieux de leur arabisme.' Michel 'Aflaq, 'Fi dhikri al-rasul al-'arabi' (1943), trans. J. Viennot, Orient 9, no. 35 (1965), pp. 147–158.

11. 'The relation between Arabism and the movement of overthrow' (1950); 'The Arab Ba'th is the will of life' (1950) in Michel 'Aflaq, *Choice of Texts from the Ba'th Party Founder's Thought*, (Florence, 1977) pp. 59, 60.

12. See 'The Party of the Arab Ba'th: Constitution', in Sylvia Haim op. cit., pp. 233–241.

13. Adolf Hitler, 28 July 1922, quoted in William Shirer, *The Rise and Fall of the Third Reich*, (London, 1970) p. 85.

14. Devlin, op. cit., p. 31.

15. See Patrick Seale, *The Struggle for Syria: a Study of Post-War Arab Politics 1945–1958*, (OUP, London, 1965); Itamar Rabinovich, *Syria Under the Ba'th, 1963–1966: The Army-Party Symbiosis*, (Israel UP, Jerusalem, 1972); Nikolaos Van Dam, *The Struggle for Power in Syria* (Croom Helm, London, 1979, 1981); Elisabeth Picard, 'La Syrie de 1946 à 1979' and Olivier Carré, 'Le mouvement idéologique ba'thiste', in André Raymond (ed.) *La Syrie d'Aujourd'hui* (Paris, 1980) pp. 143–184, 185–224; R.W. Olson, *The Ba'th and Syria 1947–1982*, (Kingston Press, Princeton, 1982).

16. See Devlin, op. cit., Chapter VII, and Hanna Batatu, *The Old Social Classes and the Revolutionary Movements of Iraq: A Study of Iraq's Old Landed and Commercial Classes and of its Communists, Ba'thists and Free Officers*, (Princeton, 1978) pp. 742–743.

17. See Devlin, op. cit., *passim*.

18. Batatu, op. cit., p. 808.

19. Maxime Rodinson, *Marxism and the Muslim World*, (Zed Press, London, 1979).

20. Batatu, op. cit., p. 750.

21. Abu Jaber, op. cit., pp. 43–44; Batatu op. cit., pp. 822–823.

22. Batatu, op. cit., p. 828.

23. See Marion Farouk-Sluglett, 'Contemporary Iraq; Some Recent Writings Reconsidered', *Review of Middle Eastern Studies*, no. 3, 1978, pp. 82–104.

24. For details see Batatu, op. cit., pp. 866–889, 912–921.

25. Ibid., p. 991.

26. Ibid., p. 1012.

27. ABSP, *Revolutionary Iraq 1968–1973; The Political Report Adopted by the Eighth Regional Congress of the Arab Ba'th Socialist Party – Iraq*,

(Baghdad, 1974) pp. 59–60.

28. See Marion Farouk-Sluglett, '"Socialist" Iraq 1963–1978 — Towards a Reappraisal', *Orient*, 23, no. 2 (1982), pp. 206–219.

29. *al-Thawra* (Baghdad), 9 February 1980.

30. *Political Report of the 8th Regional Congress of the Arab Ba'th Socialist Party*, p. 11.

31. Ibid., pp. 24–25.

32. Ibid., p. 12.

33. Ibid., p. 9.

34. Ibid., p. 75.

35. Ibid., p. 89.

6. Ba'th Terror —
Two Personal Accounts
An Iraqi Mother
Su'ad Khairi

This chapter gives two accounts of the experience of Ba'th terror in Iraq. The first is an interview with an Iraqi woman who has had two sons taken from her by Saddam Husain's regime. The second is the speech given to the 1982 CARDRI Conference by Dr Su'ad Khairi, a well-known political opponent of the Ba'thists and herself one of their many torture victims.

1. Interview with an Iraqi Mother
(First published by CARDRI in 1983)

Q. *How many sons do you have?*
A. Two — Salim and Amir.
Q. *Can you say something about them?*
A. Salim, the older, is an engineer in Sha'iba, the younger, Amir is a fourth year medical student.
Q. *When was Amir taken?*
A. On 29 December 1981. He was then a fourth year medical student. He went out to college in the morning and didn't come back. When we contacted one of his colleagues, he said that the security vehicle came to the college and they took him away.
Q. *Were you informed of why they took him away?*
A. No. The security never came and have not questioned us at any time and we do not know anything about him.
Q. *Were you told by any other source, judicial or governmental, of why they took him away?*
A. No. We know nothing about him since they took him away. Nobody told us why they took him away or what the charges against him are.
Q. *Do you know where he was taken to?*
A. No, we do not know where he was taken to.
Q. *Did Amir's colleagues mention any other arrests?*
A. Yes, they said Amir was not alone and that 38 fourth year medical students were arrested with him. Six arrests were made on the same day that Amir was taken.
Q. *From your information, were there other arrests made during this period?*
A. Yes. During this period of time the arrests included other medical students (not only from the fourth year). The wave of arrests extended to other

colleges and the university and even secondary and intermediate schools. It also included secondary and intermediate school teachers as well as university teachers. During this period of time ordinary people like small housekeepers and reserve soldiers who own small shops were also arrested.

Q. *What is your estimate of the number arrested during this period?*

A. In Basra during this period about 1,500 were detained.

Q. *Have you done anything to find out where your son is kept?*

A. Yes I tried. I wrote a petition. Up till now I have written four petitions. Every now and then I write a petition to the security, and when I give it to them they send me to the Governor's office, they say the Governor must sign it. When I go to the Governor's office for him to sign it the security chuck me out. There I see some of the mothers and fathers who are in a similar situation to mine with their petitions. They chuck them out also. They maltreat me in the same way they maltreat the others. Some people told us to go to the transit centre and ask about them there. When we went to the transit centre I saw nearly 300 mothers, not counting fathers, asking about their sons. Definitely some of them were there in a big room. The windows of the room and doors however were covered with galvanised iron sheets, eiderdowns and blankets so that the mothers and fathers couldn't seem them. We could only see their fingers, which they poke through a small window, and their lips which looked dry and drained of blood.

Q. *What is this transit centre and where is it?*

A. The transit centre is a police detention centre. The detainees of the security cells are taken to it on their way to be taken to the capital, Baghdad. It is situated in Ma'aqil near the railway station. It is in Gizaiza. The Gizaiza prison is divided into two parts, for political prisoners and for ordinary prisoners. The ordinary prisoners could be seen through the windows and the doors which are usually open, and one could see them in full. However, the political prisoners are isolated so that we could not see them. We could see only their hands and that is all. The room in which the political prisoners are kept is five m. high, four m. wide about 10–12 m. long. We went around to the back of the prison and there were small windows at the top, but we could not see them and they could not see us because the windows are so high and right at the top of the wall.

Q. *How many times did you go to the transit centre and were you able to ascertain whether Amir was there?*

A. I went three times and got no indication at all as to whether he was there or not.

Q. *When you went for the last time to the transit centre, how long was it since Amir had been arrested?*

A. Four months.

Q. *What happened after this?*

A. After four months, one of Amir's colleagues, whose name I cannot mention, telephoned us and said 'Amir and the other students with him are all in Baghdad in the Abu Ghraib Prison. There are no charges against them and they should be released in three months' time.'

Q. *What happened after this?*

A. After this I went to Abu Ghraib with some other mothers. We were five, Abdul Kadir's mother, Abdullah's mother, Karim's mother, myself and the sister of Hassani, whose name is Abd al-Salam — we went to Abu Ghraib and met some of the prison officials and asked them about our sons. They denied they were there and demanded to know who had told us such a story. They didn't allow us to go inside. After this we went to the second gate (there were three gates in the prison); the same thing happened – we were chucked out. They said 'There is no one here at all'. Then we went to the third gate where a young officer met us. He asked where we came from and we said, 'From Basra. Our sons are students, they took them away from the college and we don't know anything about them.' He said 'I will not tell you where they are, I don't know.' He was trying to tell us that they were there in Abu Ghraib, but was afraid. He said, 'It is correct that they are here in the heavy sentences prison, but I don't know if they are in this area or not but if you are able to come on 5 July you will be able to find out if they are here or not; but I have told you nothing; you could come and try to see them.' He kept trying to tell us that they were in the prison but was afraid to say so openly. In fact he telephoned someone in front of me and asked about our sons and said, 'It is correct they are here but I myself don't know of them. In any case come on 5 July'.

Q. *What happened after this?*

A. After this we were to have travelled on 5 July to Abu Ghraib but I became ill and could not go. The other mothers went to Abu Ghraib but got nothing. When they came back to Basra another wave of arrests took place, a very big one. By the end of July – beginning of August (1982) they started distributing questionnaire forms throughout Iraq. In it they asked for the names of all our sons, names of the father and mother and anyone else living with us, they even asked about our studies or schooling and about our jobs and whether we had one or not and so on. This campaign went on for about a week.

Q. *Who distributed these forms and how?*

A. The "people's army" distributed two copies to every household. They were wearing the "people's army" uniform and carrying machine guns on their shoulders. The purpose was to know all the families that had any members in detention and to indicate this on the forms. We were given two days to have the forms ready.

Q. *What happened after this?*

A. After they collected the questionnaire forms a huge wave of arrests swept the area. From every household that had one of its members already under detention they took away either a brother or a father. When there is no brother the father is taken away. Among those taken away was my son Salim, on 14 August 1982. When he went to work in the morning, it was on Saturday, he never came back home. At 11 o'clock in the morning they telephoned me from his place of work and said, 'Salim will not come home and will be late. He is ill.' I became worried about him and telephoned them and said, 'I would like to be reassured about Salim because he is ill', and asked if he could telephone me. 'He is suffering from thyroid and heart trouble and his medicine is at home; how can he be late? He must take his pills.' At that moment they told me to stop asking about him as the security had come and taken him away.

After this I petitioned the Governor asking about my son. I explained that Salim was ill and his pills were at home and that I wanted to know where my son was because the security had taken him away and that I would like to know what the charge was against him. The Governor asked for my telephone number so that they could telephone me with any news they had about him. I waited for a week and no one telephoned. I went again to the Governor's office and explained to the secretary that a week ago I had petitioned the Governor and asked about my son who was taken away by the security from his place of work in Sha'iba. He stared at me and shouted, 'Get out of here! Do you want to follow your son to the same place? We can't allow things like this, for he attacks the party and the revolution. Do you expect us to pat him on the shoulder and tell him to go away in peace?'

Q. *How sick is Salim?*

A. Salim is suffering from toxic thyroid glands. He must take his medicine continuously for the rest of his life and his place of work must be near a hospital. It is for this reason I am anxious about him and up till now don't know anything about him.

Q. *What happened after this?*

A. After this period — after going to the Governor's and calling on his secretary who treated me so harshly and threw me out and threatened to arrest me, I went home bewildered. Some mothers came to me and asked 'What can we do for our sons? We don't know their whereabouts and we don't know what has happened to them.' We remained bewildered not knowing what to do. Then on 5 September 1982 security men were all over our district knocking on the doors of one house after another. They came to our house and knocked on the door. When I opened the door I saw three persons from security, two of them in military uniforms and carrying guns, the third in civilian clothes. He is someone from the area. We know him. His name is Abid the hairdresser. He works with the security. They said 'We are from the People's Council and we want some information.' They denied that they were from security, claiming to be from the People's Council. They entered the house and asked for my full name, name of my husband, daughters and sons, names of aunts and their sons. All the people in the neighbourhood said they had to answer the same questions for some of them came to me to ask if the security men had come to me also.

Q. *What happened after this?*

A. Two days after this, on 7 September, there was a knock at the door and when I opened it I found the security men — they had been to other people before me, to three houses. They asked me if I was Amir's mother. I said 'Yes I am'. They said, 'Go to the Medical City Mortuary and collect the carcass of your son.' I started screaming and wailing. It seems that the other people whom they went to before me were abused and threatened by the security men who ordered them to close their doors and not to breathe a word. But I could not restrain myself and went on swearing at them and crying out and wailing and heaping insults on the regime and the men at its head. When the others heard my screams they also started screaming and wailing. Later on I met them in Baghdad and they said to me, 'Had we not heard your screams we would not have been brave enough to do the same.' The security men tried to silence me but I went on screaming and wailing, and went at them and tried to get hold of some of them. They started to run away and fled the neighbourhood, driven off by the commotion I caused.

Q. *What happened after this?*

A. After this I went to Baghdad on the same day, 7 September. We arrived in the night and went straight to the Medical City Mortuary and they said to us, 'Come tomorrow morning'. We went next morning, that is on the 8th, and we found many people there. As you enter the road leading to the mortuary a strong stench assails you. The stench is so strong that people walking in the road have to cover their noses. From the beginning of the road to the mortuary is about 100 to 150 m. and the stench could be smelt at the entrance of the road. There were many people there waiting for the same thing as me. I wanted to take my son and they also wanted to take their sons. At the start there were some 10–16 families – about 30–40 persons. The number kept growing. By ten o'clock there were about 150 persons or more. Then they called for the person who had come for Amir so I went into a room. I was asked by the person in charge there if I was Amir's mother. I said I was. He asked me for my full name and asked if I lived near . . . I said I did. Then he immediately said 'Your son is a criminal.' I said to him 'I did not bring up a criminal.' Then he said 'Your son is a traitor.' I said 'I did not bring up a traitor'. He said 'It looks as though you have been crying.' I said 'I am a mother. . .' Then he said 'Even if you are a mother, he is a traitor and you should not cry for him; if you cry we will not give him to you.' I said 'I will not cry, just give him to me.' He then said 'I am your son'. I said 'Somebody else's son is not my son.' Then he again said to me 'He is a traitor. . .' He then wrote down my age, my full name and told one of the security men to go and give my son to me. At this moment one of the security men entered the room and said to the one in charge, 'Sir, those Turkomans have brought in 18 people.' He said to this man, 'Let them in and instead of one carcass I'll make them take six.' I felt pained by this because it meant that they would kill them if they were let in. I went out and told the Turkomans what I had heard and asked them not to go in as a group but that only the father should go in. All the jobs in the mortuary are carried out by security men, there are no ordinary people there; even the car that took our son was a security vehicle. Those who do these jobs are all security men.

At last I was called in to look for my son and take him away. They said to me 'We will give you your son but you must not cry, you must not hold public mourning (Fatiha), no wailing. You must take him, bury him and go home without commotion. If you cry or wail, you know what to expect. . .' I said to him 'We will not do anything.'

Then I was led to the room where my son was. When I entered and saw what was inside, I could not believe that there are people who could do such things to other human beings. The room is square and about 6 m. by 6 m. There was a door on the left and another on the right (which led to two rooms) and facing you was a big door which is that of the refrigerator. My son was not in the refrigerator but was thrown on the floor of one of the rooms. I looked around and saw nine bodies stretched out on the floor with him, but my son was in a chair form. . .that is, a sitting form, not sleeping or stretched out. He had blood all over him and his body was very eaten away and bleeding. I looked at the others stretched out on the floor alongside him. . . all burnt. . . I don't know with what. . . one of them had his chest slit with a knife, another's body carried the marks of a hot domestic iron all over his head to his feet. . . another one was burnt in such a way, even his hair, like someone who has been incinerated. . . and every one was burnt in a different way.

Then they lifted my son and put him in a coffin. As he was in a sitting position, two men climbed on him, one on his legs and the other on his arms (one of them was Egyptian) and they pressed his legs and arms to straighten them. Then they asked me to carry him out. I said 'I can't do that on my own' and went outside to get someone to help me. When my helper wanted to enter, the security men prevented him and started swearing at him: 'We will not give you the carcass of your son if you come inside the room.' I pleaded with them and he said 'Give that person there five dinars so he will agree to let him in.' I gave him five dinars and gave five dinars each to those who put my son in the coffin. Then they put him in a car and we went to Najaf to have him buried. The man in the car who was a security man said to me that he was prepared to swear any oath that those sons of ours whom they killed were innocent and there was nothing against them. He said that they had been killed for no crime that had been committed nor for anything else they might have done. When we were in Najaf, the person who buried our son said that besides our son, in the last week, they had buried 300 bodies of those who had died under torture and daily more than 30 to 40 innocent martyred students, engineers and others are buried.

Among those I remember waiting at the Medical City Mortuary is a man who works as a porter. He was wailing and beating his chest and saying 'Why on earth have I sweated so much to bring up my son to become a doctor so he could look after me? He graduated in 1981, when they took him away, and now they send for me and say "Come and take the carcass of your son." I wish I hadn't nurtured him. Four months ago they brought me my other son killed at the front. . . one killed at the front and this is the second one here. . . I wish I had never brought them up and never sweated so much for them and suffered so much for them.'

Q. *Can you describe the state of the corpses at the Medical City Mortuary?*
A. At the mortuary the bodies were on the floor. One of them had his chest cut lengthwise into three sections. . . from the neck to the bottom of the chest was slit with what must have been a knife and the flesh looked white and roasted as if cooked, and from the left shoulder all the way down to the bottom of the chest and the same thing on the right.

Another one had his legs cut off with an axe. His arms were also axed. One of them had his eyes gouged out and his nose and ears cut off. Two were severely burnt and their bodies so blackened that you couldn't recognize their faces because of the severity of the burns. One of them (most likely the Turkoman) looked hanged. His neck was long, his tongue hanging out and fresh blood was oozing out of his mouth. His body was straight.

There were nine with Amir. Amir's body from neck to feet had the skin stripped off and suppurating, there were marks on his wrists as if he had been sitting and his hands tied so that he could not move. . . marks were near his neck and shoulders, his arms and on his legs and knees . . . they were marks made by strapping . . . his body. . . *(at this point she starts to cry and sob and says ' a mother cannot imagine or describe her son in a state like this.')*

Q. *Are there any other incidents you can remember from that time?*
A. Yes, on the same day that I was collecting Amir there was another one from our neighbourhood collecting the body of his nephew whose name was Hassan, a fourth year medical student. When he went to collect the body of his nephew he found in the room the bodies of 20 young women all naked and their breasts cut off. . .their bodies mutilated. He could not look at them. The security man shouted at him, 'What is the matter with you? Are you shy or ashamed?' Then he threatened him by telling him that if he didn't look at the corpses then the carcass of his nephew would not be given to him. So he was forced to look at them and was given his nephew's corpse.

This situation went on daily at the mortuary: on 17 September, four bodies were given to families in our neighbourhood and also in other areas of Basra such as Jemhoriya, Khamsa Meel, Dakeyr and al-Ba'th as it is called. This situation at the Baghdad Medical City Mortuary continued: everyone who goes there says that large crowds collect daily and many bodies are taken away. Indeed the same day we were at the mortuary, two vans loaded with the corpses of tortured students and engineers drew up at the mortuary. The van doors were opened and one of those in the vans said, 'Let us take these corpses out in front of those waiting.' They were exchanging jokes and mocking us. They carried the corpses to the refrigerator jeering at those standing by and at the corpses they were carrying. There were 20 bodies, ten in each van.

Q. *How long did this campaign go on for?*
A. This campaign went on for about a month and a half without interruption. Corpses were returned in this horrifying manner in Basra and all over Iraq during this month and a half. There were people from the other towns of Iraq such as Karbala, Najaf, Baghdad itself, Hilla, Kut, the North of Iraq — Kurds and Turkomans. Literally every part of Iraq. Now they have stopped giving the bodies to the parents and only papers, like receipts, are given. The households that receive these death certificates are threatened with dire consequences if they talk, create a commotion or wail for their dead ones. Only papers are given.

2. Torture in Iraq: A Personal Testimony

by Dr Su'ad Khairi,
representative of the Iraqi Women's League
(Speech to the 1982 CARDRI Conference in London)

Dear Friends,

On behalf of the Iraqi Women's League and in the name of all Iraqi patriots, I greet your annual Conference and wish you success in your efforts to support the Iraqi people in its struggle against Fascism and war.

I extend deep gratitude to your esteemed organization for the moral support it is giving to our people, thus healing the deep wounds inflicted upon us by the enemies of humanity in our country. Your solidarity with our people makes us always feel that the human conscience is a living and tremendous power that can paralyse the hands of the oppressors and inspire us with determination to continue the struggle until our people are liberated from all forms of exploitation and oppression.

I thank CARDRI once again for giving me the opportunity to speak on behalf of the Iraqi Women's League about the plight of our people, women and children, especially the terror and killings, not only as a witness, but also as one of the victims.

Submerged in Blood

Dear friends, the Iraqi people are now living through the darkest period of their history, as the dictatorship threatens them with annihilation to satisfy the criminal ambitions of the dictator Saddam Husain to build an Arab empire extending from the Gulf to the Atlantic ocean under his leadership, having crushed the Iraqi people in the Nazi-style 'Ba'thization' process, employing the most vicious methods of political, national and sectarian discrimination.

Iraq today is submerged in the blood of its sons from north to south. The war of genocide against the Kurdish people has transformed Iraqi Kurdistan into a huge concentraion camp, evicting more than 600,000 people and burning down hundreds of villages. Mass executions continue and families of Kurdish partisans, fighting against the dictatorship, are held as hostages in detention centres. In the south and middle of Iraq the Shi'ite community faces bloody repression. In all parts of the country, patriots and democrats, men and women, fighting for a happy, democratic Iraq, face physical liquidation. In the torture chambers and on the gallows, by firing squads or poisoning by thallium. All this in addition to the war of aggression shedding the blood of our homeland's youth and its future hope. Furthermore, tens of thousands of political opponents have been deported under conditions exceeding in their brutality the most criminal means of Fascism. The family is abducted, regardless of the absence of some of its members, including children. All their property is seized, including children's books and toys, the refugees are then thrown into the war zones or deserts, where children are exposed to death due to hunger, cold or terror. During the past two years more than 120,000 people have been deported in this way.

Iraqi Women and Peace

Dear friends, how ugly is the war. And how ugly are its crimes! Our people have lived for hundreds of years far from the disasters of war. But they themselves are being marched to a war in which they have no interest, becoming victims of its devastation and destruction. Our people and the Iraqi women have struggled to safeguard world peace and against nuclear arms and military pacts. Today, however, the Iraqi woman is struggling for peace with greater energy and stronger determination because she has suffered the tragedies of a limited local war, and has come to realize the devastation and destruction which a world nuclear war could bring. This war of aggression has not only paralysed the energies of the Iraqi and Iranian peoples to achieve their aims in freedom and democracy but also constitutes a grave danger to world peace. It has provided imperialism with the possibility of strengthening its military presence in an unprecedented manner in the Gulf region in particular and in the Middle East in general. This in addition to weakening the struggle against Israeli aggression and exposing Iraqi territories to Israeli bombing raids and spying missions. The victims of the war exceed 200,000 dead, maimed and prisoners of war.

Woman Always the First Victim

It is true that the Iraqi people have only enjoyed freedom during a brief period of their history and if the masses of people in general suffer from terror and repression, then women have always been the first victims. For under the conditions of occupation, colonialism and superficial national independence, the Iraqi woman suffered from the consequences of backwardness and dependency, and the cruelty of the mediaeval traditions that the 'civilized' colonialists strove to maintain. Under tribal laws the woman could be murdered and the murderer escaped punishment. She faced discrimination in all fields of life, and was regarded as a deficient human being always needing a guardian, even if it was her own son. In these conditions half society was paralysed in the struggle for national liberation.

95% of Iraqi women were illiterate until the 1950s. Even in the towns women's wages were never more than half of a man's. In the countryside she received no wages at all, for her work was always included with that of the family's master — always the man. Women's education required persistent struggle by the pioneers of the women's movement and its supporters. With the emergence of the working class movement in Iraq, the movement for women's liberation acquired economic, social and political dimensions, connecting it with the liberation movement inside Iraq, and the world liberation movement in general, and the women's liberation movement abroad in particular.

The Iraqi women, therefore, fought against Fascism and entered into patriotic battles for consolidating national independence and democracy after the Second World War. I had the honour of participating in the uprising of January 1948 against the Treaty of Portsmouth. My political choice was thus based on a realistic experience.

The Iraqi Women's League

Before I finished one year of organized struggle, and before reaching 20 years of age, I was arrested, together with some of my colleagues, and was sentenced to life imprisonment with hard labour. I spent ten years in prison with my colleagues facing brutal repression and denied even the right to read and write. Our only weapon was hunger strike, which only achieved some of our demands for a short period. Our number in prison used to double many times during our people's uprisings, reaching 150 women political prisoners.

The foundation of the Iraqi Women's League in 1952 came as an objective necessity required by the patriotic movement for the participation of women in the national struggle and the need for a mass democratic organization mobilizing their efforts regardless of their national and political affiliations.

In the 14 July 1958 Revolution women, under the leadership of the Iraqi Women's League, came out to struggle alongside other democratic forces to achieve the aims of the Revolution. They were able, with the support of these forces, to issue the first *Family Law* in Iraq and abolish the backward tribal laws. Under conditions of legality, for a brief period, the Women's League held its conferences and published a journal. In 1960 the League had a membership of 42,000 women, and through it patriotic and social consciousness was spread among millions of women in the towns and countryside. It fought against illiteracy and trained and mobilized women. But as soon as the revolution suffered a setback, repression included women as well.

Repression

In the February 1963 Fascist coup the junta directed their attacks on the rights of women. They suspended the *Law of Personal Conditions* and attacked the headquarters of the Women's League. Thousands of women were arrested and exposed to barbaric torture. Dozens of women who participated in armed resistance were killed, including Mariam Ra'oof al-Kadhimi.

Dear friends, under the dictatorial terror, the woman has lost most of the gains that she won through struggle. But she has not lost her experience which makes her more conscious and determined to struggle alongside other patriotic forces for a democratic regime which will secure democratic freedoms for the people and ensure the liberation of women and their equality.

With the escalation of Ba'thist repression and the policy of Ba'thization, all democratic organizations, including the Iraqi Women's League, were made illegal. Legality became conditional on joining the Ba'th Party or one of its front organizations such as the notorious 'National Union of Iraqi Students', the NUIS, or the 'Women's Federation', the GIFW. These organizations have become part of the security apparatus of the dictatorship. Even literacy classes demanded membership of the Ba'th Party.

Finally, the enjoyment of human rights, even the right to live, became an exclusive Ba'thist right. Hundreds of thousands of citizens were arrested, and had to choose between death or joining the Ba'th Party or working for one of its security organs. Hundreds of innocent people were executed. Hundreds were poisoned, including a large number of women activists, among them Salwa al-Bahrani and the sisters Najiyah and Hadiya al-Rikabi. During these years laws which have no parallel in the world were decreed laying down execution as the only punishment for a wide range of 'political crimes'.

Our Torture

On 16 May 1979 I was arrested with hundreds of young women and even children. I shared with them a small cell in the Department of Public Security in Baghdad for 42 days. In that cell we were lined up on the floor like sardines — 48 women and sometimes even 60. We had to remain lying, blindfolded. We were not allowed even to sit. A security agent with us in the cell watched us closely. The sounds of torture in the passages and of the metal torture instruments were mixed with the screams of victims and shouts of the criminal torturers. This continued from eight o'clock in the morning until two o'clock the following morning. When the torturers got tired they switched on recordings of torture sounds to continue psychological torture and to deny us sleep.

The victim is called to interrogation, to torture, in an atmosphere of terror that is not matched even by mounting the gallows. There one faces a quick death. But here there is continuous hellish torture. They resort to sexual torture as a principal weapon to break the strong will of the women detainees, as they realize the particular effect it has on the Eastern woman.

Low Beasts

They are low beasts who enjoy torturing young women. After receiving the women detainees and making cheap offers to them, they start to undress them, and apply electric shocks to the sensitive parts of their bodies. They throw the victim down on to the floor, threatening to rape her and to take photographs of her in the nude which will be made public or sent to her family.

They practised sexual attacks on many women detainees. They also threatened to murder children in front of their mothers. All this in addition to other methods of torture, such as beating with batons or metal instruments, burning and the 'Falaka'.

I was exposed, together with the other women detainees, to all these methods, but I placed my political honour above everything. I scorned death and any physical injury that might result from torture. I tried my best to convey my experience to my colleagues despite the difficulty. For this I was exposed to additional torture and was taken to hospital under the pretext of getting treatment but in fact to separate me from the other detainees.

Even young girls did not escape this torture. The child Samoud, aged only 13, suffered with me and faced the torture heroically, surprising even her torturers. All this because she refused to disclose the hide-out of her parents. A 15-year-old boy, Ali, was also subjected to brutal torture and was thrown into the street unconscious and with several fractures which left him disabled. There were dozens of children who were run over by cars just because their parents were active political opponents. There were children who were terrified to madness by placing them in sacks with starved cats or with insects.

There are dozens of unofficial prisons where the most vicious crimes are committed against the patriots, women and men, such as the Fadhileyah prison in Baghdad and similar ones in every province, town and village.

Solidarity Campaign

Under the pressure of world public opinion, including the solidarity campaign in Britain by the trade union and democratic movement, and in an attempt to gain time, I was released with other women prisoners. But only to be arrested again any time they wanted. They don't leave activists without surveillance and don't stop pursuing them, so there is only death or surrender. I was forced to flee the country with my children in August 1979 to save them from certain death, which I was threatened with more than once.

Darkest of Nights

Now, however, the dictatorial regime does not release any political detainees, torture is carried out more brutally and death awaits those who stand firm. Dozens of women activists have been killed under torture, including Jakool Abdullah, Hasiba Karim, Maniha Sewa and Jamila Karim. Others have been executed, including Bint al-Huda, Badour Hussein Mashkour, Fa'ika Abdul Karim, Saiamat Abbas Yusif. Dozens of women have been poisoned with thallium. Hundreds have been kidnapped and their fate is still unknown. Among these are Aida Yasin, Laila Yusuf, Raja and Kowther Majid (sisters and printing workers), Sameya al-Sheikly, Sabeeha Nouri Mahdi, Wadi'a Hadi Dawud, and Shadha al-Barak (with their families).

Dear friends, our people are living through severe hardship and the darkest of nights, darker than the hour before dawn. Their potentials are bound to explode, overthrowing this Fascist regime. Millions of women, with violated dignity and wounded motherhood, shall rise to struggle with other popular forces among the ranks of the partisan movement in Kurdistan and all parts of Iraq. This intensifying struggle, this sacred hatred, against the people's enemies, is bound to sweep away the dictatorship, to establish a democratic regime which secures autonomy for Kurdistan, democratic rights for the people, liberation for women and ensures peace and happiness for childhood.

7. Women in Iraq

Deborah Cobbett

This paper is an attempt to trace the changes that have taken place in the lives of women in Iraq over the past few decades and, in particular, to study the impact of the Ba'thist dictatorship. This task has been somewhat hampered by the lack of published material on life in Iraq: no statistics are available after 1977 and research in the field is impossible owing to restrictions on movement and other measures taken by the Ba'thist security apparatus. Indeed, a recently published guidebook states that foreign visitors to Iraq are not permitted to take a typewriter with them.[1] All typewriters in Iraq have to be registered with the authorities.

In the academic literature on Iraq, there are few references to women, let alone analyses of their situation, while general studies of women in the Middle East or women in Arab countries make only fleeting references to Iraq. It would also seem that Iraqi women are less newsworthy than their sisters in Iran or Saudi Arabia. At any rate they have been largely overlooked by British journalists. Only one article on women in Iraq has appeared in the 'quality' daily press over the past 20 years[2] and that was based mainly on Ba'thist sources. It followed a lecture given at the Ba'thist government's Iraqi Cultural Centre in London, just one example of the regime's concern with its image overseas, which will be discussed later.

A further preliminary remark is necessary. Terms like 'Middle Eastern women' or 'women in the Arab world' or even 'Muslim women' are equated and bandied about all too glibly. They conceal important differences, and often gross inequalities, between regions, ethnic and religious groups, urban and rural populations, age groups and, of course, social classes. Changes which affect a minority of well-off, highly educated, city women may have little or no impact on the lives of poorer village women, for instance. It is therefore necessary to avoid sweeping generalizations about 'Iraqi women', as well as Eurocentrically-biased stereotypes of the passive and submissive Muslim woman.[3] Women in Iraq have a long history of struggle against oppression, as we shall see.

Traditional Customs and Attitudes

Nonetheless, certain traditions concerning women are common to most Arab countries, including Iraq. For instance, many writers have referred to the concepts of honour and shame.[4] Nawal El Saadawi describes the 'distorted concept of honour' in Arab societies by which a man's reputation 'is more closely related to the behaviour of the women in the family than to his own' and, in particular, whether they 'keep their hymens intact.' In the case of rape, for instance, the victim, not the rapist, is considered to have brought dishonour upon her family and she may even be murdered as a result. In Iraq, especially in the rural areas, women are still murdered by members of their own families for infringing taboos against pre- or extra-marital sexual relations. The penalty for such murders ranges from six months to three years in jail, the same as that for killing a cow. Prisoners may even be released on high days and holidays. In April 1963, that is, during the bloodbath following the first Ba'thist coup, a presidential decree lowered the sentences passed on 61 such killers, even pardoning some of them.[5] Saadawi also states that most Arab men still insist that their brides be virgins and she describes the ritual defloration and display of the blood-stained sheet from the marriage bed, supposed to be proof that the honour of the family is intact. Discussing the medical implications of all this, she refers to the *Iraqi Medical Journal*.[6] It is a custom described also by an American woman who spent two years in a village in the south of Iraq.[7] She even ran into trouble by taking a young woman out to tea unprotected by any male escort from her family, for it is not only actual sexual relations which count, but anything that might give rise to gossip. This obsession with virginity can be related historically to the development of the patriarchal family and in particular the inheritance of property after the father's death, requiring a son and heir of undisputed paternity. In such circumstances, girls are brought up to avoid men and beware of the danger they represent.

A symbol of the segregation of women is the veil, worn to hide them from the eyes of strange men. Iraqi women do not usually cover their faces but traditionally wear a black cloak known as the *abaya* over their heads. An academic couple who taught at Baghdad University in the late 1950s noted the impatience of their women students with this garment, which their families still insisted they should wear. The students solved the problem by taking off their *abayas* as they entered the college building and only putting them back on when it was time to go home.[8] Yet the *abaya* is still widely worn in rural areas and in small towns, as photographs in a recently published book show.[9] Juliette Minces points out the conflicting attitudes towards veiling: on the one hand it is discarded as a symbol of women's subjection, but on the other it represents a return to traditional values as opposed to western influences.[10] However, it is also interesting to note that veiling was originally a city custom, showing that a man was wealthy enough not to need to send his woman out to work and put her honour in jeopardy.

Veils, like the tight corsets once worn by ladies from wealthy English families, can be seen as a sign of non-involvement in heavy physical work.[11]

Once she is married, a woman is usually expected to begin producing children and in many Iraqi families, as elsewhere in the Arab world and indeed beyond, the reaction to the birth of a new baby will depend very much on its sex. A young wife's position may improve somewhat if she has a son but she may be beaten or divorced for giving birth to daughters. Her husband fears losing face but economic logic underlies the preference for sons who will contribute financially and carry on the family line. In 1909 an Englishwoman published her account of life in Iraq[12] and noted that a little boy 'becomes almost like a little god to all the women folk,' but if a girl was born things were different. 'Poor little mite, her entrance into the world is not a cause of great joy or rejoicing.' To this day, although Iraqi women do not change their surnames when they marry, both parents acquire new titles when the first son is born. So 'Ali's mother, for example, will become known as Um'Ali (mother of 'Ali) and his father as Abu 'Ali (father of 'Ali). This custom does not usually apply in the case of daughters.

Child-rearing practices still differ considerably between boys and girls.[13] Girls are usually brought up to be obedient and submissive, discreet and modest. A girl must obey her father (or brothers or other male guardians) until she is married off to the man chosen, or at least approved of, by her family. She is then expected to obey him, of course. Traditionally, endogamous marriages were preferred and the girl's cousin had first right of refusal. Most women do in fact get married sooner or later, for life without a husband's 'protection' is virtually unthinkable in Iraq: to choose to remain single is a brave step to take, and a rare one. Yet marriage can mean that the woman becomes an unpaid servant to her husband as well as to any children or elderly people living in the house.

A boy's upbringing differs greatly from that of his sisters. His birth is celebrated with greater enthusiasm. He is made a great fuss of and generally spoilt. He may even be weaned at a later age than his sisters. While they have to help in the kitchen and with other household tasks, the little boy will be allowed to play indoors and out and generally do as he likes. In particular he can give orders to his sisters and later on become their chaperone even if they are older than he is. He may also arrange marriages for his sisters, subject only to his parents' approval.

Traditional child-rearing practices thus reinforce differences in gender role. Femininity means weakness, naivety, negativeness and resignation in a society which expects women to behave passively in their roles as wives and mothers, whereas men (and boys) are expected to show the qualities of a master, to dominate by strength, determination, boldness and initiative. Patriarchal society creates masochistic tendencies in women and sadistic aggression in men. Traditional values are a rationalization of physical violence against women — beating, rape and varying degrees of incarceration. In the past, an unhappily married woman had no way out of her intolerable situation since according to the custom known as *bait al ta'a*, or the house of obedience, if she ran away, no matter what the provocation, her husband could force her to return to the marital home. Any changes in the law have to contend with the dead weight of tradition in such cases.

While Islam is the dominant religion in Iraq and permeates attitudes towards women as well as underlying the Family Code, which is based on the *shari'a*, or Islamic law, there are religious minorities, notably Christians. Christian women in Iraq on the whole enjoy greater personal freedom as well as being generally speaking better off materially than the Muslim majority. Examination of the findings of the 1957 Census[14] showed that standards of living for Christians were better than for Muslims in terms of housing and education, for instance. A Christian woman who made her mark on Iraqi politics was 'Red Rose' Khadduri of the Iraqi Communist Party (ICP).

Historical Background

In the days of the Ottoman Empire (circa 1500–1918), women were not recognized as complete human beings under Islamic law. As in Pakistan today, a woman's word was equivalent to half a man's. Women's rights within marriage were inferior to men's: a man could marry more than one wife, only men had the right to divorce and they had superior rights concerning the custody of children and the inheritance of property.[15] Reforms were introduced in the 19th century in the field of education, for instance, though only a small minority of upper class city women could benefit from them. This was before the so-called women's revolution from the top introduced by Atatürk (in Turkey, of course, not in Iraq) in the 1920s when Islamic law was replaced by a secular system. Women suddenly acquired equal status with men in the domain of family law although they still required their husbands' permission in order to go out to work. Developments in Iraq under the British mandate and after were rather different.

Since the terms of the mandate entrusted the administration of Iraq to Britain until such time as the Iraqi people were judged fit to govern themselves, the authorities actually had a vested interest in keeping social progress to a minimum. The British administration seems also to have taken the line of least resistance, steering clear of controversial measures affecting traditions and religious customs, avoiding reforms to improve the status of women or anything else that might lead to trouble. For instance, the Ottoman legal system was not abolished, only amended, on the grounds that changes would be both inconvenient and unpopular, though it was decided that cases of personal status between Shi'is should be tried by Shi'i jurists as this had been a grievance under Ottoman (Sunni-dominated) rule.[16] In cases of murders of women for having brought 'dishonour' on their families, one colonial administrator saw himself as having to compromise 'between the demands of civilized and of savage tribal justice.'[17] Reporting from Arbil, a Dr Williamson noted the close connections between religion and midwifery which made him reluctant to intervene in the town's obstetrics arrangements.[18] Other medical authorities were less shy: numerous reports deal with the registration and compulsory medical examination of prostitutes in campaigns against venereal diseases, said to be rampant.[19]

As for education, one of the earliest reports[20] stated: 'The Mohammedan of Iraq is naturally suspicious of any innovation connected with his women-folk.' By 1931, the Colonial Office had somewhat shifted its ground. Noting that there were 247 primary schools for boys and 44 for girls, it reported that education for girls would make them 'unfitted for tribal life. . . The tribal girl marries early; she must have several crafts at her finger-ends.'[21] Though there was an influential woman in the British administration, Gertrude Bell, she seems from her letters to have been more obsessed with antiquities or fascinated by King Faisal than deeply interested in Iraqi women's rights.[22] The opening of government schools for girls seems to have come mainly in response to local demands, noted by divisional administrators.

The 'morbid nervousness' of the authorities irked Freya Stark, whose travels took her to Baghdad in 1931. She ridiculed the regulations restricting the movements of British and American ladies, whether accompanied or not, issued by the Ministry of the Interior. 'If you get into trouble by doing this sort of thing, no other woman will ever be allowed to do it afterwards,' she was told. She set off undaunted on a visit to a rural shaikh.[23] She was also scathing in her criticism of the 'unimaginative shallowness' of education at the Iraq Government School for Girls in Baghdad, 'a place enclosed in high walls,' to which she went in order to improve her Arabic. She found the teachers mostly Syrian 'with neat Beyrouth speech and French clothes and city manners. . . which their more Eastern sisters resent and imitate.'

Women Organize in Iraq [24]

Well before that, however, important changes had been taking place. Women had participated actively in the 1920 revolt against British occupation. The story is still told of a woman whose brother was taken by the authorities. Unveiled and with her long hair flying loose, she declared that she too would fight for the freedom of Iraq. Women also took arms and food to the rebels, organized a support group in Baghdad, collected donations and handed in a petition demanding the release of nationalist detainees and protesting against their ill-treatment by the British forces. Such activities represented a crucial step forward for Iraqi women and from 1920 on they began putting demands for education for girls and the dropping of the veil. In the 1920s women began to publish magazines. The first to appear was *Leila*, published by a society called the Women's Rising, founded by Aswa Zahawi. Its demands for women's rights to work and education led to conflict with the authorities and the women were forced to restrict their activities to do-gooding. The society became a place for social gatherings of upper class women.

During the 1930s there was a further upsurge in political awareness and activity in Iraq with the struggle for national independence and the formation of political parties whose progressive programmes attracted the support of women and who were now adding economic independence for women to their other demands. Women's liberation was much discussed at this time, among educated people at least, and new publications appeared, such as *The Modern Woman* and *The Arab Woman*. The oppression of women was also discussed in articles by Yusuf Salman Yusuf (Fahd), founder of the ICP. A woman law student, Aminah ar-Rahhal, was a member of Fahd's first Central Committee 1941 to 1943. (She was later Inspectress of Education from 1959 until 1963.)

The government withheld licences from women's societies, except those with purely charitable aims, until as late as 1943 when the Women's League Against Fascism was founded. Fascist tendencies had gained some ground in Iraq through their ultra-nationalism and opposition to the British. The League's work continued after the war with literacy classes and educational meetings where the rights of women were debated. In Iraq, as elsewhere at the end of the war, socialist ideas had become very popular and until 1947 the political atmosphere in Iraq was relatively free. Then came the clampdown. Women activists were arrested, meetings were banned and literacy schools were closed down.

The following year saw the signing of the Portsmouth Treaty between Britain and Iraq. The response in Iraq was the popular uprising known as *al-Wathbah*, in which women's participation was more effective than in the past, and more organized too because of their experience in political parties. Women led demonstrations, took part in strikes and some were killed by police bullets. The situation was such that some observers expected the monarchy to fall. Using the situation in Palestine as a pretext, the Iraqi government declared a state of emergency and proceeded to arrest hundreds of activists, including women, who, contrary to traditional customs, faced long prison sentences and were subjected to torture. For several years women's organizations were outlawed, but women continued to work inside political parties such as the National Democratic Party, the Independence Party and the ICP. In 1952 the League for the Defence of Women's Rights came into being, campaigning for national liberation and democracy as well as for women's rights and children's welfare, and incurring the wrath of the authorities, who refused to recognize it. Other women's organizations existed at this time but only the League opposed the monarchy.

Members of the League were therefore among those who greeted the establishment of the Iraqi Republic in 1958 with joyful demonstrations. The League received official recognition on 29 December 1958 and its first congress was held in 1959, on 8 March, International Women's Day. The League's President, Dr Naziha Dulaimi, who became Minister for Municipalities in 1959, was the first woman cabinet minister in the whole of the Arab world. Membership of the League rose to 42,000 (out of a total population of 8 million) and included working women, peasants, housewives and intellectuals of different national, religious and political groups.

For two years its work went well despite the obstacles put forward by reactionary elements, particularly in Mosul, but also in government offices themselves. A notable achievement was the passing of a law on the status of women based on a draft put forward by the League. It protected women from the tyranny of arranged marriages at an early age and amended other provisions to do with marriage and the family. But conditions soon became difficult, with activists facing harassment and assaults. From mid-1960 most of the League's branches were gradually closed down, together with their educational and training activities.[25]

In February 1963 the Ba'thists seized power. The League's offices were closed and thousands of its members arrested and tortured. Death sentences were imposed on three members of the League and their lives were only saved as a result of international pressure. In Iraq today the Ba'th regime has its own organization for women, the General Federation of Iraqi Women, the only officially recognized organization for women in Iraq. Under article 200 of the Iraqi penal code, membership of any organization outside those of the Ba'th Party is an offence which may be punished by death.

The General Federation of Iraqi Women

The National Action Charter, proclaimed by President Ahmad Hasan al-Bakr on 15 November 1971, had this to say on women: 'The liberation of woman from the feudalistic and bourgeois thinking and from the conditions and terms under which she was a sheer pleasure object or second-class citizen, is a sacred hope and national duty for which one should struggle faithfully and keenly.'[26] On 19 December 1972, the Revolutionary Command Council (RCC) promulgated Law 139 specifying the status, duties and functions of its women's organization, the GFIW. Its first role was to mobilize Iraqi women 'in the battle of the Arab nation against imperialism, Zionism, reactionism and backwardness.' This came before 'raising the level of the Iraqi woman by all possible means.' The first amendment to this law, promulgated in 1976, also by the RCC, 'focused upon the objectives of struggle that shall be realized by the Federation.' Prominence is also given by the GFIW to Ba'th Party ideology stressing the importance of the family. The party's constitution of 1947, formulated by 'Aflaq, sees the family as 'the nation's basic cell' which the state 'must protect, encourage and cherish.' Moreover, 'procreation is primarily the family's responsibility and secondly the State's' and 'the state must encourage its intensification.' Marriage is no less than 'a national duty that must be encouraged and guided.' It is in this context that 'the family has enjoyed special care since the July 17 1968 Revolution.'

Before going any further the reader should note that most of the information in this section is taken from the propaganda of the GFIW itself.[27] Each of their booklets has a portrait of Saddam Husain on the first page but contains no reference to any woman by name. They seem unaware of the incongruity of promoting this male personality cult and of developing 'brotherly ties among Arab women.' Still less do they register any surprise at the RCC, whose membership is entirely male, laying down the objectives to be aimed for by a women's organization. It is clear that the GFIW is in no way a women's liberation organization. It is not striving to improve the position of women in Iraq but to mobilize and control them in line with the aims of the Ba'thist regime. Its claim to be the only popular organization that represents Iraqi women is completely hollow: its programme is laid down by the men of the RCC, who have, in additon, banned all other women's organizations.

At the same time the Federation has been used for propaganda purposes to promote the regime's would-be progressive image abroad. The GFIW's most preposterous propaganda is its claim not only to have eliminated illiteracy, which stood at over 80% among women in Iraq in the 1970s, but to have eliminated it in the space of only 14 months! In fact literacy classes used for inculcating Ba'thist doctrines were compulsory and attendance was strictly enforced, causing great problems. As other examples of its activities it cites its Peasant Tent and Peasant Caravan which tour the countryside dispensing medicines, for people and livestock, as well as propaganda and 'presents.' It prides itself on its efforts to encourage girls to play basketball and women to take up paid employment with 100 nurseries to 'take care of that great national treasure, children.' Much is made in all the propaganda of a cooperative farm near Baghdad said to be run by women, but, as a Swiss writer wryly observed, nobody says anything about opening a second one.[28] They also claim to have set up small enterprises employing women workers, but only two examples are given: the 'Revolution Rosebuds' factory in Baghdad, opened in 1977 and employing only 20 women, and another small factory which produces wall carpets with traditional views or political slogans! Despite their pride at seeing token women employed on the buses, in traffic control, filling stations, courts of justice, the armed forces and so on, they see no anomaly in the fact that other areas, notably teaching very young children, are 100% women's work.

Saddam Husain gave a clear statement of how he saw the role of women in his speech to the third conference of the GFIW: 'an enlightened mother who is educated and liberated can give the country a generation of conscious and committed fighters.' He told women not to seek 'bourgeois' emancipation but to find liberation through 'commitment to the Revolution.' On another occasion he advised Iraqi women not to try to prove that women can do anything that men can.[29] In particular, he opposed women's participation in the armed forces, for 'men are better suited than women in the army, women are better suited than men in child care.' This was later forgotten: women's demands are important only in so far as they suit the needs of Ba'thism.

Women Victims of Ba'thist Terror

It has often been said, with great irony, that in Iraq women have been granted equal rights with men only in detention and torture. Victims of Ba'thist terror include thousands of women and their children who have been subjected to the same brutal treatment as men: murder, execution, thallium poisoning, detention and torture. Among women who have disappeared are Aida Yasin, a member of the Supreme Committee of the Iraqi Women's League, and many other activists, including Laila Yusuf, Ramzia al-Shaybani, Firyal Abbas, Nidhal al-Jawahiri, Shadha al-Barak, Samirah Jawad al-Musawi and Laila 'Abd al-Baqi. Badria Dakhil Allawi disappeared in 1980 with her family. The family of another woman who disappeared then, Raja Majid Muhammad, have since been informed that she is dead.

Many other women have been killed by the regime. In April 1980 Amina al-Sadr, known as Bint al-Huda, was executed in public, together with her brother, the leader of the Shi'i religious opposition. Thirteen women were killed by the security forces during the popular uprising that swept Iraqi Kurdistan in the spring of 1982. They included Sinobar Mahmud, a teacher, and Amina Sour, an elderly widow, both killed on 24 April in Qalat Dizah, three school students and other women killed in demonstrations in various towns. In March 1984 people killed by the security forces in reprisals against the Kurdish village of Liko included two girls, Amirah Audisho, aged 12, and Baghilah Ali Ahmed, aged 10.[30]

Atrocities in Kurdistan are nothing new. Since 1975 the authorities have been evacuating and destroying Kurdish villages, allegedly to prevent infiltration by *peshmerga* forces across the borders. By 1981, 1266 villages had been evacuated and their inhabitants deported to the south, with no regard for keeping families together despite the regime's propaganda which stresses the importance of the family. Another ploy is to arrest the relatives of *peshmerga* fighters whom the regime's forces cannot find and detain them instead. By 1978 Amnesty International had collected the names of over 600 men, women and children arrested in this way.[31]

Thallium, a rat poison, became internationally known among toxicologists as 'the Iraqi poison' when it was given, usually in fruit juice or yoghurt drinks, to Iraqis held in detention centres. Like men, women have died as a result of thallium poisoning. Dr Salwa al-Bahrani, aged 43, was a teacher at Baghdad University and the daughter of a former minister under the monarchy. She was taken hostage in an attempt to make her son, suspected of being a member of the Islamic *Da'wa* party, give himself up. After her 'release' she went to Yarmuk Hospital in Baghdad, where she died some days later, from poisoning. Another woman victim of thallium poisoning was Najia Hatim al-Rikabi, a student member of the ICP, arrested in May 1980. She resisted brutal torture, including threats to kill her 14-month-old daughter, who had been taken prisoner too. Najia died three days after being 'freed' and her sister Hadia was also poisoned.

Torture, in theory, is not permitted in Iraq. Any kind of physical or psychological torture is forbidden by Article 22(a) of the Iraqi Constitution and Article 127 of the Code of Criminal Procedures. Articles 332 and 333 of the Penal Code provide for a maximum of one year's imprisonment or a maximum fine of ID100, or both, for the use of torture in obtaining information or confessions from detainees. In reality, the use of torture is all too common, as is clear from Amnesty International's annual reports as well as their two special reports on Iraq.[32] Many women activists have been tortured while in detention. The testimony of a survivor, Dr Su'ad Khairi, is given in Chapter Six. Detainees do not survive so often these days, for torture is carried out more brutally and those who resist are killed. Women activists who have been killed under torture include Hasiba Karim, Maniha Siwa and Jamila Karim.

In many cases, women are tortured in front of other members of their family, husbands or children, and sometimes children are tortured in front of their mothers. There are no limits to the torturers' bestiality save perhaps their own imagination. When Fatima al-Muhsin, a journalist, was detained, her baby was deprived of food in an attempt to put pressure on her. In 1982 Su'ad Khairi told the CARDRI conference of the use of sexual torture against women and children and of children being placed in sacks with starving cats. A man who went to collect the body of his nephew from Baghdad's Medical City Mortuary saw the bodies of 20 young women all naked with their breasts cut off and their bodies mutilated. He was forced to look at them or he would not be given his nephew's body.

In the southern town of 'Amara there is a special women's jail which consists of three large halls plus cells for solitary confinement. It houses over 200 women and children, many of whom have been there since the early days of the war, hostages for their husbands or sons who have deserted the army or otherwise opposed the regime. No charges have been brought against them and they are denied the right of legal defence. Conditions in the jail are appalling. Despite the over-crowding the detainees are admitted only half an hour daily to the prison yard, when exercise is not denied altogether as a means of further pressure. Basic sanitary arrangements are lacking and the food is insufficient and often dirty. As a result of ill-treatment and under-nourishment most of the children are suffering from chronic diseases, but milk and medicines are often withheld – another form of psychological pressure – and the doctor's monthly visit is merely for a routine check.[33]

The treatment of women who oppose the regime, or whose men do, is thus in complete contempt of traditional norms and sentimental Ba'thist propaganda about the sanctity of the family, as well as being a gross violation of human rights. The cooperation of the GFIW with the security forces makes a mockery of their propaganda about women's liberation.

Women Against the Ba'th

This high level of repression indicates that women are active in opposition to the Ba'thist regime. They work with great courage in clandestine organizations and have been active throughout Iraq and beyond its frontiers in protest against oppression and in exposing the Ba'thist regime and in particular the GFIW and its false propaganda. Women's role in the struggle is becoming more and more important.

In Iraqi Kurdistan women and schoolgirls played a leading part in the popular uprising during the spring of 1982. Many demonstrations were organized and led by women at that time and again in 1984. In many towns in Iraq the cemeteries where women visit the graves of those lost in the war or killed by the regime have become places to meet and organize. Demonstrations initiated by women also take place outside prisons to demand the release of political detainees and outside hospitals in protest at the war casualties. Since 1981 women have also been active in the armed stuggle being waged in Iraqi Kurdistan against the regime. They face the same dangers as the men and live under the same rough conditions, but in addition they challenge sexist ways of thinking among their male comrades as well as among Kurdish villagers. In the marshlands of southern Iraq women have also taken up arms against the regime.[34]

In Syria women's organizations are working to improve the lot of Iraqis expelled by the Ba'thists for being allegedly of Iranian origin. In many cases families have been split up: parents were not allowed to wait for children who were away from home when the police came, for instance. Methods used to expel these people, depriving them of their property and citizenship, are reminiscent of Israeli actions against the Arab people of Palestine, except that in this case the culprits are not foreign occupants but the Iraqi regime, acting with the full cooperation of the GFIW, whose premises were used as staging posts for the deportees on their way out of Iraq. Organizations active among the deportees are the Union of Iraqi Women, the Union of Women of the Iraqi Republic–Mujahidin, the Iraqi Women's League and the League of Muslim Women. The latter is the most influential and has the resources to provide material help for the deportees.[35]

The Iraqi Women's League has worked to build links with women's organizations throughout the world and to expose the repressive Ba'thist regime and in particular its effects on women's lives in Iraq itself and elsewhere. They have been supported by international women's groups such as the Arab Women's Union and the World Federation of Democratic Women. In 1984 an International Committee for the Release of Detained and Disappeared Women in Iraq was formed.

Changes in the Law

We have seen that there are at present many obstacles to genuine liberation for women in Iraq. While education has brought some changes for younger generations of women, conditions in the family and at home have been slow to change. It should be noted that since Iraq, like other Arab countries, is not a secular state, reforms in the legal status of women can only take place within the context of the *shari'a*, or Islamic law. Important changes introduced under the Qasim regime were subsequently modified and there now exist plenty of loopholes for the benefit of men. For instance, polygamy is now only allowed with the consent of the first wife, unless a man's reasons are approved by the court: he may claim that his first wife is sterile or very ill. He may, however, simply threaten to divorce her or otherwise bully her into giving her consent. Though polygamy is disappearing this is probably because it is expensive rather than because of legal changes. This is just one example of changes in women's status coming about as a result of economic pressure, not through any kind of reforming zeal.

In the past Muslim women faced perpetual marital insecurity since a man could divorce his wife, simply by repudiating her, whenever he chose. No effective steps have been taken against this in Iraq. Though the procedures have been altered, it still remains easy for a man to obtain a divorce. It is extremely difficult for a woman to do so. The problem of the custody of children arises if a marriage breaks up. Traditionally, the mother had custody of the children until the age of seven and the father could then claim them. In Iraq, Islamic law has been amended so that the wife has custody until the child is ten. This may then be extended by a People's Committee on which the notorious GFIW has two representatives. At the age of 15, children can decide for themselves, supposedly, with whom they prefer to live.

A divorced woman could be seen as being rather better off than a widow, for her status as a divorcee is seen as temporary and traditionally the family assist with childcare and housework so as to facilitate her speedy remarriage if she is still young. A widow, on the other hand, has to look after her children herself and her chances of remarriage are slim. She may be cajoled into marrying her brother-in-law on the grounds that the children should be kept in the family. This custom is still common practice in some communities. The woman's wishes are considered to be of no importance. The regime is now bribing men to marry war widows. A man is awarded a substantial sum of money if he marries a war widow, though she is not entitled to a pension in her own right.

The effect of changes in the law, including important steps such as the abolition of forced marriages and the raising of the minimum age for marriage, achieved under the Qasim regime, depends on enforcing and publicizing them in a country where many women are still illiterate and also on giving women the confidence to demand their rights. Women are still victims of social pressures which work against any new ideas and may often be intimidated by threats of violence. More importantly, the Ba'thists' desire to present a progressive image to the world at large should never be forgotten. 'How could we expect the world to look upon us as a progressive regime?' moaned Deputy Premier 'Ali Salih al-Sa'di when provisions in the *Personal*

Status Law 'inconsistent with Islamic law' were repealed by 'Arif and al-Bakr.[36] The Ba'thists are notorious for sanctimoniously saying one thing while doing the opposite.

In addition to modifications in the law outlined above, the regime has decreed a number of measures in line with their chauvinistic policies against the Kurds and the Iranians. On 15 April 1982 the RCC decreed that any Iraqi national who is married to a woman 'of Iranian origin' is eligible to ID4,000 if a member of the armed forces or ID2,500 if a civilian if he divorces his wife or if she has been deported. Other measures aim to destroy Kurdish national identity. If an Arab man marries a Kurdish woman he is awarded the equivalent of £1,000. In addition to this, the regime's policy of destroying Kurdish villages and deporting villagers to southern Iraq is carried out without any attempt to keep families together, despite the Ba thist duty to 'protect, encourage and cherish' the family unit. The same goes, of course, for deportations of so-called Iranians.

Women in the Iraqi 'Parliament'

The boast that Iraqi women have the right to vote and that there are women in the National Assembly is ludicrous. This is another Ba'thist propaganda exercise. The value of a vote depends of course on the quality of the elections in which it is exercised. It was stipulated that any candidate for the National Assembly in 1980 'must believe in the principles and objectives of the July 17-30 Revolution' (1968 Ba'th coup) as well as being of Iraqi nationality and not married to a foreigner. Of the 974 candidates nominated, only 824 were approved.[37] In any case, the assembly is a powerless institution which can in no way be considered as a legislative body since its only role is to rubberstamp the decrees of the RCC. There are, significantly, no women in the RCC. Yet in 1959, as we have seen, the Qasim regime made history by appointing the first woman cabinet minister in the whole of the Arab world.

Women and Education

Some progress in education has undoubtedly taken place under the Ba'thist regime in the sense that more schools have been built and the number of pupils has risen. Although there has been an undeniable increase in both the numbers and the percentage of girls attending school, the gap between them and boys is still far from closed. As pupils proceed through the education system, the percentage of girls falls. According to the GFIW, in 1979-80 girls were 48% of children enrolled in kindergartens, 45% in elementary schools, 31% in secondary schools and 28% in vocational education.[38] Even if they are accurate, enrolment figures say nothing about attendance nor about the numbers of students successfully completing their courses. They also conceal very serious drawbacks in the Iraqi education system, which suffers from Ba'thization at all levels.[39] It has become a means of fostering and rewarding political loyalty rather than of developing human potential. All curricula and textbooks have been re-designed to conform to the national-socialist ideology of the regime. This includes manuals designed for use at compulsory literacy classes for women. Access to higher education depends on political allegiance since only Ba'thist students may attend universities and colleges and only Ba'thists may train to be teachers. Many women are denied higher education because they refuse to conform. In addition to all this, sisters of dead soldiers are awarded bonus points in examinations taken in the final year at school, on which admission to university depends.[40] Nor does the award of a degree necessarily depend on academic merit. For instance, officers of the National Union of Iraqi Students (another Ba'thist organization) are not required to attend classes but are guaranteed a degree at the end of their courses. They may also be rewarded with scholarships for post-graduate study abroad. Progress in education must thus be seen in the context of Ba'thization and repression.

Women in the Workforce

As in many other countries the participation of women in the paid labour force is coming about as a result of economic pressure. In 1947 women were only 1% of the paid workforce in Iraq. The situation has certainly changed since then. According to official statistics, the percentage of women in the workforce rose from 5% at the beginning of the seventies to 19% at the end of the decade. However, while there may be token women in many sectors, though not at the very top, it remains the case that women are largely confined to unskilled work. In the professions their role is also limited. For instance, women teachers work in girls' schools and women doctors tend to specialize in pediatrics or obstetrics – that is, in fields where they will be in contact with women and children only. This has been stated by the GFIW and was confirmed in 1984 by an Irishwoman, the Director of Nursing at the Ibn al-Bitar Hospital in Baghdad.[41] She added that many Iraqis see nursing as a low grade profession, almost on the same level as prostitution, and compared the situation of Iraqi women, who are seen as housewives and bearers of children, with that in Ireland 20 years ago. The idea of a professional woman, she said, is alien to most Iraqis.

The effects of the long drawn out war against Iran include an increase in the number of women doing paid work. In 1983, it was reported that well-qualified, but inexperienced, women were replacing the men who had been drafted into the army.[42] The regime's difficulties in paying foreign workers were also widely reported[43] and Iraqi women have now been conscripted into the workforce, and especially into factories and offices. This phenomenon is unlikely to be of much immediate benefit to women as workers are not only expected to make donations to the war effort, but deductions of over a third are made from their wages for this purpose.

Childcare facilities are limited and women have less and less confidence in them since children are subjected to chauvinist indoctrination and acquire habits of violence and spying. A survey of publications for children in Iraq[44] reported a shift in emphasis in the values transmitted towards 'national sovereignty, unity of the Arab countries, economic security, socialism, ownership, knowledge, excitement' and away from 'love, people, activity, generosity, food, religion and manners.' The author concluded that this indicated an emphasis on 'the ideology of the 17 July Revolution and its aims.' Children are being pulled in two directions: at school they are supposed to glory in 'Saddam's Qadisiya' while at home they experience the real effects of the war, the misery of losing members of their families and the struggle to make ends meet.

Conditions for all workers have deteriorated under wartime pressures, but this is especially true for women workers, with wages slashed, hours increased and maternity leave cut. In this situation, going out to work is not a step forward for women, whatever its long-term effects may be. It subjects them to further oppression and exploitation. Many women find themselves having to combine extended hours of factory work with childcare, housework and keeping home and family on less and less money.

Women and Health

Women's limited role as workers in Iraq's medical services, as doctors working mainly with women and children and as nurses being regarded as little more than prostitutes, has been noted above. Health care for women varies enormously, from prestige private clinics in the capital to overcrowded dispensaries in the villages. For many peasant women medical treatment is still practically nil and their menfolk often view them as expendable: if a woman dies in childbirth, for example, her husband may simply marry her sister.

The pronatalist notions of the regime have already been mentioned and Minces notes that the birthrate in Iraq is 3.6%, higher than in other Arab countries. Some women buy contraceptive pills over the counter in chemists' shops; others, if they dare, seek medical advice, but the family planning network was limited even before the war and has not been encouraged since. Abortion is illegal, but many women lose their lives in backstreet abortions.

Lack of pre- and post-natal care means that many women suffer from disease related to childbirth, and infant mortality is also high, due often to gastroenteritis and malnutrition. Diseases such as bilharzia and malaria are prevalent in the rural areas where medical services are very limited. Women may also be inhibited from seeking medical treatment at village dispensaries with their male staff. Conditions are aggravated by the lack of clean water supplies. Outside the main towns water has generally to be fetched from small rivers and schemes to provide piped water have been abandoned because of the war.

The war has also put women under greater pressure than before by increasing their work-load, making them more liable to industrial injuries and subjecting them to greater psychological stress.

Effects of the War Against Iran

Some effects of the war on the situation of Iraqi women have already been discussed, since they have been forced to go out to work to replace male workers who have been drafted. Many women now find themselves in the position of sole family breadwinner, with husbands and sons killed, wounded or missing. Yet at the same time wages have been cut and prices have risen, making conditions more difficult than ever before. As well as deducting 'donations' from wages and salaries the regime set out to rob women of their gold and jewellery. These are very important to Iraqi women, not for their sentimental value, but as a form of insurance, to be sold only in a dire emergency. The regime has pressurized women into 'donating' their gold to help the war effort. Like other levies, these were portrayed by the media in Iraq as gifts to Saddam from his loyal people. In fact, uniformed soldiers were going from door to door bullying women into parting with their gold.[45] Receipts for donations of gold were required in order to have other official documents processed. Whereas a dead Iraqi soldier used to earn his family ID10,000 as a war hero,[46] the regime can no longer afford such handouts as the war drags on. Widows, and women whose husbands and sons are away fighting, have to cope alone as the struggle to make ends meet becomes harder for all working people in Iraq.

Conclusions

We have seen that some women at least managed to achieve a measure of progress in Iraq, mostly thanks to their own efforts in keeping demands for women's liberation alive despite formidable opposition and often in clandestine organizations. Advances won after years of struggle have been undermined by the Ba'thist regime. Despite claims to the contrary, they simply make use of women to serve the interests of the ruling clique. Women have to participate in the work-force on Ba'thist terms, including low wages and pledges of loyalty to the ruling party. Progress in education has also to be seen in the context of repression and control. Decrees on Kurdish and so-called Iranian women, as well as the torture meted out to women detainees, show how little the regime really cares about women's rights. In such conditions it is hardly surprising that many Iraqi women give priority to their struggle against the Ba'thist regime, which they feel must be overthrown before any advances in women's liberation can be gained.

References

1. Peter and Magda Hall, *The Penguin International Travel Handbook*, 2nd edition (Penguin, 1984), p. 219.
2. 'Beyond the Veil', *The Times*, 15 March 1978.
3. See, for example, *Feminist Review*, no. 17, Summer 1984, for criticisms of white feminists' prejudiced views on Asian women.
4. Daniel Bates and Amal Rassam, *Peoples and Cultures of the Middle East*, (Prentice Hall, 1983).
   Nawal El Saadawi, *The Hidden Face of Eve: Women in the Arab World*, (Zed Press, London, 1980).
5. Reported in *al-Nahar*, a Beirut daily newspaper, 17 April 1963.
6. Saadawi, op. cit., chapter 5. She refers to the *Iraqi Medical Journal*, 21 February 1972.
7. Elizabeth Warnock Fernea, *Guests of the Sheikh: an Ethnography of an Iraqi Village*, (Anchor Books, New York, 1969).
8. Edith and E.F. Penrose, *Iraq: International Relations and National Development*, (Benn, London, 1978) p. 189.
9. Gavin Young, *Iraq*, (Collins, London, 1980).
10. Juliette Minces, *The House of Obedience: Women in Arab Society*, (Zed Press, London, 1980) p. 51.
11. Lois Beck and Nikki Keddie (eds.), *Women in the Muslim World*, (Harvard University Press, 1978) pp. 5–6.
12. M.E. Hume-Griffith, *Behind the veil in Persia and Turkish Arabia: an Account of an Englishwoman's eight years' residence amongst the women of the East* (Seeley & Co, London, 1909).
13. See Minces and El Saadawi. Also Patai, *The Arab Mind*, (Scribners, New York, 1973).
14. R.B. Betts, *Christians in the Arab East*, (SPCK, London, 1979).
15. Pembenaz Yorgun, 'The Women's Question and difficulties of feminism in Turkey,' *Khamsin*, no. 11, 1984, p. 70 et seq.
16. Colonial Office, Sessional Papers, CO 696/3, *Administrative Reports for Iraq 1920*, Mesopotamian Ministry of Justice Report for 1920.
17. Ibid., Administrative Report for the Amarah Division, p. 7.
18. Ibid., Medical Reports, Arbil Report.
19. Ibid., Medical Reports for Baghdad, Basra, etc.
20. Colonial Office, *Administrative Reports for Occupied Territories of Iraq*, 1917 Department of Education Annual Report.
21. Colonial Office, *Special Report by His Majesty's Government on the Progress of Iraq 1920–1931* (HMSO for the League of Nations, 1931).
22. Lady Bell, *The Letters of Gertrude Bell*, selected and edited, 2 vols. (Benn, London, 1927).
23. Freya Stark, *Baghdad Sketches* (John Murray, London, 1937).
24. The Iraqi Women's League's forthcoming *Brief History of Iraqi Women* provided most of the information in this section.
25. Hanna Batatu, *The Old Social Classes and Revolutionary Movements in Iraq*, (Princeton, 1978) p. 946 reporting a conversation with Rose Khadduri.
26. *National Action Charter*, (Ministry of Information, Baghdad, 1971) p. 49.
27. *A Practical Translation to the Objectives of the Revolution in Work*

and Creativity (General Federation of Iraqi Women, January 1980); and *The Working Program of the Iraqi Republic to Improve the Woman's Status, presented to the International Congress for the UN Women's Contract in Copenhagen* (1980); and *Papers of the General Federation of Iraqi Women presented to the World Congress of Women Held in Prague Czechoslovakia October 8–13* (1981).

28. Liesl Graz, *l'Irak au Présent* (Editions des trois continents, 1979).

29. Saddam Husain, 'The Revolution and the Historical Role of Women', speech no. 5 in *On Social and Foreign Affairs in Iraq*, (Croom Helm, London, 1979).

30. Reported in *CARDRI News*, June 1984, p. 14.

31. Amnesty International, *Annual Report* (1978) p. 258.

32. Amnesty International, *Iraq: Evidence of Torture* (AI, 1981); and *Report and Recommendations of Amnesty International Mission to the Government of the Republic of Iraq* (AI, 1983).

33. Iraqi Women's League leaflet.

34. Report by Barbara MacDermott in *The Morning Star*, 17 April 1984.

35. Report by Iraqi Women's League (Syria Branch).

36. Batatu, op. cit., p. 1018.

37. Abida Samiuddin, 'The Beginning of Parliamentary Democracy in Iraq: a case study,' *Middle East Studies*, October 1982, pp. 400–410.

38. GFIW, *Working Program*.

39. CARDRI, *Iraq: Education in the Grip of the Secret Police* (1983).

40. *Times Higher Education Supplement*, 21 September 1984, p. 10.

41. 'An Irish Nurse Takes Charge in Baghdad', *Irish Times*, 28 July 1984.

42. 'Iraq's Economy Under Siege', *Middle East Economic Digest*, 5–11 August 1983, p. 15.

43. For example, in *Time*, 27 June 1983.

44. Khalaf Nassar Muhaisin al Hiti, *Dominant Values in Iraqi Journals for Children*, (Wizarat al-Thaqafah wa al-Funun, Baghdad, 1978).

45. *International Herald Tribune*, 3 May 1983.

46. Tim Hodlin, 'Saddam the Ruthless: protector of Western interests in the Gulf', *The Listener*, 14 October 1982.

8. The Opposition

U. Zaher

Introduction

During the past few years opposition to the Ba'th dictatorship in Iraq has gathered momentum and acquired increased strength. The fragmentation and disarray which previously plagued the opposition camp and enabled the Ba'th regime to maintain its terrorist rule are gradually giving way to a complex process of polarization and re-alignment, influenced by a host of internal, regional and international factors.

These factors include: the deep structural changes in Iraqi society brought about by the post-1973 hike in oil revenues; the Algiers Accord with the Shah of Iran and the suppression of the Kurdish armed struggle in 1975; the ruthless clamp-down on the Iraqi Communist Party, particularly after 1978; the bloody purge in the Ba'th Party following Saddam's ascendency to the Presidency in 1979; and the confrontation with the new Islamic regime in neighbouring Iran leading to an all-out war since September 1980. The current war impasse (March 1985) and deep internal crisis gripping the regime have given a strong impetus to the opposition forces.

The constituent forces in the opposition camp are: the Iraqi Communist Party; the Kurdish movement; the Arab nationalists and the Islamic movement. An exposition of the origin and development of these opposition forces is essential for a deeper understanding of the current situation and interrelations between them. The Kurdish national movement is thoroughly dealt with in Chapter Nine. Chapters One and Two give the political history which is the context in which the opposition forces must be viewed. This chapter looks at the Communist Movement, the Islamic Movement and the Arab Nationalist Movement in Iraq.

Today there exists among the opposition forces a greater unanimity than ever before over the need for a broad front uniting their struggle to overthrow the dictatorship and set up a coalition patriotic government committed to ending the war and achieving democracy for Iraq and true autonomy for Iraqi Kurdistan. The expansion in November 1984 of the Democratic Patriotic Front, which linked the Iraqi Communist Party and the Kurdistan Democratic Party, to encompass some Arab nationalist forces and another Kurdish grouping, and also the continuing growth of popular resistance, including armed struggle in Iraqi Kurdistan, are significant steps along the Iraqi opposition forces' tortuous and difficult path towards triumph over terror and dictatorship.

The Communist Movement

Since its foundation in 1934, the Iraqi Communist Party (ICP) has dominated the left in Iraqi politics. It has played a fundamental role in shaping the modern political history of Iraq since independence. In his fascinating book on Iraq, Hanna Batatu[1] has shown conclusively that the Communist Party led and inspired the national movement in the 1940s, and 1950s, and derived much of its own impetus from it. The Party was involved in and generally led all the most important national uprisings and demonstrations. Communism had thus become a 'powerful passion' in Iraq by the mid-1950s. After the revolution of July 1958, the ICP emerged as the most influential political organization in the country. In their review of Batatu's book, Marion Farouk-Sluglett and Peter Sluglett point out:

> Although the Party has never held power, it has had sufficient impact to ensure that its various rivals have found it necessary to graft elements of Marxist economic and social thought onto their nationalist or Ba'thist ideologies: every government which has come to power since 1958 has had at least to pay lip service to ideas of economic and social reform in order to achieve some degree of legitimacy.[2]

In addition, the Communist Party bore the brunt of the repression by successive governments under the monarchy. In 1949, after the suppression of the revolutionary upsurge expressed in *al-Wathbah* (The Leap) of 1948, the leader and founder of the Party, Fahd, and two prominent Political Bureau members, were executed. The Party was also to become the prime target for attacks by enemies of the 1958 revolution under Qasim's dictatorial rule. Hundreds of its cadres and members were imprisoned, executed or assassinated during those turbulent years. After the Ba'thist coup of 8 February 1963, the ICP suffered an unprecedented campaign of mass physical liquidation. Leading figures and cadres of the Party were tortured to death, including its First Secretary Salam 'Adil. But despite enormous losses, the Party remained a leading force in the fight against the Ba'th's rule, and joined in the armed struggle waged by the Kurdish national movement in Iraqi Kurdistan. The courageous suffering and heroism of Party cadres and members in the face of tyranny and terror won it admiration and respect among the people as the 'Party of Martyrs', and even among its enemies. Instead of achieving their dream of uprooting communism from the soil of Iraq, successive rulers have been forced to confess to their failure.

The late 1970s saw the Ba'th Party attempting once again to crush the Communist Party, which it always viewed as a potential competitor for power and a threat to its policy of imposing total hegemony over the whole of Iraqi society. Despite their boast that by 1980 the Communist Party no longer existed in Iraq, Ba'th leaders have recently admitted the existence of armed communist resistance in the north of the country and even accused the Communists of 'national betrayal' for their opposition to the war with Iran.[3]

The outstanding prestige enjoyed by the ICP and its deep roots within Iraqi society were largely due to its ability to merge the national with the social question in an almost unique manner. Its role in the national movement and among the young working class, the peasantry and the intellectuals in the early stages of its life left an indelible impression on Iraq's recent history. The history of Iraq's Communist movement is to a large extent also that of its contemporary revolutionary movement. The following historical outline of the Iraqi Communist Party must therefore be viewed against the political set-up and other developments which have been dealt with extensively in other parts of this book.

Working Class: Early Years

During the mandate period (1920–32), the working class grew at a faster rate than the national bourgeoisie. The industries set up by the British colonial power multiplied and were generally bigger than the national industries. The number of workers in the foreign sector, including the railways, Basra port and the Iraq Petroleum Company, exceeded 13,000. Manual workers in governmental and private enterprises were, however, not more than 6,000.[4] Early strikes, such as the dockyard strike by port workers in 1918 were violently suppressed. The first big organized strike in Baghdad was by railway workers in 1927 who demanded, for the first time, the enacting of a Labour Law and the freedom of trade union organization. Its success had a great impact on the development of the workers movement in Iraq. The Railway Workers Union was the first union to be formed in 1929. It became a focus for all workers and even for artisans. Its name was later changed to *Jam'iyyat Ashab al-Sana'a* (Artisans' Association). Conscious of the need for political work, since trade union rights could only be achieved through struggle and the achievement of political freedom, this union worked with the existing national bourgeois parties such as *Hizb al-Ikha' al-Watani* and *al-Hizb al-Watani al-Iraqi*. But relations were not strong due to the vacillations and weakness of the national bourgeoisie. A joint stand was only adopted during some strikes and events such as the general strike of July 1931. Although the immediate cause of the *Jam'iyyat's* action was opposition to the *Municipal Fees Law*, a revised scale of taxation of tradesmen's premises, it was also a powerful expression of the widespread anger felt by the Iraqi people against the terms of the Anglo-Iraqi Treaty of 1930.

Despite the fact that the working class at the time did not possess an independent political organization, that important strike demonstrated vividly that its class organization, i.e. the trade union movement, was far superior, in numbers and cohesion, to that of other social classes. The organizational qualities and high militant spirit among the young working class were also evident. The British High Commission was apparently taken by surprise: 'Situation reveals surprising lack of support for present government, and un-popularity of King Faisal. Republican cries have been openly raised in the streets . . . except in the Government newspapers, there has been no sign of loyalty to King or support for Government'.[5] After presenting a petition to the Regent, demanding the release of those arrested for demonstrating, the founder of the *Jam'iyyat* was arrested and the union was closed on the orders of the Ministry of Interior. The strike spread from Baghdad to the towns of the Middle Euphrates and to Basra. The opposition parties took a hesitant stand during the first days of the strike. Although liaison with the *Jam'iyyat* developed later on, their inability to take a firm stand against the 1930 Treaty, and the limitation of their protests to complaining against the harsh measures taken by the police and raids on their party headquarters, helped the government to break the strike.

Attempts by the government to set up yellow unions soon afterwards were defeated by the workers and a Workers Trade Union Federation was formed which led the boycott in December 1933 against the increased charges levied by the British-owned Baghdad Electric Light and Power Company.[6] The fact that the company was British-owned gave the protest strong nationalist overtones. The boycott was almost total and the whole city used light and electricity only in emergencies. The government was forced to lower prices slightly, but it banned the labour union on 2 January 1934 and imprisoned its leaders. The movement was forced almost completely underground for the next ten years.

The young working class thus demonstrated at an early stage its patriotic consciousness and its preparedness to sacrifice in defence of the national interest, while the national bourgeoisie displayed narrow self-interest and vacillations during critical periods of national struggle. Furthermore, the politicization of economic grievances was to be a constant feature of similar events over the following decades.

The Foundation of the Iraqi Communist Party

The triumph of the Soviet Revolution in 1917 was the primary motivating factor behind the spread of the ideas of Marxism-Leninism in Iraq during the early 1920s. Some intellectuals, who had witnessed the impact of the revolutionary events in Europe, returned to Iraq strongly inspired by socialist ideals. Among them was Husain al-Rahhal. Marxist groups were set up, and in December 1924 a bi-monthly journal entitled *al-Sahifa* was issued. It only published four editions and contained articles on dialectical materialism and Lenin's works. During the 1920s, translations into Arabic of the works of Marx, Engels and Lenin were published in Egypt, Palestine and Syria.

Efforts by early Marxists to establish a Communist Party in 1927 were unsuccessful. The trade union organization existing at the time was weak and included small businessmen and artisans. In addition, Marxist groups had weak links with the working class and the mass movement, and lacked dedicated professional cadres.

In the south of Iraq, however, the organized communist movement made a new start. The name of the prominent Communist leader Yusuf Salman Yusuf (known as Fahd, 'the Leopard') had emerged since 1927 as one of the local leaders of *al-Hizb al-Watani* (Nasiriya branch) and also as an active organizer, directing workers struggles in Basra and Nasiriya, particularly during the general strike of July 1931. Fahd studied Marxism and began forming groups among workers, peasants and revolutionary intellectuals in the south. On 23–24 December 1932, he issued a statement entitled 'Long Live the Union of Workers and Peasant Masses of Arab Countries', and signed it 'a Communist Worker'. As the activity of those groups increased, some of their members were arrested. One of Fahd's comrades, the worker Hasan 'Ayyash, was poisoned and died in prison on 25 July 1931 after playing a leading role in the general strike in Basra. He was the first martyr of the Iraqi working class.[7] In 1933, Fahd was arrested in Nasiriya and became the first Iraqi to defend himself in front of a court as a Communist.

On the eve of the foundation of the Iraqi Communist Party, the national bourgeois parties disbanded themselves, as they regarded the ending of the mandate and Iraq's membership of the League of Nations as their ultimate national objective. On 20 March 1932, *Hizb al-Ikha' al-Watani* headed the Cabinet and pledged in its foreign policy programme to 'respect international commitments' instead of abolishing the 1930 Treaty or even just amending it as had been stipulated in the Joint Action Charter it had signed with *al-Hizb al-Watani al-Iraqi* in November 1930. The latter issued a statement on 5 November 1933 that declared: 'due to the conditions and circumstances which prevent *al-Hizb al-Watani* from undertaking its national duty, we see that it is necessary to suspend the party's political activity, hoping that conditions will come about under which we can resume political activity'.[8]

The national movement was therefore deprived by the national bourgeoisie of any forum for legitimate organization or means of expression. There was thus an objective necessity for a political organization capable of leading class and national struggles, and principally of embodying the interests of the growing working class movement. The labour unions had been banned and the national bourgeois party did not dare to legalize them when it headed the government.

The Iraqi Communist Party was founded on 31 March 1934, initially under the name *Lajna Mukafahat al-'Isti'mar wa al-'Istiqlal* (Committee for Combatting Colonialism and Exploitation) and elected a Central Committee. On 14 June 1935, on the eve of the 7th Congress of the Third International, the Central Committee took the decision to change its name to 'The Iraqi Communist Party'. The Party also issued its first central journal *Kifah al-Sha'b* (People's Struggle). Among the slogans it carried were calls for: the abolition of the 1930 Treaty; the elimination of British military bases; the distribution of land among peasants; the enactment of a Labour Law and an 8-hour working day; the granting of democratic freedoms; the

Kurdish people's right to independence; the dissolution of the Chamber of Deputies and the holding of genuinely free elections.

In November 1935, the authorities dealt a blow to the young Party by arresting a number of its cadres including its Secretary 'Asim Flayyeh. Its printing equipment was also confiscated. Following the coup d'état of General Bakr Sidqi in October 1936, which brought to power a coalition government including reformers belonging to the liberal-democratic *al-Ahali* group (formed in 1931 and named after its daily newspaper *al-Ahali*), the Communist Party declared its support for the new regime and organized strikes demanding the implementation and improvement of Labour Law 72. It also opposed the dictatorial tendency within the military leadership. Some Communists joined the Popular Reform Society, formed in late 1936, and took part in formulating its programme together with democratic elements within the *al-Ahali* group. The Society's programme, issued on 15 November 1936, called for the state ownership of certain public resources and institutions; the distribution of land to the peasants; the protection of the rights of the working class by limiting working hours; and the legalization of trade union organization.[9] The Society dissolved itself in mid-1937.

After the collapse of Bakr Sidqi's government following his assassination in August 1937, the parliament declared Communism in Iraq illegal.[10] Article 89 of the Penal Code and Article 1 of the Supplementary Penal Code were amended. According to a newly introduced Article 89a, the approval of or dissemination of Bolshevik Socialism (Communism) among the armed forces or police could be punished with death or with penal servitude for life.

During World War II, the Communist Party under the leadership of its General Secretary Fahd, consolidated its organization and enhanced its prestige. The heroic struggle of the Soviet people against Nazi occupation inspired the Iraqi people and the ideas of Communism became widespread. In February 1944, the First Party Conference was held, which drafted the Party's National Charter. This Charter, which was endorsed by the First National Congress in April 1945, stressed the Party's opposition to imperialism and foreign exploitation and advocated the establishment of a democratic form of government. The Congress also adopted the Party's internal rules and elected a Central Committee.

During the period 1944–46, restrictions on trade union activity were relaxed and permission was granted for the formation of 16 labour unions. Of these, twelve were controlled by members of the Communist Party.[11] The Party played an active role in the gradual politicization of the growing working class. The workers and the urban population which was growing in numbers (Baghdad's population doubled between 1927 and 1947) suffered considerable hardships as a result of the severe rise in the cost of living.

Union activity and workers' strikes during that period acquired a strong national character and gained widespread popular support. In April 1945, the Party organized the first railway workers' strike which paralysed all military and civilian transport by rail.[12] The strike committee was arrested and the union itself suppressed. The most important strike by 5,000 workers in the Kirkuk oilfields took place in July 1946. It was called in protest against the British company's rejection of a demand for higher wages and was organized at the initiative of the Communist Party. It was only suppressed when the mounted police opened fire on striking workers, killing at least ten in what became known as the 'massacre of Gawurbaghi'.

In order to combat Zionism and to expose the collusion of Arab rulers with colonialist powers against the Arab people of Palestine, the Party established the 'Anti-Zionist League'. It was licensed on 12 September 1945 and it published a daily newspaper called *al-'Usbah* (The League). Though it was banned after only six months, *al-'Usbah* became a focus for mass meetings and gatherings. In a memorandum addressed to the head of the Iraqi state and parliament in November 1945, Fahd attacked the government's stand towards Zionism:

> The Iraqi government is attempting to hide the real cause of the catastrophe suffered by the Arab people of Palestine. It wants to cover up for British colonialism which is the first to blame, and to hide Zionism . . . Thus it portrays the Arab Jews, who have no connection whatsoever with colonialist Zionism and with whom we have lived together for many generations without any conflict, as if they were its cause, and it therefore directs the people's wrath against them.[13]

A request to establish a legal party, *Hizb al-Taharrur al-Watani* (National Liberation Party) was refused by the government in 1945. *Hizb al-Taharrur* continued, however, under Communist leadership to propagate its programme and organize mass actions. On 28 June 1946, the Anti-Zionist League and the unlicensed *Hizb al-Taharrur* organized a demonstration in Baghdad in which more than 3,000 workers and students took part. The demonstrators denounced injustices in Palestine and called for the expulsion of the British from Iraq. As they approached the British Embassy, the police opened fire at close range killing a Communist Party member and wounding others. Batatu commented that the incident was historic, 'marking as it does the opening of the storm that was to reach its climax in the *Wathbah* of 1948'.[14] A particular aspect which deeply alarmed the government and the British Embassy was that it was the first time that soldiers took part in such a demonstration.[15]

In Iraqi Kurdistan, the first Communist cells were set up in 1941-42 in Arbil and then in Sulaimaniya in 1943.[16] The Party issued the first Kurdish political paper *Azadi* (Salvation) in 1944 as the clandestine organ of its branch. The National Charter endorsed by the First Congress in 1945 stressed the equality of rights of the Arab and Kurdish peoples and the national rights of the Kurdish people. The internal rules approved by the Congress also stipulated the formation of a branch under the name 'The Kurdish Branch of the Iraqi Communist Party'.[17] An example of Communist activity in Kurdistan was described by Batatu. He considered a peasant uprising in the village of 'Arbat in 1947 as historically significant because it 'added up to the first uprising of its kind in the Iraqi countryside — against the landed shaikh instead of under his leadership'.[18]

A severe blow was dealt to the Communist Party when Fahd and several leading cadres were arrested on 18 January 1947. They were brought to trial and charged with illegal activities and conspiring to overthrow the government and propagating Communism among civilians and members of the armed forces. By March 1947, following a campaign of arrests, over 500 alleged Communists were in jail throughout the country.[19] The new Prime Minister, Salih Jabr, publicly announced his government's 'firmest resistance to Communism'.[20] On 24 June 1947, the Supreme Court in Baghdad sentenced to death Fahd and his comrade Zaki Basim, a member of the Politbureau. Under the pressure of an international campaign to save the lives of the Communist leaders, the sentence was commuted to life imprisonment on 23 July 1947.

Despite those blows, the Communist Party emerged as the fundamental political force during the great national rising known as *al-Wathbah* (The Leap) in January 1948. The immediate cause of this uprising was the signing of the so-called Portsmouth Treaty with Britain (signed at Portsmouth on 16 January 1948). Iraqi Communists led mass demonstrations in Baghdad and other large urban centres. Demonstrators were fired on by the police. On 27 January a total of 400 people were killed in the streets of Baghdad.[21] The Prime Minister, Salih Jabr, was forced to resign and flee for his life. A mammoth march of a hundred thousand people led by Communists with banners attended the funerals of 'the Martyrs'.[22] On the initiative of the ICP, a Committee for National Cooperation was formed, which included the left wing of the National Democratic Party and the Kurdistan Democratic Party, to lead the mass struggle.[23]

In the wake of the repudiation of the Treaty, there was a wave of workers' strikes. In April 1948, the Communist Party organized a strike at the K3 oil pumping station near Haditha which involved over 3,000 workers. After three weeks, the strikers, under Party leadership, marched on Baghdad, some 250 km. away. The 'great march' (*al-Masirah al-Kubra*) was halted by the police about 70 km. from the capital. Workers were at the heart of the mass democratic movement and provided protection for mass meetings and demonstrations, such as the first congress of the General Union of Iraqi Students (GUIS) on 14 April 1948 held in the open air in Baghdad.

The government gradually regained control after declaring a State of Emergency on 1 May 1948 under the pretext of protecting the rear of the Iraqi troops sent to Palestine. The Communist Party bore the brunt of the repression that followed. Hundreds of alleged Communists were brought to summary trials. On 10 February 1949, Fahd and two members of the Party Politbureau, Zaki Basim and Muhammed Husain al-Shabibi, were re-tried and sentenced to death. They were charged with having led the Party from their prison and with organizing armed insurrection.[24] The sentences were carried out at daybreak on 14 and 15 February. As he was led to the gallows Fahd exclaimed defiantly: 'We are bodies and thoughts; if you destroy our bodies, you will not destroy our thoughts'.[25]

By the early 1950s the Party had reorganized its ranks and resumed its clandestine activity. In August 1949, it acquired a stencil printing machine, smuggled in with one of the army units returning from Palestine. On 24 August 1949, it issued the first political communiqué since the setback.

Despite the limited experience of the youthful Party leadership in the following years, it showed a tremendous vigour and a determination to re-build the Party. Communist workers set up the 'Workers' Unions' Permanent Bureau' in early 1951.

The Party was instrumental in reorganizing and activating student and women's organizations. It established the Peace Partisans Movement in 1950 which mobilized public opinion against military pacts. The Central Committee endorsed a new National Charter in 1952 which advocated national independence and a popular republican regime representing the will of workers, peasants and the popular masses.[26] By the time of the uprising of November 1952, the *intifadha*, the Party was an active partici-pant in the mass struggles.

The *intifadha* was preceded by a series of workers' strikes at the British bases (June 1952) and at the ports (August 1952), which were brutally suppressed. In late 1952, nearly 6,000 peasants among al-'Azairij in 'Amarah province rose against the landlords under the leadership of the Peasant Societies organized by the Communist Party. On 17 November 1952, the Peace Partisans joined the United Popular Front and National Democrats in setting up a 'Contact Committee' with the object of facilitating the ex-change of views and ensuring uniformity of action.[27]

When the army was called in and the Chief-of-Staff formed a new govern-ment on 24 November 1952 to suppress the opposition, the ICP published a statement which called upon members of the armed forces to unite with the people against colonialism and its hirelings. The uprising and the realiza-tion of the need to win over the army politically was the principal motivating force behind the formation of the 'National Committee for the Union of Soldiers and Officers' in December 1954 by the Party.

In June 1953, Communists imprisoned in the Baghdad Central Jail staged an insurrection which was ruthlessly suppressed. Seven prisoners were killed and 81 others were wounded.[28] A month later, an insurrection by Com-munists held in Kut prison in protest at worsening conditions, was suppressed with machine gun fire. Eight prisoners were killed and 94 wounded.[29] These incidents aroused public indignation against the rulers and stirred many people into support for the Communists.

During the turbulent revolutionary period in the late 1940s and early 1950s, the authorities were advised by officials at the British Embassy to exploit religion for the purpose of stemming the advance of Communism. In a meeting with a chief Shi'i leader, Ayatullah Kashif al-Ghita', at his school in Najaf in October 1953, the British ambassador was reported to have said that 'combatting communism is dependent upon the awakening of the "ulama" and the spiritual leaders, . . . warning the young against these principles that upset the conditions of the world . . . and their proper guidance in the schools and the clubs'.[30] But the Ayatullah, expressing alarm over the deep penetration of Communism into Najaf itself, noted wth a sense of danger that 'wide nests' of 'spirited and ardent young men' functioned successfully in the holiest of Shi'i cities, even though it was 'without logic or proof and unassisted by funds or patronage or dignity of rank'.[31]

During the following years, the Communist Party led the popular opposition to the Baghdad Pact and championed the cause of peace. In the summer of 1954, the first conference of the Peace Movement in Iraq was held, attended by 70 delegates. The Party also called for united action to foil the Iraqi-Turkish pact signed in 1955.

In June 1955, an enlarged Central Committee meeting elected Salam 'Adil as Party Secretary, adopted a large number of organizational measures to enhance party discipline and dealt firmly with problems of ideological and political unity. By mid-1956, a number of factions which had split from the Party in the early 1950s, dissolved themselves and rejoined the Party. The Party's central organ, *al-Qa'idah*, was renamed *Ittihad al-Sha'b* (People's Unity). In September 1956, the Second Party Conference endorsed a document entitled 'Our Political Plan for Patriotic and National Liberation'. It specified that the immediate task was 'the formation of a patriotic government' which would put an end to Iraq's isolation from the Arab liberation movement and pursue an independent patriotic Arab policy.

During the political agitation which swept Iraq in autumn 1956 following the Tripartite attack on Egypt, the Communist Party took part in the joint 'Field Command' set up on 29 October 1956 which comprised the National Democrats, the Istiqlal Party, the Ba'th Party and independent democrats. The parties organized more than 200 demonstrations in 30 towns during the following two months. The Communists participated actively in all demonstrations and uprisings. Their slogans called for an end to the Baghdad Pact, cutting off oil supplies to the colonialists and the refusal of credits from the West. The first martyr of the uprising was a Communist, Awad Ridha al-Saffar.

Amid ruthless suppression by the authorities under the regime of martial law, the Central Committee issued a statement in December 1956 which stressed that 'violence' was now the predominant form of the people's struggle in order 'to overcome decisively the aggressiveness and violence of colonialism and its hireling regime in Iraq'. In the town of Hai, some 225 km. southeast of Baghdad, Communists led an armed uprising on 17 December 1956. Revolutionary committees and 'people's guards' organized resistance and erected barricades, and the insurrection was only put down after much bloodshed. On 10 January 1957, the authorities executed the secretary of the Hai Party Committee and another Communist leader. The gallows were mounted in the public square to terrorize the population.[32]

The Communist Party considered the stand of the Arab national bourgeois parties on the question of the national rights of the Kurdish people as one of the reasons for the failure of the 1956 uprising. It stressed the need for drawing the Kurdish masses into the joint struggle for the liberation of the Arab and Kurdish peoples.[33]

Following the suppression of the uprising, the Party continued to mobilize popular opposition to the Baghdad Pack and the 'Eisenhower Doctrine'. *Ittihad al-Sha'b* pointed out that the main aim of that Doctrine was 'to put an end to the Arab liberation movement under guise of combatting the "Communist danger" '.[34]

In late February 1957, the National Unity Front was formed, which included the Communist Party, the National Democrats, the Istiqlal Party and the Ba'th Party. Its 5-point programme came from the secret printing press of the Communist Party on 9 March 1957. A Supreme Committee was set up with representatives of the four parties. This alliance inspired a similar process among the Free Officers. The Communist Party developed relations and maintained contacts with the Free Officer Movement and its Supreme Committee till the eve of the 14 July 1958 revolution.[35] The Party also maintained a bi-lateral alliance with the United Kurdistan Democratic Party which was not admitted into the Front due to the nationalist reservations on the part of the other parties.

At the end of May 1958, *Ittihad al-Sha'b* declared: 'The rule of the traitors is collapsing. Let us prepare ourselves for the awaited moment'. On the night of 13–14 July 1958, the Party leadership placed its clandestine organizations on the alert. 'General directives' issued on 12 July also stressed 'the need for great vigilance towards various kinds of intrigues and conspiracies' and considered 'the mobilization of the widest popular masses in support of the correct slogans at any given moment and around the paramount watchwords of our patriotic democratic movement as our fundamental task under all conditions'.[36]

On the first day of the revolution, the Party declared its determination to defend it, and called upon the people to set up committees for the defence of the revolution. In a memorandum to the Prime Minister, Brigadier Qasim, on the same day it warned against aborting the revolutionary tide under the pretext of calls for 'preserving calm and tranquillity'. Subsequent memoranda on 20 and 27 July 1958 underlined the need for a complete purge of the whole state administration, abolishing the security apparatus, and organizing the people in defence of the revolution.

The Party machine emerged from clandestinity to lead within a few months the biggest revolutionary mass movement ever witnessed in the contemporary history of Iraq. Despite its exclusion from representation in the government, the Party continued to be the most influential political force in the country. Tens of thousands of people responded to its calls and joined the ranks of the democratic vocational organizations, which were still unlicensed at the time. During the first year of the revolution, more than a quarter of a million workers joined trade unions. After the promulgation of the *Land Reform Law 30* on 1 October 1958, under pressure of the revolutionary upsurge in the countryside, the Party raised the slogan of 'a peasant association for every village'. By April 1959, when the Union of Peasant Associations held its first conference, 3,000 such associations had been formed representing 200,000 peasants. By March 1959, membership of the Iraqi Women's League reached 20,000[37] and that of the Democratic Youth Federation reached 84,000.[38]

Despite the polarization of political forces which developed soon after the revolution, the Communist Party attempted to revive the National Unity Front. On 23 November 1958, its Supreme Committee issued a statement pledging to close ranks and settle differences democratically over the question of relations with the United Arab Republic. On 27 January 1959, the Front held its first public meeting in Baghdad and issued a Charter in March 1959.[39]

In January 1959, the Party organ *Ittihad al-Sha'b* was licensed and became a daily paper. The Party's own application for a licence in January 1960 was, however, rejected. It was the only party to be denied legality despite public pressure as demonstrated by petitions carrying 184,960 signatures collected in less than one month.[40]

The mass revolutionary upsurge and the leading role of the Communist Party in the struggle for radical socio-economic reforms aroused deep alarm among the national bourgeoisie which monopolized political power. On 1 May, 1959, a procession through Baghdad of more than 300,000 people reiterated popular demands for the participation of the Communist Party in the government. But the Party soon afterwards withdrew the demand for its inclusion in the government. A Central Committee resolution in July 1959 pointed out that this demand created misgivings 'among considerable sectors of the Iraqi and Arab bourgeoisie and many moderate forces', and thus increased the division within the national ranks. This retreat provided a golden opportunity for the regime and the anti-Communist forces which were hostile to the reforms brought about by the revolution. Repressive measures and restrictions on democratic freedoms, won after the revolution, were introduced. Under Qasim the regime turned into an autocratic dictatorship. Repeated promises by Qasim to 'end the transitional period' were not fulfilled. The Second National Congress of the Party in September 1970, in its re-appraisal of that period, pointed out:

> In the revolutionary situation which began on 14 July 1958 our Party should have pursued the struggle at the head of the revolutionary masses to change the government and set up a revolutionary democratic government, representing the patriotic parties and the forces concerned with fulfilling the national democratic revolution without any compromise in achieving this central slogan.

Democratic organizations were gradually banned and elections to trade unions, peasant societies and professional organizations were rigged and falsified. In November 1960, *Ittihad al-Sha'b* was closed down.

During the terror campaign, Communists were assassinated and many were executed after facing court martial. In his speech at the 22nd Congress of the Communist Party of the Soviet Union on 23 October 1961, the First Secretary of the ICP declared that up to that date 286 'Communists and democrats' had died 'in broad daylight' at the hands of assassins.[41] One source estimated that by the end of Qasim's regime, no fewer than 400 people had been killed in Mosul alone, and as many as 50,000 had been forced to migrate to Baghdad and other places.[42]

The Communist Party condemned the military actions against the Kurdish national movement in autumn 1961 and organized a big campaign demanding peace in Kurdistan. In a statement published on 23 March 1962, the Party demanded that the Constitution should stipulate the right of autonomy for Kurdistan within the framework of a democratic government of Iraq.[43] A demonstration by about 10,000 people in Baghdad on 29 April 1962 was violently dispersed by the police.

The Ba'th coup on 8 February 1963 unleashed a massacre of Communists. The 'Guardian' of 15 February 1963 estimated that '15,000 Communists have been rounded up and sent to unknown destinations'. A week later, on 22 February, the 'Times' reported that 'the new regime had killed or jailed 2,500 Communists'. King Husain of Jordan revealed in a press interview seven months later that 'numerous meetings were held between the Ba'th Party and American Intelligence' and that 'on 8 February a secret radio beamed to Iraq was supplying the men who pulled the coup with the names and addresses of the Communists there so that they could be arrested or executed'.[44]

The Communist Party organized armed resistance against the coup and battles raged in Baghdad and other towns for several days. Salam 'Adil, the Party's First Secretary, was arrested in late February and tortured to death. His 'execution' was announced on 7 March 1963. Communist cadres who had withdrawn to Iraqi Kurdistan formed partisan units which later joined in the armed struggle of the Kurdish national movement after the resumption of the fighting against government forces in June 1963.

Despite these severe blows, Communist soldiers and NCOs courageously attempted on 3 July 1963 to seize the most sensitive of Iraq's military camps – that of al-Rashid – in Baghdad. The uprising was headed by Sergeant Hasan Sirei. The uprising was unsuccessful and its leaders were executed. In the terror campaign that followed, two members of the Polit-bureau, Jamal al-Haidari and Muhammad Salih al-Aballi were arrested and executed. By the time of the first Ba'th regime's fall in November 1963, no fewer than 7,000 Communists were held in various prisons.[45] The Party's clandestine paper *Tariq al-Sha'b* and its radio station 'The Voice of the Iraqi People' played an active role in the anti-fascist agitation and the Party re-organization.

During the following years, the Party continued to struggle against the military-nationalist rule of the 'Arif brothers. The Central Committee meeting held in April 1965 called upon all opposition forces to unite their efforts to overthrow 'Arif's military regime and regarded armed actions as the principal form of people's struggle. The Third Party Conference in November-December 1967 re-emphasized calls for the overthrow of the reactionary regime, the setting up of coalition government and fulfilment of the tasks of the national democratic revolution. It endorsed armed struggle as the means of struggle. The policy outlined in the Conference helped to develop joint actions with other opposition forces. As the regime's crisis and isolation deepened, and was further aggravated following the June 1967 Israeli attack on Egypt, signs of a maturing revolutionary situation were detected by the Party. Communists were actively involved in workers' strikes and popular resistance.

After the Ba'th Party seized power again in the 17 July 1968 coup d'état, the Central Committee of the ICP held a meeting on 29 July 1968 to assess the new situation. It identified the Ba'th Party as 'a petty bourgeois nationalist party' and accordingly characterized the regime as anti-imperialist, anti-feudal, but also with dictatorial and anti-democratic tendencies. The meeting formulated the most outstanding demands and tasks. These included the elimination of terror and the restoration of democratic constitutional life; the democratic solution of the Kurdish problem on the basis of autonomy; securing the people's welfare and their economic interests; regaining Iraq's rights which had been usurped by the oil companies; eliminating spy networks and cleaning the state apparatus; strengthening the struggle against imperialism and Zionism, and forging close cooperation with the Socialist countries.

In October 1968, the Party called for a united front on the basis of equality, and the formation of a coalition government representing all patriotic parties and forces. It also stressed the principle of the recognition of the Party's independence and its right to legal political activity, and called for the abolition of the State of Emergency and anti-democratic laws. It declared its opposition to the notion of 'One-Party rule' and warned against attempts to impose it. A draft Charter for the Front, proposed by the Party in September 1968, was regarded by some forces as a suitable basis for dialogue.

During that period, the Communist Party followed a policy of general support for the positive steps taken by the regime in the field of socio-economic reforms and in foreign policy, but strongly criticized its anti-democratic policies and measures to monopolize power. The ICP called for the liberation of the oil wealth from the fetters of the foreign monopolies and for the setting up of a national oil sector with the help of the Socialist countries, particularly the Soviet Union. It supported the agreements signed by the government with the Soviet Union in July 1969 to develop the North Rumaila oil-field and with Poland and Hungary. When the Ba'thist regime resumed the war in Kurdistan in early 1969, the ICP called for a peaceful solution based on autonomous rule for the Kurdish people. It organized various mass activities and collected 18,000 signatures on a petition calling for an immediate halt to the fighting and for negotiations with representatives of the Kurdish people.

Meanwhile, the Ba'th Party was resuming its anti-Communist propaganda and terror to paralyse the Communist Party and other political forces. After the signing of the 11 March 1970 Agreement between the Ba'th Party and the Kurdistan Democratic Party (KDP), hundreds of Communists and their supporters were arrested and tortured. In a memorandum dated 27 April 1970 and addressed to the leadership of the KDP, the Central Committee of the ICP hailed the 11 March Agreement as 'a great victory of the Kurdish people and revolution' and stressed the importance of an alliance between the two parties. It also expressed the hope that the KDP would play 'its role in condemning the anti-communist campaign directed against our Party and the repression of the masses and patriotic forces'.[46]

A statement issued by the Communist Party in mid-May 1970 pointed out that the campaign of arrests was continuing: 'In order to show the extent reached by this campaign, we mention that in the province of Kut alone 150 communists and democrats were arrested'.[47] The statement demanded an end to torture and the abolition of the infamous 'Palace of the End' (*Qasr al-Nihayah*).

In September 1970, the ICP held its Second National Congress in Iraqi Kurdistan. Three leading cadres and delegates to the Congress – Sattar Khudhayyir, Muhammad al-Khudairi and 'Abd al-'Amir Sa'id – were assassinated or tortured to death just before that. The programme endorsed by the Congress pointed out that 'the 17–30 July 1968 coup d'etat did not change the character of the bourgeois regime but it transferred power to the hands of the petty and middle bourgeoisie, which despite some of the progressive steps it took, was not willing to put an end to despotic military rule but rather gave it a party (Ba'thist) character'.[48] The Congress declared that the party policy towards the regime

> will continue on the same basis of opposition and criticism of whatever is negative and wrong, opposing the anti-democratic and anti-communist policy of the government and its suppression of all the parties of the patriotic opposition, its violation of human rights and dignity, and of the manifestations of chauvinism, narrow nationalism and sectarianism. But at the same time, we shall support and back any progressive measure or any firm stand against colonialism, Zionism, feudalism and reaction.[49]

On the policy of alliances, the Congress called for continued efforts to set up the United Patriotic Front through a dialogue between all parties. But it stressed that it was essential for any serious move towards patriotic cooperation that the ruling Ba'th party should halt all forms of repression and provide a democratic climate.

The anti-Communist campaign continued unabated and in June 1971 over 40 members and cadres, including a member of the Central Committee, were arrested in Kirkuk and many were tortured to death. In response to calls by the Ba'th Party to set up the Front, the ICP replied that only in a democratic climate created by 'ending police terror . . . abolishing the "National Security" apparatus and the slaughter at *Qasr al-Nihayah* and its annexes. . . respecting human rights . . . and unfolding political and trade union rights, can there be any talk about cooperation and the United Front'.[50]

By late 1971, the regime was facing increasing isolation, and relations with the KDP became sour as deep differences arose with regard to the implementation of the 11 March 1970 Agreement. In a tactical move designed to bolster its position at home and withstand external pressures, the Ba'th Party made overtures to the Communist Party and signalled its readiness to enter into a dialogue for setting up a Patriotic Front.

After the Ba'th Party issued the draft National Action Charter on 15 November 1971, a prolonged dialogue between the two parties began. A special statement issued by the Communist Party Politburo on 27 November, while welcoming the proposed draft charter, stressed the necessity for the various parties 'to respect one another as parties that are independent ideologically, politically and organizationally'. It also highlighted, as a matter of 'great importance' for the Communists, that the regime should put a 'decisive end' to 'all forms of oppression' against them or 'against any other national forces'.[51]

The following period was marked by the confrontation with the Iraq Petroleum Company, which together with increasing internal political and economic difficulties forced the regime to adopt a number of measures in order to mobilize public support and overcome external pressures. On 9 April 1972, it signed a Treaty of Friendship and Cooperation with the Soviet Union. Two Communist ministers also joined the cabinet. On 1 June 1972, the Iraq Petroleum Company was nationalized. These developments, as well as signs of an improvement in the internal political climate, were evaluated positively by the Communist Party as a contribution to the creation of more suitable conditions for the alliance of patriotic forces.[52]

On 17 July 1973, the Communist and Ba'th parties signed the National Action Charter, only ten days after the failure of an attempted coup by Nadhim Kazzar, the head of the security apparatus, and the government's decision to tear down the notorious torture prison of *Qasr al-Nihayah* in Baghdad. The issue of the 'leading role' of the Ba'th in the Front, which was opposed by the Communist Party, was resolved and the final Charter stipulated that: 'The relations between the parties of the Progressive and National Front are based on mutual respect for the independence of each party, ideologically, politically and organizationally'.[53] In September 1973, official permission was granted for the clandestine organ of the Party, *Tariq al-Sha'b* (People's Path), to appear as a daily, in additon to the weekly *al-Fikr al-Jadid* (New Thought).

When fighting broke out between the Ba'thist regime and the Kurdish national movement in 1973, the ICP called for the peaceful and democratic implementation of the March 1970 Agreement and denounced the interference by imperialism and the Shah of Iran.

The Third National Congress of the ICP was held from 4–6 May 1976 under semi-clandestine conditions in Baghdad. The Congress pointed out the conditions for Iraq's advance along a socialist-orientated path. Measures were needed to block the development of capitalism and the growth of private capital, both in the towns and the countryside. The Congress also called for the promotion of democratic life and the establishment of constitutional democratic organs. On the Kurdish question, it called for the implementation of autonomy through reliance on the Kurdish people, the preservation of the local national structure of the population and respect for their national feelings and cultural rights and language.[54]

However, following the 1975 Algiers Accord with the Shah of Iran and the defeat inflicted on the Kurdish national movement, the Ba'th Party embarked upon a policy of extending its political and ideological hegemony in all spheres of life. In this endeavour, it was helped by the enormous rise in oil revenues which increased tenfold between 1972 and 1974. A substantial proportion of these revenues went to strengthen the state machinery, especially the organs of repression, intelligence and propaganda. The Communist Party thus came to be viewed as a serious obstacle and a potential threat to the Ba'th Party's aim of imposing one-party rule.

The Central Report of the 9th Regional Congress of the Ba'th Party (June 1982) provides a revealing account of how it viewed its relationship with the Communist Party during the period of alliance (1973–1978). One criticism was that

> the Communist party's activity among the masses and the orientation of its press paid no attention to the defence of the revolutionary regime and safeguarding the great revolutionary gains it achieved. It was most rare to find Communists evaluate positively the Arab Ba'th Socialist Party and the 17–30 July revolution, and its achievements and leadership . . they tended to concentrate on a few negative aspects and mistakes which are a natural manifestation in a big revolutionary march.[55]

The same Report also attacked the Communist Party's policy on the Kurdish problem and accused it of striving to impose its hegemony in Kurdistan after the defeat suffered by the Kurdish national movement in 1975.[56] The Report made a striking admission of its fear of Communist influence when it claimed that 'it was not possible within the framework of this unstable relationship' with the ICP leadership 'to set up democratic institutions . . . It would not have been correct, frankly speaking, to provide a new platform which the ICP leadership could use under the cover of the Front to defame the Party and the Revolution and implement foreign strategies. The delay in setting up the National Assembly is thus partly due to this reason'.[57]

By 1979 the anti-Communist campaign intensified, and detained Communists were subjected to torture to force them to recant and pledge not to engage in any political activity other than through the ruling Ba'th Party. The campaign was stepped up following the publication of the report of the Central Committee plenum of 10 March 1978 which sharply criticized Ba'thist political and economic policies. It called for an end to the State of Emergency, for free general elections and a constituent National Assembly, and for a halt to the process of Arabization and Ba'thization of Iraqi Kurdistan. In May 1978, 31 Communist Party members and supporters were executed in army camps under the pretext that they had set up party cells in the armed forces. Some of the victims, among them Suhail Sharhan and 'Abd al-Zahra Muhsin, had been languishing in prison for several years. The Ba'thist leadership claimed, a few years later, in an attempt to justify the executions, that these had been delayed because of 'an error committed by one of the specialized organs'.[58]

In addition to the deep differences between the two parties over the issues of political democracy and the solution of the Kurdish national question, differences also developed over a wide range of Arab and regional issues. The ICP was strongly critical of Ba'th Party policy towards Syria and the PLO, which culminated in attacks and assassinations of representatives of the latter abroad. The ICP also opposed the negative stand of the regime towards the Steadfastness and Confrontation Front which emerged after Sadat's visit to Jerusalem and included Syria, Algeria, Libya and Democratic Yemen. Instead, the Ba'th Party advocated the so-called 'minimum programme' of the Baghdad Arab Summit of 1978. In contrast to the deep concern of the Ba'th regime at the triumph of the Iranian revolution and the overthrow of its ally the Shah, the ICP Central Committee sent warm telegrams of congratulations to the leaders of the new regime in Tehran.[59] An article by a member of the Politburo of the Communist Party and the editor-in-chief of *Tariq al-Sha'b*, stated that the victory of the Iranian people aroused 'optimism and joy in the circles of progressive forces the world over; meanwhile, it caused fear and panic in the circles of imperialism, reaction and Zionism which are behind the Shah's regime, giving it support and assistance.'[60]

In mid-May 1979, the Central Committee of the ICP issued a statement giving a detailed account of the anti-Communist campaign. It pointed out that

> all Communist party offices have been closed down in all provinces; the central organ of the party has been banned; the party no longer has representatives, either in the Cabinet or in the Patriotic Front, and with that the very existence of the Front has come to an end and our party is no longer bound to any decision taken in the name of the Front. . . For the Ba'th Party, the Patriotic Front is no longer anything but a propaganda office serving its own ends'.

On the economic front, the statement said that the Ba'thist concept of socialism 'has come to mean perpetuation of the private sector along with state capitalism'.[61]

In late July 1979, the Central Committee of the ICP held a meeting and declared the Party's open opposition to the Ba'th regime under the slogan: 'For a Democratic Patriotic Front to End the Dictatorship and Establish a Democratic System of Government in Iraq'. Communist partisan units were formed later that year in Iraqi Kurdistan.

The July 1979 plenum had forecast the regime's course towards a head-on clash with Iran. Its statement pointed out that the regime was 'provoking a deliberate conflict with the Iranian revolution', and that 'this course of hostility. . has been met with the encouragement and the instigation of the imperialist quarters and their mass media'. A communiqué issued by the Central Committee plenary meeting in June 1980 recalled the efforts made by the ruling clique 'to win US imperialist support for assuming the role of gendarme in the Gulf as a substitute for the regime of the Shah'.

Two days after the start of the war against Iran on 24 September 1980, the ICP issued a statement holding the Ba'th regime fully responsible for it. After analysing the motives behind the war, it affirmed that 'the ruling clique in Baghdad also aims at finding a way out of its grave crisis by engaging our people in this dirty war and fomenting national prejudice and bigotry'. Two months later, on 24 November 1980, another statement remarked with foresight that 'the terrorist clique which has ventured to unleash this war . . has also been bogged down in a predicament of which it can never come out unscathed'.[62]

In November 1980, the Communist Party established the Democratic Patriotic Front (DPF) which also included the Kurdistan Democratic Party and the Kurdistan Socialist Party. The DPF's programme called for the overthrow of the dictatorship and a democratic coalition government, the end of repression and terror, and true autonomy for Kurdistan in Iraq. The alliance also initiated a higher level of coordination between Communist partisans and Kurdish Pesh Merga fighters.

At the Central Committee plenum of November 1981, armed struggle was adopted as the main form of struggle along with other forms of struggle. It stressed that 'the only revolutionary solution to the crisis that is blowing in the country and mercilessly grinding the people, will depend, above all, on stepping up the struggle in its various forms, on preparing the masses for a victorious popular revolution that will overthrow the dictatorship and set up on its ruins a national democratic coalition government'. When the Ba'th rulers announced the withdrawal of their armed forces from most of the occupied Iranian territories in summer 1982, after successive defeats, the Communist Party concluded that 'this measure did not change the aggressive nature of the war, nor did it absolve the fascist dictatorship of the crime of starting it'.[63] It also stressed that the central task in struggle, i.e. the overthrow of the dictatorship and the setting up of a democratic coalition government, will remain 'an internal affair and an inalienable right of our people which cannot be encroached upon by imposing an alternative that falls short of realizing their rights and democratic freedoms, above all, the right to decide the form of government they want'.[64] In a comprehensive interview, published in August 1983, 'Aziz Muhammad, the First Secretary of the Central Committee, pointed out that 'the predominant sentiment among the masses in Iraq is one that generally rejects the Iranian model of political system in favour of the slogan "A Democratic Coalition Government"'.[65]

In early May 1983, forces of the Patriotic Union of Kurdistan (PUK), led by Jalal Talabani, attacked the headquarters of the ICP and its DPF allies in the region of Pesht Ashan, killing 62 partisans and wounding many others. The PUK, a nationalist organization incorporating a pseudo-Marxist faction, had vied for the leadership of the Kurdish national movement after the collapse of the armed movement led by the KDP in 1975. It adopted a hostile attitude towards the Democratic Patriotic Front and sabotaged various attempts by the ICP to reconcile it with the KDP. Despite claims to the contrary, the PUK had entered into secret negotiations with the Ba'th rulers in 1982. The PUK attack was seen by the Democratic Patriotic Front forces as a treacherous move carried out in collusion with the Ba'th regime. Subsequent developments and the negotiations between the PUK leadership and the regime confirmed this interpretation.

In summer 1984, the Communist partisans and the party's clandestine radio station 'Voice of the Iraqi People' played an active role in the student and popular rising which swept Iraqi Kurdistan.

In 1984, the ICP celebrated its Golden Jubilee Year. A plenary meeting of its Central Committee held in late June and early July 1984 called for 'intensified struggle to overthrow the fascist dictatorship' and an end to the Iraq–Iran war 'on the basis of a just democratic peace founded on: a) Non-annexation by either side of the other side's territory b) Respect for the international border of the two countries as it was before the war c) Respect for the national sovereignty of the two peoples over their territory d) Recognition of every people's right to choose the socio-political system that meets their free will'.[66]

The Central Committee statement also re-iterated the determination to step up the struggle for a democratic alternative represented by a democratic coalition government, open to all anti-Fascist patriotic forces, 'that will redress the consequences and tragic aftermath of the war, unfold the people's democratic freedoms, eliminate all forms of national, ethnic or sectarian discrimination, and enable the popular masses to build a democratic Iraq in which the Kurdish people will enjoy genuine autonomy'.[67]

The Islamic Movement

Iraqi society contains a multitude of ethnic groups and sects. In addition to the two principal ethnic groups, Arabs and Kurds, there are ethnic minorities such as the Assyrians, Armenians, Turkomans and Yazidis. Besides the Muslims, who constitute the majority of the population, there exists a number of smaller religious groups, including Christians and Jews. The Christian community constitutes about 5% of the population.

The majority of the Arab population follows the Shi'i sect of Islam and constitute nearly 55% of Iraq's population. There are no precise statistics to refer to, since no census provides details of Sunni and Shi'i, but the following rough geographical distribution of the three groups, Sunni Arabs,

Shi'i Arabs, and Kurds (the majority of whom are Sunni) may be useful. The south, below Baghdad, is predominantly Shi'i, the centre-west is predominantly Sunni Arabs, and the north-east is predominantly Kurdish. Estimates provided by Farouk-Sluglett and Sluglett based on the 1956 census, indicate that the Sunnis constituted the bulk of the urban population and in particular of the population of the capital Baghdad (850,000 inhabitants). Eighty per cent of the south was classified as rural.[68] The population of the whole country in 1957 was 6.4 million of whom 39% were classified as urban and 61% rural. By 1978, however, the population had reached about 12 million, with 63% urban and 37% rural. The population of metropolitan Baghdad increased sharply from 856,000 in 1956 to 1.5 million in 1965 and 3.2 million in 1981. The inhabitants of al-Thawra township in Baghdad, which now accounts for more than a quarter of the entire population of the capital, are mainly peasant tribal migrants from the rural south of Kut and 'Amarah and thus predominantly Shi'i.

Sunnism is the larger of the two Muslim sects and its followers from the majority of the population in most Islamic countries except Iran and Iraq. Sunnis are strictly orthodox in their obedience to the Qur'an and in the emphasis they place on following the deeds and utterances of the Prophet Muhammad. The distinctive belief of the Shi'i sect, which differentiates it from Sunnism, is that 'Ali, the fourth caliph, and his own descendants, are considered the only legitimate successors of Muhammad. Imam 'Ali was the son-in-law and cousin of the Prophet, and was the first male to accept Islam. His caliphate lasted almost five years and ended in 661 AD when he was stabbed while praying in the mosque at Kufa in southern Iraq. According to Shi'i doctrine, the leader of Islam, the Imam, must be a descendant of 'Ali and has exclusive authority in secular and religious matters. Infallibility is considered a necessary attribute of an Imam. He should also be free of sin as well as infallible.[69] The Shi'is differ among themselves as to the true line of Imams after a certain stage. Some, known as the 'twelvers', expect the return of the twelfth Imam (who disappeared in the 9th century) at the end of time, while others recognize a different line from the seventh Imam onwards. Afterwards, the Imamate was extended to the institution of the indirect representatives of the Hidden Imam, the *marji'iya*.[70] The *marji's* ('authorities') are the most important *mujtahids* (legists capable of giving a *fatwa* or binding legal or religious opinion) who are addressed as *Ayatullah al-'Uzma* ('the Great Sign of God'). Their *fatwas* are, as a rule, final unless revoked by the highest *marji'*, which is unusual.[71]

In the 8th century AD, a group of Shi'is recognized Isma'il the son of Ja'far al-Sadiq as the true Imam, while the rest of the Shi'is supported his brother Musa. In 909, the Fatimid caliphate was established and its rulers were Isma'ili Imams. Fatimid rule in Egypt and North Africa continued until 1171, contesting control of the Muslim world with the 'Abbasid dynasty of Baghdad. The Isma'ilis developed several doctrines and eventually split into many subsects. One of the best organized Isma'ili sects was the Carmathian movement which came into being in Kufa in the late 9th Century AD. It set up a clandestine organization and later established its state in Bahrain which lasted till the end of the 11th century. The Isma'ili and Carmathian movements illustrate that Shi'ism was identified, at an early stage, with the rebellion and struggle of the downtrodden and oppressed in the Islamic empire, and its doctrines accommodated their aspirations for social justice and equality.

Some contemporary Shi'i writers argue that Shi'ism existed even during the lifetime of the Prophet Muhammad as a devotional trend, 'believing in devotion to the religion and its arbitration, and in total submission to the religious texts, in every sphere of life.'[72] They consider it opposed to a second trend, 'which believed that belief in the Religion did not necessitate devotion except in the special scope of religious observances and metaphysics, and believed in the possibility of *ijtihad* (independent judgement), and the permissibility of making judgements on this basis with changes and modifications in the religious texts according to their interests in matters other than in the above in the sphere of life'.

Southern Iraq is the heartland of Shi'ism as it was here that the first Imam, 'Ali, and his son Husain, fought and died. The main Shi'i shrines are located in Najaf, Karbala', Kadhimain (in Baghdad) and Samarra' in Iraq, and in Qum and Mashhad in Iran. Among the most important occasions for the Shi'a is *'ashura*, the tenth of the Islamic month of Muharram, when they commemorate the martyrdom of Imam Husain in 680 AD on the plains of Karbala in a battle with the forces sent to Iraq by the second Umayyad caliph, Yazid. His tomb in Karbala has become a major shrine.

Because of the nature of Shi'i religious belief, the *'ulama* or religious scholars occupied a particularly vital place in the Holy Cities. Thus Najaf, Karbala and Kadhimain were not only religious seminaries but the centres of a living religious organization, in the sense that the *mujtahids,* individually or collectively, could pronounce authoritatively on matters of faith and doctrine affecting their followers. The *mujtahids* could and do still function as the guardians-of-the-day of a living tradition; they were consulted, or gave their views spontaneously, on a wide variety of issues.

Although the Shi'is predominate in Iraq and Iran, the majority of Muslims are, and always have been, Sunnis. As no guidelines for the succession of the Prophet Muhammad were laid down in the Qur'an, the question of legitimacy has always been open. In broad terms, two major Sunni dynasties ruled over most of the classical Islamic world; the Umayyads (661–750), with their capital at Damascus, and their successors the 'Abbasids, who ruled in Baghdad until the time of their overthrow by the Mongols in 1258. After 1258 — although signs of decay and disunity had already manifested themselves since the mid-10th century — no single dynasty could claim to represent all Muslims. The most extensive Islamic empire to follow the 'Abbasids was that of the Ottomans, which, at the height of its power in the 16th and early 17th centuries, extended over most of southern Europe, what is now Turkey, the Arab Middle East and North Africa excluding Morocco. An important Shi'i dynasty, the Fatimids, ruled Egypt and most of Syria between the 10th and 13th centuries and the first wholly Shi'i dynasty to come to power in Iran was that of the Safavids, whose rule between 1501 and 1732 ensured the primacy of Shi'ism in Iran which it has held ever since. Although the men of religion generally tended to co-operate with the Safavids and their successors, an important theme in the history of the 'twelver' Shi'ism has always been the notion that worldly government is a necessary evil, to tide mankind over until the twelfth Imam returns from occulation, when some final day of judgement will take place. This often led to the adoption of an oppositional role on the part of the Shi'i clergy, as expressed in the national protest of Iran over the tobacco monopoly being given to a foreign company in 1891–92, the Constitutional Revolution of 1905-09, throughout the 1960s and of course most recently in Iran since 1978.

Shi'ism in 20th Century Iraq

According to Sluglett, the Shi'is in the Ottoman Empire as a whole occupied a position very roughly analogous to that of Roman Catholics in England before 1829.[73] They were excluded from public office, and not able, except in internal matters in their own centres, to use their own code of law. Apart from the expeditions to destroy the powers of the clans of Karbala and Najaf in the middle 19th century, the Ottoman authorities did not exert particularly forcible control over the Holy Cities. Najaf and Karbala were more or less independent enclaves in which the Ottomans tended not to intervene unless provoked.

In the period before 1914, the position of the traditional Shi'i religious leadership, as well as that of the tribal shaikhs, had been undergoing a gradual transformation as fragmentation accompanied the process of agricultural and pastoral settlement. *Fatwas* were still pronounced by the *'ulama* in the Holy Cities whose effect was binding. Here, however, the apparatus of authority existed more to issue condemnation against established governments elsewhere than to act as an alternative political body.

After the outbreak of World War I, Turkish requisitioning and conscription caused risings in Karbala and Najaf, which ousted the Turks. By 1915-16 autonomous regimes had been instituted by the townspeople in both cities, and tactful overtures, together with payments of subsidies, had been made by the British political staffs of the Mesopotamia Expeditionary Force.[74] After the capture of Baghdad in March 1917, the British apparently intended that the Shi'i Holy Places should form a separate enclave not under direct British control, but in fact British political officers were sent to Najaf and Karbala later in the year. Although there were no signs of serious resistance to the British authorities at the time, there were disturbances at the end of March 1918 and a British officer was killed. Fines were levied and some eleven people were publicly executed for their alleged complicity in the officer's murder. Sluglett notes that the difficulties encountered by the British there probably derived from a power struggle between the *'ulama* and the rest of the community which had begun long before the Political Officers arrived, during the townspeople's brief period of power, in an attempt to curb the power of the clergy within the city. During soundings known as the 'plebiscite' of late 1918 and early 1919, there was clearly very little enthusiasm within the Holy Cities for any kind of British controlled regime for Iraq as a whole.[75]

Under British occupation, the situation in the towns changed relatively little from what it had been under Ottoman rule. Townsmen continued to supply the main cadres for the administration and the army, either from the notable families of Baghdad and Mosul or the so-called nationalists, many of whom were ex-Ottoman officers and officials. As urban Shi'is worked mainly in commerce or in the theological centres, there was no pool of trained Ottoman Shi'i officials to draw on.

During the period of uncertainty between the end of the war and the establishment of the Provisional Government in 1920, strong anti-British sentiments developed in Iraq. There was no sign of the self-determination promised by President Wilson's 14 Points and in the Anglo-French Declaration of November 1918, nor of the formation of any national assembly. The Shi'i and Sunni *'ulama* supported the nationalists in the anti-British rising in June 1920, an alliance which was vital in order to involve the tribal leaders and incite them to revolt. Subsequently, many Karbala'i *'ulama* were arrested in June 1922 and sent to the prison island of Henjam for circulating a letter purporting to originate from the premier *mujtahid* of Karbala, Mirza Taqi al-Din al-Shirazi, urging the defence of Islam against 'the infidels'.[76]

After regaining control of the country by late 1920, the British High Commissioner Sir Percy Cox initiated direct contacts with the tribal leaders, refusing to allow the *'ulama* to act as intermediaries to arrange a truce on behalf of the tribes. The regime introduced after the 1920 rising took little account of the Shi'i leadership, and until January 1921, when al-Tabataba'i was given the Ministry of Education, no Shi'i had been offered a portfolio in the National Government.[77]

Amid opposition to the treaty with Britain and widespread nationalist agitation, a leading *'alim* of Kadhimain, Shaikh Mahdi al-Khalisi, declared a number of anti-mandate demands in April 1922. But he also included demands for half the Cabinet and half the government officials to be Shi'i. In the autumn of 1922, the elderly and conservative *mujtahids* al-Na'ini and al-Isfahani signed a *fatwa* forbidding Shi'i participation in the coming elections. To silence them, al-Khalisi was deported and al-Na'ini and al-Isfahani were asked to leave. They were all regarded as Persian subjects. al-Khalisi never returned, but the two latter *mujtahids* were allowed to re-enter Iraq on condition that they revoked their anti-election *fatwas* and undertook not to take an active part in politics.[78]

During that period, according to the information in the files of the British political police, some of the *'ulama* were among the first Iraqis to make connections with the Bolsheviks in Russia. In particular, Mirza Muhammad Ridha, son of the chief religious authority of the Shi'i sect, was reported to have advocated the idea of Muslim-Bolshevik cooperation during 1920 and 1921.[79] In January 1920, a pamphlet entitled 'Bolshevism and Islam' was in circulation in Baghdad. It represented one of the earliest attempts to create sympathy among the Muslim peoples for the Bolshevik revolution.[80] Contacts and meetings were also reported between exiled Iraqi *'ulama* in Persia and Soviet representatives in the winter of 1922-23.[81] The great *mujtahid* Shaikh Mahdi al-Khalisi in Kadhimain is reported to have paid a tribute to Lenin, published by the Soviet periodical 'New Times' in the 1950s: 'The East awakened by you waits for the moment to translate into reality your cherished ideas of alliance of the Eastern nations, of the right of every individual and every nation, big or small, cultured or backward, to life and independence.'[82] Sluglett notes that before 1923, the *'ulama* tended to encourage rather than actually instigate action by tribal leaders:

> apart from the direct encouragement given to tribal leaders in 1920 by the *'ulama* it was frequently the case that the tribal leaders themselves sought validation of their anti-British or anti-Government activities rather than passively accepting the dictates of their religious leaders.[83]

In 1925, Shi'i tribal leaders did not respond to appeals by religious leaders, like Muhammad al-Sadr, to support the Government's campaign to introduce conscription and against increased British influence in the army. Fearing that conscription would deprive them of their own corps of armed retainers they were quite content that the British should continue to command.

Some Shi'i leaders, particularly the founders of *Hizb al-Nahdha* (Renaissance Party) also attempted to bargain with the government, trying to obtain their demands for a higher proporton of places in the civil service in return for their support for the conscription bill. The formation of *Hizb al-Nahdha* in 1927 had been encouraged by the British authorities to press for Shi'i rights in an attempt to make use of the conflict potential which the sectarian divisions contained. It was led by Amin al-Charchafchi and included the *'alim* Muhammad Kashif al-Ghita' and tribal leaders. When their demands were not met by the Government, they turned almost unanimously to Britain to look after their interests.[84] The government, while not conceding Shi'i demands, paid off the noisier and more powerful shaikhs with tax remissions and beneficial land legislation, frightened the *'ulama* into silence and paid attention to the urban politicians as and when the need arose. Tribal revolts during the 1920s and 1930s were often struggles for power between different levels of the tribal leadership.

For the next few years, the Shi'i opposition ceased to be an active source of danger to the regime, and by the time of the next serious revolt, in 1935, the Iraqi Army had become sufficiently powerful to crush all but the most carefully organized tribal forces.

An important factor in the weakened influence of the Shi'i *'ulama* among tribal leaders was the policy pursued by the British soon after the occupation. In order to create a social base for the new regime, individuals were nominated by the British intelligence services to act as tribal shaikhs, and were officially invested with juridical, and later financial, authority over their tribes. Some were 'tribal shaikhs' whose position had waned considerably by World War I. This policy was continued by the Iraqi government in the 1920s and 1930s, and in return for their cooperation and support, the Shi'i shaikhs were given influence, authority, membership of parliament, and so forth.[85] Numerous peasant revolts against the despotic powers of the shaikhs were put down with great ferocity. As Farouk-Sluglett and Sluglett correctly point out, over the following decades until the 1958 Revolution, the real conflict in the south was between the landlords and the peasants, both of which happened to be Shi'i. 'The conflict is thus one of class and not one of sect'.[86]

Batatu also points out that many of the rural Shi'is were relatively recently converted to Shi'ism, and many of the more important tribes had turned to Shi'ism only within the last 180 years or so.[87] An important factor in the conversion of the tribespeople turned peasants was that the anti-government motif of Shi'ism, its preoccupation with oppression, its grief-laden symbols, accorded with their instincts and sufferings. The agricultural, sheep-tending, or marsh-dwelling tribespeople are not strict in their Shi'ism or well versed in their faith. On the whole they conform to certain traditional rites and participate in the great religious rituals, such as the *'ashura*, but are by and large lax about their prayers or in keeping the Ramadan fast. Until the 1958 Revolution and even afterwards they continued to be governed more by their ancient tribal customs than by the *shari'a* (Islamic Law) as developed and interpreted by the highest authoritative legists of the day.[88]

The fact that religion was very feebly organized in the overwhelmingly Shi'i rural districts in the 1940s is clearly borne out by figures from the census of 1947. In the southern districts which accounted for more than 49% of the total rural population of Iraq at the time, there were only 39 religious institutions, an average of one for every 37,000 persons.[89] A Shi'i 'religious institution' refers to such things as mosques, religious schools and *husayniyahs* (places for lamenting the martyrdom of Imam Husain in the Muslim month of Muharram). The Kurdish Sunni rural belt, however, had large numbers of *takiyahs* and *khanaqas* (dervish places of retreat and prayer). The 1947 census also showed that when the population was about 4.5 million (it is about 14 million at present), the number of persons employed in the 'religious services' of all denominations did not exceed 7,763. More than one-sixth of the total were concentrated in the Shi'i Holy Cities. Another sign of the dwindling influence of the Shi'i *'ulama* (men of religion) was the continuing decrease in the number of students of religion. While no fewer than 6,000 students attended the theological schools of Najaf in 1918, the number had declined to 1,954 by 1957, of whom only 326 were Iraqis (896 were from Iran, 665 from the Indian sub-continent and the rest from Arab countries).[90]

The scarcity of religious institutions can partly be explained by the fact that vast segments of the countryside were the home of semi-mobile tribal societies. Large areas also consisted of permanent or seasonal marshland. Another important factor in weakening the influence of religion in general, and of the traditional Shi'i clergy in particular, was the rise of Communism and its widespread influence among the poor peasants in the countryside, who suffered under their feudal landlords and tribal shaikhs, and also among the urban population whose ranks were swelled by hundreds of thousands of peasant tribespeople migrants from the countryside. The population of Baghdad doubled between 1927 and 1947. The Iraqi Communist Party challenged the authority of the landlords and highlighted the misery suffered by poor peasants and championed their right to own the land they worked. In the towns, the Communists championed the rights of the urban poor who lived in miserable conditions.

Organized Political Activity

Despite the active role of the *'ulama* in the 1920 rising, the religious movement did not constitute an organized political movement with clear and definite programmes and aims. It was rather the case that prominent religious figures sometimes played an active role in the political struggles. As the influence of the Shi'i *'ulama* dwindled in the following decades, some *ayatullahs* collaborated with the British, and were thus labelled as *al-'ulama al-Hafiz* (*al-Hafiz* is a corruption of the English word 'office' and is a term of opprobrium).[92] The religious movement as an 'organized political force' thus had no role in the uprisings of 1948, 1952 and 1956. It was not represented in the National Unity Front set up in 1957, prior to the July 1958 Revolution. It is noteworthy that Sunni political movements such as the Muslim Brotherhood, which exercise greater influence in other countries such as Egypt and Jordan, were virtually non-existent in Iraq.

After the 14 July 1958 Revolution, and in the face of the revolutionary mass upsurge, the more reactionary religious leaders — both Sunni and Shi'i — began to oppose democratic reforms. *Fatwas* were given which considered land reform, nationalization and other socio-economic measures as *haram* (religiously forbidden). Calls were made by some of the clergy to combat Communism, to the extent of legitimizing the killing of Communists, at a time when the term 'Communist' was used to describe all supporters of the July Revolution.[93] A number of Islamic organizations attempted to attain legality and applied to the Ministry of Interior in February 1960 for a license. The programme of one such group, *al-Hizb al-Islami al-'Iraqi* (Iraqi Islamic Party) declared its hostility to 'all the atheistic ideas and concepts which only recognized materialism' and considered the dissemination of such ideas as 'destructive for society and cannot be tolerated'.[94] Another group, *Hizb al-Tahrir* (Liberation Party) advocated a closely similar programme that also called for the full and universal application of Islamic rules and teachings in all spheres of life. The applications of both parties for licences were rejected by the Ministry of Interior. But the Islamic Party appealed against the Ministry's ruling and was granted legality. It was fiercely anti-Communist and used its paper *al-Heyad* (Neutrality) to attack Communists and democratic forces.[95] It continued its activity till 1961 when all political parties ceased functioning legally and their papers were suppressed.

The pronounced sectarian policy of the 'Arif regime (1963–66), manifested in increased discrimination against the Shi'i majority of the population, gave rise to widespread resentment. The emergence of the Fatimiyah group in 1964 reflected the earliest signs of restlessness on the part of the *'ulama*. But it was soon penetrated by the political police and effectively dispersed.[96] A special branch was set up within the Directorate of Public Security devoted exclusively to combatting underground Shi'i activities.

In 1964, Ayatullah Khomeini was expelled from his native Iran to Turkey and was then granted asylum in Najaf. His stern and unswerving idealism is reported to have had a significant influence within the circle of *'ulama* at Najaf.

According to Batatu, it was not 'Islamic revival' or ascendant Shi'ism that prompted the clergy in Najaf to organize ranks in the late 1960s, and set up the *Da'wa* (Islamic Call) Party. Instead, they were moved by a growing fear that the old faith was receding, especially among the educated and the urban Shi'i masses, and that their prestige and material influence was declining.[97] But an important factor was also that under the rule of the Ba'th Party, which came to power in 1968, Shi'i resentment increased as a reaction to the regime's efforts to interfere with some of the religious rituals, to weaken the authority of the religious hierarchy, and to impose certain political slogans on them.

The founding of the *Da'wa* Party in 1968 or 1969 is identified by many Shi'is with Sayyid Muhsin al-Hakim, the highest *marji'* of the day. In 1969, he was subjected to surveillance and harassment by the authorities. His son, Mahdi al-Hakim, who was accused by the government of 'spying on behalf of the CIA', was associated with the *Da'wa* from the very beginning.[98] Ayatullah Khomeini apparently had no hand in the rise of the *Da'wa* Party. One reason could be that in the earliest phase of its history the *Da'wa* had links, probably of an indirect nature, with the Shah of Iran who was at loggerheads with the Ba'th at the time.[99]

A major clash with the regime occurred in February 1977 when attempts by the police forces to interfere with the religious processions, halfway between Najaf and Karbala, triggered off massive demonstrations. Order was only restored after a large army contingent had been sent in and many arrests were made. Later, eight Shi'i dignitaries, five clergy and three laymen, were sentenced to death and executed.[100]

The second half of the 1970s witnessed the intensified application of the policy of Ba'thization, imposing the total hegemony of the Ba'th Party in all spheres of life. This process was accompanied by a policy of escalating repression of the Iraqi Communist Party, including the liquidation of scores of its cadres and members in 1978. The severe blows dealt to the Communist Party organizations thus helped to produce a temporary void in the political underground movement. The revolutionary upheaval in Iran also had a significant impact and provided an inspiring example that generated sympathy and support for the religious forces. In October 1978, as the anti-Shah movement intensified in Iran, the Ba'th regime expelled Ayatullah Khomeini. This provocative step was soon followed up by a visit to Baghdad by the Shah's wife, Empress Farah Diba, who was escorted around the Holy Places by Saddam Husain.[101]

Early in 1980, after a number of grenade attacks in Baghdad blamed on the *Da'wa* Party, tens of thousands of people were expelled to Iran, in brutal conditions, under the pretext that they were of 'Iranian origin'. On 19 April 1980, the Shi'a leader Sayyid Muhammad Baqir al-Sadr, and his sister Bint al-Huda, were executed after being held under house arrest in Najaf. A decree by the ruling Revolution Command Council banned the *Da'wa* Party and made *Da'wa* membership punishable by death. al-Sadr had no political or organizational connection with either the *Da'wah* or other groups. But as he was the most distinguished Shi'i legist, he was looked upon for political leadership.[102] After the Iranian revolution he was increasingly regarded by the Ba'th regime as a potential threat. The other Iraqi chief *marji'*, Abu'l-Qasim al-Khu'i, remained wrapped up in religion and was determined not to sanction or oppose the government.

Among other more recent active Islamic organizations is the Organization of Islamic Action which was formed in 1979, nearly five months after the victory of the Iranian revolution. *Jam'iyyat al-'Ulama al-Mujahidin* (The Community of Combatant 'Ulama), which is more like an umbrella organization, was formed in 1981 by Ayatullah Muhammad Baqir al-Hakim, with the blessing of Iran, in an attempt to close Shi'i ranks.

It is difficult to assess the real strength of the various Shi'i underground forces, but the scale of opposition to the regime and the latter's ruthless clampdown indicate that the *Da'wa* was the strongest group. During the past few years, the Islamic Action Organization has been noted for carrying out a number of successful armed operations in Baghdad. There is, however, no evidence available of any level of activity by the third group, *Jam'iyyat al-'Ulama*.

The ideological basis of these organizations is generally fairly similar. They all consider that the process of historical development is merely a conflict between 'atheism' and belief.[103] They tend to exaggerate the role of the religious movement and its real potential, and also avoid entering into economic analyses. In their political organization and outlook the movements have been influenced to a great extent by the revolutionary upheaval in Iran. During recent years, they have been increasingly subjugated, organizationally and politically, to the influence of the ruling clergy in Iran. All Iraqi Islamic organizations are now based in Tehran and are entirely dependent on the material and financial support of the Iranian regime. Rivalry and in-fighting are rife, and the setting up of the Supreme Assembly for the Islamic Revolution in Iraq (SAIRI) on 17 November 1982 'as a step along the path of uniting their political and military work' was seen as an attempt to unify the various groupings by force under a single command directly supervised by their Iranian counterparts. SAIRI has declared its unequivocal subordination to Ayatullah Khomeini as the supreme commander of the

Islamic nation.

The *Da'wa* Party has advanced some political views and statements, addressed to the political forces in Iraq, calling for the unity of the opposition ranks in order to overthrow Saddam's dictatorship.[104] However, after joining SAIRI, the *Da'wa* Party retreated fully from some of its more positive stands and from the call for a dialogue among the opposition forces which was included in its 'Manifesto for Mutual Understanding' of 1980. The Islamic Action Organization seems not to recognize the need for a patriotic alliance, but rather to put emphasis on the unity of Islamic organizations. However, it stipulates as a condition for such unity acceptance of the principle of *wilayat al-Faqih*, 'vice-regency of the Islamic jurist', and the establishment of an Islamic government in Iraq under the leadership of Imam Khomeini. A representative of this organization justified absolute dependence on Iran by claiming 'it is based on our relationship to the sole Islam, the sole leader and the sole state.'[105] Iraq is seen as part of the 'great Islamic homeland'. The official organ of this organization, *al-Jihad*, attributed the emergence of political parties and movements, and right-wing and left ideological trends in Iraq, to the absence of Islamic religious organization in the past.[106] SAIRI, which includes the three above-mentioned organizations, is based in Tehran and issues a weekly paper *al-Shahadah*. It has Muhammad Baqir al-Hakim of Najaf as its official spokesman. He is the son of the late Sayyid Muhsin al-Hakim of Najaf, a senior Shi'i *marji'* who died in 1970.

It is noteworthy that the impetus given to these organizations by the victory of the Iranian revolution in 1979, as manifested by their armed operations inside Iraq (particularly in Baghdad), has receded for a number of reasons. The most significant among these is their diminished influence inside Iraq following ruthless campaigns of repression and deportation, which has weakened their organizations. The execution of Muhammad Baqir al-Sadr has also dealt a heavy blow to the movement and caused it to lack an effective overall guidance and unifying symbol, as well as any intellectual significance. Developments in Iran and the suppression of democratic freedoms have also had a profound impact. The Iranian Islamic system is no longer an inspiring example for the Iraqi people who have long been deprived of their fundamental rights and are longing to enjoy political democracy and the freedoms which have been ruthlessly suppressed under Ba'thist rule. Furthermore, the intensified struggles of the patriotic and democratic forces has helped to unite broad sections of the people, from a variety of ethnic groups and sects, and rally them under their slogans, particularly the main slogan calling for democracy in Iraq and true autonomy for Iraqi Kurdistan. Another important factor is the dependence of the religious organizations on the support and backing of the Iranian regime and calls for 'merging with its state', 'integration within the leadership of the *'umma* (i.e. Islamic nation)',[107] and the 'export of the Islamic revolution'.

The Iraqi Islamic forces have stated their clear stand regarding the overthrow of the dictatorship in Iraq, but the methods and means advocated for overthrowing this dictatorship, the alternative they support, and their stand on the war unleashed against Iran in September 1980, have undergone significant changes. Following the failure of the acts of individual terror, the blows dealt to several of their clandestine units, the physical liquidation of hundreds of cadres and supporters at the hands of the security apparatus, and the transfer of their headquarters to Iran, they have started to advocate exploiting the war to weaken the regime and then 'revolutionize' (incite to revolution) the masses of people through a 'Popular Islamic Revolution'. However, the response to the calls made by these forces has been almost nil. Iraq did not witness any mass anti-regime activity organized on a religious basis, whereas the political forces allied in the Democratic Patriotic Front (DPF) have escalated their activity to include armed struggle in Kurdistan. The religious forces have thus come to pin their hopes on 'a decisive conquest'.[108] This stand was elaborated in the statement of SAIRI after an explosion at the Iraqi News Agency in Baghdad on 16 December 1982, which declared the Council as 'the legitimate and sole representative of the Iraqi people'. While pointing out that the alternative to the dictatorial regime 'would be determined by the people following the overthrow of the rule of despotism', it went on to declare that 'this people will only choose the Islamic system and Islamic leadership'. Such a stand contradicts the slogans raised by the other opposition forces which have called for a broad patriotic front open to all anti-dictatorship forces, and a democratic coalition government to replace the regime.

The spirit of hegemony, monopoly of political power, the imposition of an Islamic alternative against the will of the people, and total subjugation to the Iranian regime, and its repressive policies and covetous designs towards Iraq, in addition to its vague stands towards the Kurdish people and other national minorities, and its blind hostility towards the democratic forces, have increasingly isolated the organized religious opposition movement. On the other hand, the policies and slogans advocated by the patriotic and democratic movement have gained increasing support. The religious forces now face the choice between adhering to their present policies or working side by side with other opposition forces, not for 'an Islamic alternative versus the atheistic alternative'[109] but rather for a democratic alternative versus other alternatives hostile to the interests of the Iraqi people and the national sovereignty and independence of Iraq.

The Arab Nationalist Movement in Iraq

An extensive exposition of the historical roots of Arab nationalism and the evolution of the ideological and political thought of the pan-Arab movements is given in Chapter Five ('Iraqi Ba'thism: Nationalism, Socialism and National Socialism'). Here, light is shed on the role in the contem]orary history of Iraq of Arab nationalist parties and forces other than the Ba'th.

The pan-Arab movement which sprang up in Iraq at the beginning of the 20th century was influenced by the Young Turk Revolution of 1908.

In the 1920s many of its adherents identified themselves fully with the monarchy. It also existed as a trend within *al-Hizb al-Watani* (National Party) led by Ja'far Abu'l-Timman between 1928 and 1933. In 1935, the Muthanna Club was founded and declared its commitment to 'disseminating the spirit of Arab nationalism . . . preserving Arab traditions . . . strengthening the sense of Arab manhood in youth, and creating a new Arab culture which would unite to the Arab heritage what is worthy in the civilization of the West.'[110] It had close links with a pan-Arab faction of young army officers centered around a group known as the Golden Square, led by Colonel Salah-al-Din al-Sabbagh, the moving spirit in the coups d'état of 1938 and 1941. The Muthanna Club developed leanings towards authoritarianism and derived its strength from Sabbagh's group which had a dominant voice in the army and the administration of the country. The destruction of this group brought about by the defeat of the 1941 military movement and British military intervention, led to the breakup of the club. Surviving leaders of the Club later constituted the central nucleus of the right-wing Independence Party (*Hizb al-Istiqlal*), founded on 2 April 1946. Muhammad Mahdi Kubbah, the vice-chairman from 1935 to 1941 of the Muthanna Club, became the chairman of the Independence Party from 1946 to 1959. While declaring its opposition to 'the class standpoint' and to 'regional, sectarian and religious fanaticism,' and its support for 'an adaptation to spirit of the time even while clinging to the old and venerable distinguishing attributes and high principles,' the Party called for a fully independent Iraq and for the eventual establishment of a federated Arab state.[111] The Party membership grew rapidly, counting in 1947 no fewer than 5,450 members drawn mainly from the middle strata, with the legal profession being well represented. The Party had no intensive inner life and from the late 1940s it revolved around its leading figures, such as the secretary, Siddiq Shanshal.[112]

During the 1948 popular uprising of *al-Wathbah* (The Leap), the policy of the Independence Party was characterized by vacillation. As mass pressure continued to build up against Salih Jabr's government, a statement issued in its name on 22 January 1948 pleaded that 'his Highness and loyal personages must be given time to deal with the situation.'[113] During the uprising of November 1952, the Independents drew closer to other anti-governmental forces – the National Democrats, the United Popular Front, and the Partisans of Peace – and joined the 'Contact Committee' formed to coordinate joint action. The Party advocated reforms and the granting of liberties and together with the National Democrats called for a limit on ownership in land, a policy of non-alignment, and the termination of the treaty with Britain.[114] After the mid-1950s, the Party suffered from immobility, a drift of its younger elements into the Ba'th Party and the general swing of the political mood of young people in Iraq towards the left. During the anti-government upsurge following the Tripartite aggression on Egypt in October 1956, the Independence Party joined other opposition forces in a joint 'Field

Command'. A few months later, in February 1957, the National Unity Front was set up and the Party was represented in its Supreme Committee by its leader Muhammad Mahdi Kubbah. Some of the Party leaders had personal connections with the clandestine Free Officer movement. After the Revolution of 14 July 1958 and the overthrow of the monarchy, Siddiq Shanshal joined the cabinet as Minister of Guidance. The Party supported the calls for unity with the United Arab Republic, and in February 1959 Shanshal resigned together with the other nationalists in the cabinet. It collaborated with the Ba'th Party and the Movement of Arab Nationalists. During that period, it had no official or clandestine newspaper. By mid-1959, after a highly turbulent revolutionary period, the Independence Party was dying away.

A more significant nationalist grouping was the *Harakiyyin* (Movement of Arab Nationalists), which had its beginnings in a small group of Arab students which was founded in 1948 at the American University of Beirut by George Habash and others. Its main driving force was its ardour for Arab national unity and later its adulation of the person of Nasser after the Revolution in Egypt in July 1952. It was first organized in Iraq in 1955, recruiting mainly among students, but it did not play any significant role in Iraqi politics before 1958. The Movement laid emphasis on Arab unity and strongly attacked the Communists in its clandestine publications after the July Revolution. In August 1958, *al-Rabitah al-Qawmiyyah* (Nationalist League) was set up and raised the slogan 'One Arab people . . . One Arab State'. It claimed to be a pan-Arab non-partisan organization, and conducted mainly anti-communist propaganda.[115] In 1960, a diminutive Nasserist party, the Arab Socialist Party, came into being under the slogan 'Struggle-Unity-Socialism', and was led by the president of the Bar Association, 'Abd al-Razzaq Shabib.[116]

Iraqi nationalist exiles in Egypt formed the Iraqi Nationalist Grouping in 1959, which included representatives of various nationalist parties and movements. It was in reality connected to the Refugee Affairs Bureau of the Egyptian government, and carried out a propaganda campaign against Qasim's regime, in radio broadcasts and publications, until the coup d'état of 8 February 1963.[117] Attempts were made to establish an alliance between the various nationalist forces but these were shortlived due to rivalries and fragmentation. In 1961, a Nationalist Front was set up which included the Ba'th Party, the Independence Party and the Movement of Arab Nationalists. But only a few months later, in July 1961, sharp differences erupted following Qasim's claims on Kuwait, as some members of the Front regarded the move as a positive step towards Arab unity.

Soon after the bloody coup d'état of February 1963, attempts by the Ba'th Party to impose one-party rule, in addition to mounting internal opposition, combined to deepen the rift between the Ba'th and its nationalist allies who had earlier supported and participated in its anti-Communist campaign. The clash with the Nasserists worsened after the collapse of unity talks with Egypt in July 1963, and the unsuccessful experiment of the

United Arab Republic of 1958–61 had already divided Nasser and the Ba'th of Syria. Military Nasserists later played an active role in ousting the Ba'th Party in a coup d'état led by the President, 'Abd al-Salam 'Arif, who gave them a free hand in an attempt to model Iraq's political system on that of Egypt. In July 1964, 'the Arab Socialist Union – Iraqi Region' was announced and embraced, in addition to the *Harakiyyin*, various nationalist groupings of little significance and some ex-Independents and ex-Ba'thists who had become Nasserists.[118] However, by the spring of 1965, Nasser's fervour for unity had begun to fade, and the Nasserists began losing ground rapidly. In an attempt to avoid a complete break, the commander of the air force, 'Arif 'Abd al-Razzaq, who was closely associated with the *Harakiyyin*, was appointed Premier and Defence Minister in September 1965. Despite that, the *Harakiyyin* and other Nasserists staged a coup attempt which backfired and the principal plotters fled the country. During the following years till July 1968, when the Ba'th Party seized power once again, Nasserists and Independent nationalists joined successive cabinets. After the June 1967 War many Nasserists were set free and reinstated in their former posts.[119]

By July 1968, the nationalist forces were no longer in any serious position to challenge the Ba'th; they had become too fragmented and ineffective. No fewer than nine mutually antagonistic pan-Arab organizations were in the field: the Arab Socialist Movement, The Congress of Socialist Nationalists, the Party of Arab Toilers, the Party of Revolutionary Workers, the Socialist Party of Unity, the Nationalist League, the Nationalist Congress, the Movement of Socialist Unionists, and the Arab Socialist Party.[120] The largest, the Arab Socialist Movement, had just split into two factions, one following the line of the UAR and the other advocating Marxism-Leninism and 'popular armed struggle'.[121] After seizing power in July 1968, the Ba'th Party endeavoured to crush all other nationalist forces and emerge as the sole and undisputed leader of the pan-Arab movement. During the first few months, it settled scores with the Nasserists and former Ba'thists who had collaborated with the 'Arif regimes after the collapse of the first Ba'th experience in power in 1963. It purged from the armed forces high-ranking officers whose allegiance to the new regime was in doubt and who had been instrumental in palace coups and plots during the 1960s. Potential nationalist rivals were liquidated at the hands of assassination squads directed by Saddam Husain through the head of the security apparatus Nadhim Kazzar. In mid-February 1969, the Arab Socialist Movement, now led by the former Ba'thist Fu ad al-Rikabi, issued a joint statement with the Iraqi Communist Party which called for putting an end to the prevailing 'state of emergency' and all manifestations of political terror and repression. The campaign against other nationalist forces was coupled with a fiercely hostile stance towards Nasser and his policy on the Middle East and the Palestine question, which was officially maintained until Nasser's death in September 1970.

The task of suppressing other nationalist forces proved to be far easier than the futile attempts to crush the Kurdish national movement led by

Mulla Mustafa Barzani and the Iraqi Communist Party. Nationalist groupings were fragmented and torn apart by the political and ideological in-fighting which had plagued the pan-Arab movement after the defeat suffered by Egypt in the June 1967 War. Furthermore, they lacked a mass base and their organizations could not withstand systematic state terror. Many such groupings existed only in name and were centred around a few leading figures; they were no match for the Ba'th party which had a relatively coherent organization and could draw on the experience it had gained after the February 1963 coup. The Ba'th gradually consolidated its hold on political power through a policy combining terror with socio-economic reforms. By the end of 1971, the nationalist parties had virtually ceased to exist. Many of their cadres were coerced or bribed into joining the Ba'th party and relinquishing their previous political affiliations. Some were physically liquidated or assassinated. Thus Fu'ad al-Rikabi, the leader of the Nasserist Socialist Party, who had split from the Arab Socialist Movement, was killed while in Ba'quba prison in November 1971. He had been the first Secretary General of the Iraqi Ba'th party between 1952 and 1959 and a Minister in the first cabinet after the 14 July 1958 Revolution. After denouncing the pan-Arab command of the Ba'th Party in 1961, he had turned to Nasserism. Remnants of various nationalist and Nasserist forces who fled the country sought refuge in Syria, Egypt and Libya. Some came together in the Iraqi National Grouping which operated from Damascus during the early 1970's and carried out mainly propaganda work. They were however virtually non-existent inside Iraq as the Ba'th party gradually imposed its total hegemony over the nationalist movement. When the Patriotic Front was announced in July 1973, a few former Nasserists served on its Supreme Committee as 'independent' nationalists and some joined the cabinet. Throughout the 1970s, the position of the nationalist forces did not change and they did not constitute a real threat to Ba'th power. Some became associated with Palestinian organizations in Lebanon, but in general their policies were dictated to a large extent by their host states on which they were heavily dependent for material support.

The purge in the Ba'th party hierarchy and the crisis it faced after Saddam Husain became president in July 1979, coupled with the collapse of unity talks with Syria and the final showdown with the Iraqi Communist Party, gave a new impetus to opposition forces, including the nationalist movement. The latter hoped to cultivate dissent within the Ba'th and win over support among sections of the armed forces in the case of a possible collapse of the dictatorship. On 12 November 1980, less than two months after the start of Saddam's war against neighbouring Iran, an alliance of opposition forces, the Democratic Patriotic and National Front (DPNF), was announced in Damascus which included nationalist Arab and Kurdish forces together with the Iraqi Communist Party. The nationalist forces included the Socialist Party, the Arab Socialist Movement and the pro-Syrian Ba'th party (Iraqi Regional Command). The Front advocated 'the overthrow of the dictatorial regime and the setting up of a patriotic coalition government which achieves democracy for Iraq and autonomy for Iraqi Kurdistan'. The Arab nationalist parties objected to the inclusion of the Kurdistan Democratic Party (KDP) in the DPNF and supported the other major Kurdish party, the Patriotic Union of Kurdistan (PUK). As a result they adopted a hostile attitude towards the Democratic Patriotic Front (DPF) which was set up on 28 November 1980 at the initiative of the Iraqi Communist Party and included the KDP. As a result, the Communist Party announced in early 1981 that it had suspended its membership in the DPNF.

In general, the nationalist forces are still plagued by fragmentation and personal rivalries for leadership. A meeting in Tripoli, Libya, in February 1983 which aimed at setting up a broad front of opposition forces, broke up after nationalist forces and groupings were unable to reach agreement. However, in November 1984, the Socialist Party, together with two other forces, announced that it would join the DPF. Policy documents of nationalist forces are generally scarce and it is difficult to provide a comprehensive review of their policies and to follow the path of their development. In common with the Arab Nationalist Movement and Nasserism generally, they have undergone a process of ideological and political radicalization, but a number of constraints have impeded this process, particularly the lack of an effective mass base inside Iraq and also extensive interference from various Arab quarters.

References

1. Hanna Batatu, *The Old Social Classes and the Revolutionary Movements of Imperialism* (Princeton, 1978).
2. Marion Farouk-Sluglett and Peter Sluglett, 'Conflict and Communism in Iraq', *Gazelle Review of Literature on the Middle East, Gazelle Review*, No. 8, 1980, p. 17.
3. *al-Sharq al-Awsat* (Arabic daily in London), 21 August 1984.
4. Ibrahim Husain, *Lamahat Mujazah min Ta'rikh al-Harakah al-Naqabiyyah al-'Iraqiyyah* (A Brief Look at the History of the Iraqi Trade Union Movement), 1984, p. 18.
5. Acting High Commissioner, Baghdad, to Secretary of State for Colonies, London, July 11, 1931. Delhi, National Archives of India, Baghdad High Commission File 7/4/22, Part II.
6. Su'ad Khairi, *Min Ta'rikh al-Haraka al-thawriyyah fi'l-'Iraq – Thawrat 14 Tammuz* (From the History of the Revolutionary Movement in Iraq – 14 July Revolution), Beirut, 1980, p. 21.
7. *al-Thaqafa al-Jadida*, No. 152, March 1984, p. 76.
8. 'Abd al-Razzaq al-Hasani, *Ta'rikh al-Wizarat al-'Iraqiyya* (History of Cabinets), Vol. 3, p. 230.
9. Rony Gabbay, *Communism and Agrarian Reform in Iraq* (London 1978), p. 50.
10. Ibid., p. 52.
11. Marion Farouk-Sluglett and Peter Sluglett, 'Labour and National

Liberation: The Trade Union Movement in Iraq, 1920–1958', *Arab Studies Quarterly*, Vol. 5, No. 2, p. 151.

12. Hanna Batatu, op. cit., p. 529.
13. *Works of Comrade Fahd* (in Arabic), 1974, pp. 309–310.
14. Hanna Batatu, op. cit., p. 532.
15. *al-Thaqafa al-Jadida*, No. 154, May 1984, p. 17.
16. Majid 'Abd al-Ridha, *al-Mas'ala al-Kurdiyya fi'l-'Iraq* (The Kurdish Question in Iraq), Publications of al-Tareeq al-Jadid, Baghdad, 1975, p. 82.
17. Ibid., p. 183.
18. Hanna Batatu, op. cit., pp. 611–614.
19. Rony Gabbay, op. cit., p. 57.
20. *al-Zaman*, 3 April 1947 (Iraqi daily).
21. Sluglett and Farouk-Sluglett, op. cit. 1980. p. 153.
22. Rony Gabbay, op. cit., p. 57.
23. Su'ad Khairi, op. cit., p. 33.
24. *Middle East News Letter*, Published by the Middle East Committee of the Communist Party of Great Britain, January-February 1949, Vol. III, No. 1, p. 43.
25. *Ittihad al-Sha'b*, 20 February 1959.
26. Su'ad Khairy, op. cit., p. 38.
27. Hanna Batatu, op. cit., p. 667.
28. ibid., p. 691.
29. Ibid., p. 693.
30. Ibid., p. 694.
31. 'Iraq's Underground Shi'i Movements', *Merip Reports*, No. 102, January 1982, p. 6.
32. *1956 Uprising and our Tasks in the Current Situation* (in Arabic), 1957.
33. Hanna Batatu, op. cit., p. 756.
34. *Ittihad al-Sha'b*, mid-February 1957.
35. Hanna Batatu, op. cit., pp. 793, 803.
36. Su'ad Khairi, op. cit., p. 82.
37. Ibid., p. 173.
38. Hanna Batatu, op. cit., p. 945.
39. Su'ad Khairi, op. cit., pp. 194–195.
40. Ibid., p. 198.
41. *Tareeq al-Sha'ab*, early November 1961.
42. Hanna Batatu, op. cit., p. 13, Para 2.
43. *Iraqi Letter – Information Bulletin*, published by the Iraqi Communist Party, No. 4–5, April-May 1962, p. 10.
44. Hanna Batatu, op. cit., pp. 985–986.
45. Ibid., p. 988.
46. *Iraqi Letter*, No. 1, July 1970, p. 13.
47. Ibid., p. 14.
48. *Documents of the 2nd National Congress of ICP*, September 1970, p. 80 (in Arabic).
49. Ibid., p. 48.
50. *Tariq al-Sha'b*, August 1971.
51. Hanna Batatu, op. cit., pp. 1108–1109.
52. *Iraqi Letter* (Special Issue), No. 4–5, May 1976, p. 51.

53. *National Action Charter and the Rules of Action of the Progressive Patriotic and National Front*, Publication of the Ministry of Information, Documentary Series (29), al-Huriyyah Printing House, Government House, Baghdad, 1974.

54. Ibid., p. 70.

55. *Central Report of the 9th Regional Congress of the Arab Ba'th Socialist Party (June 1982)*, Baghdad, January 1983, p. 68.

56. Ibid., pp. 70–71.

57. Ibid., p. 78.

58. Ibid., p. 72.

59. *Iraqi Letter*, No. 2, April 1979, p. 19.

60. *Tariq al-Sha'b*, article by 'Abd al-Razzq al-Safi, editor-in-chief, 15 February 1979.

61. *Iraqi Letter*, No. 4, mid-May 1979, pp. 1–2.

62. *Iraqi Letter*, No. 1, March 1981, p. 7.

63. Statement of CC Plenum of ICP, late September 1982, *Iraqi Letter*, No. 3, November 1982, p. 2.

64. Ibid., p. 3.

65. *Iraqi Letter*, No. 5, December 1983, p. 14.

66. *Iraqi Letter*, No. 4, September 1984, pp. 9–10.

67. Ibid., p. 10.

68. Peter Sluglett and Marion Farouk-Sluglett, 'Some Reflections on the Sunni/Shi'i Question in Iraq', *British Society for Middle Eastern Studies*, Vol. 5, No. 2, 1978, p. 80.

69. Dr. Abu'l-Quasim Jurji, 'Shi'ism in Relation to Various Islamic Sects', *al-Tawhid*, a quarterly journal of Islamic Thought and Culture, published by the Islamic Propagation Organization – Vol. I, No. 2, January 1984, p. 47.

70. Ayatullah Muhammad Baqir al-Sadr, *A Preparatory Legal View of the Scheme for an Islamic Constitution*, (1979), published by al-Tawhid Institute, London, p. 3.

71. Hanna Batatu, 'Iraq's Underground Shi'i Movements: Characteristics, Causes and Prospects', *The Middle East Journal*, Autumn 1981, p. 589.

72. Ayatullah Muhammad Baqir al-Sadr, *A Study on the Question of al-Wilaya*, published by al-Tawhid Institute, London, p. 21.

73. Peter Sluglett, *Britain in Iraq 1914–32*, 'A Note on Shia Politics', (London, 1976), p. 301.

74. Ibid., p. 302.

75. Ibid., p. 302–303.

76. Ibid., p. 304.

77. Ibid., p. 304.

78. Ibid., pp. 306–307.

79. Hanna Batatu, op. cit., 1978, pp. 1142–1143.

80. Ibid., p. 1137.

81. Ibid., p. 1143.

82. Ibid., pp. 1145–1146; *New Times*, No. 17 of 23 April 1955, p. 13.

83. Peter Sluglett, op. cit., p. 309.

84. Ibid., p. 313.

85. Sluglett and Farouk-Sluglett, op. cit., 1978, p. 82.

86. Ibid., p. 82.

87. Hanna Batatu, op. cit. 1987, p. 584.
88. Ibid., pp. 585–586.
89. Ibid., p. 583.
90. Ibid., p. 586.
91. Ibid., pp. 587–588.
92. Ibid., p. 592.
93. Dr. Majid al-Radi, *Islam: Historic and Contemporary Experience*, published by al-Hadaf, 1983, p. 71 (in Arabic).
94. Laith 'Abd al-Hasan al-Zubaidi, *Thawra Arba'at 'ashar Tammuz f'il-'Iraq The 14th July 1958 Revolution in Iraq*, Baghdad, 1981, pp. 240–241.
95. Ibid., p. 248.
96. Hanna Batatu, op. cit., 1981, p. 588.
97. Ibid., p. 586.
98. Ibid., p. 588.
99. Ibid., p. 588.
100. Dilip Hiro, *Inside the Middle East*, 1982, pp. 144–145.
101. Ibid., p. 145.
102. Hanna Batatu, p. 590.
103. *Sawt al-'Iraq* (Voice of Iraq), organ of Vanguards of Islamic Da'wa in Europe, No. 1, Sept. 1980. (in Arabic).
104. *Bayan al-Tafahum* (The Manifesto for Mutual Understanding) issued by the Da'wa Party, 1980 (in Arabic).
105. Interview published in *al-Shahid* (The Martyr), No. 75, 9 January 1981, p. 32 (in Arabic).
106. *al-Jihad*, organ of the Islamic Action Organization, 3rd Year, No. 32, p. 31. (in Arabic).
107. Final Communique of Imam al-Mahdi Congress of the Islamic Da'wa Party, the Third Session, Iraq Region, 1983.
108. *al-Shahid* (The Martyr), No. 91, 25 August 1982.
109. Ibid.
110. Hanna Batatu, *Old Social Classes*, op. cit., 1978, p. 298
111. Ibid., p. 299.
112. Ibid., p. 299.
113. Ibid., p. 552.
114. Ibid., p. 667.
115. Laith 'Abd al-Hasan al-Zubaidi, op. cit., p. 427.
116. Batatu, op. cit., 1978, p. 1014.
117. al-Zubaidi, op. cit., pp. 428–430.
118. Batatu, op. cit., 1978, p. 1031.
119. Ibid., p. 1074.
120. Ibid., p. 1098.
121. Ibid., p. 1098.

9. The Kurds

Peter Sluglett

The name 'Kurdistan' designates an area on the present borders of Turkey, Iran, Iraq and Syria, the homeland of the Kurds, a pastoral nomadic people of Indo-European origin. The Kurdish people 'have the unfortunate distinction of being probably the only community of over 15 million persons which has not achieved some form of national statehood, despite a struggle extending back over several decades.'[1] Although there are at least four major Kurdish dialect groups, Minorsky's contention that the similarities between them indicate a common origin,[2] probably Median, has not been challenged. All varieties of Kurdish are Indo-European, and thus belong to the same linguistic family as Persian, although there are many important differences of syntax and vocabulary. There is thus no *structural* relationship whatever between Kurdish and Arabic or Kurdish and Turkish, and of course Arabic and Turkish are themselves members of two very different linguistic families, the Semitic and Altaic groups.

Extrapolating on the latest census figures for the provinces in each of the four countries in which the Kurds form the majority of the population (18 provinces in Turkey, 3 provinces in Iran, 3 provinces and parts of 2 others in Iraq, parts of 2 provinces in Syria), plus some 140,000 in the Soviet Union, the total number of Kurds in the Middle East and Central Asia today is an estimated 17 million. Since three of the four countries (Iraq is the exception) have never 'recognized' the Kurds as a separate ethnic entity, this figure is naturally open to question, but the lowest estimates have been taken in all cases, with nominal additions for the large Kurdish populations in cities outside the Kurdish area such as Baghdad and Istanbul. If these figures are broadly correct, the Kurdish percentage of the population is 18.6% in Turkey, 16% in Iran, 23% in Iraq and 11% in Syria.[3] Most Kurds can trace their origins to particular tribes, although increasing rural to urban migration (and, in the case of the Turkish Kurds, migration to West Germany) has tended to weaken tribal bonds. Furthermore, the passage of time and the political constraints on cross-frontier transhumance have combined to increase the tendency to sedentarization.

History

Until the end of the First World War, the Kurds were generally subject to what was at least the nominal jurisdiction either of the Shah of Iran or the Ottoman sultan, with a few small communities in the Russian Caucasus. The boundary between Iran and the Ottoman Empire was not finally charted until 1913, which meant that attempts on the part of either government to assert its authority in the Kurdish areas could be kept in check by reinforcements from the 'other side'. In general terms, the Ottomans attempted to extend their authority over all parts of the Empire after the dissolution of the janissaries in 1826, and their efforts to do so caused major risings in the Kurdish areas in 1837-52 and 1880-81. By the end of the century, the Ottomans had managed to recruit many Kurdish tribesmen into the Hamidiyya cavalry, named after Sultan 'Abd al-Hamid (1876-1909), which was used to put down Armenian risings in Eastern Anatolia in the 1890's.[4] Nevertheless, it is clear that government authority had not been universally accepted in either the Iranian or Ottoman Kurdish areas by the First World War.

In common with the other non-Turkish peoples of the Ottoman Empire, the Kurds were affected by the currents of nationalism in Europe and Asia in the second part of the 19th century. Kurdish intellectuals began to form secret societies aiming either at some form of decentralized administration of the Kurdish provinces, or (more rarely) for complete independence from the Ottoman government. In an essentially rural and tribal society, however, such activities were generally to have little effect unless they were accompanied by the support of powerful tribes and their leaders, who could produce the weapons and the men necessary to effect the political changes desired by the intellectuals.

During the First World War, the Turks and the Russians were on opposite sides, while Iran remained neutral. However, Russian troops had been stationed in Iran since 1909 (when they had intervened on the Shah's side in the Constitutional Revolution), and Turkish troops actually captured Tabriz from the Russians for 10 days early in 1915. After the Treaty of Brest-Litovsk in December 1917, when Russia withdrew from the war, there was a virtual power vacuum in eastern Turkey until well into 1919, and also in western Iran until Reza Khan's seizure of power in 1921. In general, the absence of any centralized authority in the area permitted widespread disorder and the massacre or expulsion of most of the Assyrian and some of the Armenian populations, who, as Christians, had tended to take the Russian side.[5] Further south, Mosul town was occupied a little after the Treaty of Mudros (30 October 1918), and the area of British occupation was soon afterwards held to extend over the whole of Mosul province.[6] Kurdish nationalists in exile outside Turkey, and local tribal leaders in ex-Ottoman Kurdistan, saw the defeat of the Ottomans and the occupation of Mosul as a golden opportunity for pressing their claims, encouraged by President Woodrow Wilson's 14 Points (8 January 1918), the Twelfth of which states

---

that 'the nationalities now under Turkish rule should (sc. in the event of an Allied victory) be assured an undoubted security of life and an absolutely unmolested opportunity of autonomous development.'

At this time, it will be remembered, the two southern Iraqi provinces were under direct British administration. Because of the circumstances of the occupation of Mosul province, and because of its mountainous terrain, it could not be occupied in the same way. In fact, the whole question of the future of Mosul, and whether it was to be 'returned' to Turkey, or be part of the new state of Iraq, was not to be settled finally until 1925. In mid-November 1918, it was British policy to encourage the appointment of suitable local figures to administer the area with British political advisors. The most prominent of these notables was Shaikh Mahmud Barzinji, who was installed as governor of Sulaimaniya.[7]

A variety of factors combined to ensure that this was not to be the prelude to the creation of an independent or quasi-independent Kurdish state. In the first place, although this took some time to emerge clearly, the British government gradually became committed to the establishment of an Arab state under British auspices in Iraq, and to the inclusion of the oil-bearing province of Mosul within that state. Secondly, the defeat of the Ottomans was followed by the rise of a national resistance movement in Anatolia in the spring of 1919, the prelude to the war of independence, which ended with Atatürk and his forces victorious, compelling the British and Greek occupying armies to withdraw by October 1922.[8] In these changing circumstances the Kurds both north and south of the present Turco-Iraqi frontier naturally hesitated over whether to throw in their lot with Britain or with Turkey, since Britain's *locus standi* in the area was by no means clear. Finally, and very significantly for the future, the whole concept of an 'independent Kurdistan' or 'self-determination for the Kurds' required a degree of consensus in the recognition, on the part of the Kurds themselves, of suitable representatives. At this stage, the desire for Kurdish autonomy did not, because of traditional clan and tribal rivalries, produce any coherent movement towards Kurdish unity; Shaikh Mahmud was removed by the British in May 1919 because his support base was so inadequate that he could not control areas less than 20 miles from Sulaimaniya.[9]

Throughout 1919 and for most of 1920, there were constant risings in northern Iraq. Some were inspired by the Turks in an attempt to drive British forces out of the Mosul area, but some were the normal Kurdish expression of distaste at the imposition of outside authority.[10] By the summer of 1920, a few months after the award of the mandates for Palestine and Iraq to Britain and Syria and Lebanon to France, the Istanbul government accepted the Treaty of Sèvres,[11] against the wish of the Grand National Assembly convened by Atatürk and his supporters in Ankara. The Treaty amounted to the dismemberment of what was left of Turkey and its partition between Italy and Greece, with 'independent states' in Armenia and Kurdistan. Although the rise of Atatürk ensured that Sèvres was never ratified, it marked an important turning point in the history of the evolution of the Kurdish movement, as the first formal declaration of intent to set up a separate and specifically Kurdish political entity.

By the early 1920s, therefore, the political geography of the Kurdish areas had begun to assume much of the shape that it does today, with the Kurds divided between Turkey, Iran, Iraq and Syria. In general terms, the Turkish government under Atatürk pursued consistently repressive policies towards the Kurdish population, which amounted to a virtual denial of the separate ethnic or linguistic identity of the Kurds, and drastic reprisals, involving executions, massacres and mass deportations were taken against any attempts to assert Kurdish nationalism or independence. The risings led by Shaikh Sa'id (1925), the Khoybun revolt (1929–30) and the Dersim rebellion (1937) were all put down with great ferocity.[12] In Iran, the early 1920s were filled with uncertainty. The Iranian Kurds were told firmly by the British to respect the rule of the Iranian government, meaning that they should expect no assistance from Britain in setting up a Kurdish political entity. However, the Russian revolution had removed the Iranian monarchy's main support, which meant that there was anarchy throughout most of the country. In the Kurdish area Simko Agha, the chief of the Shakkak tribe, seized power in Western Azerbaijan shortly after the end of the war. Although checked by the Cossack brigade, he managed to gain the support of several Kurdish tribes in the Mahabad region, and began to talk of creating a Kurdish state, taking the towns of Mahabad and Khoi in the autumn of 1921. By July 1922, however, the Iranian Army had been sufficiently reorganized to defeat Simko and his allies, and he was forced to flee across the border into Turkey.[13]

In Iraq, the situation of the Kurds was more complex. In 1922, the British mandatory authorities promised the Kurds a form of autonomy in Northern Iraq; but by this time Shaikh Mahmud Barzinji, whom the British had re-instated, *faute de mieux*, in Sulaimaniya, seems to have decided against accepting any form of Iraqi suzerainty. By the spring, Shaikh Mahmud's movement had gathered sufficient momentum for the British authorities to decide that it could only be put down by force, and British troops were moved into Rowanduz and Koi Sanjak by the end of April. It was not until July 1924 that Sulaimaniya itself was occupied, and Shaikh Mahmud was still considered enough of a danger for the bombing of the town by the RAF to be authorized in December 1924.[14]

By this time, the League of Nations had decided to send a special Commission to decide whether the Mosul *wilayet* should be part of Iraq or of Turkey. After several months' deliberation, the Commissioners decided that Mosul should be part of Iraq, a recommendation which seems to have found general favour.[15] Early in 1926, the Prime Minister of Iraq declared that civil servants in the Kurdish area should be Kurds, that Kurdish and Arabic should be the official languages of the area, and that Kurdish children should be educated in Kurdish.[16] Although these provisions were only half-heartedly carried out, it is fair to say that the Kurds' separate ethnic identity has generally been recognized to a greater or lesser extent by all Iraqi governments since then, and token Kurds served as ministers in virtually all the governments under the monarchy. However, the Anglo-Iraqi treaty of 1930, under which Iraq became at least nominally independent from Britain, did not contain any specific minority guarantees, much to the consternation of many Kurds. Shaikh Mahmud was technically exiled from Iraq between 1926 and 1930, but seems to have been able to enter the country from Iran and meet frequently with British officials without any difficulty. By 1929, some of the Kurdish deputies in the Iraqi parliament sent a memorandum to the Prime Minister, expressing their concern that nothing had been done in any very tangible way to implement the promises he had made in 1926.[17] In the circumstances, the announcement by Britain that she would support Iraq's application for independence in 1932 naturally caused serious misgivings, especially when, as has been mentioned, it became known that the treaty contained no minority guarantees.

At this stage, there was very little that the British authorities were prepared to do to force the Iraq government to make concessions. After serious rioting in Sulaimaniya in September 1930, Shaikh Mahmud indicated that he was once more prepared to go on the offensive, and fighting broke out again in the spring of 1931.[18] This time, Mahmud was decisively defeated, but, almost simultaneously, a new and generally more effective nucleus of Kurdish opposition was developing, in the Barzani tribal lands in the subdistrict of Baradost. Mulla Mustafa Barzani, the younger brother of the Barzani religious and tribal leader Shaikh Ahmad, emerged in the early 1930s as the principal figure in Iraqi Kurdish politics, a position he was to retain until his death in exile in 1979.[19]

After organizing a series of revolts against the Iraq government in the Barzan area, the Barzani brothers were finally forced to surrender and eventually made to live under a loose form of house arrest in Sulaimaniya in 1936. In the course of his stay in Sulaimaniya, which is still regarded as the intellectual centre of 'southern Kurdistan', Barzani came into contact with Kurdish political writers and thinkers, some of whom joined together to form the clandestine *Héwa* (Hope) Party in 1939.[20] *Héwa* was a fairly loose grouping and included both left-wing and right-wing factions, that is, those who believed that revolution and socialism were essential ingredients if the Kurds were to achieve their national rights, and those who felt that the key to obtaining Kurdish rights lay in Britain's hands, and that some form of alliance or association with Britain was necessary. Since such differences were to form the basis of important splits within the Kurdish movement later on, it is as well to indicate their emergence, at least in a tacit form, at this stage. As was to be expected of a traditional tribal leader Barzani himself was more inclined to favour some sort of accommodation with Britain.

In addition to *Héwa*, the Iraqi Communist Party had become active in Kurdistan almost from the time of its foundation in 1934. The earliest Communist newspaper, *Kifah al-Sha'b*, carried slogans in favour of Kurdish rights, and Communist organizations were set up in Arbil and other Kurdish centres in 1941 and 1942. In addition, *Azadi*, the first Kurdish political paper, was edited by members of the Communist Party. An editorial in the first issue of the paper in 1944 declared:

> We urge the politically conscious among the sons of our people and every sincere Kurd who loves his people and his homeland, not to leave his people unorganized and unprepared . . . we urge him to struggle for democratic parties and associations to organize the Kurdish people, to prepare them and enable them to achieve self-determination so that their unity with the Arabs in Iraq would be a voluntary union based on equality of rights.[21]

The Party consistently stressed Kurdish rights in its National Charter, which was endorsed by the first Party Conference in 1944 and subsequently by the National Congress in 1945. In broad terms, the ICP was the first political party to develop a coherent policy on the Kurdish question, which generally amounted to a plan for autonomy based on Kurdish self-determination. During and after the Second World War the ICP continued to have a wide following in the Kurdish area, and was particularly influential in the period before the revolution of 1958.[22]

In 1941, the Iraq government under Rashid 'Ali al-Gailani was making what appeared to the British Embassy to be over-friendly overtures to the Axis powers, and as a result a British military force was sent to occupy Iraq at the end of April.[23] For the rest of the war Britain kept a tight rein on political developments in Iraq, through the close relationship between the Prime Minister, Nuri al-Sa'id, and the British Ambassador, Sir Kinahan Cornwallis, who had previously served as Adviser to the Iraqi Ministry of Interior from 1921 to 1935. Since many Iraqis continued to believe that an Allied defeat was possible at least until the major victories of 1943, the British and Iraqi authorities were inclined to concentrate most of their efforts in the southern parts of the country, leaving the north more or less to its own devices.[24] In July 1943, Barzani managed to escape from Sulaimaniya, and made his way back to Barzan, where he raised a revolt in the autumn. In the course of November-December 1943, he made several overtures to the British authorities in an attempt to induce Britain to support Kurdish autonomy. In the course of a remarkable correspondence with Cornwallis, Barzani declared his willingness to obey him 'whatever your orders may be'.[25] For his part, Cornwallis, presumably realizing that Barzani's strong position in the north could be used as an additional lever against any signs of recalcitrance on the part of the Iraq government, encouraged Nuri al-Sa'id to make contact with the Kurdish leader to try to work out a settlement.[26] However, both Cornwallis and Nuri seem to have reckoned without the extremely spirited reaction of the Regent of Iraq and many members of the cabinet, who saw, or purported to see, that any concessions in the direction of autonomy were simply a prelude to separatism, and thus a derogation of the sovereignty of the Iraqi state which, it should be remembered, had only assumed its final form in 1926, some 17 years earlier.

In fact, the plans for a Kurdish settlement found so little favour that Nuri was forced into temporary retirement. For a time (June 1944–April 1945) a tacit truce prevailed, but by the summer of 1945 the Iraq government seems to have felt sufficiently confident to launch a campaign to restore its authority in the north. 14,000 troops were assembled, and this large force, aided by the defection of Barzani's father-in-law, Mahmud Agha Zibari, succeeded in chasing Barzani out of Iraq and into Iran in October 1945.[27]

The Republic of Mahabad[28]

In June 1941, Nazi Germany invaded the Soviet Union, which immediately joined the Allied side. In order to be able to supply the Soviet Union, the Allies needed to be able to use the land routes across Iran, and when Reza Shah attempted to resist this he was deposed and exiled. The Anglo-Russian occupation of Iran in August 1941 inaugurated a brief period of political liberty, which lasted some six years. As the Iranian Army collapsed, the Kurdish tribes were once more virtually autonomous in their own areas, a situation reminiscent of the hiatus between the end of the First World War and the assumption of power by Reza Khan in 1921. By May 1943, then, the authority of the Iranian government in north-western Iran, never particularly strong since the invasion, had collapsed altogether, and Soviet officials had begun to make approaches to influential Kurdish figures in the area. The political centre of the region of Western Azerbaijan was the small town of Mahabad, formerly Sauj Bulagh, south of Lake Urmia, which had a population of some 16,000 inhabitants in 1945.

In 1942, some 15 citizens of Mahabad met secretly to form a nationalist association, the *Komala*, which gradually extended its activities to embrace most of the region round the town, particularly to the north and north-west. The *Komala* had links with *Héwa* (Mahabad is about 80 miles from Sulaimaniya as the crow flies, and 170 miles by road), the political group which had influenced Mulla Mustafa in Sulaimaniya in 1939–43. In October 1944 the leading citizen and judge of Mahabad, Qadhi Muhammad, was asked to become a member of the *Komala*. These events coincided with the rise of another separatist movement in the adjoining province of eastern Azerbaijan, where the population was of Turkish, and thus non-Iranian, origin. The Azeri separatist movement was encouraged by Soviet officials from across the border, and a number of members of the Iranian Communist (Tudeh) Party. For both the Kurds and the Azeris, the Soviets were regarded as natural partners, since they were encouraging the autonomous movements in both areas and were also instrumental in keeping the Iranian military and civil administration out of Kurdistan and Azerbaijan. In the autumn of 1945, after a meeting with Soviet officials in Nakhichevan, just across the frontier (some 200 miles by road and rail from Mahabad), Qadhi Muhammad and a number of other prominent citizens of Mahabad founded the Kurdistan Democratic Party, at almost exactly the same time as Mulla Mustafa Barzani and his supporters were preparing to enter Iraq from Iran.

For Qadhi Muhammad and the Kurdistan Democratic Party (KDP), the arrival of Barzani meant the addition of some 3,000 fighting men pledged to the Kurdish cause. Accordingly, the Iranian Kurds decided to proclaim an autonomous Republic of Mahabad, which was duly inaugurated by Qadhi Muhammad on 22 January 1946. A cabinet was soon formed, composed of fairly representative elements from the surrounding area. However, the main factor enabling the republic to function at all was the Soviet presence, which of course acted as the main stumbling block to the re-establishment of Iranian authority in the area. By the beginning of 1946, with the beginning of the Cold War, the British and Americans were starting to press for a withdrawal of all foreign troops from Iran, which would naturally imply the eventual restoration of the authority of the Iranian government over all parts of the country, including, of course, the north-west.

The effects of this pressure took some time to be felt in Mahabad, where the republic was building up a defence force, composed partly of Mulla Mustafa Barzani's tribal irregulars but also including 12 Kurdish former officers of the Iraqi Army, some of whom had been involved in the *pourparlers* initiated by Nuri al-Sa'id in 1943–44.[29]. The Soviet Union provided equipment and a military advisor; Barzani and three senior Kurds from Iran were given the rank of general. At this stage, the Soviet government had promised the Iranian government that its troops would be withdrawn some time in May.

One of the first difficulties facing the Mahabad Republic was the regulation of its relations with the much larger Azerbaijan autonomous state, based on Tabriz, not least because of the presence of large numbers of Azeris within Mahabad territory. Accordingly, the political leaders of both sides met in Tabriz in April 1946 to sign a treaty of friendship and alliance. The Azeri Republic was much larger and more powerful militarily than the Kurdish Republic, which made the alliance fairly attractive for the Kurds in spite of the evidently more leftward leanings of the Tabriz government. Another problem, that of finance, was soon solved when the Soviet government bought up the entire Mahabad tobacco crop for about $800,000.

Meanwhile, the Soviet Union had agreed to evacuate its troops from Iran on two conditions, first, that a satisfactory agreement would be made between the autonomous government of Azerbaijan in Tabriz and the central government in Tehran, and secondly that the Iranian parliament would ratify an oil concession in northern Iran in favour of the Soviets.[30] The agreement between Tehran and Tabriz was signed in mid-June, which, in essence, provided for the reintegration of Azerbaijan into Iran. This would also, it was felt, pave the way for elections in which the Tudeh Party, then at the peak of its popularity, would gain a substantial number of seats, and this, together with a contingent of pro-Soviet Azeri deputies, would ensure the ratification of the Soviet oil concession. The agreement with Tehran made only passing mention of the Kurds, and no mention at all of the Treaty of Friendship between Tabriz and Mahabad which had been signed in April.

As the short-lived Republic of Mahabad remains the sole instance of the actual implementation of a project of Kurdish autonomy, it is interesting to summarize Qadhi Muhammad's own views, as conveyed to a correspondent of AFP in June 1946. In sum, he wanted some kind of federal association with the government in Tehran which would not involve the entry of Iranian troops into the territory of the republic; he wanted education to be conducted in Kurdish, a locally based administration and a locally controlled military force. He did not seek, and in fact actively opposed, foreign military intervention; unlike Azerbaijan, the area of Mahabad had never been occupied by the Soviets, and had in fact enjoyed a degree of de facto independence for some five years, since the deposition of Reza Shah. As far as Qadhi Muhammad's long term socio-economic ideas are concerned, it is difficult to form a very clear picture, but, in contrast to the Azeri Republic, there were no nationalizations and no land reforms in Mahabad. Qadhi Muhammad was essentially a nationalist leader, seeking independence and autonomy from the central government. To this end, he spent several days in Tehran in August, under a Soviet safe conduct, attempting to negotiate an agreed settlement on the lines of the Tehran-Tabriz agreement concluded in April.

At this stage, the prospects of the Soviet Union in Iran looked distinctly encouraging. Three members of the Tudeh were appointed to the cabinet; a major Tudeh-inspired strike had been organized against the Anglo-Iranian Oil Company, much to Britain's alarm. However, this triumph was short-lived; by October, conservative elements had rallied, and an anti-left campaign was organized in the south, supported by the Bakhtiari and Qashqa'i tribes. One of the main objectives of the new cabinet (appointed in October) was to restore central authority in Azerbaijan, and in mid-December, Iranian troops entered Tabriz. Faced with the collapse of the Republic of Azerbaijan, and the unwelcome but clear realization that no Soviet support would be forthcoming, the leaders of Mahabad quickly grasped that their turn too would soon come. On 16 December, Qadhi Muhammad and his associates formerly surrendered to the Iranian army: resistance, as they correctly perceived, would be futile.

By this time, the only uncertain element in the Kurdish area was Barzani's tribal army, which was still capable of offering resistance, and which, as we have seen, exerted considerable influence in the Kurdish areas. In brief, Barzani himself seems to have decided against this, and sought to come to an accommodation with the Iranian government through the good offices of the British Embassy in Tehran. Eventually after two months in Tehran, he rejoined his tribesmen near the Iraqi frontier, and the Iranian Army launched a major offensive against them in mid March 1947, which lasted until the Barzanis crossed into Iraq some five weeks later. Meanwhile, on 31 March, Qadhi Muhammad together with two of his close relatives and political allies, were hanged in public in the main square of Mahabad. Later in the year, four Kurdish ex-officers of the Iraqi army who had accompanied Barzani to Mahabad were also executed, even though they had voluntarily surrendered to the Iraqi authorities. By mid-May, Barzani and his closest associates had come to the conclusion that it was not safe for them to stay in Iraq. Some 600 men accompanied Mulla Mustafa on a daring journey to the Soviet Union across Turkey and Iran, crossing the Aras River between 15 and 18 June, covering 220 miles over very mountainous country in about a fortnight. They stayed in the Soviet Union until 1958.

Kurdish Politics 1947–58

With the fall of Mahabad, and the departure of Barzani, Kurdish politics remained virtually in limbo until the overthrow of the Iraqi monarchy. In Iran, the KDP was proscribed; it reappeared briefly in support of the government of Muhammad Musaddiq in 1951–53, but it suffered along with the Tudeh, with whom it was closely associated, in the reprisals against the left that followed Musaddiq's fall. In 1956, still underground, it published a draft programme, in which the emphasis was very much on the struggle against imperialism and Zionism, and calling for Kurdish autonomy.[31] In broad terms, the history of the Kurdish movement since 1947 is largely the history of the Kurdish movement in Iraq. As has already been mentioned, in spite of the unwillingness of successive Iraqi governments to render more than lipservice to the principle, the Iraqi Kurds enjoyed certain basic freedoms denied to their fellows in Iran and Turkey, perhaps most significantly the recognition, tacit and grudging though it may often have been, of their separate ethnic status. In Turkey, and to a lesser extent in Iran, Kurds were persecuted as Kurds; in Iraq, provided that they did not actually engage in activities directed against the central government, the Kurds were generally free to do as they pleased, and were no more – and no less – deprived of civil liberties than their Arab fellow citizens.

At this point, one important generalization is appropriate. Whatever one may think of the various regimes that have been or are in power in Baghdad, Ankara or Tehran, the fact remains that these countries are all (even Iran, in many important ways), in the form in which they exist today, modern geopolitical creations, and do not antedate 1920. Largely, of course, because of the policies that these governments have pursued, it has not been easy for them to co-exist with a well-armed and potentially, if not actually, hostile ethno-linguistic entity living compactly together in what may be a strategically or economically vital part of the country. Furthermore, as we have seen, it has often been the case (and this was to continue to be so until comparatively recently) that the Kurdish leadership has on occasions resorted to attempting to obtain assistance from foreign powers, whose attitudes towards the relevant national government in Baghdad (or Tehran or Ankara) have ranged from simply suspect to downright hostile. The fact that certain Kurdish leaders have often been in touch to a greater or lesser extent with 'enemies of the state' has made it easy for the states concerned to allege that the only solution to the Kurdish problem is to batter the Kurds into submission; any moves towards autonomy, this argument runs, will only be interpreted as weakness; in any case, it continues, although the Kurds may *claim* that they only want autonomy or administrative decentralization, this is simply a cover for their real aim, which is either (at least) separatism or (at most) incorporation in a Grand Kurdistan, which, because of the oil deposits in Iraqi Kurdistan, will certainly menace the security of the existing regimes in the region.

In addition, another important issue has emerged, certainly since the Second World War and possibly even earlier. Kurdish history has often been represented as the struggle of a national liberation movement, of a people seeking its independence from external control. After Mahabad, however, a simple Kurds-versus-regime polarity is not a sufficient description, since it does not take into account the splits within the Kurdish movement, and the different ideological orientations of the various groups which it has come to include. In Iraq, for example, after Barzani's return in 1958, a serious rift developed between the Iraqi Kurdistan Democratic Party, which had a political and economic programme for the Kurdish areas, and Barzani, whose principal aim was to try to ensure that he, rather than the Iraq government, ruled Iraqi Kurdistan or at least parts of it, and who therefore had no scruples in attacking the 'revolutionary', 'progressive' and 'anti-imperialist' Qasim government in 1961 in an attempt to achieve that aim.

The most important development in Kurdish politics between Mahabad and 1958 was undoubtedly the foundation and rise to maturity of the *Iraqi* KDP.[32] At first, an Iraqi branch of the Iranian KDP had been founded in Mahabad in 1946 by Barzani and his close associate Hamza 'Abdullah; 'Abdullah was charged with organizing the Party in Iraq, although, as events turned out, his mission ended in the creation of a separate *Iraqi* KDP. This detail may seem trivial, but it had the effect of formalizing a permanent administrative separation in terms of Kurdish politics between Iraqi and Iranian Kurdistan. Thus in August 1946 the Iraqi KDP was formally inaugurated, with 'Abdullah as secretary-general, and Mulla Mustafa, who was then still in Mahabad, as president. At the same time, of course, there was a branch of the *Iranian* KDP in Iraqi Kurdistan, based at Sulaimaniya, under the leadership of Ibrahim Ahmad, which denounced the new Iraqi KDP as a potentially dangerous derogation of the authority of Qadhi Muhammad and the Mahabad Republic, which, in the eyes of Ahmad and his supporters, constituted the most viable vehicle for Kurdish national aspirations at the time. Ahmad's suspicions of the Iraqi KDP were well founded, but after the fall of Mahabad his own Mahabad-linked organization ceased to have much relevance. With some reluctance, he joined the Iraqi KDP, attempting to push it towards the left, a task which was facilitated by Barzani's absence in the Soviet Union. By 1951, Ahmad was elected secretary-general of the Party (always known in Iraq as the *Hizb al-Party*, since the Kurds themselves used a transliteration of the English word Party — *hizb* is the Arabic translation — calling the organization the Parti Democrati Kurdistan), having successfully ousted Hamza 'Abdullah. Because of the nature of its political orientation under Ibrahim Ahmad, the KDP worked mainly among students and intellectuals, and had little support in the Kurdish countryside, which remained dominated by the tribal leaders and landlords.

When the Free Officers seized power in July 1958, the KDP, in common with the other non-Kurdish political organizations, was not directly involved, but welcomed the Revolution in the belief that the new regime would be generally sympathetic to their cause. Ibrahim Ahmad, who was under house arrest in Kirkuk at the time, immediately telegraphed a message of congratulations and support to the Free Officers.[33] The new constitution promulgated at the end of July stated that 'Arabs and Kurds are partners in the Iraqi homeland, and their national rights are recognized within the Iraqi state.'[34] In October 1958, Ibrahim Ahmad was despatched to Prague with four Iraqi passports for Barzani and three of his closest associates. On 6 October, Barzani returned from exile to a rapturous welcome from his Kurdish supporters and what seemed to be expressions of genuine cordiality from the Prime Minister, 'Abd al-Karim Qasim. A new era in Arab-Kurdish relations appeared to have begun.

The Kurds under Qasim, 1958-63

It is clear that the Free Officers who came to power in Iraq in 1958 had no special interest in or commitment to the Kurdish question – none of them was actually Kurdish – but their general attitude towards the Kurds was friendly, if not in any way actively sympathetic. The three-man 'sovereignty council', which was to exercise the ceremonial functions of a president, contained a Sunni Arab, a Shi'i Arab, and a Kurd from a well-known religious and land-owning family, Khalid al-Naqshbandi, a former Army officer who had been governor of Arbil province before the Revolution. Although this body enjoyed virtually no executive power, al-Naqshbandi's appointment to it was clearly a gesture of good will towards the Kurds.

Although the Revolution of July 1958 was widely welcomed by Iraqis of all classes, the country's new rulers were almost entirely without political or administrative experience, and with few exceptions had no clear and certainly no unanimous vision of Iraq's future. Most of the officers, who had been profoundly influenced by the seizure of power in Egypt by Nasser and his military colleagues in 1952 and the nationalization of the Suez Canal four years later, shared varying degrees of enthusiasm for the idea of pan-Arab nationalism much in vogue at the time, which favoured the creation, preferably as soon as possible, of a single Arab state from the Atlantic to the Gulf, in which the Arabs, arbitrarily divided by the imperialist powers in the 19th and 20th centuries, could reassert their strength and restore their former glory. In the eyes of some Arab nationalists, the first steps in this direction had already been taken with the creation, in February 1958, of the United Arab Republic, a merger of Egypt and Syria. In the immediate aftermath of the July Revolution in Iraq there was mounting pressure for Iraq to join the Union.

As has been explained, the coup which became the Revolution was actually carried out by a group of key military officers who were not directly connected with any political party. In pre-revolutionary Iraq the only formal political organization which had any sort of popular following in the country as a whole was the Communist Party, which had been established in 1934. In brief, after the Revolution came, the Communists, many of whom had emerged from long prison sentences, felt that the time was not ripe for the immediate advocacy of a socialist revolution, and called instead for the re-establishment of democracy, which meant a constitutional government and free elections in which they would be able to participate. On the other hand, those who recognized, and feared, the Communists' very widespread popular appeal, tended to side with the Arab nationalists, who were calling for Iraq to join the UAR.[35]

For their part, the Communists, although not opposed to the *principle* of a unified Arab political entity, could not but view the United Arab Republic as it was actually constituted as a grave threat to them. The UAR, in general terms, was largely the very hurried and ill-thought out product of the Syrian Ba'th Party's fears that it would be overtaken in popularity in Syria by the Syrian Communist Party, which had gained greatly in strength throughout the 1950s, particularly after the Syrian government had begun to forge closer military and diplomatic ties with the Soviet Union. One of the great merits of the Union, as far as the Ba'th was concerned, was that all parties would be dissolved in Syria, thus bringing Syria into line with Egypt.[36] Hence the Communists were resolutely opposed to union under, let it be stressed, such conditions. On the other side, many of those Iraqis who had enjoyed positions of privilege, and particularly those who had prospered economically, under the monarchy, now pronounced themselves in favour of Arab nationalism, and supported union either as a gut anti-Communist reaction or because they feared the growing strength of Communist pressure on the government. In this conflict, the leader of the Free Officers, 'Abd al-Karim Qasim, although certainly no Communist, was quick to realize that Iraq's adhesion to the UAR would mean that he would have to defer to Nasser, which would not have accorded with his own ambitions. This in part explains the uneasy, and for the Communists ultimately fatal, partnership between themselves and Qasim.

Thus in the early months of the new republic, the struggle for power centred round the question of whether to join, or not to join, the UAR, although it will now be clear that this was only the superstructural symbol of a far more profound conflict. It will be equally clear that the Kurds' attitude to 'unity' was bound to be negative. Quite apart from the fact that the Kurds in post-revolutionary Syria did not enjoy even the inadequate recognition of Kurdish linguistic, ethnic and educational rights which had been afforded to the Kurds in pre-revolutionary Iraq,[37] it would have been unrealistic in the extreme for the Iraqi Kurds to imagine that the UAR was in any sense likely to be a suitable vehicle for the furthering of their aspirations, however defined. The only prominent Kurd to doubt the wisdom of a policy of unrelenting opposition to Iraqi adhesion to the UAR was Ibrahim Ahmad, who was on good terms with Nasser, and was apparently genuinely convinced that Iraq's joining the Union was inevitable, and hence that the Kurds should work for it in order to win the right to participate fully in it.[38]

However, by the autumn of 1958, Qasim had gained the upper hand over his most vociferously pro-Unionist colleague, 'Abd al-Salam 'Arif, with the result that there was no longer any question of the government itself proceeding with any unity scheme. This did not dampen the ardour of the nationalists, but it did mean that their ambitions were not going to be satisfied while Qasim remained in office. For a while, the amicable relations between the new regime and the Kurds continued. In March 1959, a group of unionist officers attempted a coup in Mosul with Syrian backing; Barzani gave his unqualified support to the Qasim regime, despatching thousands of armed tribesmen to Mosul, where they took advantage of the situation both to put down the coup and to settle old scores with some of the great landowners of the city.[39] A little earlier, Barzani had taken over the leadership of the KDP, removed Ibrahim Ahmad, whose advocacy of the UAR had made his position somewhat incongruous, and installed his own nominees on the central committee, including Hamza 'Abdullah. At the same time, the KDP had signed a pact with the Communists.[40] In such company, the 'new-look' KDP put forward a left-wing Manifesto in May 1959, whose attacks on 'feudalism' and 'reaction' were difficult to square with the fact that the party was led by a tribal chief who was also a member of an important land-owning family.[41]

In a very short time, this incongruity came to the surface, because Barzani and others like him were not slow to realize the implications for their own positions of the social content of such a programme. In addition, the alliance with the Communists meant that the latter were now relatively free to operate in the Kurdish areas, where many of the aghas and shaikhs were at least as repressive of their peasants and tribesmen as their Arab counterparts further south. The prospect of the extension of the provisions of the new (September 1958) land reform to Kurdistan were viewed by Barzani and his circle with considerable alarm, especially as there was little doubt that such policies would have widespread popularity in the region as a whole. It goes without saying that these and other contradictions have acted as a major brake on the effectiveness of the Kurdish movement over the past quarter century.

Quite fortuitously, Barzani's unease about the KDP's orientation and what he saw as the increasing disadvantage of the alliance with the Communist Party, coincided with Qasim's own desire to distance himself from the Communists, whose reputation had suffered from allegations of their involvement in the riots in Kirkuk in July 1959, in which at least 30 people were killed and about 130 injured. The real extent of Communist involvement is not clear, partly because what actually happened was a battle with Kurds on one side and members of the Turkoman minority (two groups who had traditionally been at loggerheads) on the other.[42] Nevertheless, Qasim took advantage of the situation to accuse the Communists of trying to terrorize their way to office in his government, and sought a closer alliance with Mulla Mustafa. A few months later, in January 1960, the KDP was legalized, but the Communist Party was refused permission to register. At the same time, Mulla Mustafa found Hamza 'Abdullah's generally supportive attitude towards the Communists increasingly out of tune with his own ambitions; eventually, he sent a group of tribesmen round to KDP headquarters to eject 'Abdullah physically. In the course of the year Ibrahim Ahmad and his ally Jalal Talabani managed to find their way back into Barzani's favour, and by October Ahmad had been 're-elected' secretary-general of the party.[43]

However, it soon became clear that Qasim's commitment to the Kurds was both limited and very much dependent on the other groups and factions with whom he was attempting to ally at the same time. Easing away from the Communists meant moving closer to the conservative military officers, many of whom were opposed to any genuine concessions to Kurdish national sentiment. Hence, although the KDP was given an official license in January 1960, Ahmad discovered to his surprise that the 'party programme' which the government returned to him differed considerably from the one he had submitted originally, particularly as far as any mention of Kurdish autonomy was concerned. References to Marxist-Leninism, the 'Kurdish people' and 'Kurdistan' had also been omitted.[44] This caused considerable friction between the Kurdish 'politicals', and Qasim, but, as it does not seem to have been a matter of particularly grave concern to Barzani, Ahmad and his friends accepted the changes. In general, of course, Barzani's basic instincts and attitudes were those of a tribal leader; although he was naturally interested in gaining the support of Kurdish intellectuals, his real power base lay in his own tribe, and his force of some 2,000 fighting men. In an important sense, the precise wording of the programme of the KDP was less significant to him than to those who saw the Party as a means of political and ideological mobilization for the goal of a form of progressive autonomy for the Kurdish areas. For their part, both at this point and at many times between 1961 and 1975, the 'politicals' were forced, often against their better judgement, to defer to Barzani, precisely because he was the only Kurdish figure with sufficient magnetism, tribal following and military experience to be able to carry the day in Kurdistan.

Thus, in March 1960, Barzani accepted, more or less without demur, the expulsion by Qasim of the leaders of the Iranian KDP who had taken refuge in Iraq after the 1958 Revolution.[45] However, although apparently lacking the political sophistication to see where such a policy might logically lead, Barzani was quick to understand a much more direct threat, Qasim's favourable reception of his enemies, the leaders of the Herki and Surchi tribes, in the autumn of 1960. Barzani had already left for a courtesy visit to the Soviet Union; when he returned to Baghdad in mid-January 1961, the rupture with Qasim was almost complete. By the end of March, all the Kurdish newspapers and magazines had been banned, and Barzani himself had left the capital for Barzan. For his part, it seems that Qasim had also not forgotten Ahmad's early espousal of 'Arif and the nationalist cause, and always remained intensely suspicious of him: this distrust was naturally enhanced when Ahmad was reappointed secretary-general of the KDP in place of Hamza 'Abdullah in the autumn of 1959.

Like any other ruler of modern Iraq, Qasim was simply not willing to grant real autonomy to the Kurds, particularly when they were represented, or led, by a figure who had already attained the status of a national hero when Qasim was still an unknown junior officer. However, the split between Qasim and Mulla Mustafa was almost certainly not simply based on differences of personality and reputation, but was fundamentally the product of what seems to have been a fairly generally held notion among Iraqis of a variety of different political opinions, that concessions to Kurdish nationalism were ultimately equivalent in some imprecisely articulated but deeply felt sense to a fundamental derogation of Iraqi sovereignty, which had itself been so recently and so hardly won. Even among progressives and liberals, who might believe in notions of minority rights and the granting of self-determination to ethno-linguistic groups, the fact that the Kurds' most visible leader was a figure who seemed to represent many of the least desirable aspects of the old order symbolized by the monarchy and its entourage of shaikhs and landlords, meant that the credibility of the whole Kurdish cause was somehow always open to question. For a while at least, the conflict between Qasim and Mulla Mustafa, which broke out in earnest in the autumn of 1961, could be regarded as a profound breach of faith, an attack on the Revolution of 1958 by elements which the new regime had been unwise enough to encourage in the first place.

For a while, Barzani was content to bide his time in the north, and let Qasim arrest or harass the urban leadership. Thus Ahmad and another member of the politbureau, 'Umar Mustafa, were arrested in March 1961, and the KDP was refused permission to hold its annual congress in July. The Kurdish newspapers, as has already been mentioned, were all banned in the first few months of 1961. However, when the government began to give clear encouragements to Barzani's tribal enemies, the Zibaris, Barzani reacted vigorously, chasing the Zibari leaders across the Turkish border in July 1961. By September 1961, the fighting had started in earnest, with government forces heavily involved, aided by the Baradost, Herki and Zibari tribes, all of whom had a long history of opposition to the Barzanis.[46]

The tribal character of the conflict was readily apparent, and was underlined by the KDP's initial unwillingness to become involved. Ahmad expressed a strong suspicion that Iran was supporting the revolt for the ultimate purpose of undermining the 1958 Revolution, to which the KDP remained committed,[47] and considered that Barzani was using the kinds of tactics employed in the 1920s and 1930s, which were out of place in post-Revolutionary Iraq. It was also clear that Barzani's supporters among the other tribal leaders in Kurdistan were as anxious as he was to resist the imposition of land reform in the area. Other leftist groups in the country, notably the Communists, were also opposed to the revolt, which they thought might precipitate Qasim's fall. Here again, many of the contradictions inherent in the Kurdish movement are revealed; most Iraqi leftists and progressives wanted the government to take active steps to grant the Kurds their national rights, but few were prepared to support Mulla Mustafa if this meant rocking the extremely fragile apparatus over which Qasim was presiding, whose vulnerability was to become increasingly apparent over the next two years.

The war which began between the central government and the Kurds in 1961 continued intermittently until 1975. It was, as Kutschera correctly points out, less a war than a series of 'mini-wars', with periods of truce of varying length between them, both affecting, and being effected by, the twists and turns of Iraqi politics.[48] The attack on the Barzanis began in earnest in September 1961, although at this stage the KDP chose not to commit itself and did not become fully involved until much later. It is possible that Ahmad and Talabani hoped that Qasim and the army might actually succeed in smashing the Barzanis, and that this would make the Kurds more likely to look to the KDP for leadership. By the end of 1961, however, the KDP had judged it wiser to declare itself, and brought its 750 fighting men into the conflict. This inaugurated a period of uneasy cooperation with Barzani which was possible largely because the two groups controlled different parts of Kurdistan.

For the first few months the fighting was inconclusive, although – as was always to be the case – the Kurds were vastly outnumbered by the government forces. However, Qasim was also involved at the time in what can only be described as a senseless confrontation with Kuwait, which reduced the numbers he could deploy in the north. By May 1962, Barzani had gained control of the Hamilton road between Rowanduz and the Iranian frontier; the Iraqi army was only able to return to this area after the collapse of the Kurdish movement in 1975. As has already been explained, these operations were taking place at a time when Qasim was becoming increasingly isolated, having jettisoned his allies on the left and having failed to consolidate his relations with their opponents. As early as April 1962, Ibrahim Ahmad had 'accepted the principle of cooperation with forces opposed to Qasim', laying down a series of conditions for such cooperation.[49] In fact, when the Ba'th-Nationalist alliance eventually overthrew Qasim in February 1963, they had had previous assurances from both Barzani and the KDP leaders that if they were successful the Kurds would announce a ceasefire, which duly materialized.[50] Talabani and Salah al-Yusufi were despatched to Baghdad a few days later to negotiate with the new regime, but as the enthusiasm of the Ba'thists and Nationalists for Kurdish autonomy had been assumed for purely tactical purposes, the KDP leaders soon realized that any hopes they may have entertained were purely wishful thinking. Fighting broke out again in June, and continued until the beginning of 1964, by which time the nationalists had already succeeded in pushing their Ba'thist partners out of the coalition, and 'Abd al-Salam 'Arif had emerged as unchallenged leader.

The Kurds since 1963

For the next few years, some elements of a pattern are discernible.[51] The conflict was generally a three cornered one, with the participants being the government, the KDP and Barzani; sometimes the KDP would cooperate with the government, sometimes with Barzani, and sometimes, though rather more rarely, Barzani and the government would join forces to attack the KDP. Thus in August 1964, Barzani chased Ahmad and Talabani out of Iraq, across the Iranian border, in revenge for the KDP's attack on his truce with 'Arif (April 1964). In July 1964 he had set up his 'own' KDP, with a new politburo including Mahmud 'Uthman and Habib Karim, from which all supporters of the Ahmad-Talabani group had been purged. This rupture between Barzani and the politicals had the effect of handing over the day to day control of the Kurdish movement on the ground to Barzani alone; while Barzani's military talents can hardly be questioned, his political acumen was so limited that this development put the Kurdish national cause at a grave disadvantage from then on.

The cease-fire arranged by Barzani and 'Arif in February 1964 lasted some 15 months, until the beginning of April 1965. Virtually the entire Iraqi army (40–50,000 men) was despatched to the north in another desperate attempt to reassert the authority of the government in the area. During this round of fighting Barzani began to receive large (and eventually essential) quantities of military aid from Iran, perhaps Barzani's major miscalculation as Kurdish leader. To forge a close relationship with a power vigorously opposed to the 'progressive' government in Baghdad enabled the Kurds' critics to portray them as being prepared to consort with the enemies of Iraq; it caused an almost irreparable breach with the 'politicals', and finally it left the Kurds profoundly exposed to any changes of heart in Tehran. Partly, perhaps, as a consequence of this, the KDP leaders now made their peace with Baghdad (Barzani had allowed them to return to Iraq from Iran in the summer of 1965, on condition that they would live under a form of house arrest in the north, from which they managed to escape in January 1966), and set up anti-Barzani Kurdish military units, largely from tribes traditionally hostile to Barzani, sponsored and paid for by Baghdad, which actually fought alongside the Iraqi army in the north. However, by mid-May 1966, Barzani and his followers inflicted a crushing defeat on the Iraqi army and the pro-government Kurds at Mount Handrin, between Rowanduz and the Iranian frontier. At this point the government began to negotiate seriously with Barzani again, and a 'third interlude' began, which lasted between June 1966 and January 1969.

On 29 June 1966, the Iraqi Prime Minister, 'Abd al-Rahman al-Bazzaz, announced a cease-fire on television, and also put forward a peace plan for Kurdistan, which, although honoured largely in the breach over the following years, has generally formed the basis for most subsequent peace initiatives for the area. It recognized the principle of Kurdish autonomy, provided for elections to a legislative council, the use of Kurdish as an official language in schools and in the local administration, a general amnesty, and the maintenance of armed tribal units (taken from Barzani's forces) as a kind of government gendarmerie until the situation in the area returned to normal. In addition, Kurdish political prisoners were to be released, and Kurdish newspapers permitted.[52]

Unfortunately for the Kurds, al-Bazzaz was forced out of office a few months later, and the more hawkish elements once more carried the day. Many such peace initiatives broke down (both before and after 1966) largely because of the opposition of the various governments' military supporters, who felt that the honour of the armed forces required that no real concessions should be made to the Kurds. At this stage, however, Barzani's relations with Iran were excellent, and any campaign against him would have stood little chance of success. Nevertheless, opposition to the al-Bazzaz agreement from various quarters in Baghdad was strong enough to ensure that it remained largely a dead letter.

In July 1968, the government of 'Abd al-Rahman 'Arif was overthrown, and the Ba'th came to power, with the tacit support of the Ahmad-Talabani faction of the KDP, some of whom were appointed to the cabinet.[53] In the first few weeks, the new regime and Barzani attempted to reach an agreement, although Barzani was naturally suspicious of the Ba'th's Kurdish associates. These efforts failed, and severe fighting broke out once more in the spring of 1969, beginning with a daring raid on the IPC installations at Kirkuk. The damage was considerable; IPC had to reduce production by some 70% and incurred losses of about $10 million. The government replied by sending four divisions to Kurdistan, and the fighting continued for most of that year. In order to consolidate his own position, Barzani promoted his younger sons Idris and Mas'ud to positions of major responsibility within the KDP, as well as 'Sami' (the *nom de guerre* of Muhammad Mahmud 'Abd al-Rahman) and 'Aziz 'Aqrawi.

In August 1969, a major offensive was launched by the government, once more without any visible success, in spite of atrocities on the government side designed to terrorize the inhabitants of the Kurdish area into submission.[54] At this stage the Ba'th regime was not yet sufficiently firmly established to continue the campaign indefinitely, and approached Barzani with a view to opening negotiations. These took place between mid-December 1969 and March 1970, and ended with the publication of the Manifesto of 11 March 1970. If implemented, this agreement would have gone as far as, if not further than the al-Bazzaz declaration of 1966 towards a solution of the Kurdish question. In essence, it recognized 'the legitimacy of the Kurdish nationality', and promised Kurdish linguistic rights, Kurdish participation in government, Kurdish administrators for the Kurdish area, and a new province based on Dohuk. It also envisaged the implementation of the Agrarian Reform Law in the north, and, perhaps most controversially, as future events were to show, stated that 'necessary steps shall be taken . . . to unify the governorates and administrative units populated by a Kurdish majority as shown by the *official census to be carried out* . . .' (my italics).[55]

As Kelidar has pointed out, the Manifesto had two main drawbacks for the Ba'th. In the first place, it was specifically concluded with Barzani himself, not with 'the Kurds' or 'the Kurdish people', which meant that it gave, at least by implication, recognition to Barzani and the KDP as the sole political (and, *de facto*, administrative) authority in an area extending from Zakho to north of Halabja. Secondly, this recognition had the effect of undermining 'the writ of the Iraqi State in the Kurdish areas.'[56] Essentially, therefore, it must be seen as a device enabling the Ba'th to gain time and establish itself sufficiently to be able to recast its Kurdish policy more to its own advantage at some future point. One minor consequence of the agreement was that the Ahmad-Talabani faction of 'pro-government Kurds' now became redundant, and in fact dissolved itself in the course of 1970.[57]

Almost immediately after the publication of the Manifesto, the government's bad faith became apparent. Large numbers of families were forcibly removed from their homes to change the ethnic balance of particular areas, especially around Kirkuk, which the Kurdish leadership had insisted should form part of the Kurdish area and which the government wanted to retain for itself. Again, in September 1971 some 40,000 Faili Kurds were expelled to Iran from the border area near Khaniqin on the grounds that they were not really Iraqis. In these and other ways the government showed that they were intent on limiting the extent of 'Kurdistan' as far as possible. In an interview some years later, perhaps with hindsight, Barzani said: 'At first (the Ba'thists) came to us and said, "We will grant you self-rule." I said this was a ruse. I knew it even before I signed the agreement. But (our) people asked me, "How can you refuse self-rule for the Kurdish people?" '[58] In September 1971, the government attempted to assassinate Barzani; this had been preceded by an attempt on the life of his son Idris, and similar attacks took place in 1972. After the execution of Nadhim Kazzar the notorious head of the security police, in July 1973,[59] such incidents could always be conveniently ascribed to his personal malevolence, but there is little doubt that Saddam Husain was closely implicated in all Kazzar's activities. Tension gradually rose throughout 1972 and 1973, with a series of articles attacking the KDP appearing in the regime's *al-Thawra* between October and November 1972. After the nationalization of the Iraq Petroleum Company in June 1972, there were clashes between Kurds and government forces in Sulaimaniya, and a number of incidents in Jabal Sinjar, where several thousands of Yazidis were to be forced to leave their homes in February-March 1973 in another of the internal 'redistributions' of population engineered by the Ba'th. In June 1973, Barzani gave an interview to the Washington Post, in which he announced his readiness to entrust the exploitation of the Kirkuk oilfields to an American company: 'it is our homeland, and the nationalization (of IPC) was a blow against the Kurds',[60] which showed how narrow his political aspirations had become.

In the circumstances, it was not surprising that Barzani and the KDP refused to join the National Front between the Ba'th and the Communists in July 1973. However, members of the front met a KDP delegation in Baghdad in January 1974 apparently to try to come to an agreement before the Manifesto was to be officially applied in March. No progress was made, although some members of the KDP ('Aziz 'Aqrawi, Hashim 'Aqrawi and Barzani's eldest son 'Ubaidullah) now broke with Barzani and joined the government side. Both in words and deeds, Barzani himself was moving steadily closer to Iran, the CIA and Israel,[61] from which the Kurds obtained both supplies and military instructors — another potent stick with which their enemies could beat them both at the time and in the future.

Although a major breakdown seemed inevitable, negotiations between the parties continued throughout the end of 1973 and the beginning of 1974. However, by the end of February, the five Kurdish ministers had left Baghdad and sought refuge with Barzani; they were replaced by 'Ubaidullah Barzani, 'Aziz 'Aqrawi, Hashim 'Aqrawi, 'Abdullah Isma'il and 'Abd al-Sattar Tahir Sharif, who founded the Kurdish Revolutionary Party, which proceeded to join the National Patriotic Front. Although perhaps not entirely justly characterized as bogus,[62] in the sense that the KRP did represent those Kurds who genuinely believed in the Ba'th's 'socialist' objectives, the KRP's presence in the Front did not alter the fact that a very much larger number of Kurds were solidly behind Barzani and the KDP. In April 1974, fighting broke out in earnest, with the Iraqi Air Force bombing Qala Diza, Halabja and Galala at the end of April, killing 193 civilians.[63] A mass exodus of refugees took place to Iran, where there were over 110,000 in the autumn and about 275,000 by the spring of 1975. For a few months, the Kurds had the upper hand; in spite of their vast numerical superiority, the government forces had as usual become seriously bogged down, and no end seemed in sight.

This time, however, the Iraqis' desire and need to get the better of the Kurds coincided with the Iranians' desire to end frontier disputes and other hostilities with Iraq, which had enflamed relations between the two countries over the previous decade. Hence, in March 1975, in the course of the OPEC conference at Algiers, the Iraqis and Iranians signed an agreement which, on the Iraqi side, effectively abrogated the Sa'dabad Pact of 1937, and thus gave the Iranians free rights of navigation in the Shatt al-'Arab, and, on the Iranian side, closed the Iran-Iraq frontier in the north, thus preventing aid reaching the Kurds from Iran, and equally preventing the Kurds themselves from regrouping and rearming in and from Iran.[64] The Iranian artillery withdrew within 24 hours, and the Kurdish resistance collapsed almost immediately. Barzani left for Iran, and then for the United States, where he died in 1979.

The Algiers agreement was a devastating blow, which Barzani had simply never foreseen, believing as he did in the 'moral obligation and political responsibility' of the United States towards the Kurdish people, as he wrote in a letter to Kissinger which was later leaked with the rest of the Pike

Report.[65] In the months that followed, most of the refugees trickled back to Iraq under a series of amnesties. On a visit to Iraq in August and September 1985, it was quite clear to Ismet Sharif Vanly, a Kurdish activist long resident in Geneva who had been invited to Iraq by the government, that the government was forcibly Arabizing the area, and that 'Kurdish autonomy' was a farce. In addition the inhabitants of the more remote areas were being removed from their homes and 'resettled' in newly constructed villages on the sides of roads where surveillance would be easier. Kurdish was clearly not being taught in the schools, and Kurdish teachers and administrators were being sent to work in southern Iraq, and replaced in the Kurdish area by Arabs.[66] By 1979, an estimated 200,000 Kurds had been deported from the frontier area, and some 700 villages burnt down as part of a scorched earth policy which aimed to clear a strip along the borders with Iran and Turkey some 20km. deep and 800km. long.[67]

It has taken some time for the Kurdish movement to recover from the disaster of 1975. Almost immediately after the defeat, it split once more into two main factions, the KDP-Provisional Command, led by Barzani's sons Idris and Mas'ud, who claim to be more radical than their father, and the Patriotic Union of Kurdistan (PUK) led by Jalal Talabani, who returned from several years exile in Syria.[68] For a while, the Iranian Revolution brought new hope to the Kurds in both Iran and Iraq, but this was soon dashed by the increasingly repressive and anti-minority stance of the new regime in Tehran. The Ba'th in Baghdad had tended to support the Iranian KDP, now led by 'Abd al-Rahman Qasimlu, while the Iranian regime supports the KDP-Provisional Command, which means that the Kurdish movement is effectively divided along 'national' lines. Hence the Kurds in Iran and Iraq will tend to favour a victory by the 'other side' in the present conflict, although as most Kurds are Sunni Muslims, their enthusiasm for a Shi'i 'Islamic government' is naturally somewhat limited.

The most important development in Kurdistan in recent years has been the revival of armed struggle in the area. In addition, the deportations, executions and other atrocities perpetrated by the Ba'th have served to sharpen the political consciousness of many Kurds. Kurdistan has emerged as the main focus of opposition to the dictatorship in Baghdad, although, alas, the old factional struggles between the Barzanis and Talabani continue. How successful the Kurds and their Communist partners will be is an open question: Talabani in particular is an unknown quantity, since the PUK oscillates between opposition to and cooperation with Baghdad, according to how Talabani sees his own interests best served.[69] In 1981, there were strikes and demonstrations throughout the Kurdish area. Vengeance was swift; hundreds of executions and many thousands of deportations and 'relocations' followed.[70] The Ba'th clearly cannot afford to risk a second hostile front in Kurdistan, but the extent of the repression gives some indication of the strength of the resistance.

In general terms, however, the struggle is likely to be a long and bitter one. The Iraqi Kurds have been, and to some extent still are, badly served by their leaders, and of course by every regime which has come to power in Baghdad. Overall, Kurdish history in the 20th century is a tragic record of the progressive erosion of a people's independence and its identity as an ethno-linguistic entity, punctuated by several outstanding instances of heroism and sacrifice, which have alas produced few positive or lasting results. On the other hand, Rodinson has implied *à propos* Marx's dictum that 'a people oppressing another cannot be free',[71] it is quite clear in the Iraqi case that the regime's oppression of the Kurds is part and parcel of its oppression of the whole Iraqi people. At the present time, the overthrow of the Ba'th dictatorship represents the only hope for the restoration of democracy and civil liberties in Iraq, for Arabs and Kurds alike.

References

1. 'Introduction', by Gerard Chaliand, in G. Chaliand (ed) *People without a Country: the Kurds and Kurdistan* (trs. Michael Pallis), (Zed Press, London, 1980) pp. 8–18.

2. V. Minorsky, 'Kurds', *Encyclopedia of Islam*, (Leiden, 1918–1934).

3. These figures are based on those in M. van Bruinessen, *Agha, Shaikh and State: on the Social and Political Organization of Kurdistan*, (Rijswijk, Utrecht, 1978) pp. 20–22; see also the various country by country articles in Chaliand, op. cit.; compare the latest estimates given by Ferhad Ibrahim, *Die Kurdische Nationalbewegung im Irak: eine Fallstudie zur Problematik Ethnischer Konflikte in der Dritten Welt* (Schwarz, Berlin, 1983) pp. 100–103.

4. The history of the Kurds in the 19th century is discussed briefly in B. Nikitine, *Les Kurdes: Étude Sociologique et Historique* (Klincsieck, Paris, 1956), pp. 185–194, and in 'The Kurds under the Ottoman Empire', in Chaliand, op. cit., pp. 19–37. See also van Bruinessen, op. cit., pp. 220–232.

5. See William Eagleton Jr., *The Kurdish Republic of Mahabad,* (O.U.P., London, 1963) pp. 14–24, and Sir Arnold Wilson, *Mesopotamia 1917–1920, a Clash of Loyalties*, (O.U.P., London, 1931) pp. 29–38.

6. Peter Sluglett, *Britain in Iraq 1914–1932*, (Ithaca Press, London, 1976) p. 14.

7. Ibid., pp. 116–117.

8. For further details, see S.J. and E.K. Shaw, *History of the Ottoman Empire and Modern Turkey: Volume II, Reform, Revolution and Republic: The Rise of Modern Turkey, 1808–1975*, (C.U.P., Cambridge 1977) Chapter V, 'The Turkish War for Independence, 1918–1923', pp. 340–372.

9. Sluglett, op. cit., p. 117; see also C.J. Edmonds, *Kurds, Turks and Arabs,* (O.U.P., London, 1957) pp. 28–78.

10. Ibid.

11. The text of the articles relating to 'Kurdistan' (nos. 62–64) is reproduced in Chaliand, op. cit., pp. 42–43.

12. For these events, see Kendal, 'The Kurds in Turkey', in Chaliand, op. cit., pp. 47–80; C. Kutschéra, *Le Mouvement National Kurde*, (Flammarion, Paris, 1979), pp. 79–105, 121–129, and the useful map of the

risings in Turkey in Hasan Arfa, *The Kurds: An Historical and Political Study*, (O.U.P., London, 1966) p. 35. van Bruinessen (op. cit., pp. 353–406) gives a detailed account of Shaikh Sa'id of Piran's revolt. In general, Kutschéra and van Bruinessen are impressively documented.

13. See Kutschéra. op cit., pp. 43–56; Eagleton, op. cit., pp. 9–11; Arfa, op. cit., pp. 47–64. As an Iranian officer, Arfa was personally involved in many operations against the Kurds in Iran.

14. Sluglett, op. cit., pp. 116–125; Edmonds, op. cit., pp. 116–124, 298–384.

15. Edmonds, op. cit., pp. 386–435. Edmonds was an Administrative Inspector in northern Iraq, and accompanied the boundary commissioners on their tours of the area early in 1925. The episode is summarized in Sluglett, op. cit., pp. 114–125.

16. This speech is quoted in Sluglett, op. cit., pp. 182–183.

17. Ibid., p. 186.

18. Ibid., pp. 186–194, 211–212.

19. See Kutschéra, op. cit., pp. 113–121.

20. Sa'd Jawad, *Iraq and the Kurdish Question 1958–1970*, (Ithaca Press, London, 1981) pp. 13–14; Kutschéra, op. cit., pp. 136–137; F. Ibrahim, op. cit., pp. 387–390; 'Hizbi Hiwa war wie die meisten irakischen Parteien, die vor dem Zweiten Weltkrieg enstanden waren, eine Partei der Elite.' (387).

21. Majid 'Abd al-Ridha, *al-Mas'ala al-Kurdiya fi'l-'Iraq* (The Kurdish Question in Iraq), (al-Tariq al-Jadid, Baghdad, 1975) p. 83.

22. For further information on Kurdish Communist politics under the monarchy and the activities of the ICP in Kurdistan see Majid 'Abd al-Ridha, op. cit., and Su'ad Khairi, *Min Ta'rikh al-Haraka al-Thawriya fi'l-'Iraq: Thawra 14 Tammuz* (The History of the Revolutionary Movement in Iraq; the Revolution of 14 July [1958]), (Dar Ibn Khaldun, Beirut, 1980).

23. S.H. Longrigg, *Iraq 1900-1950*, (O.U.P., London, 1953) pp. 277–302, Mohammad Tarbush, *The Role of the Military in Politics: a Case Study of Iraq to 1941*, (Kegan Paul International, London, 1982) pp. 150–187.

24. Longrigg, *loc. cit.*

25. Quoted from Barzani to Cornwallis, 25 December 1943, FO 371/40038, in Kutschéra, op. cit., pp. 139–140.

26. Ibid., pp. 140–146; see also Jawad, op. cit., pp. 14–16.

27. Kutschéra, op. cit., pp. 146–152.

28. The most complete account of Mahabad is by W. Eagleton, op. cit.; see also Archie Rosevelt Jr., 'The Kurdish Republic of Mahabad', *Middle East Journal*, vol. 1, no. 3, 1947, (reprinted in Chaliand, op. cit., pp. 135–152). The following paragraphs are largely based on Eagleton.

29. See note 24 above.

30. This period in Iranian history is best followed in Ervand Abrahamian, *Iran between Two Revolutions* (Princeton UP, Princeton, 1982) and in Nikki R. Keddie, *Roots of Revolution: an Interpretive History of Modern Iran*, (Yale U.P., New Haven and London, 1981) pp. 113–141.

31. Ibid., and Kutschéra, op. cit., pp. 188–189.

32. Kutschéra, op. cit., pp. 189–200; Ibrahim, op. cit., pp. 406–427; Jawad, op. cit., pp. 18–24.

33. Jawad, op. cit., p. 37.

34. Uriel Dann, *Iraq under Qassem; a Political History, 1958-1963*, (New York: Praeger 1969) p. 36. The most comprehensive and reliable account

of this period is in Hanna Batatu, *The Old Social Classes and Revolutionary Movements of Iraq; a Study of Iraq's Old Landed and Commercial Classes, its Communists, Ba'thists and Free Officers*, (Princeton U.P., Princeton, 1978) pp. 764–807.

35. This is discussed in more detail in 'Iraqi Ba'thism: Nationalism, Socialism, and National Socialism', in this volume.

36. The Syrian Ba'th leaders themselves felt that their own nationalist credentials would be sufficiently strong for them not to be passed over for high office in the new Republic – a miscalculation on their part, as events were to show. See Elisabeth Picard, 'La Syrie de 1946 à 1979', in André Raymond (ed.) *La Syrie d'Aujourd'hui*, (Editions du C.N.R.S., Paris, 1980) pp. 143–184.

37. See Mustafa Nazdar, 'The Kurds in Syria', in Chaliand, op. cit., pp. 211–219.

38. Jawad, op. cit., p. 45; Ibrahim, op. cit., pp. 463–469.

39. See Batatu, op. cit., pp. 866–889.

40. Jawad, op. cit., pp. 46–50; Ibrahim, *loc. cit.*

41. Reproduced in part in Kutschéra, op. cit., pp. 207–208.

42. See Batatu, op. cit., pp. 912–921. Ibrahim quotes the Kurdish journal *Xebat*, deploring the violence at Kirkuk (*Xebat*, 11 August 1959); op. cit., pp. 475–477.

43. Jawad, op. cit., pp. 46–47.

44. Ibid., pp. 49–50.

45. Kutschéra, op. cit., p. 210.

46. Ibid., pp. 210–213.

47. Jawad, op cit., p. 80; this period is dealt with in some detail by Ibrahim, op. cit., pp. 478–491.

48. op. cit., p. 213.

49. Ibid., p. 226.

50. For Ibrahim Ahmad's contacts with Tahir Yahya, see Jawad, op. cit., pp. 108–112.

51. The clearest source for these years is Kutschéra; for a more detailed account, see Ibrahim.

52. For a discussion of the peace plan, see Edith and E.F. Penrose, *Iraq: International Relations and National Development*, (Benn, London, 1978) pp. 338–340.

53. For further details, see Batatu, op. cit., pp. 1073–1093.

54. See Kutschéra, op. cit., p. 272, quoting incidents at Dakan and Sorya.

55. For the text of the March Manifesto, see Majid Khadduri, *Socialist Iraq: a Study in Iraqi Politics since 1968*, (Washington, 1978) pp. 231–240.

56. Abbas Kelidar, 'Iraq, the Search for Stability', *Conflict Studies* no. 59, Middle East Institute, July 1975, p. 11.

57. Ibrahim, op. cit., p. 578. Ahmad retired finally from Kurdish politics in 1975 to exile in London; Jalal Talabani heads the Patriotic Union of Kurdistan (PUK), see below.

58. Edmund Ghareeb, *The Kurdish Question in Iraq*, (Syracuse U.P., Syracuse, 1981) p. 89. The interview is dated September 1976. Ghareeb's pro-Ba'thist stance makes his account both unreliable and one-sided.

59. See Penrose and Penrose, op. cit., pp. 364–366.

60. Quoted by Kutschéra, op. cit., p. 286.

61. The details were revealed in the Pike Report, which was leaked to the *Village Voice* in February 1976, where it was published in full. Kurdish-Israeli relations are discussed in Ibrahim, op. cit., pp. 711–714; cf. Ghareeb, op. cit., pp. 142–145.

62. This is Kutschéra's view; see op. cit., p. 302.

63. David Hirst's report, quoted by Ibrahim, op. cit., p. 621, and Kutschéra, op. cit., p. 303.

64. For details of the preparations for the agreement, and the involvement of Egypt and Algeria, see I.C. Vanly, 'Kurdistan in Iraq', in Chaliand, op. cit., pp. 184–186. The text of the agreement is reproduced in Khadduri, op. cit., pp. 245–260 (Iran-Iraq Treaty on International Borders and Good Neighbourly Relations, 13 June 1975).

65. See note 59 above.

66. I.C. Vanly, op. cit., pp. 192–203. In October 1976, the Ba'th attempted – unsuccessfully – to assassinate Vanly.

67. Ibrahim, op. cit., pp. 635–638.

68. See Ghareeb, op. cit., p. 182.

69. Ibid; see also Marion Farouk-Sluglett, Peter Sluglett and Joe Stork, 'Not Quite Armageddon: the Impact of the (Gulf) War on Iraq', *MERIP Reports*, no. 125/126 (July-September 1984), p. 26.

70. C. Legum, H. Shaked and D. Dishon (eds.), *Middle East Contemporary Survey*, vol. VI, 1981–82 (Holmes / Meier, New York, 1984) pp. 596–598.

71. M. Rodinson, 'Preface', in Chaliand, op. cit., pp. 1–8.

10. The Iraqi Armed Forces, Past and Present

A. Abbas

Particularly since the Second World War many Third World countries have experienced the installation of repressive military regimes by means of plots, coups d'état and assassinations. These phenomena arouse much interest and scholars have sought their causes.[1] Some studies explore the relationship between the armed forces and different social and political systems.[2] Publications on the Iraqi Army are, however, scarce. It is a politically sensitive topic and research into it is discouraged by the Iraqi authorities who view such interest as hostile and a threat to Iraq's national security.

This chapter examines the Iraqi armed forces from both historical and political aspects, with special emphasis on the periods of Ba'th rule in Iraq, and the effect on the armed forces of the Ba'th Party's national socialist ideology. It looks first at the formation of the Iraqi army and its early social structure. It then traces the army's involvement in politics, through the coups d'état of 1937 to 1941, the national democratic revolution of July 1958, the coup of February 1963 which brought the Ba'th Party to power for the first time, and the various coups d'état from 1963 to 1968. The role of political parties in the Iraqi army is then looked at in detail, particularly the role of the Iraqi Communist Party (ICP). This is followed by an account of the ruthless Ba'thization of the army by the Ba'th Party since it came to power in 1968 with the concept of *al-Jaish al-'Aqa'idi* ('the ideological army'). After an examination of the structure and weaponry of the Iraqi army forces today the chapter concludes with a summary of the reasons given by military analysts for Iraq's poor performance in the Gulf War.

Formation of the Iraqi Army

The Iraqi Army was formed on 6 June 1921. King Faisal, the first of the Hashemite family to rule Iraq (1921–33), considered the army to be 'the spinal column for forming a nation'[3] and was to raise its strength from 7,500 in 1925 to 11,500 in 1933.[4] According to Khairi[5] the king felt the need for a 'protective force' which the government could use as a deterrent and to deal with any popular resistance or uprising, and, further, to ensure acknowledgement of the monarch's legitimacy and authority. Hemphill[6] argues that an army was needed to provide Iraq with a symbol of national identity and integrity.

At the time of the setting up of the Ministry of Defence under Ja'far al-'Askari in 1921, there were two types of armed forces: the British (33 battalions of the British imperial troops and a detachment of RAF) and 4,000 Iraqi Levies composed mainly of Assyrians. Both were controlled and financed by Britain. The British government had already seen the need for a joint approach with the Iraqi leaders in dealing with the internal defence of Iraq, and this was spelled out in the resolutions of the March 1921 Cairo Conference, chaired by Winston Churchill.[7] The Cairo Conference decided to maintain the Levies and at the same time to create a local army whose basis and terms of service would be voluntary, with Britain providing training and equipment;[8] from that time the Army expanded. First, the number of recruits was substantially increased following a cabinet decision in 1922. Then, in June 1927, al-'Askari introduced a conscription bill, although this was deferred because of opposition from Britain. In 1934, however, the king issued the Decree of Civil Defence,[9] according to which, every Iraqi man was required to serve in the army. On 1 January 1936 the first call-up was made.[10]

From its formation the Iraqi Army's military training followed the British model. British military advisers provided the supervision, and promising graduates were sent to Britain for further military studies.

The Social Structure of the Iraqi Army

The Sharifians

The Iraqi army was dominated in its early years by the Sharifians, former Ottoman officers who had served with Faisal and his brothers in the Arab Revolt in the First World War. It was estimated that during the late Ottoman period some 60–70 Iraqi cadets were accepted each year into the military academy of Istanbul.[11] Batatu[12] discusses in detail the role and status of these Sharifian officers. The majority were Sunni Muslims from Baghdad or northern Iraq and after the founding of the monarchy many of them assumed important posts in the army and government. Mahmood al-Sinawi was Governor of Baghdad in 1932; Jamal Baban was Minister of Justice; Rashid Mahmud al-Sinawi Khoja was Minister of Defence 1932–33 and 1934–35; Jamil al-Wadi was Minister of Justice 1932–33; Shakir al-Wadi was Minister of Defence 1946–47. Other Sharifians who held important posts included 'Ali Jawdat al-'Ayyubi, Ja'far al-'Askari and Jamil al-Midfa'i.

Nuri Al-Sa'id, also an ex-Sharifian officer, was appointed as the first Director General of the Police in 1921. King Faisal and Nuri al-Sa'id increased the role of the ex-Sharifians in the Iraqi army and by 1936 twelve out of the 19 senior military staff were ex-Sharifians. Nuri al-Sa'id's rise to power was possibly only because he had the support of the king and many of his fellow ex-Sharifians as well as having strong ties with Britain. He became Prime Minister in 1930 and again in 1932. By that time he was the second most powerful man in the country after the King.

Class Origins of Officers

Analysing the social origins of Iraqi officers from the 1930s, Be'eri[13] discerns three distinct categories. First, there were those from the privileged and wealthy families. A number of officers came from the distinguished 'Umari family of Mosul. One of these was Amin al-'Umari, who was Commander of Baghdad and the First Division from 1937 to 1940, and Chief-of-Staff in 1941, after the Rashid 'Ali revolt. Another was Major General Husain al-'Umari, who was involved in the al-Shawwaf rebellion of 1959 and became an administrative inspector of the Ministry of the Interior during the rule of 'Abd al-Salam 'Arif, 1963 to 1966. Naji Suwaydi, from the Suwaydi family of Baghdad was first an Ottoman officer and later an officer in the Sharifian army; in the spring of 1930 became Prime Minister and finally one of Rashid 'Ali's associates. From the Daghistani family of Baghdad there was Major General Ghazi Daghistani, who was Deputy Chief-of-Staff until July 1958. From the Rawi family came Ibrahim Rawi, commander of the 4th division (1937–41), and 'abd al-Ghani al-Rawi, who in 1958 held the rank of Colonel and was one of the Free Officers. In 1959, after the Shawwaf rebellion, he was dismissed from the army.[14] Najib Ruba'i, head of the Presidential Council in Qasim's time, was also from a very prominent and wealthy Baghdadi family. His brother, Hasib, who died in 1956, was a Major General and Deputy Chief-of-Staff in charge of administration. From the al-Sa'duns, a wealthy family in southern Iraq, came 'Abd al-Khaliq al-Sa'dun, who was Air Attaché in London in 1959, and Mumtaz al-Sa'dun, a Captain in the Air Force, who was the pilot of the military plane in which 'Arif 'Abd al-Razzaq fled to Cairo after his abortive coup in September 1965.

Secondly, there were the sons of the Muslim clergy. To this group belonged 'Abd al-Wahhab Shawwaf and his brother Major General Muhammad, who was minister of Health under Qasim. Nadhim Tabaqjali was also the son of an influential clerical family.

Thirdly, there were those who came from middle-class urban families, sons of junior officials and small traders. From 1958 they formed the bulk of the Iraqi officers corps.

The Rank and File

The rank and file soldiers were from the lower strata of Iraqi society, both from urban and rural areas. During the mandate they were volunteers; after the 1934 decree they were conscripts. Conscription was unpopular and people tried to avoid it by any available means. Those from rich families were able to do this by paying a financial indemnity of ID50, know as *al-badal*. Soldiers were expected to blindly obey their superior officers. Those who failed to remain unquestioningly obedient and disciplined faced severe penalties. Soldiers were isolated from civilians, being kept in remote barracks and their meagre salaries drained by fines for trivial offences.

Changes

The original social structure of the Iraqi army changed over the years. As a result of the conscription law the army expanded and increasing numbers of officers were needed. But the most important factor influencing the change in the social structure of the army was the 1958 Revolution. Qasim's Government attempted to purge the army of supporters of the monarchy and replaced them by officers from the middle class. There was an influx of middle-class cadets into the military academic and teaching institutions. However, workers and peasants continued to make up the vast majority of the soldiers. A further incentive for them was the Qasim government's offer of a plot of land from the agrarian reform.[15]

The Army and Politics

The First Coup d'État

From the beginning, the monarchy tried to isolate the Iraqi Army, on the grounds that 'the Army is above politics'.[16] However, nationalist feelings inspired many army officers, and some joined early political societies. The first major involvement of the Iraqi armed forces in politics was the 1936 coup d'état. On 29 October 1936 eleven aeroplanes flew over Baghdad dropping a statement signed by General Bakr Sidqi. The statement criticized the government for disregarding public interest and, on behalf of the army, appealed to the King to ask Hikmat Sulaiman to form a new government. The statement also contained a threat to bomb the capital if these demands were not met. While negotiations and consultation continued, Bakr Sidqi, in an attempt to indicate the seriousness of his threats to the Prime Minister and King Ghazi, authorized limited bombing of Baghdad near the office of the Prime Minister. King Ghazi, following the advice of the British Ambassador not to allow the army a victorious entry, ordered Hikmat Sulaiman to form the new government[17] which, for the first time, included leaders of the left such as Kamil al-Chadirchi and other supporters of the *al-Ahali* group. Some Iraqi cities witnessed a wave of sympathy demonstrations organized by members of the clandestine Iraqi Communist Party, which provided all the necessary popular support.[18] The Iraqi Communists were the first to spread organized political activity inside the armed forces and to foster links with the rank and file to the extent that on 17 March 1937 Sidqi unexpectedly launched an attack on them.

Bakr Sidqi's was the first coup d'état in the Middle East, and was described by a perceptive British author as an 'innovation of the most startling kind'.[20] On 11 August 1937 Bakr Sidqi was assassinated by Sergeant Muhammad

Salih Tal-'Afari, and this was the signal for a counter-coup. General Amin al-'Umari occupied Mosul and, with the support of local commanders in Baghdad and Kirkuk, presented the weak government with a list of demands, some of which called for the banishment of all officers who supported Bakr Sidqi's coup. The Prime Minister resigned and on 16 August 1937 Jamil al-Midfa'i formed the new government.[21] Significantly, he was selected because of the support he enjoyed from senior army officers.

Years of Discontent

Between 1937 and 1941 the Iraqi army was the decisive factor in the formation and downfall of many Iraqi governments.[22] This was true even in cases where the Prime Ministers accepted office on condition that the army remained out of politics. Such a case was Jamil al-Midfa'i's government. Its initial success was owing to the support it had from a group of prominent officers; it was overthrown on 24 December 1938, after an army detachment moved in on the outskirts of Baghdad. A new government was then installed by Nuri al-Sa'id in Iraq's third coup d'état. This was followed by a succession of governments, none of which could have been formed or dismissed without the consent of the army.[23]

In 1940, after the fifth Nuri al-Sa'id government, Rashid 'Ali al-Gailani formed a coalition government, which followed an anti-British line in foreign policy. A power struggle started which concluded with his resignation on 31 January 1941 after dramatic events in which the Regent, Prince 'Abd al-Ilah, fled from Baghdad to Diwaniah. However, al-Gailani continued to be motivated by anti-British feeling and nationalist aspirations, and in this he had the support of four powerful colonels. On 1 April 1941 they met in al-Rashid barracks, and were joined by the Deputy Chief-of-Staff; they planned a coup d'état and the declaration of a state of emergency if the Hashemite government refused to dissolve itself. The seventh coup followed after military detachments moved in and occupied key positions in the capital. A 'government of national defence' was formed by al-Gailani on 3 April, while the Regent again fled, this time to Basra.[24] Later, however, al-Gailani's government was overthrown after British military intervention, al-Gailani himself escaped to Germany, but the four colonels were captured and subsequently executed.

Politics and the Rank and File

Army involvement in politics was not only through coups d'état organized by senior military officers. Soldiers, inspired by patriotic ideals, actively supported popular demonstrations and events. When, in June 1946, there was a huge demonstration in Baghdad, against injustices in Palestine and to demand the expulsion of the British in Iraq, rank and file soldiers played a paramount role in protecting the crowds from police attacks. In the uprisings of 1948 and 1952 many soldiers disobeyed orders for the army to intervene and quell the demonstrators.[25]

The Free Officers Movement

Dissatisfaction among officers—arising from the execution of the four colonels in 1941, and by 1943, the subsequent purge of three-quarters of the army's 44,217 men—increased with the failure of the Palestinian campaign, particularly because of the inactivity of the Iraqi troops during the decisive months of October and December 1948. There was also growing discontent with the Hashemite royal family, ruling in lofty isolation.

In 1952 these factors, together with economic hardship, led scores of army officers to organize themselves into 'Free Officers', modelled on the Egyptian free officer movement. Detailed information about the Iraqi free officer movement is lacking and what exists is mainly based on subjective and often contradictory accounts. Anti-British and anti-monarchy sentiment was heightened after Nuri al-Sa'id signed the Baghdad Pact in 1955. The 1956 uprising gave the free officers movement a boost and, later that year, a Supreme Committee was formed. It selected as chairman, Staff Brigadier Muhyi al-Din 'Abd al-Hamid, who was the most senior member in rank, and Engineer Colonel Rajab 'Abd al-Majid as secretary, and adopted a constitution. Membership was open to all loyal officers, preferably from active units. It was very centralized. The Supreme Committee formed three committees — military, political and economic—plus a coordinating committee.[26] At that time Staff Brigadier 'Abd al-Karim Qasim, Commander of the 19th Infantry Third Division, was in Mafraq in Jordan. He was already a member of another dissident army group, but maintained contact with the main movement until summer 1956. Later, in April 1957, Lieutenant Colonel Wasfi Tahir approached Qasim and in June, after taking an oath, he joined the Supreme Committee.

By late 1957–58 the Supreme Committee had established contacts with the political parties, delegating Colonel Rajab 'Abd al-Majid for this task, particularly in relation to the Iraqi Communist Party (ICP) which had its own military organization. The ICP advocated that a main commitment for all patriotic forces should be to gain the army's support; the ICP itself, unreservedly opposed to any isolation of the army from other patriots, worked strenuously towards this end.

Preparations for the coup continued. The timing was influenced by the 20th Infantry Brigade's orders to move from Jalawla' to Mafraq in Jordan. They had to pass through Baghdad and near to the Palace. There were, however, tensions and splits within the movement. Young officers were eager to begin the coup and there was rivalry among the Free Officers;[28] as a result Qasim initiated the coup on his own. On the night of 13–14 July 1958, the 20th Infantry Brigade's Commander was overcome and detained, and later, the Brigade headed towards Baghdad and occupied key positions. At 6.30am on 14 July 'Proclamation No. 1 was broadcast, and at 7.45am the Royal Guard surrendered.

The Military in Government

One of the first decrees of the 14 July 1958 Revolution formed the Council of Sovereignty, consisting mainly of senior army officers. 'Abd al-Karim Qasim was installed as Prime Minister, Defence Minister and Chief-of-Staff, 'Abd al-Salam 'Arif as Deputy Prime Minister and Minister of the Interior.[29] Under martial law Brigadier Ahmad Salih al-'Abdi was appointed General Military Governor and Colonel Tahir Yahya Chief of Police.[30]

Qasim based himself at the Ministry of Defence rather than at the Prime Minister's Office, and embarked on a radical programme of reorganizing the state and the army.[31] There were extensive changes among the senior military staff with the aim of selecting trustworthy military cadres. A new Chief-of-Staff was appointed as well as new commanders of the four army divisions. Numerous senior army officers were retired and a few were demoted and moved to distant posts. The army was once again at the centre of politics.[32]

Sensitive government positions occupied by members of the military included two seats on the Council of Sovereignty (held by General Najib al-Rubai'i and Colonel Khalid al-Naqshabandi) and four out of 14 ministerial posts, namely Prime Minister, Minister of Defence, Minister of the Interior and Minister of Social Affairs. (Ministerial posts held by members of the military were to be increased to six in the February 1959 cabinet reshuffle.)

In August 1958 a special supreme military court was established – the People's Court – presided over by Colonel F.A. al-Mahdawi. Its purpose was to try defendants charged with offences against the state or with corruption. On 1 August 1958 a decree was issued declaring the formation of the Popular Militia from Iraqi volunteers, to train people in civil defence and to help the army maintain law and order inside the country and to be mobilized against external aggressors. Brigadier Taha Mustafa Bamarni was appointed as the commander of the Popular Militia, accountable directly to the Minister of Defence.[33]

The first incidence of rivalry was between Qasim and 'Arif. 'Arif was not a bright student, had no distinguished military career and was described as naive and immature. Whilst he was engaged on a nationwide tour in Iraq, Qasim started to transfer more army officers who supported 'Arif to less important posts. On 30 September 1958 'Arif was removed as Deputy Prime Minister. He persisted in resisting Qasim's attempts to send him on a diplomatic mission to Bonn and at the same time fostered his links with the Ba'thists and other anti-Communist groups conspiring against the Prime Minister. In early December 1958 'Arif was arrested and later appeared in the People's Court on 27 December 1958. On 5 February 1959 the Court sentenced him to death but Qasim did not sign the death warrant and 'Arif was released in the autumn of 1961.

New attempts were now made to overthrow Qasim. Rashid 'Ali al-Gailani, who returned to Iraq after 1958, was seeking political influence. He started to incite and conspire with the tribes of the Middle Euphrates. He was caught, tried and imprisoned but pardoned and released in July 1962.

On 8 March 1959 Colonel 'Abd al-Wahhab al-Shawwaf, commander of the armed forces in Mosul, proclaimed a rebellion and attacked participants in a peaceful demonstration of the Partisans of Peace. He did this in collusion with Colonel Rifa'at al-Hajj Sirri, Chief of the Military Intelligence Service and Brigadier Nazim al-Tabaqchali, Commander of the Second Division in Kirkuk, all of whom were in touch with the Egyptian authorities. The rebellion met with stiff resistance from the non-commissioned officers and the rank and file of the army in Mosul. The air force prevented attempts by the conspirators to send planes on a bombing mission from Mosul to Baghdad. Instead planes flew from Baghdad and bombed the al-Shawwaf headquarters; al-Shawwaf was wounded and later killed. Those involved in this conspiracy were tried in the People's Court.

The revolutionary mood prevailing after 1958 had affected the army in many ways. Some of the bureaucratic differences between officers and rank-and-file soldiers were abolished. Small libraries were introduced into all the army barracks. Soldiers were able to join in political discussions and freely express their political views. This brought an outcry from senior army officers at the lack of discipline in the army and the spirit of anarchy among the soldiers, especially after 1961 when those who had earlier been retired for their reactionary or anti-revolutionary activities were reinstated following an amnesty decree.[34]

But Qasim was frightened by the immense growth of the democratic movement in the army. He wanted the military establishment fully under his personal control and isolated from the people and politics. However, his personal influence lessened as those who had been expelled in the past assumed control over military affairs again. Progressives and democrats were expelled from the army and the military became more and more opposed to Qasim.

The February 1963 Ba'th Coup

The Ba'th Party, despite its smallness, began collaborating with some army officers and also, according to the Penroses,[35] with the CIA, to overthrow Qasim, utilizing the anti-democratic nature of Qasim's regime, the discontent among the people and the popular disapproval of his anti-Kurdish campaign.

The coup began on 8 February 1963 with the murder of al-Awqati—a Communist and distinguished air force supreme commander—and the movement of troops from the Abu Ghraib Camp towards Baghdad. The coup's Revolutionary Command Council issued a decree forming the National Guard, a Nazi-style paramilitary organization, effectively a Ba'th Party private army. Its commander was Colonel 'Abd al-Karim Mustafa Nasrat, and other Ba'th Party members involved included Ahmad Hasan al-Bakr al-Takriti. The main task of this force was to hunt Communists, their sympathizers and other democrats in a campaign of kidnapping, torture and murder. The murder of Qasim on 9 February was followed by what Penrose and Penrose described as an 'orgy of revenge against known and suspected opponents of the Ba'th [which] knew no bound or restraints'. It was accompanied by a breakdown of law and order on an unprecedented scale.

There were many army officers in Iraq's first Ba'th Government, which the February 1963 coup installed, but none with a distinguished military record. 'Abd al-Salam 'Arif, a nationalist who collaborated with the Ba'thists, was President, Ahmad Hasan al-Bakr al-Takriti was Prime Minister, Salih Mahdi 'Ammash was Minister of Defence, Tahir Yahya was Chief-of-Staff and Hardan al-Takriti was Commander of the Air Force. Colonel Rashid Muslih (later to be executed as a CIA agent, after the 1968 Ba'thist coup) was appointed as the General Military Governor.

The regime published a list of many army officers who were to be compulsorily retired or arrested and tried. Some of the officers who were tried and executed were brought straight from the prisons to which Qasim's regime had condemned them. Soon a struggle started among different factions of the Ba'th Party which resulted in the loss of central government control over the armed forces.[36] One faction was keen to extend its influence within the army and to rally its support to save the regime from deepening crisis and isolation.[37]

The November 1963 Coup

In November 1963 another coup was staged, led by a group of army officers. The 16th and 17th army divisions were moved to occupy strategic positions in Baghdad and in the early morning of 18 November the headquarters of the National Guard was bombed and Baghdad came under the control of the new army group. President 'Abd al-Salam 'Arif asked Chief of Staff Tahir Yahya to form a new government, of which at least a third were to be army officers occupying the most important posts. It also included civilian nationalists, the Nasserists.

The new regime remained divided, and in July 1965, culminated in the resignation of the Nasserist ministers. In an attempt to reduce the Nasserist animosity towards the regime, 'Arif appointed 'Arif 'Abd al-Razzaq, Commander of the Air Force, as Prime Minister and Minister of Defence, after the resignation of Tahir Yahya in September 1965. A civilian, 'Abd al-Rahman al-Bazzaz was appointed as Deputy Prime Minister.

Six days after his appointment Razzaq, supported by air force officers and a number of army units, attempted a coup d'état, but he failed to secure the support of other army units. He escaped to Cairo, and al-Bazzaz became the new Prime Minister. al-Bazzaz's government lasted until August 1966, surviving many problems, including the military campaign against the Kurdish people renewed in spring 1965 by the notorious Brigadier 'Abd al-'Aziz al-'Uqaili. al-'Uqaili planned and executed a bloody war often referred to as 'the spring offensive' which was a total failure but led to heavy casualties in the Iraqi army.

President 'Abd al-Salam 'Arif died in obscure circumstances when a helicopter in which he was travelling from Qurna to Basra crashed on the night of 13–14 April 1966. A curfew was imposed. 'Arif's death was followed by a civilian-military confrontation. After some delay a meeting was held to select a new President, the majority of those present being army officers in the National Defence Council and cabinet. Against the wishes of Prime Minister al-Bazzaz, they pressed for al-'Uqaili or 'Arif's brother 'Abd al-Rahman 'Arif. On the second vote the civilians gave their support to 'Abd al-Rahman 'Arif. He was limited intellectually, unambitious, weak and inadequate, but he was appointed because he was the only candidate the rival factions could agree upon.[38]

Another coup soon followed, planned by 'Arif 'Abd al-Razzaq (who returned from Cairo in June 1966) and some Nasserists, in an attempt to oust Prime Minister al-Bazzaz. Under this pressure President 'Abd al-Rahman 'Arif replaced al-Bazzaz with Brigadier Naji Talib (a Shi'i who had been Minister for Social Affairs in Qasim's regime). Talib was Prime Minister from 6 August 1966 to 10 May 1967, during which time there was a continuous power struggle between the military and the civilians, which ended in Talib's removal. 'Abd al-Rahman 'Arif then assumed both the Presidency and the Premiership. Following the Arab-Israeli war of June 1967, with its disastrous effects, and increased pressure on 'Arif for radical change, he gave up the Premiership to Tahir Yahya.

The Coups of 17 and 30 July 1968
With opposition to 'Abd al-Rahman 'Arif's regime increasing it became more isolated, weakened by a power struggle. Colonel 'Abd al-Razzaq al-Na'if, Chief of Military Intelligence, and Colonel Ibrahim al-Da'ud, Commander of the Republican Guard, were planning with the Ba'thists to overthrow the 'Arif government in a military coup. The coup was carried out on 17 July 1968.

The conspirators had the support of the three major military units: the Republican Guard (al-Da'ud was assisted by Colonel Sa'dun Ghaidan al-Takriti Commander of the Tank Brigade, who became Minister of the Interior after the Ba'thists had disposed of al-Na'if and al-Da'ud); the Baghdad Garrison headed by Colonel Hammad Shihab al-Takriti; and the Military Intelligence. Al-Na'if and al-Da'ud negotiated the distribution of the ministerial posts with the Ba'thists.[39] A new government was formed and a Revolutionary Command Council was established to assume supreme authority. Its self-appointed membership was drawn from the Ba'th Party and the al-Na'if/al-Da'ud group. Colonel Ahmad Hasan al-Bakr al-Takriti was President, al-Na'if was Prime Minister with most of the important ministerial posts held by the al-Na'if/al-Da'ud group.[40]

From the start there were contradictions and acute differences between the Ba'th Party and the al-Na'if/al-Da'ud group. The Ba'thists planned another coup to displace the al-Na'if group. On 30 July 1968 Colonel Hammad Shihab al-Takriti encircled the Presidential Palace with the Armoured Brigade he commanded. Al-Na'if and al-Da'ud were arrested and later deported. A new chapter in Iraqi history began, in which the Ba'th regime embarked on a ruthless policy of Ba'thization and indoctrination of the armed forces.

Political Parties and the Army

The Iraqi army's involvement in politics has not been limited to senior officers at government level. Throughout its history the Iraqi army has been much influenced by party politics. Iraqi officers were enthusiastic supporters of the nationalist cause and were leaders of clandestine societies; *al-'Ahd*, the Covenant, was one of these societies. It was formed in 1913 and Iraqi officers formed a sizeable part of its membership. In 1915 even Nuri al-Sa'id joined *al-'Ahd*. The early nationalist aspirations were for an Arab state within the Ottoman Empire.[41]

Later, in the 1930s, the National Party was active in fostering contacts with the armed forces. It saw the army as a tool for changing the regime, which was savagely repressing anti-government uprisings, both in Kurdistan and in the southern areas of Iraq. Their contacts were limited to senior officers, but were enough to provide political support for the 1936 coup d'état.[42]

Similar influence was seen in the 1940s. This influence was mainly related to nationalist feelings and aspirations demanding independence and pan-Arab unity. It was shown by the four colonels — Salah al-Din al-Sabbagh, Mahmud Salman, Fahim Sa'id and Kamal Shabib — who were responsible for installing Jamil al-Midfa'i in government after the assassination of Bakr Sidqi in 1937. They and many others, motivated by Arab nationalist aspirations, were actively pursuing political goals, and their conspiracies resulted in the coups and counter-coups of 1936–41.

Salah al-Din al-Sabbagh, one of the four colonels, is a good example of this line of political influence. His writings glorify the Arab race and Arab brotherhood.[43] He had no concern for social or economic problems but considered the military factor to be decisive both during war and peace. His pan-Arab nationalism was interwoven with anti-imperialism.[44]

The Influence of the Communist Party

The Iraqi Communist Party pioneered and established the most organized and efficient political influence in the armed forces. The first Communist cell inside the army was founded in 1931. The Communist Party issued its first special declaration in the 'honest soldiers and officers' group in the spring of 1935 at the time when the regime directed the Iraqi army to crush the peasants' uprising in Suq al-Shuyukh. It called upon them to direct their weapons against the enemies of the people, namely the ruling traitors, and not against their brethren, the peasants.

The Iraqi Communist Party established a Communist military committee entrusted with responsibility for agitation and propaganda in the army. Communists had cells in the Communication Battalion and in selected army units.[45] Communist organization in the army was first attacked by the government in 1937, when the regime arrested 65 soldiers and NCOs, and sentenced three of them to death. It also sentenced the civilians responsible for the military organization to imprisonment for two years, to be followed by two years under surveillance.

To counteract the increasing Communist influence inside the army the government issued an appendix to the Baghdad Penal Code, Article (a) 1938, which stated that any officer, NCO or soldier who joined the Communist Party would be sentenced to death. Similarly, any civilian who advocated Communist ideas among five or more military persons would be sentenced to death. Combatting Communism has been an important and central part of the ideological education in the army from its very early days.[46]

In spite of that, the Communist organizations in the army developed. In the 1940s the known membership of the military organization of the Communist Party constituted 15.6% of its total membership.[47] This increased to 18.1% during the period 1949-55.[48] The Communist Party paid great attention to the soldiers' welfare. Its newspaper *al-Qa'idah* published many articles that exposed the poor conditions—as a result of deliberate government policy—under which they lived, and demanded not only decent living conditions for them, but full democratic rights. The ICP's first programme, endorsed by its first Congress in 1944, included a section on the army. It stated that: 'We struggle to give every care to the conscripted Iraqi soldier, for his health, food and general education, to give him also a democratic education, to abolish all the inhuman methods followed in the army such as physical punishment and imprisonment, to introduce democratic discipline into the army, to purge it of its "fifth column" of reactionary elements. Moreover, we struggle for an army which serves the interests of the people and defends their national independence.'[49]

During the severe attack on the ICP in 1949 many soldiers, NCOs and students of the military academy were arrested and punished.

The regime was forced to use the army to crush the November 1952 uprising since the police failed to do so. On 22 November, the ICP issued a proclamation directed at the soldiers and officers, asking them to support the people against the regime.

Late in 1954 the ICP formed the 'Union of Soldiers and Officers'.[50] This organization included non-Communists, and published the first edition of its newspaper *Hurriya al-Watan*(Freedom of the Homeland) in January 1955. In 1956 the Second Congress of the ICP took a decision to direct attention towards army officers and to win as many members and supporters among them as possible.[51] It also fostered links with the Free Officers Movement and had separate links with Qasim.[52]

The 1958 Revolution brought a major movement towards the ICP by soldiers and officers from all units of the army. Batatu estimates the minimum number of army officers who were Communists at 235 including three brigadiers, 18 colonels, 27 lieutenant colonels. Furthermore, the Communists had a major presence in the people's resistance force.[53] However, the Qasim regime was frightened by the influence of the ICP in the armed forces and removed Communist officers from the more sensitive positions, retired them or transferred them to civilian jobs.[54]

During the first few days of the 1963 coup hundreds of Communist officers and soldiers were murdered and imprisoned. However, the organization of the ICP in the army was deeprooted and very secret, to the degree that on 3 July 1963 the Communist soldiers and NCOs, led by Sergeant Hasan Sirei, were able to carry out an uprising in the al-Rashid military camp in Baghdad. Its objective was to overthrow the Ba'th regime and to hand over power to the ICP. But this uprising failed because of weaknesses in the preparation and execution of the coup. The uprising was ruthlessly crushed by the Ba'th regime. Many soldiers and NCOs were executed, the leaders being publicly hanged in the poorer areas of the town from which they originated.

In the subsequent years the ICP continued its organization and propaganda work inside the military establishment. The Second[55] and Third[56] Congresses, in 1970 and 1976, discussed the issue and incorporated policy on it in their final documents. After the transformation of the Ba'th Party into an organization to rubber stamp the national socialist ideology of its leadership, the ICP adopted armed struggle as the main form of political opposition.[57] This meant more emphasis on military work both inside and outside the army. In 1984 a declaration published by the ICP on the 63rd anniversary of the foundation of the Iraqi army spelt out its immediate tasks in this sphere: increased organization within the army and 'popular' army, with the development of appropriate forms of organization and methods of agitation to encourage soldiers and members of the armed forces to reject the war and establish relations with the Patriotic Democratic Front, and to join the armed partisans with their arms, ammunition and other military provisions; securing contact with deserters; and destroying the Ba'th Party structures in the army.[58]

From the strategic point of view the ICP's approach to work inside the armed forces was to unite its political and organizational activities there with those in civilian life, especially among the working class.[59]

The Ba'thization of the Iraqi Armed Forces

al-Jaish al-'Aqa'idi

After the February 1963 coup the Ba'thists tried to purge the army and form *al-jaish al-'aqa'idi* ('the ideological army'). Many military ranks were granted to civilians who were later given a very important role in running the army. This created resentment among the senior army officers since many of them were denied promotion. The purge concentrated on the more important military commands such as the general command, military intelligence, the department of administration, and commanders of some of the army divisions, especially the armoured tank units and the air force. Many non-Ba'thist officers were sent on active duty in Kurdistan, where the regime was waging a savage war against the Kurdish people. Many civilians were admitted to the military college for short courses to replace the retired officers. As part of their propaganda the Ba'thists issued a pamphlet entitled 'Our Army is a Popular Revolutionary Sector' which was distributed to soldiers and officers. Ba'thist officers gave lectures to many army units, and especially to the air force.[60] This venture failed and the Ba'thists were removed in the November 1963 counter-coup.

Once it regained state power in the 30 July 1968 coup d'état the Ba'th Party set about imposing its ideological, political and administrative control over the army, in a process of Ba'thization. The aims of Ba'thization were set out in the Ba'th Party conference of 1974: consolidation of Ba'th Party leadership over the army; strengthening of military discipline; protection of the army from deviation and error; ensuring the army's total adherence to the people's movement led by the Ba'th Party; and continuation of emergency measures guaranteeing party control and supervision. The conference report clearly stated: 'In the next five years we must maintain the policy of tightening the Party's control over the other branches of the army —the security services, the police and the frontier guard.'[61] The Ba'th Party spelled out clearly its monopoly over the armed forces as a condition for any alliance with other political parties.

The strategy adopted to achieve these objectives was as follows. Admission to military colleges and institutions was restricted to members of the Ba'th Party. Those accepted had to sign a pledge to work for the interest of the Ba'th Party and to expect the death penalty if they broke the pledge. All officers and NCOs had to join the Ba'th Party. Those who refused were removed from military service and severely punished. All whose loyalty to the Ba'th Party was in doubt were discharged, put under surveillance and in some cases liquidated. Discrimination in recruitment and promotion on religious and nationality grounds was made more severe, and later all senior posts were restricted to officers related to Saddam Husain and the Takriti clan. The Military Intelligence Department was expanded to include informers in every unit, covering the military and civilian life of army personnel. A comprehensive programme of propaganda and Ba'thist ideological indoctrination was introduced into every sector of military education and life. A system of severe punishments and generous financial rewards was introduced to ensure the loyalty of officers and NCOs towards the Ba'th Party.

The process of Ba'thization of the army was aimed at building *al-jaish al-'aqa'idi* ('the ideological army') with the force to protect its power. In 1979 al-Barrak, ex-Director of al-Amn al-'Amm (General Security Bureau) spelled out more clearly than ever before the Ba'thist concepts of such an army in a study on the role of the Iraqi army in politics.[62] The 'ideological army' advocates national socialist ideology. It is the militant tool of the 'leading Ba'th Party' to fulfill its aims and objectives. It is an organized and modern force capable of rapid and active movement and 'enriched' with the overwhelming feeling of 'historical responsibility'. The officers have firm convictions about their elitist role as the leading 'patriotic' force in Iraqi society. It is an army inspired by 'national ideas' and carries on the 'historical mission'. In short, the fascist elements in the Ba'th Party's approach to the army are: national socialist indoctrination; worship of brute force; and a vision of 'historical mission'.

Organization
Organizationally the Ba'th Party formed the 'Military Bureau' in the provinces and sectors (North, South, Central and Baghdad). The Military Bureau is dominated by civilians and deals with indoctrination and propaganda.[63] Furthermore a network of cells and Ba'th party organizers was set up in every military unit with responsibility for: propaganda for the aims and objectives of the 'revolution and party'; surveillance of 'hostile elements'; immediate reports to the Ba'th Party of any 'trends' or 'moves' by 'hostile elements'. This clearly indicates the role of the Ba'th Party organization as an additional intelligence system to suppress any dissident member of the armed forces.

An additional apparatus for Ba'thization is the 'Department of Political Orientation'. The aims of this department are to 'prepare the fighters ideologically and psychologically in accordance with the principles of our revolution, the Party and the Leader, Saddam Husain'. The department also organizes special training courses for officers to select them for these functions, and is involved in planning psychological warfare.[64]

Army Victims of Ba'thization
The names and occupations of those who died as a result of Ba'thist terror and repression between 1968 and 1978, published by CARDRI[65] include 31 army and police personnel, ten junior army and police personnel, ten junior officials, five retired soldiers and junior army officers. Between 24 and 27 May 1978, 38 Iraqis were executed, of whom the majority were members of the armed forces, and all of whom were accused of political activity inside the Iraqi army. The death sentences were imposed by special court martials whose decisions were not subject to any review or appeal.[66]

Structure and Arms Supplies

From the late 1970s to the mid 1980s there have been many qualitative and quantitative changes in the Iraqi armed forces, in size, structure, arms supplies, hierarchy, use and political character.

Structure
The army, now with a million men under arms, has four corps, six armoured divisions (each with two armoured and one mechanized brigade), and three mechanized divisions (each with one armoured and two or more mechanized brigades). There are also four infantry divisions, one Republican Guard armoured brigade, three special forces brigades, nine reserve brigades and

ten 'Popular Army' brigades.[67] The army's small arms are mainly 7.63 mm. AK–47 (Kalashnikovs), 7.62 mm. SKS (Simonovs), 7.62 mm. RPD (Degtyarevs), 7.62 mm. SGM (Goryunovs), 12.7 mm. DShK 38/46 (Degtyarevs), 82 mm. M–37 and RPG–7. The tanks are mainly T–72, T–62, T55, T54, PT 76 and Chieftain. The majority APCs and ARVs are BMP–1 and Engessa EE–9/11/17. It has 2,000 different types of artillery, 1,000 anti-tank missile launchers and 36 surface-to-surface missiles or rockets.[68]

The navy consists of 4,350 men, 3,200 of them conscripts, and is mainly based in Basra, Umm Qasr and Fao.[69] Its weaponry includes ten combat vessels, eight mine warfare vessels, twelve gunboats, 28 patrol crafts, eight or nine landing craft and two auxiliary ships. Four Lupo class missile frigates and six Wadi class missile corvettes were on order in late 1984.[70]

The air force consists of 38,000 servicemen, including 10,000 administrative personnel and 10,000 conscripts.[71] It is equipped with 500 combat aircraft, 30 bombers, 52 transport aircraft, 110 training liaison aircraft and 320 helicopters of different kinds. These include MiG–21s, MiG–25s, MiG–23s, SU–20s, MIRAGE F1s, SU–7Bs and Hawker Hunters. The Iraqi air force's advanced weaponry includes air-to-air missiles, air-to-ground missiles and 200 anti-aircraft defences. There are 20 military airfields in Iraq, the most important being Basra, H–3, Habbaniyah, Kirkuk, Mosul, Rashid and Shaiba.[72]

The paramilitary forces include 20,000 from other Arab countries, mainly Egypt and Jordan. The so-called 'People's' or 'Popular' Army was 35,000 in 1980 and 400,000 in February 1982.[73]

Arms Supplies

After the 1958 Revolution the Soviet Union replaced Britain as Iraq's main supplier of arms. Supplies included MiG–21 interceptors, TU–22 bombers, and MiG–23 ground-attack aircraft.[74] The only major disturbance to this association was after the 1963 coup d'état which installed the Fascist Ba'th regime for the first time, for a few months only. The trend for the USSR to be the main arms supplier then continued.[75] From 1972–79, however, the percentage of Iraq's military equipment supplied by the Soviet Union declined from 95% to 63%, with France a major supplier after 1975. In 1978 the Ba'th regime started actively to improve relations with the USA, inviting senior American officials to Baghdad. Iraqi trade with Eastern Europe began to decline[76] while trade with Western Europe and Japan soared. The regime adopted a policy of diversifying the source of its arms, and huge deals were signed with many Western countries, especially France, Italy and Brazil. In 1978, France supplied 18 Mirage F1 interceptors and 30 helicopters and negotiated a share in the production of Mirage 2000[77] in addition to a major $2 billion arms deal for aircraft, tanks and other military hardware.[78] Recent surveys of Iraq's sources of arms indicate that France is now the leading Western European supplier of arms to Iraq, which takes 40% of France's total arms exports. France's arms sales to Iraq were $2,148 million in 1981, $1,925 million in 1982 and $2,000 million in 1983. The 1983 deal included helicopters and 29 Mirage F1 fighter bombers. A contract was later signed for the supply of five Super-Etendard attack aircraft[79] equipped with AM39 Exocet air-to-surface missiles.[80]

Britain has been involved in supplying reconnaissance equipment and in training Iraqi army officers[81] including special courses for Iraqi air force cadets.

Despite huge sums of money being spent on weaponry Iraq's military performance has so far been a particularly grim demonstration of how useless arms expenditure can be.[82]

Iraqi Armed Forces and the Gulf War

The Iraqi army invaded Iran on 22 September 1980, after a period of massive military preparation and build-up. Although Iraq had prior planning consultation with European and even US military personnel and had the element of surprise, its initial air attacks failed to achieve superiority. More than that, the ground force underestimated the level of the Iranian forces, while the armoured units manoeuvred to no real effect. In the initial stage of the war Iraq launched 80,000 men on the ground, occupying hundreds of square miles of Iranian territory. However, it moved very slowly, with poor logistics, deployment and combat support, and failure in tank utilization, with troops advancing only during slight or non-existent Iranian resistance.[83] Repeated Iraqi defeats and huge losses of equipment and men have led military analysts to explore the preparedness of the Iraqi armed forces prior to the war, focussing on issues of leadership, combat experience, training, logistics and command and control. In early 1983 Iraq needed 1,500 new tanks fully equipped with fire control and advanced armour, several hundred advanced attack helicopters, surface-to-air missiles and 250–400 advanced fighters of F20R or Mirage 2000 calibre.[84] The human losses for Iraq alone are estimated at 75,000 to 150,000 casualties.[85] This section highlights some of the military analysts' findings.

Poor Military Leadership and Command

In a personality cult unprecedented in Iraq's modern history Saddam Husain is the country's Head of State, Premier and Chairman of both the Revolutionary Command Council (RCC) and the Ba'th Party. Moreover he has conferred upon himself the rank of Field Marshal and appointed himself Commander-in-Chief of the Iraqi armed forces.[86] Saddam Husain's military leadership has been much glorified in the Ba'th and military propaganda produced in Iraq. From these and other sources it is clear that he has been directly involved in both strategic and tactical military decisions. It is claimed that he has developed new military ideas and theories of global importance.

We have to be proud [it was stated in the main Ba'th Party journal in

August 1980 that our beloved leader has developed new concepts in military principles which hitherto were viewed in an unbalanced way during war time. We have to be proud that His Excellency is enriching the military ideology and drawing new experience from the lessons of the war.[87]

This quotation came from one of many similar articles being published regularly.[88] Western military analysts, however, consider that the main reason for Iraq's military failures is the quality of its military leadership and command. This is shown in the lack of clear orders and in the poor responses by the army. The occupation of Susangerd was an example of this. Armoured units advanced and withdrew twice in October 1980, and later in the same operation strategic positions near Dizful were given up.[89] Rigid control of NCOs and junior officers frustrated their initiative and transformed them into pawns waiting for orders. This was the reason for the high casualty figures in the infantry during the fighting in built-up areas, where initiative and spontaneity in decision-making are of paramount importance. The paramilitary 'Popular Army' was the first part of the army to collapse under the stress and pressure of the war. Its detachments have 'political' commanders and their command structure is particularly rigid, inflexible and slow.

The poor quality of leadership and command is largely the result of the continuous purges of the armed forces before and during the war. The Ba'thization policy rigorously pursued before the war put those deemed politically reliable in key positions throughout the armed forces, regardless of their military competence. Their incompetence has been revealed by the war.[90] In summing up the issue of military leadership a retired British officer who still holds senior military responsibility in the Gulf said of Iraq's military leaders:

They seem to have launched the war with only token planning, no real objectives and no contingency plans. They seem to lie in each other throughout their command and control structure. The junior officers and enlisted men on both sides are damned good fighters, as good as any. The command level is unbelievably bad. I can't speak about the Iranian, but the Iraqi General Staff seems to be a farce. They used to refer to the British army in World War One as 'lions led by donkeys'; the Iraqi soldiers are 'tigers led by a pack of jackasses.'[91]

Inadequate Training and Lack of Combat Experience
Although there has been rapid expansion and modernization of the Iraqi army, financed by the income from increased oil production and loans from the Gulf states, it lacks administrative abilities and technological expertise. Diversification of the sources of arms supplies has created many difficulties, since great skill is required to use a combination of arms, especially air power and tanks which are important in offensive warfare.[92] Iraq's huge arsenal

of military hardware has been inefficiently and ineffectively used. The use of tanks and armoured vehicles has been slow and tedious, and never co-ordinated with other elements of war-fighting. The tendency was to dig in and attempt to avoid anti-tank weapons. This approach militated against exploiting the potential of the military hardware. A symptom of the inefficiency, poor training and command was the abandonment of armour intact in the battle zone because of inability to carry out minor repairs. This also indicates the poor quality of training in battlefield techniques and the use of modern arms. As an example of incompetence in training Staudenmaier cites the fact that the land computing sights on the Iraqi tanks have seldom been used. This lowers the accuracy of the T–62 tanks to World War Two standard.[93]

Tactical Mistakes

One common tactical mistake made by the Iraqi commanders was to send armour to attack well defended infantry forces in built-up areas or rough terrain without infantry support. This tactic, carried out with low officer initiative and a lack of the aggressiveness essential for modern mid-intensity offensive warfare, resulted in high casualties.[94] Furthermore, when the Iraqi armed forces used defensive tactics against Iranian counter-attacks there were disastrous weaknesses in reinforcing and redeploying defensive positions once they were penetrated or outflanked.

Military analysts also observe that the Iraqi armed forces have tended to use conventional warfare in situations where it was inappropriate. For example, in the attack on Abadan, the Iraqi armed forces tried to occupy the island by mass artillery fire and conventional tactics rather than responding to the defensive warfare adopted by the Iranian forces.

Many other problems have been cited such as failure to co-ordinate naval and army operations; air warfare being poor in tactics and ineffective, showing an inability to sustain long operations[95]; and the use of reserves being limited, with the Iraqi regime focussing on mass and morale rather than on tactics, training and technical factors.[96]

Despair, Low Morale and Desertion

Many of the Iraqi military detachments failed to cope with combat stress, and huge losses were experienced as a result of psychological casualties.[97] Furthermore, the largest scale of collapse or surrender was among the volunteer units led by senior Ba'th Party members. They surrendered without even being defeated in military engagements.[98]

Low morale prevailed all along the chain of command after the diastrous military defeats suffered by the Iraqi regime at the war front. This, in addition to the general conditions of repression, purges and murder, and in an atmosphere of overall economic, social and political crisis, led to numerous signs of mutiny against the war. This was demonstrated on an individual and spontaneous level. The number of deserters reached 100,000 and they formed armed groups opposed to the regime in the middle and south of Iraq. Many soldiers refused to fight in Kurdistan and some used their weapons against members of the military intelligence, while many more joined the armed partisan movement. Acts of sabotage and deliberately burning arms depots occurred. Other signs of lack of support for the war in the army have included trading in government weapons and ammunition, defeatism and surrender to the Iranian forces.[99]

Conclusion

The contemporary history of Iraq has provided numerous examples of the vital and decisive role of the army in the various political upheavals. The army has always been an arena of struggle between the different political forces aiming to win it over to their side or at least to neutralize it in the fight to seize power.

Aware of this the Ba'thists set out after seizing power in 1968 to exercise full control over the army by ideological indoctrination, dismissal of non-Ba'thist officers and a combination of generous handouts and privileges with repression and a tight military intelligence network directly loyal to Saddam Husain. Although this policy succeeded in isolating the armed forces temporarily from the arena of direct political struggle they have remained a source of deep concern for the Ba'th rulers.

From the mid-1970s there was a significant expansion in the numbers of the armed forces, with the additional armaments paid for by increased oil revenues, and the purchase of sophisticated weapons from the West, particularly France. This policy reached a peak on the eve of the war against Iran in September 1980, when Saddam Husain believed that a military blitzkreig across the Iranian borders would fulfil his dream of replacing the Shah as the policeman of the Gulf and extend his leadership over the Arab world.

Saddam's miscalculations, however, turned this adventure into a military catastrophe which almost led to his downfall in 1982. It was averted only because of the Iranians' inability to force a defeat. Since then the Iraqi army has apparently withstood Iranian attacks, reorganizing its ranks and strengthening its defences.

Significant changes, however, have affected the armed forces during the war, which will leave their mark on the subsequent role of the army in Iraqi political life. The influence and status of the armed forces have been bolstered, and resentment against the political leadership has become widespread, even amongst the officer corps. The huge expansion of the army, to almost a half a million people, as well as the three-quarters of a million in the paramilitary 'People's Army' has brought about fundamental changes in the rank-and-file. The original 'ideological army' which entered the war in 1980 was crushed when the Iranians took the initiative to push the Iraqis out of Iranian territory, and now the army is composed mainly of men forced to fight as a consequence of wartime mass conscription. The regime can no longer exercise the same tight control over the rank-and-file as it did before the war and the army is no longer immune to the growing influence of popular opposition to the war and the activities of the opposition forces. The regime's fate will largely be decided by the army's stand and the extent to which the opposition forces succeed in winning it over to their side.

While the armed forces can see no prospect of a political settlement of the war, the stresses and strains within them will tend to be aggravated by the stalemate on the battlefield (March 1985) coupled with other aspects of the regime's crisis such as the economic and human costs of the war and growing realization that it has been a huge blunder. The army's morale is low and now that the war has become a war to defend Saddam Husain's dictatorship its ability to withstand the impact of a successful Iranian military penetration of the war front is doubtful. Under all circumstances it can be expected to play a decisive role in any forthcoming political change in Iraq.

References

1. Jack Woddis, *Armies and Politics*, (London, 1977) pp. 7–8.
2. G. Harris-Jenkins and C.C. Moskor Jnr, 'Armed Forces and Society', *Current Sociology*, vol. 29, no. 3, Winter, 1981.
3. Hanna Batatu, *The Old Social Classes and Revolutionary Movements in Iraq: a Study of Iraq's Old Landed and Commercial Classes and of its Communists, Ba'thists and Free Officers*, (Princeton, 1978).
4. S.H. Longrigg, *Iraq 1900–1950: a Political, Social and Economic History*, (Oxford, 1953).
5. S. Khairi, *The Iraqi Army and the Current Situation in Iraq*, unpublished, 1984.
6. P.P. Hemphill, 'The Formation of the Iraqi Army,' in *Integration of Modern Iraq*, ed. A. Kelidar (London, 1979) p. 90.
7. M.A. Tarbush, *The Role of the Military in Politics: A case study of Iraq to 1941*, (London, 1982) p. 75.
8. M.A. Tarbush, op. cit., p. 76.
9. P.P. Hemphill, op. cit., p. 95.
10. *al-Thawra*, 6 January 1983.
11. E. Be'eri, *Army Officers in Arab Politics and Society*, (London, 1970) p. 327.
12. Hanna Batatu, op. cit., p. 319.
13. E. Be'eri, op. cit., p. 330.
14. *Mahkamat al-Sha'b*, vol. 5, (Baghdad, 1959) p. 2187.
15. S. Khairi, op. cit.
16. Abu Sa'd, *al-Thaqafa al-Jadida*, no. 154, 1984.
17. M.A. Tarbush, op. cit., p. 122.
18. Hanna Batatu, op. cit., p. 439.
19. Hanna Batatu, op. cit., p. 442.
20. K. Williams, *Great Britain in the East*, (London, 1963).

21. M.A. Tarbush, op. cit., p. 151.

22. A. Yaghi, *Harakat Rashid 'Ali al-Gailani, diras fitatawur al-haraka al-watania al-'Iraqia*, (Beirut, 1974) p. 21.

23. M.A. Tarbush, op. cit., p. 95.

24. A. Yaghi, op. cit., p. 95.

25. S. Khairi, *Min ta'rikh al-haraka al-thawriya al-mu'asira fi'il-'Iraq 1929–1958*, (Baghdad, 1975) p. 199.

26. Hanna Batatu, op. cit., p. 782.

27. S. Khairi, *Min tar'rikh al-haraka al-thawriya fi'il-'Iraq, Thawra 14 Tammuz*, (Beirut, 1980) p. 86.

28. Hanna Batatu, op. cit., p. 799.

29. Majid Khadduri, *Republican Iraq*, (OUP 1969) p. 49.

30. Majid Khadduri, op. cit., p. 70.

31. Majid Khadduri, op. cit., p. 67.

32. E. & E.F. Penrose, *Iraq: International Relations and National Development*, (London, 1978) p. 208.

33. Majid Khadduri, op. cit., p. 83.

34. Abu Sa'd, op. cit.

35. E. & E.F. Penrose, op. cit., p. 288.

36. E. & E.F. Penrose, op. cit., p. 309.

37. Majid Khadduri, op. cit., p. 210.

38. Majid Khadduri, *Socialist Iraq: a Study in Iraqi Politics since 1968*, (1978) p. 17.

39. Majid Khadduri, *Socialist Iraq*, op. cit., p. 23.

40. Majid Khadduri, *Socialist Iraq*, op. cit., p. 25.

41. E. Be'eri, op. cit., p. 24.

42. A. Yaghi, op. cit., p. 23.

43. Salah al-Din al-Sabbagh, *Fursan al-'Uruba fi'l-'Iraq*, (Damascus 1956).

44. E. Be'eri, op. cit., pp. 15–40.

45. Hanna Batatu, op. cit., p. 651.

46. S. Khairi, *The Iraqi Army and the Current Situation in Iraq*, op. cit.

47. Hanna Batatu, op. cit., p. 445.

48. Hanna Batatu, op. cit., p. 704.

49. Iraqi Communist Party, *The Works of Comrade Fahd*, al-Thaqafa al-Jadida, (Baghdad, 1974) p. 125.

50. Hanna Batatu, op. cit., p. 792.

51. S. Khairi, op. cit., p. 281.

52. Hanna Batatu, op. cit., p. 789.

53. Hanna Batatu, op. cit., p. 894.

54. S. Khairi, *The Iraqi Army and the Current Situation in Iraq*, op. cit.

55. Iraqi Communist Party, *Documents of the Second National Congress*, August 1970, p. 108.

56. Iraqi Communist Party, *Documents of the Third National Congress*, May 1976, p. 156.

57. Iraqi Communist Party, *Report of the Central Committee*, November 1982.

58. Iraqi Communist Party, 'Whither the Army?' *Iraqi Letter*, no. 3, May 1984.

59. Abu Sa'd, op. cit.

60. Amin Houadi, *Kuntu safferaa fi al'Iraq 1963--1965*, (Cairo, 1983) p. 144.

61. The Ba'th Party, *Political Report of the Eighth Congress*, (London, 1979) p. 168.

62. Fadhil al-Barak, *Dawr al-jaish al'Iraqi fi hokomat al-difa' al-watani wa'al-harb ma Biritania 1941*, (Iraq, 1979) pp. 129–138.

63. Phebe Marr, 'Iraq: socio-political development', AEI, *Foreign Policy and Defence Review*, vol. 2, no. 3–4, 1980 p. 35.

64. *Alef Baa*, no. 745, January 1983 (Iraqi monthly journal controlled by the Iraqi Ministry of Information).

65. *Iraq Solidarity Voice no. 2*, published by CARDRI.

66. *Iraq Solidarity Voice no. 1*, March–April 1979.

67. Institute of Strategic Studies, *Military Balance 1982–1983*, (London) p. 55.

68. Jaffa Centre for Strategic Studies, *The Middle East Military Balance 1983*, eds. Mark Heller, Dov Tamari and Zeev Eyban, (Tel Aviv, 1984) p. 102.

69. Institute of Strategic Studies, op. cit., p. 55.

70. Institute of Strategic Studies, op. cit.

71. Institute of Strategic Studies, op. cit., p. 55.

72. Jaffa Centre for Strategic Studies, op. cit.

73. Anthony H. Cordesman, 'Lessons of the Iran–Iraq War Part Two—Tactics, Technology and Training', *Armed Forces Journal International*, June 1982, p. 69.

74. Adelphi Papers, *The Soviet Foreign Policy towards Iran and the Gulf*, (USA, 1983) p. 26.

75. Centre for Defense Information, 'Soviet Geopolitical Momentum, Myth or Menace?' *The Defense Monitor*, vol IX, no. 1, January 1980.

76. K. Dawisha, 'Iraq, the West's Opportunity'. *Foreign Policy*, no. 41, 1980–1981.

77. R.O. Freedman, *Soviet Policy towards Ba'thist Iraq 1968–1979*, Paper delivered at the Strategic Studies Institute of the US Army War College Carlisle Barracks, Pennsylvania, 10 June 1980.

78. Ibid.

79. Adelphi Papers, op. cit.

80. Institute of Strategic Studies, op. cit., p. 77.

81. Frank Allaun MP, *Iraq Solidarity Voice no. 10*. (CARDRI).

82. A.K. Mansur (pseud), 'The Military Balance in the Persian Gulf: Who Will Guard the Gulf States from Their Guardian?' *Armed Forces Journal International*, November 1980, p. 45.

83. Ibid.

84. Anthony H. Cordesman, *Armed Forces Journal International*, May 1983, op. cit.

85. Institute of Strategic Studies, op. cit., p. 77.

86. A. Hottinger, 'Personality Cult', *Swiss Review*, June 1984.

87. *al-Thawra*, 14 August 1984.

88. *al-Thawra*, 21 September 1984 and 25 September 1984.

89. A. Cordesman, op. cit.

90. W.J. Alson, 'The Iraq–Iran war and the future of the Gulf', *Military Review*, March 1984.

91. A.K. Mansur, op. cit.

92. W.O. Staudenmaier, *A Strategic Analysis of the Gulf War*, Strategic Studies Institute, US Army War College Carlisle Barracks, Pennsylvania, 25 January 1982, p. 6.

93. Ibid.

94. A. Cordesman, op. cit.

95. W.O. Staudenmaier, op. cit.

96. A. Cordesman, op. cit.

97. G.H. Jansen, 'Iraq: Bleak Outlook', *Middle East International*, 4 February 1983, p. 6.

98. A. Cordesman, op. cit.

99. S. Khairi, *The Iraqi Army and the Current Situation*, op. cit.

11. The Gulf War

Jabr Muhsin

On 22 September 1980, after repeated incidents along the border between Iraq and Iran, the war officially started. Four years later it had not only claimed the lives of hundreds of thousands of people and maimed hundreds of thousands more, but over ten towns and cities had been flattened and in Iraq at least, factories destroyed. The war's far-reaching political, economic and social implications will be discussed here, as well as the dangers posed to world peace and security. Before considering these aspects, a review of developments preceding the outbreak of war is necessary: contrary to official propaganda, it is not simply a border disagreement, nor is it rooted in eternal hostility between Arabs and Persians.

Before the War

In 1979 Saddam Husain forced president Ahmad Hasan al-Bakr into retirement and assumed absolute control of the Ba'th Party and of the state. The new President also embarked on a purge of the leadership of the Ba'th Party. This was the culmination of a process of monopolization of power by the Ba'th and the elimination from the state apparatus of elements which had joined them in the coup of 1968. The early rapprochement with progressive forces had given way to a bloody repression reminiscent of Hitler's Germany or Mussolini's Italy. At the same time, there had emerged a parasitic bourgeoisie composed of merchants, speculators, contractors and estate owners, as well as a bureaucratic bourgeoisie, which had assumed greater influence in the decision-making process, in the direction and implementation of economic plans and the exploitation of Iraq's enormous oil wealth. As the political struggle intensified, so did the repression against the opposition forces. Signs of dissent within the ruling Ba'th Party also began to increase. In Iraqi Kurdistan the regime left nothing untried in provoking the national feeling of the Kurdish people by its policy of forced Arabization and Ba'thization, in total violation of the 11 March 1970 Manifesto which had defined the principles of autonomy for Iraqi Kurdistan.

In the Arab world the regime adopted a policy of collaboration with reactionary regimes and accommodation with imperialism, and though it claimed to be the 'unifier of the Arab ranks' it proved in practice to have a divisive and disruptive influence. The Iraqi regime signed a security agreement with Saudi Arabia, and the Iraqi-Jordanian-Saudi axis became the bastion of the reactionary forces in the Arab world and the Middle East as a whole. Saddam's declaration of the 'National Arab Charter' in February 1980 assured the reactionary Arab states of his allegiance and led David Hirst to comment in the *Guardian*: 'the unmistakeable pro-western orientation of the regime. . . . . has taken another step forward with Saddam Hussein's proposal for a national charter.'[1] In April 1980 Iraq ordered the closure of the offices of the Democratic Front for the Liberation of Palestine and then became a leading advocate of the return of Egypt to the Arab fold.

Iraq also went on an arms-buying spree, euphemistically called 'diversification of arms sources.' Huge arms deals were concluded with France, Italy, Spain and Brazil. Ties with Turkey, a member of NATO, were strengthened. Baghdad was full of Western salesmen, contractors, consultants, bankers and finance ministers.

The Iraqi regime put a two-page advertisement in the *Observer* on 20 July 1980 which spelt out for readers in Britain the dreams of Saddam and his clique:

> Iraq was more than once the springboard for a new civilization in the Middle East and the question is now pertinently asked, with a leader like this man (Saddam), the wealth of the oil resources and a forceful people like the Iraqis, will she repeat her former glories and the name of Saddam Hussein link up with that of Hamurabi, Ashurbanipal, al-Mansur and Harun al-Rashid?

The Iranian Revolution

The popular revolution in Iran in the late 1970s had sent shock waves through the reactionary and dictatorial regimes in the Middle East. The *Times* commented: 'Implicitly, the Iranian revolution threatened every established regime in the Muslim world, just as the French revolution threatened all the crowned heads of Europe.'[2] Huge numbers of Iranians, most of them unarmed, took to the streets in a popular uprising and defeated one of the most ruthless and heavily armed regimes in the world: that of the Shah and his notorious SAVAK security forces. The strength of the Iranian revolution was not that of an Islamic threat but mainly because it showed that an oppressed people could rise up against their oppressors and defeat them. It contributed to the revolutionary mood already developing in the region.

When the struggle in Iran was at a critical stage, the Iraqi regime deported the father figure of the Iranian revolution, Khomeini, who was still living in exile in Najaf and not willing at that time to return to Iran. He went instead to France. At the same time the Iraqi regime embarked on another of its chauvinistic policies, that of deporting thousands of Iraqi families, particularly Shi'is, because of their 'Iranian origin'. (Iranian nationals living in Iraq, and Iraqis with Iranian ancestry were given a B-status after the collapse of the Ottoman Empire when the modern nationality law was introduced; their children and grandchildren retain that status.) In the most appalling conditions men, women and children, whole families, were escorted to the border and ordered to march towards Iran. A spokesman at the Iraqi Embassy in London called it a 'very humane procedure' for the 'repatriation of some Iranians. . . taking into consideration the reunion of the family in their original country.'[3] Other Iranians were more welcome: Iraq was soon to become a centre for counter-revolutionaries and officers from the Shah's army who played a direct role in planning the war from the Iraqi side.

The social direction of the Iranian revolution was yet to be determined. Signs of internal conflicts were emerging. The army was neutral and in some areas its ranks disintegrated. Iran was thus vulnerable to any attack from Iraq. Such aggression was encouraged by the United States and its allies, Saudi Arabia and Jordan, as well as the Shah's generals living in Iraq, all of whom wanted to contain the Iranian revolution. It was calculated that a quick and decisive invasion would bring Iran to its knees. At the same time Iraq's rulers hoped to fulfil their dreams of a new role for Iraq as policeman of the Gulf, to replace the Shah. They also wanted full control of the Shatt al-'Arab waterway and to annex the oil-rich province of Khuzistan which the Ba'thists call 'Arabistan.' Nor should one forget the Iraqi regime's domestic and internal political difficulties which, as we have seen, manifested themselves in ruthless repression of all opponents, national oppression and sectarian discrimination.

At least three factors, therefore, underlay Iraq's invasion of Iran: first, the Iraqi regime aimed to exploit Iran's difficulties and fulfil its own expansionist ambitions; second, it was encouraged in this by those who sought to contain the Iranian revolution; and third, the invasion was an attempt to divert attention from the emerging political crisis within Iraq itself.

The Eve of the War

Before the start of the war, Iraq abrogated the Algiers Agreement, which had been signed between Saddam Husain (then Vice-President of Iraq) and the Shah of Iran during the Non-Aligned Summit in Algiers in 1975. In return for some territorial concessions, the Iranians had undertaken to end their support for Iraqi Kurdish nationalists in their revolt against the Iraqi government. Weeks after the signing of the agreement, the Barzani uprising ended and thousands of Kurdish people were exiled to other parts of Iraq. In September 1980, Saddam told the 'National Assembly': 'The Iranian leaders have disregarded the agreement by their open and premeditated interference in the internal affairs of Iraq as did the Shah before them.'[4] He declared Iraq's intention of 'liberating' areas claimed to be allocated to Iraq under the Algiers agreement, such as Zain al-Qaws and Saif Sa'ad.

During 1980 there were numerous claims and counter-claims of frontier violations as well as 'sabotage' and 'terrorist attacks' inside both countries.

Bani-Sadr, then President of Iran, threatened to invade Iraq if 'the Baghdad government causes more trouble along their common frontier'[5] while in April the political correspondent of the official Iraqi News Agency declared that 'Iraq does not only demand the return of the Arab islands (Greater Tunb, Minor Tunb and Abu Musa, occupied by Iran in 1971) but is acting positively for their return.'[6] By the beginning of September 1980 the Iraqi army was actively engaged on the border. An Iraqi press release stated that 'in accordance with the Revolutionary Command Council's directives for the return of the lands stolen by Iran, the Iraqi army went into a quick decisive battle with the Iranian forces in Maisan province and liberated the land stolen by Iran.'[7] There were also air and sea skirmishes as well as land activities in Mandali province. Saddam Husain sent three members of the Revolutionary Command Council to Saudi Arabia and the Gulf states with personal letters to their rulers 'analysing' the situation of 'the eastern flank of the Arab homeland.'

The Course of the War
Iraq's full offensive against Iran came on 22 September 1980 along some 200 miles, from Khorramshahr in the south to Qasr-e-Shirin north of Baghdad. Within days the Iraqi army was occupying Qasr-e-Shirin and pushing the Iranian army back. Iraq had military superiority on land, but the country is landlocked, apart from Shatt al- Arab at the top of the Gulf, and Iran succeeded in blocking Iraqi oil exports through this outlet. From the air, Iran launched attacks on industrial and commercial installations in Baghdad, Basra and Kirkuk. These attacks were, however, virtually brought to a halt because of lack of spares and servicing support for the Iranians' American planes.

On the political side many countries declared their neutrality and the United Nations demanded an immediate halt to the fighting. The Non-Aligned and the Islamic mediating teams shuttled between Baghdad and Tehran. Jordan, Egypt, Sudan and France declared their support for the Iraqi government while Syria and Libya supported Iran.

In October 1980 the fighting was concentrated north of Khorramshahr around Dizful, Bustan and Susangerd. The Iraqi aim was the oil-rich province of Khuzistan, which the regime boasted of 'liberating'. The Iraqi army crossed the river Karun, claiming the destruction of the Abadan-Tehran oil pipeline. The prize of the war came when the Iraqi army occupied Khorranshahr on 24 October 1980, and beseiged Abadan.

When Iranian resistance stiffened the Iraqi advance slowed down, the Iraqi government declared a ceasefire on 5 October, but the Iranians did not respond. This was to be repeated many times. The Iraqi army was over-stretched and showing signs of dissent, by deserting or evading conscription. On the other hand, the Iranians were reorganizing, and morale was high with the influx of volunteers to the front. The Iranian Revolutionary Guard's human wave tactics pinned down the Iraqi army. Iranian television started to show prisoners of war, some 2,000 of whom were captured in January alone.

It was obvious that the war was not going to end in a few months let alone a few weeks. Time was on Iran's side and the Iraqi regime was desperate to end the conflict while victorious.

From Occupation to Retreat
At the beginning of 1981 Iraqi forces were 10–20 miles inside Iranian territory along the whole front and occupied at least five towns. The Iraqi government had deployed five divisions in the northern sector of the front and seven divisions in the south, four of them at Khorramshahr and around Abadan. The Iranians, for their part, massed an estimated 15 divisions. They were expected to launch their offensive from Kermanshah and Dizful towards Mehran, possibly with the objective of cutting the route from Baghdad to Basra north of Kut. The first major counter-attack by Iran, on 11 January 1981, failed to achieve its objectives and it took the Iranians a full year to reverse the Iraqi successes. However, Susangerd was recaptured by Iran in January 1981 and so was Ahwaz, which changed hands three times. An Arab from the town, appointed as mayor by the Iraqis, faced the firing squad when the Iranians came back. After battles for Dizful in April the Iraqi army was forced to abandon some strategic positions but they also had some limited successes, such as Serbil and Zahab in April and May.

In September, after heavy fighting with both sides claiming to have inflicted severe casualties, the Iranian army successfully lifted the seige from Abadan. More than 1,500 Iraqi soldiers were captured. The Iraqis were also driven from areas east of the Karun river from Darkoveyn to Abadan and the roads from Mahshar and Ahwaz to Abadan were reopened. The Iraqi government sent in its 10th Armoured Brigade but in the end had to admit pulling back east of Karun 'from a position of strength'. They proposed a Muharram ceasefire in November, as they had for Ramadan in July. Both were rejected by Iran. Bustan was recaptured on 7 December following the Iranians' successful offensive in Khuzistan province in November. Seventy villages were occupied with the now familiar human waves and heavy casualties.

To gain some momentum, in January 1982 the Iraqi army launched a major offensive in the central sector. They captured the Iranian town of Gilan al-Gharb, some 80 miles north of Bustan. Iraq also formed a special task force involving commando training for hundreds of thousands of people. But they could not hide the fact that the initiative lay with the Iranian army. In March 1982, for instance, the Iranians recaptured 250 sq. miles west of Dizful, claiming to have killed 5,000 Iraqis and to have taken 3,000 prisoners of war including 60 high-ranking officers. Iraqi counter-claims were no less spectacular: 10,000 Iranians were said to have been killed.

The Battle for Khorramshahr

At Khorramshahr the Iraqi army was prepared for a long siege with three divisions inside the city and a fourth defending the road north-west of the city along the Shatt al-'Arab. 70,000 Iranian troops were massed for the battle including an estimated 20,000 teenage volunteers. The Iranians attacked the road on 21 May 1982 and the defending division disintegrated, sapping the morale of those inside the city which the Iranians recaptured on 25 May taking over 30,000 prisoners. Iraq remained silent at first and when it admitted the defeat the Iraqi communiqué said: 'Iraq's main task in the war was to inflict the heaviest possible losses on the Iranians. This has been achieved.'[8]

Khorramshahr was renamed 'the city of blood.' It was the last city to be recaptured by Iran in an offensive code-named 'The Holy City' (Jerusalem). The Iranians had reached the border with Iraq for the first time since the start of the war and Basra came within range of their artillery. Indeed, Basra has been under heavy fire since 28 May 1982.

The Final Retreat

This was an enormous blow to the Iraqi regime which had named the war 'the second Qadisiya' after a seventh century battle in which the Arabs defeated the Persians. 'Saddam's Qadisiya', as it is more often called, was turning sour. In desperation, Iraq declared a unilateral ceasefire and offered on 9 June to pull back to the pre-war border within two weeks if Iran would agree to end the war. When no response came from Iran, Iraq announced on 21 June that its troops were withdrawing nevertheless.

When Iraq was winning the war Saddam had promised his soldiers and officers that 'the Iraq army would not go back to the status quo before the war without recovering from Iran Iraq's outstanding claims and rights and that the blood shed by the Iraqis would not go without a price.'[9] On 14 March 1981 in a speech to a contingent of the 'people's army' he had said that if Iran did not agree to stop the war and accept Iraq's demands, then his forces would add new towns and territories to the Iranian territories they have already occupied and that the liberation of lands and waters from the hands of the corrupt Khomeini clique was equal to the liberation of parts of Palestine'.[10] As for the form of government in Iran, Saddam was clear about his links with anti-revolutionary elements in Iran. He stressed Iraq's willingness 'to extend all forms of assistance, from weapons to other materials as might be needed by such Iranian people in order that they might attain their national and patriotic rights.' Indicating his willingness to aid national minorities fighting inside Iran, he said that in any case 'Iraq would no longer care about Iran's unity.'[11]

In 1982, after the defeat of the Iraqi army Saddam changed his line. On 30 March 1982 in a speech to the Fourth Army Corps, he declared: 'the General Command have decided to rearrange your defensive positions to the rear after your strong blows absorbed the advance of the enemy.' But demagogic slogans which talked of a 'stationary offensive,' or 'rearranging defences' and 'withdrawing from a position of strength' were too flimsy to cover up the Iraqi army's retreat. By this time all attacks were initiated by the Iranians, who launched another offensive 'Ramadan' against Basra on 14 July 1982 and were reported to have crossed the border north of the city. This was followed on 1 October by the Muslim Ibn 'Aqil offensive in the Mandali area and on 1 November by the Muharram offensive in the Mehran sector. The many assaults in both offensives by infantry backed by tanks and artillery failed to make any significant advance in the marshlands of southern Iraq. The superior Iraqi firepower mowed down the ill-trained Revolutionary Guard, which was composed mainly of teenagers. Iraq, however, admitted for the first time that the fighting had shifted to the Iraqi side of the frontier and in mid-November suffered another setback when one of its brigades, estimated at 4,000 men, fled from their defensive lines before the Iraqi cities of Kut and 'Amara.

In retaliation Iraq declared a military exclusion zone at the head of the Gulf around the Iranian oil-exporting terminal of Kharg Island. In mid-August Iraq sank two commercial ships near the entrance to Bandar Khomeini, the Greek 15,000 tonne freighter *Litsion* and the South Korean 16,000 tonne *Sambow*. This was followed by three attacks on the oil installations at Kharg Island which started a fire there. Attacks on commercial ships in the Gulf inside and outside the exclusion zone were later to become the Iraqis' main strategy. Fighting died down until 6 February 1983, when the Iranians launched their Val Fajr offensive in the Fakkeh area in the southern sector. When this was unsuccessful, Val Fajr II was launched in the north of Iraq on 22 July and was later extended to the southern sector. Yet another offensive east of Penjwin was launched in October 1983.

The war had become bogged down and there were no significant developments until 1984 when attacks on cities and on commercial shipping in the Gulf were intensified and chemical weapons were used by Iraq.

Intensification of the War in 1984

In early February 1984, Iraq threatened to launch a barrage of air and missile attacks against seven Iranian towns and cities and gave the date of such an attack as 6 February. The cities named were Dizful, Shrish, Andimeshk, Ahwaz, Kermanshah, Ilam and Abadan. When the attack materialized, Iran retaliated by shelling Basra, Khanaqin and Mandali in mid-February. They also moved 15 miles inside north-eastern Iraq. They code-named their operation 'Road to Jerusalem.' After mediations from the UN, the Islamic Council, the Saudis and the Kuwaitis, the attacks on civilian targets subsided.

Iran's biggest gain in this offensive was the man-made, 76 sq. miles oil-rich island of Majnun in the al-Hawizh marshes, with 50 unworked oil wells. In order to dislodge the Iranians the Iraqi army used chemical weapons against the Iranians and also the remaining Iraqis, soldiers and civilians, in the area.

Chemical weapons were banned under the Geneva Protocol of 1925 and their use by Iraq, confirmed by the International Red Cross and the UN teams which visited Iran, brought an international outcry. Britain was involved in the sale of ingredients for the production of the mustard gas used by Iraq. It was suggested that the chemicals sold were originally intended for the production of agricultural pesticides but in fact Iraq had been planning to use chemical weapons for some time. In 1981, the British Ministry of Defence's sales organization approved the sale of 10,000 protective kits and breathing equipment made to Iraq's specification by Primary Medical Aid Limited of Farnham in Hampshire.[12]

In the Gulf, Iraq intensified its attacks on commercial ships serving Iranian ports in an attempt to internationalize the conflict. The intensive campaign lasted from March to June 1984. Iraq's declaration of a maritime exclusion zone around Kharg Island on 12 August 1982 had been intended to disrupt Iranian oil exports. Iran had threatened to close the Strait of Hormuz if its oil exports were halted. The danger of escalation was increased when in late 1983, France supplied Iraq with Mirage F-1 fighter-bombers and Super-Etendard aircraft equipped with Exocet missiles. The United States, Britain and France rushed their naval forces to the region. In the event, however, the strait was never closed. Iran declared that it was not its intention to harm the West. But the danger of foreign intervention was not removed.

When the Iraqi campaign intensified in 1984, Arab ships were not spared from attack. The Saudi ships *Safina al-Arab* and *al-Ahood* were hit on 25 April and 7 May respectively. Nor were the attacks limited to the exclusion zone. Many ships were hit by Iraqi and Iranian attacks outside the zone, the first being the Kuwaiti tanker *Umm Cashah* on 13 May. Iran retaliated and was blamed for the attacks on the Kuwaiti ship *Bahrah* on 14 May, the Saudi ship *Yanbu Pride* on 16 May and *Chemical Venture* on 24 May. Iranian jets were involved in a dog fight over Saudi waters on 5 June and at least one F4 Phantom jet was shot down.

International Implications

The war was a menace to international peace and security from the start, given the reasons for Iraq's aggression discussed above - Ba'thist expansionism and a general desire to contain the Iranian revolution. Even when Iraq withdrew from Iranian territory, the danger of foreign intervention remained because of the likelihood of escalation at any moment and because of the intensification of the internal struggle in both countries. The stance of other Arab countries, of Turkey and of her NATO allies will now be considered.

The Arab Countries and Saddam's War

From the start of the war the regime of Saddam Husain had the full support of Jordan, Egypt and the Sudan. Sudanese troops were sent as volunteers after President Nimeiry had decided in October to send troops to 'sister Iraq.' In 1982 Egypt had 20,000 men fighting alongside the Iraqis, 'three quarters of them . . . Egyptian workers whom the outbreak of the Gulf war in 1980 found in Iraq. In the summer of 1981 Saddam Husain secretly asked the late Egyptian president, Anwar Sadat, for permission to call them up. Sadat agreed.'[13] Egypt is also one of the main suppliers of arms to Iraq. In 1982 war equipment including 105mm and 155mm guns, anti-tank missiles and armoured personnel carriers was airlifted from Egypt to Iraq.

Saudi Arabia and the Gulf states declared their neutrality but nevertheless gave considerable financial assistance and moral support. Saddam declared that he was fighting his war on behalf of the Gulf states and Saudi Arabia in particular against the danger of an Iranian invasion. However, after the series of military setbacks in 1982 culminating in the withdrawal of Iraqi forces from Iranian territory, it was rumoured that the Saudis had a plan to find a replacement for Saddam Husain.

Turkish Plans

On 26 May 1983, troops of the Turkish military dictatorship (a member of NATO) launched an attack on northern Iraq with 15,000 men, including paratroops and special task forces, backed by 30,000 regulars massed along the border and covering an area of over 12,000 sq. km. The attack coincided with wide-scale manoeuvres by NATO forces in Turkey close to the Iraqi border, overseen by the US Chief-of-Staff, General G.C. Jones, who was in Ankara just before the attack. Directed against the resistance forces in Iraqi Kurdistan to allow the Iraqi army to concentrate on the war with Iran, the attack took place with full co-operation and agreement between the two Fascist regimes of Turkey and Iraq. The frontier was declared a free-fire zone and all Iraqi troops were pulled back to give the Turkish troops a free field of fire. Collusion was admitted by Iraq's ambassador to Turkey, who stated that it was based on the border agreement concluded between the two countries in 1979. It took place despite the knowledge that Turkey still had claims on some parts of northern Iraq. While Tariq 'Aziz (Iraq's Vice-Premier) said of the policies of the Ba'th Party: 'the first concern is the sovereignty of Iraq over its territories,' the regime invited another army to invade those same territories.

In autumn 1984, Turkish troops launched another attack on the same territory, preceded this time by an incursion into Iranian Kurdistan. In early September, 4,000 Turkish troops crossed the Turkish-Iranian border, and it was no coincidence that the Iranian government itself had started a military offensive against its Kurdish opponents in the same area on 1 September 1984.

On 17 October, Turkish forces began a large-scale military operation code-named 'Operation Sun' along an 85-mile by 18-mile stretch inside Iraqi Kurdistan. This new invasion took place with the full approval of the Ba'th leadership which had agreed to upgrade the security agreement of 1979 with Turkey following talks between Saddam Husain and the Turkish Foreign Minister and Deputy Chief-of-Staff in the first half of October 1984.

Clearly, the lull in the fighting on the Iraqi southern front provided an opportunity for an offensive against the Kurds and their allies who remained an obstacle to the political and military aims of both the Iranian and the Iraqi regimes.

How far the US military chiefs in Turkey were involved in this operation was not immediately clear. But there is no doubt that the US would not easily abandon its hope to bring oil-rich Iraqi Kurdistan under its control, directly or indirectly.

In July 1983 the *New Statesman* revealed close US-Turkish high level military planning to take control of the oil-field of Kirkuk. The article sheds light on a top-secret plan for an invasion of Iraq code-named CANNONBONE, first drafted by the US in 1958, to be put into operation if Saddam is toppled.[14]

The US Stance

Indeed the US has repeatedly made it clear that it would not allow a change in the balance of power in the area. The 1979 Carter doctrine stated that the Gulf was considered to be a zone of vital interest to the US and the West and that no challenge to their influence would be permitted. The US Rapid Deployment Force formed in the 1970s was strengthened during the war and a Central Command (Centcom) was formed covering the Gulf region, Somalia, the Arabian Sea and part of the Indian Ocean with 300,000 troops at its disposal and bases in Saudi Arabia, Oman and Somalia. AWACS surveillance planes cover the Gulf area to give early warning of the approach of enemy planes so that they could be shot down within minutes of take-off.

When the attacks on commercial ships in the Gulf started, the US sent in a battle group including the San Diego-based carrier *Ranger*; six escort ships followed in October 1983 by despatching the 40,000 ton assault ship *Tarawa* to the Indian Ocean together with two other amphibious ships carrying 2,000 marines.[15] A French naval force was in the Gulf in September 1983 and Britain, with two destroyers in the Arabian Sea, was reported to have agreed to take part in a convoy system for tankers going into the Gulf.[16] Centcom manoeuvres took place in Egypt, the Sudan, Somalia and Oman in early 1984, and in May the US reiterated its willingness to intervene to defend tankers in the Gulf.

Results of the War

Rather than resolve the crisis faced by the Iraqi regime on the eve of the war, the war itself deepened it. The regime became entangled in its own policies, struggling to release itself from the web of political, social and economic crises. The war, planned to last a few weeks or months at most, dragged on for years. The magnitude of human losses and destruction is reminiscent of the First World War and the effects will be felt for generations to come.

Human Tragedy

The most horrific effect of the war has been in the human losses: more than 100,000 people killed and over 100,000 wounded and maimed. In the fierce battles east of Basra in July 1982 alone, 10,000 people were killed. In 1984, chemical weapons left the island of Majnun strewn with the corpses of Iranian soldiers and Iraqis. In every Iraqi family at least one member has been killed or maimed. Black fabric for mourners to wear has become a sought-after commodity on the Iraqi market though the regime's reaction to the loss of lives has been to discourage people from mourning. In the Ba'thists' vocabulary, 'discourage' means 'force' and the dead are the 'heroes' of the nation 'willingly' giving their lives to defend their 'leader' and their country. Families, we are told, are proud to lose a son or a member of the family in 'Saddam's Qadisiya.' It is an honour to receive Saddam, who visits the families to join in their celebration for having given a martyr. The regime boasted of a woman who committed suicide out of 'shame' because her son deserted from the army and another who did the same because her son failed to detect enemy planes.[17] The Iraqi propaganda machine brands retreating soldiers 'traitors' or 'cowards' and these words are usually written on their coffins. Saddam formed special units behind the front lines with the objective of eliminating retreating soldiers and boasted that if any coward were to retreat or desert his post, his son would hear about it at school!

When the financial going was good, the regime rewarded the families of 'martyrs' with 'free agricultural land, houses and pensions.'[18] The dead husbands were paid for by gifts of money and cars. The final insult came when the regime began to extend its rewards to anyone marrying a widow. The markets, for the first year of the war, were flooded with every kind of imported goods, from eggs and frozen chickens to videos and commodities of all kinds. To what extent these bribes softened the impact of the war is arguable. Clearly, some people cashed in on all this, but as Fred Halliday remarked, 'no amount of videos and frozen meat can hide the coffins.'[19] But all this soon stopped, the market faced acute shortages and people were asked—or usually coerced—forcibly to donate to Saddam's Qadisiya.

The human tragedy of the war went hand in hand with the escalation of repression against the democratic forces and against any opposition to the war or its direction. Not even Ba'thist leaders and army officers escaped this repression. News of purges at the top emerged after every defeat suffered by the Iraqi army. Saddam's direct control of military operations gave rise to desertions within the armed forces, particularly when many senior officers were eliminated as scapegoats for the defeats suffered by the army. The armed forces, including the police and the paramilitary organizations, were given powers to shoot deserters on sight and many were publicly executed during 1983. In one incident deserters were executed in front of school children. Desertion from the army continues, however, with an estimated 100,000 deserters concentrating in the marshland of southern Iraq or in Iraqi Kurdistan.

From Oil Riches to Bankruptcy

The Iraqi budget of $48 billion for 1980, which constituted a 49% increase on the budget of 1979, 'can make an outsider feel like Alice in Wonderland', commented the *Middle Eastern Economic Digest*.[20] The riches came mainly from oil, for in 1979 Iraq was the second largest oil exporter in the Middle East (after Saudi Arabia). Monetary reserves stood at $17 billion and increased to $37 billion in 1980.

Exports of oil suffered enormously during the first few months of the war, dropping to 560,000 barrels a day (b/d) but recovered somewhat to 830,000 b/d during 1981, though the closure of the pipeline through Syria in 1980 aggravated the situation. The Iraqi regime was left with only one outlet through Turkey with a capacity of up to 600,000 b/d which increased during the war to 960,000 b/d. Despite all its difficulties the regime continued to boast about its economic capabilities, continuing its development plans, 'without difficulties or obstacles' and 'no matter how long the war would take'—but this was another dream soon to be dispelled.

As early as 1981 when the Director of the Central Bank of Iraq was claiming that Iraqi monetary reserves were $38 billion, the Iraqi Minister of Finance visited Saudi Arabia and the Gulf States begging for financial assistance 'to preserve the level of the balance,' it was claimed. At the same time the regime was spending huge sums on 'beautifying Baghdad' for the Non-Aligned Summit scheduled to be held there in 1982. With all these commitments, as well as sums drawn to be used at the discretion of Ba'th Party leaders, it is easy to understand why reserves had fallen to $2 billion at best estimates. The Iraqi regime turned to its Arab allies, the Gulf States and, in particular, Saudi Arabia, which contributed $1 billion a month to cover part of the war effort. The regime could no longer hide its bankruptcy, with projects shelved, wages cut, taxation increased and foreign contractors asked to produce credit facilities or leave. Loans from France, Britain, West Germany and the US as well as from Arab countries were mounting. In 1981 alone, the loans were estimated to be $24 billion.

One method of extorting money from the people was by 'donations' which were extracted by psychological pressure and by soldiers going from door to door to check receipts of donations. No official documents can be processed without the production of such receipts. 'Even foreigners are not immune.'[21] The government collected over 30 tons of gold in a campaign reminiscent of Mussolini's 'Day of the Wedding Rings' in 1935 during the Abyssinian war. Thousands of Iraqis lining up daily to have their 'donation' weighed or counted were shown on television, congratulated in the press or taken to meet the President. Saddam received donors in his Presidential Palace, chatting with them, kissing the children or listening to their poems praising him and his Qadisiya. One man declared: 'I wish my blood were gold so that I could give it to you to the last drop.'²² Originally Saddam promised to build a monument from this gold to celebrate this 'glorious' deed and the Iraqi women who donated their gold. But later the Finance Minister Thamir Razzuki announced that it would be kept in the Central Bank as a 'strategic cover for Iraqi currency.'

Despite all these financial difficulties and while introducing austerity measures and asking the people to tighten their belts, Saddam and his clique maintained their own lavish spending. Their 'popular' celebrations were always timed to coincide with critical events such as decisive battles at the front. The celebrations have but one aim, which is to glorify Saddam. Celebrations were even staged on the anniversary of his visit to one town and another celebrated the anniversary of Saddam passing through on his way to some other town! Public celebrations for Saddam's 46th birthday in May 1983 took place only a few days after a battle in which 4,000 Iraqis had been killed. Each government department received a cake for the occasion while a 46-layer cake 'that needed a crane to put it in position'²³ was presented at the palace.

The Fodder of the War

From what has been said so far, it is obvious that the Iraqi people are paying economically and with their own blood for Saddam's war. Three-quarters of a million Iraqis (out of a population of 14 million) are engaged in military activity in the armed forces or in Fascist-type paramilitary organizations such as the 'people's army.' This figure represents 60% of the Iraqi workforce and the gap left was filled by imported workers mainly from Arab countries. The age of conscription was lowered to under 18 when, at the beginning of 1984 all males born in 1966 were ordered to report for military service.

The chairman of the yellow trade union in Baghdad province, Shakir Ahmad, declared: 'One hundred thousand workers have volunteered in the Special Units.' He also boasted of his pride that the Iraqi working class had 'donated' the value of their work uniforms and their annual holidays for the war effort.²⁴ However, he did not mention that the Union's buildings had been used as military centres for training working people after working hours.

The average wage of ID72 was cut by ID16 for the war effort, adding to other 'donations' forcibly extracted from the workers—a million free hours of work a day, loss of weekends, holidays and other benefits such as free transport and the like. There has been no real wage increase since the start of the war. Food prices increased on the official market by 600% in one year. There are also periodic shortages of various foodstuffs. The cost of accommodation increased by 500%, transport by 50–100%, pass tickets for public infirmaries by 500% and so on.

The Iraqi Army and the War

One of the striking features of developing countries is the amount of money spent on armaments as a percentage of their national income. The army plays an important role in the history of many of these countries. In Iraq the National Democratic Revolution of 14 July 1958 was led by the Free Army Officers, assisted in planning and implementation by the democratic and national forces. The army maintained power but changed its political stance from one coup to the next. The Ba'thists themselves came to power through a coup d'état in 1963 and again in 1968. The Ba'th Party mono-polized control of the state and the army through a series of purges, and political activities within the armed forces were limited exclusively to those of the Ba th Party.

A large amount of the oil revenue was spent on enlarging and reorganizing the army and equipping it with the latest weapons and hardware. On the eve of the war the Iraqi army was made up of twelve divisions with a total strength of 330,000 men in addition to the so-called 'people's army' whose trained members numbered over 200,000. The security and intelligence services, the police machinery and the border guard were also expanded. During the war the army's numerical strength was increased to 17 divisions following the call-up of all reserves, and the 'people's army' formations were increased to 400,000 people. There are also volunteers from Jordan, Egypt and the Sudan serving alongside the Iraqi army. Military assistance came from Iraq's friends as well as from some Western 'neutral' states. The regime signed arms contracts worth billions of dollars, mainly with France.

The Iraqi army thus did not lack fire power. Yet it could not withstand Iran's volunteers and Revolutionary Guards who advanced in their human waves convinced of the justness of their cause. At the front, 'Iranian victory owes less to the fighting quality of Iran's soldiers than to the demoralization of the Iraqis,' commented the *Economist*.[25] For the Iraqi people, the Iranian revolution set an example, not by its Islamic fundamentalism, although initially many did take up that call, but in its strength in defeating the Shah's dictatorship. Opposition to the Ba'th regime and Saddam's Qadisiya intensi-fied as did the armed struggle against the regime. This all had its effect on the army rank-and-file as Iraqis learned how to evade conscription just as students used to deliberately fail their exams in order to remain in their colleges as long as possible.Over 100,000 men deserted from the army.

The ruling clique, aware of the army's limitations, protected the front lines of the fighting forces in the rear with lines of special task units whose function was to shoot retreating soldiers. While he was rewarding soldiers with good food and video sets Saddam was also rewarding them with bullets and mustard gas. For it was Saddam himself who directly controlled all military operations. A civilian, not a military man, he gave himself an honorary degree from the Military College and appointed himself Field Marshal of the armed forces. This was resented by professional army officers particularly as many of them were executed as scapegoats for his blunders. Saddam has become so fearful of the army and the 'people's army' that every unit he visits is deprived of its live ammunition until he leaves.

As for deserters, most of those in the Kurdish areas of Iraq have joined the partisans but the majority are concentrated in the marshlands of the centre and southern parts. At first they were passive, only defending themselves and evading capture. Gradually they became a force to be reckoned with, a force of opposition and active resistance, so that the regime offered an 'amnesty' with threats from the head of the regime that 'families should bear the responsibility for the return of their sons.' On the morning of 2 May 1983 the inhabitants of the marshes in southern Iraq around Amara, Nasiriya and Basra were given a few hours to evacuate their villages before the place was heavily bombarded with rocket, artillery and air fire in a mopping up operation in which poison gas is reported to have been used. The deserters fought for three hours with limited machine guns, rifles and small mortar fire. The losses of the civilians and deserters were more than 250 killed or injured and 600 captured. The deserters' resistance did not cease: they reorganized and are taking a more active role against the regime.

The armed forces, police and security units have been given power to shoot deserters on sight and courts are banned from hearing cases of bodily or material harm inflicted on innocent people by the regime's forces while in pursuit of deserters. The degree of repression exercised against any sign of dissent is one of the important factors explaining why the army has not moved against Saddam's regime. There is no lack of such actions as assassination attempts, but an overall organized move is difficult to plan and co-ordinate because of the fear of traps set by the regime. An example of reprisals against any move by the army is the fate of the town of al-Dujayl, where an attempt on the life of Saddam was made in July 1982. The town was razed and its inhabitants dispersed.

Political Crisis

Saddam's seizure of the Presidency in 1979 marked the victory of the most reactionary and ruthless faction of the Ba'th Party in the struggle for power. Within two weeks 21 leading members of the party including ministers, 'trade union' leaders and members of the Revolutionary Command Council were tried *in camera* and executed. This demonstrated how Saddam intended to deal with every crisis. The war was a continuation of these policies, and resolved nothing. On the contrary the war highlighted the crisis which intensified as the war continued.

The war is extremely unpopular and opposition parties have condemned the regime and stated on many occasions that the conditions created by the war should be exploited in order to rid the country of the most vicious regime ever known in Iraq. The resistance forces intensified their armed struggle, particularly in Iraqi Kurdistan where the partisans and *peshmerga* set up their bases. Elsewhere the deserters moved from passive and defensive action to active resistance against the regime and became an important constituent of the opposition forces, not only against the war but also against the regime.

Even members of the Ba'th Party were killed for opposing the war or Saddam himself. The Minister of Health, who suggested in 1982 that Saddam might temporarily step aside to appease Khomeini, was summarily executed. In June 1982, only a day before the scheduled withdrawal from Iranian territory, Saddam dismissed members of the Revolutionary Command Council in a far-reaching government, party and cabinet shake-up. The *Guardian* reported: 'the president delivered an address which hinted strongly at a purge, at grass roots level, of what he called "negative elements" in the party and the population.'[26] Almost all the party leaders from the time Saddam became President, had disappeared by 1984. Even his half brother Barzan Takriti, chief of the dreaded secret police, was dismissed in October 1983 after an attempted coup. His fate is unknown but, judging by Saddam's record, it is almost certain that Barzan was killed.

After four years of fighting the war had achieved none of Saddam's objectives, and his hopes of becoming the leader of the Non-Aligned Movement were shattered when the majority of its members objected to holding the summit in a country at war with another member.

The Iranian position

The Iranians shifted their ground somewhat during the course of the war. At first the Iranian leadership thought that the aggressive war by Iraq would spark a popular uprising against Saddam's regime and they called on the Iraqi people to revolt and join in with the Iranian Army. Iran put forward three conditions for ending the conflict: the withdrawal of Iraqi forces from all territories occupied since the start of the war, reparations for damages estimated at billions of dollars and the trial of Saddam Husain as a war criminal. The last condition was soon to be replaced by the demand for the replacement of the Ba'th regime.

Opposition to the war among the Iraqi people was strong and some military actions by pro-Iranian Islamic groups and parties took place. But no Iraqi 'Islamic revolt' materialized: the political map of opposition forces is different in Iraq and religious organizations are traditionally weaker than in Iran. Eventually the Iranian alternative lost its appeal as the situation developed in Iran.

This influenced Iranian strategy at the war front. Their policies changed from waiting for an Iraqi uprising and assisting Islamic elements to fighting in order to occupy and impose an alternative on the Iraqi people. As early as 1982 the Iranian President stated Iran's willingness to march to Baghdad if necessary in order to remove Saddam. Ayatullah Montazeri called for the formation of a Muslim army of 20 million men to 'liberate Iraq and Palestine.'[27]

Conclusions

Today, near the end of 1985, the war has reached a stalemate with no immediate prospect of peace. Iran appears isolated while Iraq is receiving support from many countries and has a better equipped, if smaller, army than Iran.

But five years of fighting have brought the economies of the two countries to the brink of bankruptcy. In addition to the enormous cost of the war itself, large industrial areas on both sides of the common southern border are devastated and rendered unproductive. No one in 1985 dares assess the cost of rebuilding the flattened cities, the ruined factories and port installations, or estimate the years or decades needed to return life to normal in Southern Iraq, in Kurdistan and in Iran's Khuzistan after the end of the war.

What is certain is that there can be no victor in this war, even if either of the two countries emerges from it with the same rulers as in 1980.

The high morale which sustained the Iranian people at the time of Saddam Husain's aggression gradually disappeared as the Khomeini regime used the war as a pretext for cancelling the early promises of economic and political reforms, and set aside the constitution, allowing religious obscurantism and commercial greed to rule supreme. Disenchantment with the Khomeini regime will, sooner or later, undoubtedly lead to a new popular upsurge to get rid of a regime that has flouted the hopes of the 1979 Revolution and to resume the struggle for social progress.

The mad ambitions which launched the Iraqi Ba'thist regime on its invasion of Iran soon faded. As the war dragged on, Saddam Husain and his regime became increasingly exposed as criminal adventurers and brutal tyrants over their own people. The anger of the Iraqi people mounted as every new lying propaganda ploy and every empty boast was followed by harsher and harsher sacrifices imposed on the army and the civilian population.

The Iraqi people never wanted to wage war on Iran. They would welcome peace with their neighbours and will endeavour to bring it about at the earliest possible moment. But one thing they know: there can never be peace between them and a regime that has oppressed them for long years and then plunged them into an unjust war and subjected them to its disastrous results.

References

1. *The Guardian*, London, 12 February 1980.
2. Editorial in *The Times*, London, 21 September 1981.
3. Press release of the Press Office, the Embassy of the Republic of Iraq, London, 17 April 1980.

4. Press Office Publication, Iraqi Embassy, London, 17 September 1980.
5. *The Guardian*, London, 12 April 1980.
6. Press release (in Arabic), Iraqi Embassy, London, 22 April 1980.
7. Press release (in Arabic), Iraqi Embassy, London, 17 September 1980.
8. *The Times*, 26 May 1982; see also *International Herald Tribune*, 26 May 1982.
9. *Iraq*, Weekly Bulletin of the Iraqi Press Office, no. 6, London, 30 January 1981.
10. *Iraq*, Weekly Bulletin of the Iraqi Press Office, no. 10, London, 20 March 1981.
11. Ibid.
12. The story of the sales of protective kits to Iraq was unearthed by *New Scientist* writer Judith Perera and reported in the British press 22 December 1983.
13. *Foreign Report*, the Economist Newspaper Ltd, London, 6 May 1982.
14. *New Statesman*, London, 15 July 1983.
15. *International Herald Tribune*, 12 October 1973.
16. *The Daily Telegraph*, London, 3 February 1984.
17. *Saddam's Qadisia*, Iraqi Embassy Publication No. 155, London, 17 February 1982.
18. *Iraq*, Weekly Bulletin of the Iraqi Press Office, London, 25 February 1981.
19. Fred Halliday in the *New Statesman*, 9 April 1981.
20. *Middle East Economic Digest*, London, 9 May 1980.
21. *Newsweek*, London, 15 August 1983.
22. *Le Monde*, Paris, 23 October.1983.
23. *The Economist*, London, 4 June 1983.
24. *al-Thawra*, Baghdad, 9 June 1982.
25. *The Economist*, London, 10 April 1982.
26. *The Guardian*, London, 29 June 1982.
27. *The Times*, London, 12 July 1982.

Chronology

1869 Suez Canal and powered river transport open up Mesopotamia to international trade.

1912 The Turkish Petroleum Company is formed (with British, Dutch and German participation) and acquires the concession to prospect for oil in the Ottoman provinces of Baghdad and Mosul.

1914 NOVEMBER. British Indian troops land at Shatt al-'Arab to protect the Anglo-Persian oil installations at Abadan.

1916 Tribal shaikhs are given land and financial and juridical authority by the British.

1917 MARCH. British capture Baghdad.

1918 OCTOBER. Mudros Armistice. British capture Mosul.

1919 Uprisings in Kurdistan.

1920 APRIL. In the San Remo Agreement the League of Nations awards Britain the mandate for Iraq.

JUNE. Turkey accepts the Treaty of Sèvres, which promises an independent Kurdistan, but it is never ratified.

JULY-OCTOBER. Revolt in Iraq against the British mandate.

1921 MARCH. Cairo Conference presided over by Winston Churchill makes the political, financial and military arrangements for the British mandated territories.

AUGUST. Faisal crowned King of Iraq.

1921-32 Behind a constitutional facade real power in Iraq is wielded by the British High Commissioner and the Commander of the RAF.

1922 First Anglo-Iraqi Treaty embodies Britain's mandatory powers.

1924 JUNE. The Anglo-Iraqi Treaty is ratified by Iraq's Constituent Assembly in exchange for British commitment to secure Mosul for Iraq.

DECEMBER. RAF planes bomb Sulaimaniya in Iraqi Kurdistan.

1926 JULY. Turkish-Iraqi Treaty. Mosul becomes part of the state of Iraq. Turkey to receive 10% of oil royalties.

1927 APRIL. First major oil strike, in Kirkuk.

1929 The Turkish Petroleum Company becomes a consortium of Anglo-Iranian, Shell, Mobil and Standard Oil, known as the Iraq Petroleum Company, with British, Dutch, French and US participation.

Formation of *Jam'iyyat Ashab al-Sana'a* (the Artisans Association), Iraq's first trade union.

JUNE. British Labour government decides to review the Anglo-Iraqi Treaty.

1930   JUNE. Anglo–Iraqi Treaty – "a major sacrifice of Iraqi interests for Great Britain's benefit".

IPC's oil concession area expanded from 192 sq miles to 35,000 sq miles.

Fighting in Iraqi Kurdistan.

Widespread civil unrest in response to the Municipal Fees Law, which increased taxation on small merchants.

1931   JULY. RAF flies demonstration flights over mid-Euphrates and Basra.

1932   JANUARY. Iraq joins League of Nations as an independent state but little changes. Prime Minister Nuri al-Sa'id maintains the link with Britain. British air bases remain.

1933   AUGUST. Iraqi armed forces led by Bakr Sidqi massacre Assyrians.

SEPTEMBER. Death of King Faisal.

DECEMBER–JANUARY 1934. City-wide boycott of Baghdad Electric Light Company.

1934   Iraqi Communist Party formed.

1935   JUNE. National Service Law becomes operative.

1936   OCTOBER. First military coup d'état, led by Bakr Sidqi.

1937–41   Six coups d'état. The army is virtually the sole deciding factor in the rise and fall of almost all Cabinets.

1941   MAY. Rashid 'Ali revolt. Britain resumes military control until 1945.

1944–46   Some political parties and trade unions allowed to be formed and operate legally.

1946–47   Strikes by railway workers, port workers and oil-field workers; massacre of striking oil-workers at Gawurbaghi in Kirkuk, July 1946.

1946   JANUARY–DECEMBER. Kurdish Republic of Mahabad.

AUGUST. Iraqi Kurdistan Democratic Party founded.

1947   MAY. Kurdish leader Barzani and closest associates flee to exile in the Soviet Union.

JUNE. Fahd, leader of the Iraqi Communist Party, is sentenced to death by the Supreme Court; under pressure of an international campaign the sentence is commuted to life imprisonment.

1948   JANUARY. Portsmouth Treaty attempts to renew the hated 1930 Anglo–Iraqi Treaty. Signed but never ratified because of *al-Wathbah* – The Leap – popular uprising against it.

APRIL. First Congress of the General Union of Iraqi Students (later known as GUSIR) held in the open air in Baghdad.

1949   FEBRUARY. Execution of Communist leader Fahd and others.

1951   Iraqi Ba'th Party founded.

1952   American oil companies adopt 50/50 policy.

Oil revenue becomes 60% of Iraqi government revenue.
1954 Nuri al-Saʻid's development policies favour landlords.
Repression increases.
1955 The Baghdad Pact.
1956 Widespread opposition to the Baghdad Pact and the Anglo-French–Israeli attack on Egypt.
1957 National Unity Front formed by the National Democratic Party, the Independence Party, the Communist Party and the Baʻth Party.
1958 14 JULY. Free Officers coup d'état led by Brigadier ʻAbd al-Karim Qasim becomes a national democratic revolution. The Iraqi monarchy is overthrown, Nuri al-Saʻid is killed. For a short while there is freedom for democratic activity. *Wahda* (unity with Egypt) becomes the issue over which the struggle as to how radical the revolution should be is fought.
SEPTEMBER. Land reform begins to break the economic power of the great landed shaikhs.
OCTOBER. Barzani returns from exile in Soviet Union.
1959 MARCH. First Congress of the Iraqi Women's League.
OCTOBER. The young Saddam Husain takes part in a Baʻthist attempt to assassinate Qasim.
1960 Repression of Communists begins.
SEPTEMBER. Fighting in Iraqi Kurdistan between Qasim and Barzani.
1961–75 Intermittent war between the Kurds and governments in Baghdad.
1961 Qasim makes territorial claim to Kuwait.
Law No.80 reduces the oil companies' oil concession areas to 0.5% of their size.
1963 8 FEBRUARY. Baʻth-nationalist coup d'état. 10,000 killed in one week. Nine months of bloodshed.
NOVEMBER. Military-nationalist coup d'état ousts the Baʻthists.
1963–68 Series of highly unstable Nasserist-nationalist governments.
1968 17 & 30 JULY. Military coups d'etat return Baʻth party to power.
1968–69 *Daʻwa* (Islamic Call) Party formed.
1970 MARCH. Manifesto recognises legitimacy of Kurdish nationality.
1971 Forcible removal of Kurdish population begins in some areas.
1972 APRIL. Iraqi–Soviet Friendship Treaty.
JUNE. Nationalisation of Iraq Petroleum Company.
1973 JULY. National Action Charter signed for the Progressive and Patriotic National Front between the Baʻth Party and the Communist Party.
SEPTEMBER. Kurds led by Barzani resume fighting, with backing of the Shah of Iran.
1975 MARCH. Algiers Agreement between Iraq and the Shah of Iran leads to the collapse of the Kurdish revolt.
1976 The Baʻth begin to repress Communists and others.
1977 FEBRUARY. Demonstrations in Najaf and Karbala during religious

processions. Eight Shi'i dignitaries executed.

1978   MAY. 31 Communist Party members and supporters are executed in army camps on the pretext that they have set up party cells in the armed forces.

1979   FEBRUARY. Overthrow of the Shah of Iran.

JULY. Saddam Husain becomes President, executing all potential rivals and critics within the ruling circles of the Ba'th Party. Terror and repression continue and spread wider through Iraqi society. Whole families "disappear". Mass deportations of the Shi'i Muslim community.

1980   APRIL. Shi'i leader sayyid Mohamed Baqir al-Sadr and his sister Bint al-Huda are executed.

JUNE. So-called elections are staged for a powerless "National Assembly".

17 SEPTEMBER. Iraq abrogates Algiers Treaty with Iran.

22 SEPTEMBER. Iraq invades Iran. Dissent spreads to the army, the rank-and-file of the Ba'th Party and the "people's army".

Repression extends to all sections of the Iraqi population.

NOVEMBER. Setting up of the Democratic Patriotic Front, which includes the Iraqi Communist Party, the Kurdistan Democratic Party and the Kurdistan Socialist Party. Armed struggle adopted.

1981   SEPTEMBER. Iraqi armed forces pull back east of the Karun river in Iran.

1982   APRIL. Popular uprising in Iraqi Kurdistan. Thirteen women among those killed.

JULY. Iranian troops cross into Iraqi territory.

NOVEMBER. Setting up of Muslim opposition umbrella organisation S.A.I.R.I. (Supreme Assembly for the Islamic Revolution in Iraq).

1983.   MAY. Turkey invades Iraqi Kurdistan with full cooperation of the Iraqi regime.

1984   FEBRUARY. Iraq launches air attacks on Iranian cities and uses chemical weapons.

MAY/JUNE. Commercial ships hit in the Gulf.

JULY/AUGUST. Students and villagers in popular uprising in Iraqi Kurdistan.

NOVEMBER. Expansion of the Democratic Patriotic Front to include some Arab nationalist forces and another Kurdish grouping. Continuation of armed struggle in Iraqi Kurdistan.

Bibliography

M.S. Agwani, *Communism in the Middle East*, (Asia Publishing House, New Delhi and London 1969)

Amnesty International, *Iraq: Evidence of Torture* (AI, London, 1981) and *Report and Recommendations of Amnesty International Mission to the Government of the Republic of Iraq* (AI, London, 1983)

Hanna Batatu, *The Old Social Classes and Revolutionary Movements in Iraq: A Study of Iraq's Old Landed and Commercial Classes and of its Communists, Ba'thists and Free Officers*, (Princeton U.P. 1978)

—————— 'Class Analysis and Iraqi Society', *Arab Studies Quarterly*, vol 1 no 3 Summer 1979

—————— 'Iraq's Underground Shi'a Movements: Characteristics, Causes and Prospects', *Middle East Journal*, Autumn 1981 and, ed. Joe Stork, *Merip Report* no 102 January 1982

E. Be'eri, *Army Officers in Arab Politics and Society*, (London 1970)

Gerard Chaliand (ed), *People Without a Country: the Kurds and Kurdistan*, (trans. Michael Pallis) (Zed Press, London, 1980)

Anthony H. Cordesman, 'Lessons of the Iraq–Iran War Part Two—Tactics, Technology and Training', *Armed Forces Journal International*, June 1982

Uriel Dann, *Iraq Under Qassem, a Political History 1958-1963*, (New York: Praeger 1969)

K. Dawisha, 'Iraq, the West's Opportunity', *Foreign Policy*, no 41 1980–81

William Eagleton Jnr., *The Kurdish Republic of Mahabad*, (OUP, London 1963)

C.J. Edmonds, *Kurds, Turks and Arabs*, (OUP, London, 1957)

Marion Farouk-Sluglett, 'Contemporary Iraq: Some Recent Writing Reconsidered', *Review of Middle Eastern Studies*, no 3, 1978

—————— ' "Socialist" Iraq 1963–1978—Towards a Reappraisal', *Orient* 23 no 2, 1982

Marion Farouk-Sluglett and Peter Sluglett, 'Labor and National Liberation: the Trade Union Movement in Iraq 1920–1958', *Arab Quarterly*, vol 5 no 2, 1981

—————— 'Iraq: the Path to Independence', *Gazelle Review*, no 6, 1979

—————— 'Conflict and Communism in Iraq', *Gazelle Review*, no 8, 1980

—————— 'The Transformation of Land Tenure and Rural Social Structure in Central and Southern Iraq 1870–1958', *International Journal of Middle Eastern Studies*, no 15, 1983

Marion Farouk-Sluglett, Peter Sluglett and Joe Stork, 'Not Quite Armageddon: the Impact of the (Gulf) War on Iraq', *Merip Report* no 125/126 July/September 1984

Rony Gabbay, *Communism and Agrarian Reform in Iraq*, (Croom Helm, London, 1978)

Sylvia Haim (ed. and trans), *Arab Nationalism: an Anthology*, (California U.P., London and Berkeley, 1962, 1976)

M.S. Hasan, 'The Role of Foreign Trade in the Economic Development of Iraq 1864-1964: a Study in the Growth of a Dependent Economy', *Studies in the Economic History of the Middle East*, ed. M.A. Cook (London 1970)

P.P. Hemphill, 'The Formation of the Iraqi Army', in *The Integration of Modern Iraq*, ed. A Kelidar (Croom Helm, London, 1979)

Dilip Hiro, *Inside the Middle East*, (Routledge and Kegan Paul, London 1982)

Albert Hourani, *Arabic Thought in the Liberal Age 1798-1939*, (OUP, London, 1979)

Ferhad Ibrahim, *Die Kurdische Nationalbewegung im Irak: eine Fallstudie zur Problematik Ethnischer Konflikte in der Dritten Welt*, Schwarz, Berlin 1983)

Institute of Strategic Studies, *Military Balance 1982-83*, (London 1984)

G.H. Jansen, 'Iraq: Bleak Outlook', *Middle East International*, 4 February 1983

Sa'ad Jawad, *Iraq and the Kurdish Question 1958-1970*, (Ithaca Press, London 1981)

Abbas Kelidar, 'Iraq, the Search for Stability', *Conflict Studies*, Middle East Institute no 59, July 1975

Majid Khadduri, *Independent Iraq: 1932-1958*, (London 1960)

——— *Socialist Iraq: a Study in Iraqi Politics since 1968*, (Washington 1978)

'Isam al-Khafaji, (in Arabic), *The State and Capitalist Development in Iraq 1968-1978*, (Dar al-Mustaqbal for UN University Third World Forum, Middle East Office, Cairo 1983)

Su'ad Khairi, (in Arabic), *The History of the Contemporary Revolutionary Movement in Iraq*, (Baghdad 1975)

——— (in Arabic), *The History of the Revolutionary Movement in Iraq: 14th July Revolution*, (Beirut 1980)

H.H. Kopietz, 'The Use of German and British Archives in the Study of the Middle East: the Iraqi Coup d'Etat of 1936', *The Integration of Modern Iraq*, ed. Abbas Kelidar (Croom Helm, London, 1979)

C. Kutschera, *Le Mouvement National Kurde*, (Paris 1979)

S.H. Longrigg, *Iraq 1900-1950: a Political, Social and Economic History*, (Oxford 1953)

A.K. Mansur (pseud.) 'The Military Balance in the Persian Gulf: Who Will Guard the Gulf States from their Guardian?' *Armed Forces Journal International*, November 1980

Phebe Marr, 'Iraq; Socio-Political Development', AEI *Foreign Policy and Defence Review*, vol 2, no 3-4, 1980

Elizabeth Monroe, *Britain's Moment in the Middle East 1914-1956*, (Chatto and Windus, London 1963)

Edith and E.F. Penrose, *Iraq: International Relations and National Development*, (Benn, London 1978)

Maxime Rodinson, *Marxism and the Muslim World*, (Zed Press, London, 1979)

Nawal El Saadawi, *The Hidden Face of Eve: Women in the Arab World*, (Zed Press, London, 1980)

B. Shwadran, *The Middle East, Oil and the Great Powers*, (Council for Middle Eastern Affairs Press, New York, 1969)

Peter Sluglett, *Britain in Iraq 1914-1932*, (Ithaca Press, London, 1976)

Peter Sluglett and Marion Farouk-Sluglett, 'Some Reflections on the Sunni/Shi'i Question in Iraq,' *British Society for Middle Eastern Studies Bulletin*, vol 5, no 2, 1978

G.W. Stocking, *Middle East Oil*, (Allen Lane, The Penguin Press, London 1971)

Joe Stork, 'Oil and the Penetration of Capitalism in Iraq', *Oil and the Class Struggle*, Ed. Petter Nore and Terisa Turner (Zed Press, London, 1980)

Mohammad A. Tarbush, *The Role of the Military in Politics: a Case Study of Iraq to 1941*, (Kegan Paul International, London, 1982)

Bassam Tibi, *Arab Nationalism: a Critical Enquiry*, ed. and trans. Marion Farouk-Sluglett and Peter Sluglett (Macmillan, London, 1981)

Jack Woddis, *Armies and Politics*, (London, 1977)

Z.N. Zeine, *The Emergence of Arab Nationalism*, (Khayat's, Beirut, 1966)

Index

Mahabad, Kurdish Republic of 183-6,
188
Mosul 1, 3, 6, 15, 19, 26, 55, 63, 98, 99,
126, 150, 161, 178-80, 205, 209-10

National Action Charter (1971) 45, 46,
126, 153
National Democratic Party 23-4, 26, 96-7,
125, 145-6, 148, 169
National Guard (Ba'th militia) 31, 32, 37,
99, 100, 210-11
National Union of Iraqi Students (Ba'thist
organisation) 40, 133
North Rumaila (oilfield) 34, 39, 44, 62-4,
151

Oil in Iraq 2-7, 12, 17-18, 19-20, 26-7, 34,
38, 39, 40, 44, 47, 48, 54-71, 73, 74,
78-9, 85-6, 101, 187, 228, 233, 240
Ottoman Empire, Ottomans 1-6, 10, 18,
55, 89, 90, 92, 123, 160-1, 178, 204,
229

Pan-Arab Nationalists (Nasserists,
qawmiyyun) 23, 26, 27, 37, 39, 89,
95-8, 100, 102, 170-1, 188-9, 210
Democratic Patriotic Front (founded
November 1983, alliance of ICP and
various Kurdish and other parties)
156-7, 168, 215
Patriotic Union of Kurdistan (party led
by Jalal Talabani, founded 1975)
157, 173, 198
Population (demography) 2, 19, 71, 82,
177

Revolution of 1958 1, 19, 23-7, 30, 38,
54, 56-8, 139, 163, 164, 188-90, 192,
206, 208-10, 214-15, 239

Shi'is in Iraq 4, 6, 49, 96, 123, 128, 132,
146-7, 157-8
Syria 3, 5, 25, 35-6, 40, 63, 66, 69, 70,
86, 89, 90-8, 130, 155, 171, 172, 177,
179, 188-9, 198

Trade Unions *see* Labour movement
Turkey 3, 6-7, 10, 12, 20, 50, 66, 69, 70,
86, 91, 159, 179-80, 186, 228, 234-5,
238
Turkish Petroleum Company 2, 4, 6-7, 55

Union of Soviet Socialist Republics 11, 12,
22, 44, 64, 98, 100, 141, 150, 151, 153,
183-6, 189, 191, 218
United States of America 3, 5, 6, 12, 17-18,

55, 86, 156, 197, 219, 229, 235-6

wahda ('unity' with Egypt and Syria) 25,
35-6, 96-8, 170, 189-90
Women in Iraq 108-19, 120-37